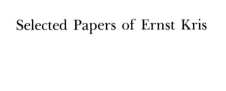

Selected Papers of Ernst Kris

Selected Papers of Ernst Kris

Ernst Kris

New Haven and London,
Yale University Press,
1975

Copyright © 1975 by Yale University.
All rights reserved. This book may not be
reproduced, in whole or in part, in any form
(except by reviewers for the public press),
without written permission from the publishers.
Library of Congress catalog card number: 74-29725
International standard book number: 0-300-01856-8

Designed by Sally Sullivan
and set in Baskerville type.
Printed in the United States of America by
Vail-Ballou Press, Inc., Binghamton, N.Y.

Published in Great Britain, Europe, and Africa by
Yale University Press, Ltd., London.
Distributed in Latin America by Kaiman & Polon,
Inc., New York City; in India by UBS Publishers'
Distributors Pvt., Ltd., Delhi; in Japan by
John Weatherhill, Inc., Tokyo.

Contents

PART II
PROBLEMS OF MEMORY

PART III
HISTORY OF PSYCHOANALYSIS

PART IV
APPLIED PSYCHOANALYSIS

Foreword

We can judge an analytic author's impact on his colleagues by the frequency with which he is quoted in the writings of his contemporaries or those who follow after him. Better still, we can measure his success by the number of his propositions and pronouncements which have entered into the body of psychoanalytic theory to the extent that they have become common psychoanalytic knowledge and that their originator ceases to receive special mention. It is, I believe, this second yardstick which can be applied profitably to assess Ernst Kris's theoretical and clinical achievement.

To enumerate a series of examples:

Studying early development today, we use not only the analytic method itself but, as a matter of course, combine it with the *direct observation* of young children, without paying tribute to the fact that Ernst Kris was the first to secure for observation outside the analytic setting a legitimate place in the armamentarium of the analyst. His view that this tool can "implement, supplement, control, and enlarge" the picture gained from analytic exploration proper has thus ceased to be a personal opinion and has become an accepted attitude.

What is true of our developmental studies as a whole extends then to many of their problematic details. It was Ernst Kris who first discussed the possibility of clinical foresight regarding the future prospects of a child by adding up the known facts about interaction of drives, application of existent defenses to developmental phases, typical danger situations, etc. If, today, we take it for granted that at times we can predict the future where formerly we could only reconstruct the past, we merely follow where Ernst Kris has led us.

Also, we are confident now that pathology in an individual child can be spotted (and hopefully prevented) before it has become manifest and threatening. It is worth remembering that this skill also has its roots in Ernst Kris's observational work at the Child Study Center of Yale University. Likewise, we take it for granted now that sublimation implies not only the displacement of a drive's aim but also its qualitative change, and are apt to forget that this view was not held before Ernst Kris (and Heinz Hartmann) applied themselves to an investigation of the problem; or, we discuss trauma, ignoring how much our present views of it owe to Ernst Kris's studies of the fate of childhood memories. Even his distinction between the good and the bad analytic hour has entered common usage, with no quotes needed.

On the other hand, some of Ernst Kris's important propositions, though not refuted, are by now in danger of being lost. He concerned himself at length with the "early features of the mother-child relationship" and stressed the child's gradual and ongoing adaptation to the changing maternal attitudes which appear in later analysis telescoped into a unified picture. This useful concept became overlaid by and submerged under the massive later literature on mother-infant interaction and now needs rescuing for further elaboration. So does his statement that "data obtained by psychoanalysis are naturally selective," i.e., weighted heavily toward areas of conflict involvement to the neglect of smooth developmental progress.

What the volume before us is intended to reveal is an image of Ernst Kris as psychoanalytic psychologist. This is not, as modern usage sometimes alleges, to be mistaken for that of an "ego psychologist" who explores ego characteristics, ego functions, ego adaptations, or ego development in pure culture. As demonstrated by the selection of papers which follow, Ernst Kris's role is that of the true analyst who sees the human ego as part of the mental apparatus, engaged in an unending struggle to maintain its integrity and efficiency in the face of the pressures exerted on the one hand by the drives and on the other hand by the environment.

Anna Freud

Editor's Note

The publication of the *Selected Papers of Ernst Kris* nearly twenty years after his death, forty years after the first of them was written, needs little explanation. They are needed. To some extent, of course, they are a continuation of his *Psychoanalytic Explorations in Art,* which appeared in 1952, covering more than twenty years of work on the creative process. To some extent they overlap, both in time and in subject matter; so much so, in fact, that it was necessary to reprint the paper On Preconscious Mental Processes (chap. 11) once more, because of its central position in a second, apparently distinct, line of inquiry on the therapeutic process.

Much of the present volume touches closely upon the author's *Papers on Psychoanalytic Psychology* (1964), written jointly with Heinz Hartmann and Rudolph M. Loewenstein. It was an important feature of their productive partnership that each of the three continued to work independently as well. In the case of Ernst Kris, this independent work covered a wide territory.*

The organization of this volume reflects Ernst Kris's main areas of interest and activities: his concern with refining psychoanalytic propositions and formulating them so that they can be tested not only in the psychoanalytic situation but also by psychoanalytically oriented observations of ongoing development (Part I); the interaction of psychoanalytic theory and technique and clinical observations, as seen especially in the area of memory formation and recall (Part II); his firm belief that an understanding of psychoanalysis can be obtained only by a study of its development (Part III); and the application of psychoanalytic knowledge and assumptions to social problems

---

* A complete list of Ernst Kris's writings appears in *The Psychoanalytic Study of the Child,* 13 : 567–573, 1958.

and creativity (Part IV). Within each section, the papers are arranged in chronological order.

The papers are presented essentially as they were written, though some obvious duplications have been eliminated. Inserts not contained in the original papers are set off in brackets.

In many instances Ernst Kris referred to works published several years after he wrote a particular paper, since he read many manuscripts by others prior to their publication. Only the bibliographical references were added. All citations from Freud's writings are now from the *Standard Edition*.

The preparation of the manuscript and the checking of proofs benefited greatly from the generous advice and active participation of Dr. Marianne Kris, Dr. Anton Kris, and Dr. Anna Wolff. It also benefited from my past association with the author himself.

I spent my years of apprenticeship as an editor working with Ernst Kris on *The Psychoanalytic Study of the Child*, the preparation of his two books, and the initial editing of most of the papers included here. I attended his courses at the New York Psychoanalytic Institute for many years, and participated as a research assistant in the Longitudinal Study at Yale. He taught me most of what I know about psychoanalysis and editing today. He also guided my reading. I well remember his all-too-frequent, "You don't know that?" And then: "How I envy you the experience reading this for the first time." In acknowledging my indebtedness and gratitude to him, I feel I can express the same sentiment for the future reader of this book.

                                                    Lottie M. Newman

Part I

PSYCHOANALYTIC CHILD PSYCHOLOGY

1 : The Nature of
Psychoanalytic Propositions
and Their Validation

(1947)

The word *psychoanalysis* will be used in the context of this paper to designate a body of hypotheses. I shall speak of *the psychoanalytic movement* in order to designate a social force, consisting mainly of the association of individuals who believe in the truth of these propositions, and who wish to propagate their acceptance, sometimes, especially early in this century, in an attitude of opposition to current social values. I shall speak of *psychoanalytic therapy* in order to designate a therapeutic technique, and of *psychoanalytic observation* in referring to the investigatory value of the *psychoanalytic interview:* the regular and frequent association of subject and observer, patient and therapist, over long stretches of time and under special rules of procedure.

Psychoanalytic hypotheses are derived from this interview situation, which is, at the same time, the most important testing ground for their validity. This leads to the crucial question: how reliable is this observational method in which the observer fulfills a threefold function: he records the behavior of his subject, he judges his own reactions to this behavior, which are part of the record, and he acts in order to produce

First published in *Freedom and Experience: Essays Presented to Horace Kallen,* ed. S. Hook and M. R. Konwitz. Ithaca, N.Y.: Cornell University Press, 1947, pp. 239–59; also in *Psychological Theory: Contemporary Readings,* ed. M. Marx. New York: Macmillan, 1951, pp. 332–351.

In the course of this paper I have liberally drawn on ideas and formulations that emerged in discussions with H. Hartmann and R. M. Loewenstein [see Hartmann, Kris, and Loewenstein (1964)].

changes in his subject? The lack of precision that results from such triple involvement of the observer is a cause for discomfort to the scientist. But there also are other grounds for discomfort: some lie in the development of psychoanalysis, and others are connected with the subject matter with which the propositions deal.

Psychoanalysis has developed outside institutionalized science and has been carried forward almost exclusively by the psychoanalytic movement. For over forty years professional associations of psychoanalysts have provided the necessary facilities for all those who have wished to study psychoanalysis and its applications, mainly they have provided facilities for the training of psychiatrists in the handling of psychoanalytic therapy. Even at the present time, when psychoanalytic propositions are permeating various psychological systems and are forming the hard core of psychiatry, psychoanalysis is taught only at few medical schools and only in exceptional cases in other departments of American universities. It seems that some of the—admittedly more superficial—difficulties with which many scientists are faced in their first contact with psychoanalysis have to do with this state of affairs. There is, for instance, a lack of trained clarifiers, who might properly coordinate the various propositions with each other or try to eliminate the inequities of language in psychoanalysis. As examples of such inequities one may mention that definitions of terms are sometimes unsatisfactory, that even their translation from German into English is not always fortunate; that in psychoanalytic writings metaphors tend to obscure the meaning of statements; and that such usages are ingrained by the fact that a generation of scientists adopted what now seems understandable as the peculiarity and privilege of one genius (Hartmann, Kris, and Loewenstein, 1946).

No other large body of hypotheses in recent science reveals to a similar extent the influence of one investigator. This has a number of consequences of varying significance. In the present context I refer to one of these consequences only: terminology and constructs of psychoanalysis reflect ideas and connotations dominant in Freud's formative years, i.e., in the 1870s and 1880s. Many interacting influences have to be considered: the humanist tradition in European education of the period, the concepts of "classical" neurology, the impact of twenty years of experiments and clinical work in the physicalist physiology of the school of Helmholtz and Du Bois-Reymond (Bernfeld, 1944), and finally the influence of evolutionism, both Darwinian and Lamarckian. It has been argued that since some of the concepts of psychoanalysis are derived from overaged connotations, for instance, from the mechanistic psychology of Herbart and his followers (Dorer, 1932), psychoanalysis itself is either in general overaged or, more specifically, limited to the viewpoints which originally suggested the terms used. The argument is clearly fallacious (Hartmann, 1927). The concepts borrowed from other sciences gained a new meaning in the new context: if in psychoanalysis reference is made to "associations"—mainly to the "free associations" of the subject—this has little to do with the traditional associationism of the nineteenth century. On the contrary, it seems that, historically speaking, the method of free associations has suggested some of the early criticism of the older association theories. Or, to use an even more significant example, Freud borrowed the term *regression* from brain pathology, but Freud's and not the neurological meaning of the term has found entrance in modern psychopathology and psychology. While it seems possible that the reverberations of overaged connotations attached to some of the psychoanalytic terms and constructs might act as a factor delaying their understanding or impeding communication, this origin does not affect their function. And in the present context I am interested in this function. How well do the constructs of psychoanalysis permit the establishment of a systematic set of propositions that review present knowledge, and how well do they function in suggesting "new" propositions that can be empirically tested—empirically tested in spite of the great number of independent variables?[1]

The subject matter of psychoanalysis was new in science

---

1. In this connection see K. W. Spence's (1942) somewhat extreme views on the relation between independent variables and constructs: "Theories come into play whenever we do not know all variables entering into a set of experimental events or the interrelation between them" (p. 281).

when Freud started on his investigation; it is new and bewildering even today. That subject matter is human behavior viewed as conflict. Before Freud it had been the exclusive province of intuitive insight, religious, poetic, or philosophic: these had created the various patterns of "the image of man" around which philosophy and the arts of Eurasian civilization have centered throughout the ages. Rapid changes of that image were under way in the outgoing nineteenth century, in the age of Darwin, Nietzsche, Dostoyevsky. The relation of psychoanalysis to this world of thought has not yet been satisfactorily investigated, a study that will clearly be one of the major assignments of a future biographer of Freud. Suffice it to say here that a distinction between tangible influences of contemporary intellectual movements on Freud's thought and "mere" similarities of his approaches to that of others working in other fields cannot always be made. However, the coincidences are often astonishing—no less astonishing and unexplored than the rapidly spreading influence that Freud's thought has exercised on the intellectual life of the twentieth century. To give only one example: the method of free association, one of the main avenues of exploration in psychoanalytic observation, has so clearly influenced literary fashions of the twentieth century that one has been inclined to assume that the "stream of consciousness," as a medium of poetic expression, was derived from it. And yet that very medium of poetic expression, was derived from it. And yet that very medium was used in France in 1887 in Edouard Dujardin's novel *Les Lauriers sont coupés* (Hoffman, 1945), several years before Freud ever applied the method of free association in his explorations. There is no evidence that Freud ever read Dujardin's novel, and there hardly need be any. Both Freud's approach and some of the literary currents of the second half of the nineteenth century are part of a general trend in the history of ideas, a trend that increasingly tended to pay tribute to the manifestations of psychopathology. The quest for the first relevant traces of this interest within science leads to the French psychiatrists of the nineteenth century, who stimulated Freud's interest in the new field (Kris, 1946).

Freud's first reaction to that field was similar to that through which many students of later generations, including our own, have passed and are passing. When, at the age of thirty, he first had contact with the study of neurosis, he reacted by a partial withdrawal. After his return from Paris, where he had studied with Charcot in 1886, and from Nancy, where he had worked with Bernheim in 1888, he renewed his interest in physiology and brain pathology. His studies on aphasia (1891), one of the first attempts at a functional approach in neurology—functional as contrasted to traditional localizationsism—were written in these years of retreat; Freud's interest and publications in the field of neurology continued until the end of his fourth decade.[2] When, at the age of almost forty, he published his first psychoanalytic case histories, he confessed to a feeling of *discomfort*. He who had been trained in the school of experimental sciences was writing what read like a novel. Not personal preference, he said, but the subject matter forced such presentation on him (Freud, 1905a; Breuer and Freud, 1893/95, p. 160). We may add that one particular property of the subject matter was responsible: the property that led to the discovery of the importance of the individual's past in relation to society, to primary and secondary groups— the clinician's role as life historian and social historian—drove him toward the novelist.

Psychoanalytic constructs and assumptions are designed to cope with this difficulty and to make the scientific study of human conflict possible. In the present context it suffices briefly to characterize some of these constructs. The first step in the formation of Freud's theories led to an application of the dynamic concepts of Herbartian psychology to the study of conflict in general, in all areas of human behavior, but especially to the already familiar problems of the stages of awareness, i.e., to the then current ideas concerning conscious and unconscious mental processes. Consequently, *unconscious* became a dynamic attribute, instead of a merely descriptive one; and a special term, *preconscious,* was introduced to designate processes that are only descriptively unconscious. The dy-

2. For a bibliography see Freud (1897).

namic concepts are supplemented by assumptions dealing with
the nature of psychic energy and its somatic source in basic
drives and needs; and by specific assumptions that deal with
the general principles regulating the functioning of the psychic apparatus in relation to discharge of tension and its post-
ponement. All these assumptions are characterized by their
relation to physiology. Contrary to the tradition of German
psychology and psychopathology of the late nineteenth century, Freud kept at a safe distance from making too close a
link between psychological and physiological assumptions. He
borrowed this approach from French psychiatrists: "The clinical observation of the French [psychiatrists]," he wrote in
1892, in his preface to the German translation of Charcot's
Tuesday Lectures, "undoubtedly gains in self-sufficiency in
that it relegates physiological considerations to a second
plane. . . . In this . . . there is no neglect, but a deliberate
exclusion which is considered expedient" (p. 135). Freud himself never lost sight of this second plane. When after many
tentative formulations he developed his structural model of
the psychic apparatus, in his assumptions regarding the development of the psychic organizations during ontogenesis, the
id, the ego, and the superego, he defined these organizations
as physiologists define organs, i.e., he defined them by their
functions (Hartmann, Kris, and Loewenstein, 1946). While
neither Freud nor the majority of later workers in the field
find it advisable to establish strict correlations between these
functions and certain parts of the nervous system, such lack of
correlation is considered provisional. Freud explicitly assumed
that the time would come when psychological constructs
would be replaced by physiological or biochemical constructs.[3]

The constructs of psychoanalysis here briefly characterized
have in the course of forty years been repeatedly revised,
sometimes so radically that older propositions were—silently—
superseded by newer ones. As a consequence, the student who
wishes to familiarize himself with the system of propositions

3. See Freud (1920, p. 60): "The deficiencies in our description would probably
vanish if we were already in a position to replace the psychological terms by physiological or chemical ones." For a similar later statement, see Freud (1933, p. 154).

has to study its history. No fully satisfactory comprehensive statement on the system itself is known to me. This is one of the reasons why random quotations from psychoanalytic writings are of particularly dubious value. A young American scholar has recently pointed to the fact that much confusion about what is believed to be a psychoanalytic proposition is due to the exclusive acquaintance with one or the other phase in the development of hypotheses as embodied in Freud's writings (Hoffman, 1945). This state of affairs is symptomatic of the social setting in which psychoanalysis is developing; the interest of psychiatrists who alone have access to the full set of observational data can hardly be expected to center on problems of semantic and systematic clarification, at a time when the rapid advance of clinical insight attracts their attention. A time lag exists between their insight and their theoretical formulations and even between clinical experience and published case histories; the clinical tradition, at the present time, is richer and both more concrete and more precise than the psychoanalytic literature tends to reveal. Since the evidence on which the handling of psychoanalytic therapy rests is on the whole convincing to those who apply it, the need for systematic clarification presents itself mostly when controversial issues arise among those who work with this therapy.

There are obviously many reasons why such controversies have been frequent since, early in the century, Freud gained his first collaborators; and there are obviously many reasons why they should have taken the specific form of "splits" of what I here call the psychoanalytic movement. One of these reasons, however, is directly relevant in the context of the present paper: it is the elusive nature of the subject matter (Waelder, 1944). The fact that there are many psychoanalytic propositions that have not yet been verified by procedures used in science seems to explain why controversies tend on the whole to be less fruitful and less centered on essential issues than they otherwise might be. Whatever the incentives to controversy, unverified propositions are readily taken as training ground by those polemically inclined.

Not all propositions currently included in psychoanalysis

can be made subject to verification. I shall mention only two examples. The large set of propositions which accounts for human behavior in using phylogenetic assumptions frequently implies another purely biological proposition, the inheritance of acquired characteristics; and so long as there is no reason to consider this proposition verified by biologists, it seems appropriate to exclude psychoanalytic propositions based on it. Similarly, Freud's assumption of a drive toward death ("death instinct") as a propensity of living matter should not be used in establishing empirical propositions, so long as the implied biological assumption has not been tested—the assumption, namely, that living matter tends toward extinction even when chemical self-intoxication is eliminated. Psychoanalysis as a science cannot, I believe, directly deal with these propositions; moreover, their value for the formulation of other empirical propositions can be seriously questioned.[4] Their place in Freud's thinking, however, and their immensely stimulating effect are matters of great concern to those interested in the history of ideas.

In turning to the problem of validation of psychoanalytic propositions, I shall distinguish validation provided by psychoanalytic observation from other "objective methods" (Sears, 1944) of verification. In discussing the latter, I shall distinguish between experimental procedures and observational evidence.

The validation of psychoanalytic propositions through psychoanalytic observation can in this context only briefly be characterized; any attempt to do so must start with the exclusion of what one might expect to be the most convincing test: the success of psychoanalytic therapy. This therapy operates with a number of agents. In many cases it remains to some extent doubtful which of these agents has produced the desired change; even if the probability is great that one particular agent can be made responsible, evidence is as a rule difficult to establish. However, this limitation does not seriously restrict our discussion since, apart from the question of the effec-

4. For one example, see Hartmann and Kris (1945, p. 21f.).

tiveness of psychoanalytic therapy, the psychoanalytic interview provides a setting of experimental character through its
rules of procedure; it covers an area and makes data accessible
that are otherwise not observable under conditions of com-
parably relative precision.[5] Not only does the total course of
the association between observer and subject provide an experimental setting and permit the testing of long-range predictions; each interview provides potentially a number of
opportunities for the testing of forecasts. Each one of the
manifold reactions of the subject to the interventions of the
observer can be described as a reaction to a deliberately introduced change in the situation between observer and subject. The reactions of acknowledgment to any interpretation
given, for instance, that of sudden insight combined with the
production of confirmatory detail or substitute reactions of a
variety of kinds, frequently—but not always—permit confirmation or refutation of the hypotheses on which the given intervention was based.

It seems appropriate to discuss the simplest example of such
confirmatory evidence: the interpretation has removed obstacles to recall; the forgotten memory can take its place
within awareness. It is naturally not assumed that in such cases
the interpretation "produced" recall; rather, the situation existing previous to the interpretation, the one which "suggested" the interpretation, must be described as one of
incomplete recall (and, therefore, as in some measure similar
to the situation in which the memory trace was laid down). Interpretation, therefore, acts here as a help in completion. Incomplete recall had announced itself by a variety of signs in
the individual's behavior. The subject may have acted in relation to an actual rival as he once acted toward a sibling, and
the interpretation of the observer merely translated the non-
verbalized into verbalized response, unconscious repetition
into conscious recollection. The similarity of the situations to
which I refer here need exist only in the meaning of the situation to the subject, for instance, in the dynamic structure of

5. For a full discussion, see Hartmann (1927) and Hermann (1934).

the constellation in his life, as this constellation may have been modified by previous interview situations.

The frequency of such experiences during analytic observation is in part due to the rules of procedure. They are designed to bring about the experience of similarity of present and past. Thus in many instances the personal relation to the observer is experienced as "similar" to the relation to one or another member of the subject's primary group—I refer here to rules concerning the relative anonymity and passivity of the observer during the interview situation. In saying that the subject exhibits behavior similar to earlier behavior patterns, behavior that would, as it were, be appropriate in another context, analysts refer to a large number of behavioral details, actions in life as well as during the interview, dreams, and verbalizations that follow the process of free association. In order to eliminate a number of problems concerning the reliability of confirmations of reconstructions by recall of the subject, it seems appropriate to mention that in a considerable number of instances in which interpretation was used to reconstruct the past, or, as one might say, to "predict the past" (Hartmann and Kris, 1945), objective verification of the reconstruction was possible. Inquiries in the environment of the subject and for recollections of members of his family brought confirmations of astonishing details.

Thus Marie Bonaparte (1945) reported a case in which confirmation was obtained for a reconstructed experience that occurred in the second year of life; the reconstruction was largely based on one dream. At least one subject, the psychologist E. Frenkel-Brunswik (1940), has published an account from her own experience under psychoanalytic observation. From her behavior, and from associations about her two sisters, the analyst had interpreted what he called a "Cordelia motive." He suggested to her that she was displaying in her life the role of Cordelia, the youngest daughter of King Lear. To her answer that she had read most of Shakespeare's dramas but not *King Lear,* the analyst replied that Cordelia was the best and most generous daughter of King Lear, who nevertheless preferred his other two daughters because of their flattering attitudes. Such an interpretation was at that time refused by the author rather emotionally. Later it was received somewhat more favorably. But she was still very surprised when much later she discovered, in looking through old notes, that at the age of about fifteen she had copied the entire role of Cordelia. Thus she must at that age have been very much concerned with the fate of Cordelia, with whom she probably had identified, later repressing not only this identification but also all other memory of the play.

The confirmation of reconstructions by objective evidence played a considerable part in the early history of psychoanalysis, at a time when Freud was constantly experimenting with new propositions. It appears that he felt ·considerably encouraged as to the validity of his theories on dream interpretations when the interpretation of one of his own dreams led to the reconstruction of an experience in his third year of life, which was subsequently confirmed by a recollection of his mother (Freud, 1950).

But even without the support of objective confirmation psychoanalytic observation has in many instances been able to decide between alternative propositions. Thus the hypothesis that there was a regular or extremely frequent occurrence of actual seduction by adults in the childhood of individuals who later in life develop hysterical symptoms, and the hypothesis that there was a regular or frequent correlation between the severity of the birth experience and the incidence of neurosis in the adult, were disproved by this procedure.

A survey of the body of psychoanalytic propositions reveals, however, that in other instances psychoanalytic observation does not provide criteria for verification. Observers using the same proposition claim different results; and even when they submit their data to each other, no decision can be reached. The number of variables and the fact that no repetition of the experimental procedure under comparable conditions is feasible limit in these cases the possibility of decision. This is, for instance, true of propositions suggested by M. Klein (1932) and Isaacs (1935), concerning earliest reactions of the infant to deprivation.[6] They claim, for instance, that in earliest in-

6. See Waelder (1936) and Glover (1945) for a discussion of these theories and methodological questions.

fancy, at the age of a few months, the child reacts with self-punitive tendencies to the extraordinarily intense destructive impulses that he feels against an environment imposing even slight and unavoidable frustrations. I select this instance because it is typical of a large number of other propositions that are indispensable in psychoanalysis: they deal with reactions of the child during the preverbal stage or during the earliest stages of development of his verbal faculties; propositions which will tend to remain controversial unless verified by objective methods. It should be added that they are not the only propositions of which it is true that a decision cannot be reached. Briefly, if I speak of verification of psychoanalytic propositions by objective methods, I do so not in order to make psychoanalytic propositions "respectable" in science, or in order to establish unity in the field of psychology, but because sooner or later the ever more precise empirical test becomes an essential element in the development of any system of scientific propositions. In the development of psychoanalysis this moment seems to have arrived.

Validation of psychoanalysis by experimental procedure has been the preoccupation of individuals and groups of writers over many years, in certain areas (relation of dream formation to percepts, symbolism in dreams) for over thirty years. The interest in this approach is growing so rapidly that recent bibliographies, though incomplete (Sears, 1943, 1944), enumerate several hundred contributions, and "experimental psychoanalysis" has come to be considered "a field of its own." The importance of this trend in experimental psychology can hardly be overestimated. The walls that a generation ago separated the psychological laboratory from "life" have been pierced; the relevance of the problems investigated has increased; experimental work is gradually moving from a concern with peripheral factors determining human behavior to the central problems, on which man's existence depends. That movement is—naturally—slow, but it is effective. And from the experimental setup there leads a way to test situations and test procedures and their ever wider application in techniques of welfare and social control.

Through this trend in experimental psychology the isolation of psychoanalysis from other systems and approaches in psychology has been considerably reduced. Furthermore, a number of psychoanalytic propositions have gained wide recognition and are moving rapidly into the area of common-sense psychology. This corresponds to a regular sequence: the greater familiarity with some psychoanalytic propositions leads to their becoming part of "what one always knew."

Before discussing the significance of these experiments for the verification of psychoanalytic propositions it seems appropriate to introduce a distinction applicable to the most frequently tested and most relevant psychoanalytic proposition (Hartmann and Kris, 1945). Psychoanalysis describes processes of conflict solution in their time sequence. It seems, therefore, necessary to organize psychoanalytic propositions according to two viewpoints: according to whether or not they deal with dynamic or genetic (ontogenetic) interrelations. Dynamic propositions "are concerned with the interaction and the conflicts of forces within the individual and with their reaction to the external world at any given time or during brief time spans" (p. 11). Genetic propositions describe how any condition under observation has grown out of an individual's past and extended through his total life span. If we take as examples of dynamic propositions defense against danger and reaction to frustration, genetic propositions state how defense and reaction come into being and are used in an individual's life. A survey of the vast number of experiments dealing with reactions to frustration indicates that they frequently test only dynamic propositions. They are concerned "with the field conditions as they exist here and now" and view the subject "who is a product of his past experiences as a static part of the field conditions" (Rapaport, 1942).[7] Thus Dollard and his collaborators (1939) have ably dealt with the proposition that frustrations sometimes lead to aggression; Barker, Dembo, and Lewin (1941) with that asserting that frustration sometimes results in primitivization of behavior, in what Freud called ego

7. For a more detailed discussion of this point and a critical discussion of K. Lewin's position, see Hartmann and Kris (1945).

regression. Both investigations have convincingly verified psychoanalytic propositions. However, these propositions are of a
general kind, and the question arises under what condition an
individual will react to frustration either with aggression or
with regression or with another mechanism of defense. Dynamic propositions alone cannot answer the question. An
example may illustrate the reasons: K. Lewin and his
collaborators investigated the reaction of children when suddenly deprived, but still in view, of highly desirable toys. Let
us transfer this laboratory situation into life: "When children
visit department stores with their mothers, [they] are in an almost equally tantalizing situation. What will their reaction
then be? It will depend on what meaning the 'You can't have
it' and the 'It is too expensive' gains for the child, by the way
in which the mother puts it to him. This depends on a variety
of factors: on the child's relation to the mother; on the
mother's own relation to similar present and past experiences;
and how, in the child's own previous development, tolerance
for deprivation in general and for certain specific deprivations
has developed" (Hartmann and Kris, 1945, p. 17).

This comparison is not meant as a criticism of the laboratory
technique; it is only an attempt to characterize the limitations
of the predictions that can be based on experiment. Lewin and
his collaborators can naturally not generalize "to what kind of
frustration and under what circumstances a child will respond
with regression" instead of with a different mechanism. However, when the data available cover the individual's past, when
both dynamic and genetic propositions are applied, such forecast frequently becomes possible. Thus, in order to prognos-
ticate the child's behavior in the department store, data on
both the mother and the child's past experience are essential,
detailed data that hardly ever are assembled outside of psychoanalytic observation.

Other experimental approaches have been singularly successful in studying genetic propositions. The experimenter
can view life as a series of learning processes (Bergmann,
1943; Mowrer and Kluckhohn, 1944). The outstanding example of an experimental setup of this kind is Hunt's article

on "The Effect of Infant Feeding Frustration upon Adult Hoarding in the Albino Rat" (1941). He found that the experience of frustration in infancy modifies adult behavior under two conditions: first, that the frustration be experienced at a certain early point during the maturational sequence; and second, that the adult animal be exposed to frustration experiences. The behavior of the satiated animal cannot be said to have been modified; nor will the behavior of the adult animal exposed to frustration be modified if the infantile frustration was experienced at a late period of maturation. This experiment reproduces not only the general proposition that under certain conditions frustration modifies subsequent behavior but also the specific interrelation between experience and predisposition, which is part of all genetic propositions in psychoanalysis. An experience, it is contended, will become effective only if the child meets it at a given moment of his development.[8]

The value of experiments such as those of Hunt's and a limited number of similar ones by Mowrer (1940) and Levy (1934) is self-evident: they have succeeded in demonstrating experimentally the validity of genetic propositions of psychoanalysis in an incontrovertible manner.

Whatever gratification one feels at such results is somewhat reduced by the fact that the proposition verified is a good deal removed from the area in which, from the point of view of psychoanalysis, verification of propositions is most urgently needed. To remain in the province covered by Hunt's experiment, we would wish to know what constitutes frustration to the human child, when does what kind of experience act how on what kind of children in what kind of environment—variables in whose effects psychoanalysis is equally interested and whose interrelations are tentatively covered by psychoanalytic propositions, which, as a rule, cannot be verified by experimental procedure.

The use of animal experiments reaches its limit when prop-

8. In speaking here of development instead of maturation, I refer to a definition: we ascribe to maturation processes relatively independent of environment; to development those highly dependent on environment (Hartmann and Kris, 1945).

ositions are so specific that they apply to one species only, to
the human animal. The limit of experiments with humans
rests on the fact that the laboratory cannot as a rule reproduce
dangers or basic needs with which the genetic propositions of
psychoanalysis deal.

A number of authors have contested this point and have
claimed that the difference between quasi needs and "true
needs" can be neglected; the study of human motivation can,
they suggest, be based exclusively upon investigations of behavior determined by quasi needs. K. Lewin (1938), who has
advanced this view, argues that tensions of low and high intensity are only quantitatively and not qualitatively different; that
the fact of this quantitative difference cannot affect the laws in
question. Henle (1942), who elaborated on Lewin's views,
argues that experiments in a variety of fields have proved that
Lewin's contentions are correct. None of these experiments
seems entirely convincing; but one of Henle's examples encourages a more detailed discussion. Henle claims that Freud's
analysis of the psychopathological phenomena of everyday
life, of slips of the tongue, and parapraxes have shown that in
an area where tensions of low intensity operate, phenomena
come into being that clearly follow the same principles as the
symptom formation in neurotic behavior, i.e., phenomena of
great intensity.

Henle's argument is misleading. Not only is it worth remembering that not all essential propositions concerning the formation of the neurotic symptom apply to parapraxes (the
theory of symptom formation was known to Freud when he
hit upon the explanation of parapraxes, and it is doubtful
whether a reversal of the sequence could have led to equally
satisfactory results); but also the assumptions that the conflicts
that lead to parapraxes are necessarily or typically of low intensity is entirely unwarranted. Evidence to the contrary is
rather suggestive. But I should like to introduce a different
kind of argument. Assuming that even in some cases the intensity of the conflict that leads to parapraxes be low, the nature of the conflicts remains significant. The conflict is of the
same kind as the conflict that leads to symptom formation in

neurosis; it may involve libidinal and aggressive impulses, love, hate, guilt, and anxiety, and the part played by the three psychic organizations may be in details comparable to that observable in symptom formation.

The quasi needs of the laboratory investigations are of a different kind. There is no doubt that, as Zeigarnik (1927) and a host of experimenters since the publication of her paper have shown, the need to complete an uncompleted task exists. But that need is of a very specific kind; [9] seen from the point of view of the psychoanalyst, it is a complex desire in which, however, two elements, that of avoiding failure, and that of feeling unsatisfied because one has not complied with a task, seem to predominate; that is to say, impulses in which the ego and the superego are predominantly involved; as a rule, no id impulses are either frustrated or gratified. Consequently, the conflict that arises when the impulse to complete is frustrated can hardly be compared to conflicts that may arise when the impulse to complete an action with aggressive or libidinal connotation is impeded. In these cases the impediment, whether external or internal, is frequently experienced as a threat and the individual frequently reacts with anxiety. The difference in the situations referred to, which Lewin described as one of mere quantitative character, can be demonstrated in terms of physiological reactions: the bodily changes (Cannon) attending anxiety states are different in kind and not in degree from other and lower tension states in the organism; their closest relative is the state of rage. Considerations of this kind must be taken into account in discussing the relation of quasi needs of the laboratory to the true needs of life, and when evaluating the bearing of certain types of experiments.

It should be added that experimental approaches to the study of "true" conflict situations have repeatedly been attempted. They were initiated by H. A. Murray (1933) who, in

9. Hartmann (1933) repeated Zeigarnik's experiments with obsessional neurotic subjects and found that contrary to Zeigarnik's expectations based on experiments with normal subjects, they did not *prefer* incomplete to completed tasks. The need to repeat, which predominates in the clinical picture of the majority of obsessional subjects, overrides the need to complete the uncompleted. The specific impulses of the obsessional neurotic "modify the structure of the quasi needs."

his paper on "The Effect of Fear upon Estimates of the Maliciousness of Other Personalities," clearly demonstrated the working of projection. Murray's method has been elaborated by others (Harrower and Grinker, 1946), and experimentation in this area is rapidly developing. The preliminary reports of various wartime setups for the selection of specialized personnel, where subjects were exposed to considerable strain, seems to indicate that the "paper and pencil" experiments are finding rivals in controlled observation of individuals exposed to real or almost real threat situations.[10]

And yet it seems doubtful whether any experimental method will ever be able to rival the confirmation of psychoanalytic hypotheses concerning human reaction to danger that can be obtained by carefully controlled data of observation. To quote a recent example (chap. 22): the fantastic prediction that bombing of civilians in the Second World War would produce mass neuroses was made by those who were unaware of psychoanalytic propositions. The result of bombing surveys, however, confirmed the latter; they state that an individual's reaction to objective danger in a clearly structured situation—under adequate leadership and morale—will depend on the state of inner tension of the individual. All surveys on reaction to bombing in England (Wolf, 1944) have shown that pathological reaction was maximized in one group of citizens, the adolescents, i.e., in those whose level of adjustment is for biological reasons least stable and in whose life conflict is supreme. Some surveys (Cyril Burt, 1941) have been interpreted as showing that a similar peak of the curve existed for the age groups three to five in which another set of psychoanalytic propositions locates a high propensity to anxiety. Verifications of this kind seem particularly significant since they are based on data selected for other purposes.

The limitations of the laboratory to quasi needs (and quasi dangers) seriously restricts the area of propositions that can be

10. At the present time only incomplete evidence as to the experimental procedure used is available. See Bion (1946) and *Fortune Magazine* (March 1946), where a cursory description of the various tests applied by Murray in the selection of personnel for the Office of Strategic Services is given.

experimentally verified. In fact, up to the present, experimental approaches have been more successful in dealing with propositions concerning substitution [11] than they have been with propositions concerning repression (Rapaport, 1942; Hartmann and Kris, 1945). The child represses an experience because the remembrance would entail conflicts of "too great intensity" in the presence of what to the child are vital threats. Situations of this type can hardly be reproduced by the experimenter, but they can be successfully studied by trained observers of behavior, who live in close contact with the child. The ideal of an intense study of the child by a team of participant observers of many skills is as yet unfulfilled, partly for organizational reasons. The communication between "academic" and "psychoanalytic" studies of child development is very incomplete. Quotation marks are used to indicate the spurious character of a division according to which one group of observers would be mainly interested in maturational aspects, the other, the psychoanalytic observer, in the "emotional" or "social" aspect of the child's life,[12] a division of interests which is bound to reduce the value of both sets of findings.

In fact, observation has been most meaningful when it covers many areas at the same time and tends to illustrate how all sides of the child's personality are interdependent. The observations by Anna Freud and Dorothy Burlingham in a wartime nursery in London may be quoted as outstanding examples (1942, 1944). Similarly, the investigations by Spitz (1945) on hospitalism have produced quantified data demonstrating how lack of stimulation by mother or mother substitute may seriously and under certain conditions irreversibly affect the total development of the infant. In both these investigations the plan to verify psychoanalytic propositions has led far afield: the investigators have not only been able to decide between alternative hypotheses but, what is even more essential, to suggest new ones. The requirements of scientific proce-

11. As an example, see Henle's experiments (1942).
12. As an example of such a division, I refer to the data on the development of the child's views on morality by Piaget (1932) and similar sets of data produced by psychoanalysis (Saussure, 1933).

dure would suggest that observation of this kind should not be limited to random groups but use representative samples, that it should be conducted over long periods of time, and that studies of child development should be extended and should form the substance of systematic studies in life histories.

Data cannot be restricted to any one cultural or subcultural area. The study of the "nursery" as a matrix of civilization has gained considerable impact from the fieldwork of anthropologists who followed the lead of the genetic propositions of psychoanalysis (Bateson, Erikson, Mead, and others) or used these propositions in their interpretation of anthropological data on child rearing (Gorer, 1942, 1943; Kardiner, 1939, 1945). While advance in this area has been rapid, one other possible field of elucidation has been neglected: the study of identical twins, which would permit access to factors of heredity.[13]

In speaking of validation of psychoanalytic hypotheses by psychoanalytic observation, experimental procedure, and systematic observation, I may have unwittingly conveyed the impression that psychoanalysis is a complete system of propositions, or one near completion. Both impressions would be equally misleading. While psychoanalysis covers a wide area, the closer one investigates the interrelation of proposi-

13. According to Freud's observation (1908), three peculiarities—orderliness, parsimony, and obstinacy (or the opposites of all or one of them)—tend to form a character triad, i.e., they frequently occur together. A further empirical finding of Freud's indicates that in the life of individuals who show that triad of characteristics, excretory function obtained accentuated importance in childhood. He furthermore assumes that under equal environmental conditions during childhood, only certain constitutionally predisposed individuals are likely to develop the indicated triads. In studying the character traits of adult identical twins, Hartmann (1934/35) found confirmation for a part of Freud's propositions. He investigated ten pairs of identical twins and found that if in one of the twins one of the three character traits forming the triads of anal erotism was of importance, in the other the same or another trait of the triads regularly predominates, either in its positive or in its negative form. The three character traits are, therefore, paravariable, i.e., they substitute for each other. No analysis of overt behavior of the twins could have established a meaningful relationship between the disorderliness of the one and the obstinacy of the other. Only the genetic proposition of Freud, which considers the triads of traits as reaction formations to experiences in the anal phase of libidinal development, made the relationship meaningful.

tions, the more "the gaps" hit one's eye; the more does it become evident that however suggestive is the sketch at which one looks, a sketch it is, richer in some parts, more general and painted with a broader brush in others.

Psychoanalysis is not static. Out of psychoanalytic observation a stream of new propositions constantly emerges; the increased number of workers, the changing conditions of observation, such as those of wartime, advances in neighboring fields, but most of all an ever more careful evaluation of the data obtained by psychoanalytic observation are all reflected in psychoanalysis. Hence the quest for verification refers to "old" and "new" propositions alike.

It cannot be a static process; it must be dynamic and continuous. Finally, I would venture the forecast that the gradual amalgamation of psychoanalysis with other sciences, mainly with psychology and psychiatry, will find its expression in the institutions of higher learning. The psychoanalytic movement will yield its function to institutionalized science—for better or worse; there are advantages and serious dangers implied in this development. The tradition of courageous exploration that lives on in psychoanalysis may well be lost in this transformation.

2: Problems in Clinical Research

(1947)

My remarks will be concerned only with those aspects of the methodology of clinical research that are related to psychoanalysis not as a therapeutic technique, but as a body of hypotheses.

Psychoanalytic hypotheses have been formulated and reformulated in constant response to clinical observations. The psychoanalytic interview itself has been the matrix of psychoanalytic research. The reformulations of hypotheses in Freud's own work coincide with the encounter with new clinical pictures in psychoanalytic therapy (chap. 1). The observations of cases of severe obsessional neuroses around 1910, of psychoses in the second decade of the century, and later encounters with character neuroses and patients who had strong self-punitive reactions to therapeutic progress, and impressions gained in child analysis, contributed each in turn not only to the development of therapeutic skills but also to a revision of hypotheses.

I therefore begin with the assumption that the constant interrelation between theory and clinical observation is one of the cornerstones of any science we build. I shall divide the discussion into three aspects: first, the *clarification* of hypotheses; second, their *verification;* and third, their *amplification.* This division is clearly artificial; the three aspects are mutually supporting and form a unit.

Contribution to Round Table Discussion on Problems in Clinical Research, held at the Annual Meeting of the American Orthopsychiatric Association in Cincinnati, Ohio, February 17, 1946. First published in the *American Journal of Orthopsychiatry,* 17 : 210–214, 1947. Copyright 1947, the American Orthopsychiatric Association, Inc. Reproduced by permission.

CLARIFICATION

Two types of clarification seem to deserve precedence: semantic and syntactic, or, as I should like to say, *systematic* clarification. Semantic clarification is concerned with the language in which hypotheses are being presented; systematic clarification with the interrelation of hypotheses.

Current psychoanalytic terminology is, by and large, that used by Freud. Freud's language bears the imprint of the physiology, neurology, psychiatry, and the classical education of his age. It is colored by its use in the therapeutic procedure, hence the richness of metaphors. Freud was not concerned with semantics. The correct use of a term had little meaning to him; it was the context that mattered. One might say that such insouciance is the hallmark of genius; it undoubtedly is its prerogative. When a generation or two of scientists arrogate such a prerogative, the lack of concern for semantics may well lead to confusion. There are three main reasons for this. (1) Gone is the time when psychoanalysis was entrusted to small teams of private practitioners, cooperating on an international scale and trained by a few instructors. (2) Not only has the number of psychoanalysts increased, but the integration of psychoanalytic hypotheses with those suggested by other research procedures imposes upon psychoanalytic terminology new obligations (and new potentialities). (3) Since the startling early discoveries are on the whole unquestioned, and their detailed elaboration is at stake, the context in which a word is used does not always eliminate ambiguity. Seen from another angle, this means that clinical research as conducted up to now has not enabled us to verify or refute *all* relevant controversial hypotheses. Failures in predictions seem to be more frequent than they need be.

Even more urgent is the *systematic* clarification. Throughout fifty years, psychoanalytic hypotheses have frequently been revised and reformulated. Rarely, however, have all previous findings been integrated with new insight. In 1926, in *Inhibitions, Symptoms and Anxiety,* Freud reformulated a considerable

set of his previous hypotheses. I am convinced that this reformulation reaches further than was realized at the time of publication, possibly by Freud himself. At present, hypotheses in
psychoanalysis are formulated in various terminologies according to the various stages of the development of psychoanalysis in which they were suggested. A systematic insight,
therefore, can only be gained by a study of the history of psychoanalysis. However valuable the study of history, systematic
formulation of hypotheses is an essential task for the progress
of science. It enables us to organize hypotheses according to
their actual importance. In this sense, systematic clarification
becomes a prerequisite of verification. There is, moreover, the
task of checking hypotheses against new findings, against what
is this connection I call amplification. This procedure is clearly
facilitated if the structural interconnection of hypotheses is established.

Verification

There is still a tendency among psychoanalysts to look upon
rigorous procedures of verification, upon what has come to be
called "experimental psychoanalysis," with a scornful or pa-
tronizing eye, an attitude I believe to be unwarranted. The
two overlapping goals of verification are: (1) to facilitate communication between scientists; and (2) to decide the "truth" or
"untruth" of a hypothesis (Kaufman, 1944). Such a distinction
is superficial and only partially valid. The procedures of experimental verifications are, as a rule, limited in scope; but
however limited, the immediate value of experimentation is at
least twofold. First, verification by experimental procedure
compels psychoanalysts to formulate their propositions
sharply, and therefore acts as an incentive to clarification of
hypotheses. Second, it makes the findings more easily demon-
strable. The clinical evidence is not accessible to all who are vi-
tally interested in psychoanalytic findings. Experiments on
projection, displacement, substitution, etc., can clearly demonstrate what certain psychoanalytic hypotheses assert. They are
bound to become an essential tool of education at a time when

departmentalization in the study of man becomes ever more obsolete.

Hartmann and I (1945) suggested that psychoanalytic hypotheses can be divided into two groups: dynamic propositions mainly concerned with reactions to a specific experience at a given time or in short-time intervals; and genetic propositions concerned with long-time perspectives. On the whole, it might be said that more dynamic than genetic propositions have been verified. Controversy in this latter field, which represents the hard core of causal explanation in psychoanalysis, is rampant.

Verification in this area can best be obtained by a systematic study of large numbers of life histories of normal people in our culture from infancy on. The usual data which the study of child development produces, however important, are not fully satisfactory. They must be supplemented by data suggested by the psychoanalytic hypothesis, the relevance of which tends to be ignored. Attempts to evaluate such data have been undertaken both in experimental psychology and in cultural anthropology, but only comparatively few of these attempts are fully satisfactory. The question is, at what distance from actual clinical experience should they be undertaken? I believe this distance should be reduced and that the clinic should have precedence over the laboratory. The reason is simple. However closely we observe the growing individual, however accurately we register what we have seen, the relative importance of an experience for the individual becomes clear only in that retrospect which the psychoanalytic interview establishes with greater precision than any other clinical method. It is therefore suggested that verification be increasingly concerned with the study of life histories in our culture, and that such studies be undertaken in close contact with clinical psychoanalysis. The retrospective study should guide the participant observer's attention.

Into what direction the interaction of these two approaches will lead cannot be predicted in detail, but it seems clear that some of the answers to urgent questions can come only from organized cooperation. Let me give one example. Psychoanal-

ysis works with the concept of infantile neurosis. It may be
defined in various ways; what we mean is disturbances of a
certain intensity which occur at various phases of the child's
development. We have not yet come to an insight as to how
far some of the phenomena which are usually classified as infantile neuroses—disturbances of sleeping, eating, and even
intellectual development at various periods—are normal. We
all know and realize that man cannot form his personality
without having experienced anxiety, and yet we frequently
behave as if anxiety in the child is a neurotic symptom. How
can we achieve what has been postulated in this discussion—a
specificity of insight into the etiology of certain types of mental disturbances—until such fundamental questions have been
answered?

There is one aspect of verification, possibly the most important, that I do not approach anew since Kubie (1947) discussed it in his comprehensive presentation. By recent
advances in recording of interviews, the interview situation
will be subjected to an ever closer scrutiny by impartial observers. Under these circumstances, one character of clinical work
may well emerge more clearly: that every interview can, in itself, be considered an experiment in verification and invalida-
tion of hypotheses.

AMPLIFICATION

In dealing with possible amplifications of psychoanalytic hypotheses, we are faced with a vast array of problems. The
most tangible results are in the advance in psychosomatic
medicine.

The fictitious division of body and mind has been eliminated. It seems that at least one side of the advance which has
recently been made may be of immediate relevance for all
other fields. The fact that certain physiological changes provide possibilities for exact measurements of concomitantly registered psychological experiences is only one of the various
consequences of these amplifications (Fenichel, 1945). In several cases it has opened up the avenue for new and more rig-

orous verifications. Let me contrast this area of progress and achievement with another, in which I feel that clinical research is deficient.

If one considers the intricacies of psychoanalytic technique and its teachings, and contrasts discussions in clinical seminars with clinical reports in psychoanalytic literature, one gains the impression of a time lag. Little in psychoanalytic writing is on the level of vividness and specificity of these clinical case discussions. Let me illustrate this by a rather superficial example. Two clinicians talking to each other will describe what a person can do, his skills and potentialities, possibilities of performance, etc. In psychoanalytic literature, such things are frequently discussed under the somewhat misleading heading of potentiality for sublimation. The problem is obviously wider. It concerns many more areas than intellectual skills or performance level. Case histories of an earlier phase, say fifteen or twenty years ago, dealt largely with those areas in which individuals were similar. One may roughly correlate this to the time when the predominant interest of the analyst was concentrated on the id. Now clinical reports start from the surface, from the character, and from what is termed defenses; individuals are treated in clinical work not only so far as they are alike, having similar desires and similar fears, but also in how they are different. In other words, in clinical work, that part of psychoanalytic theory which is called ego psychology has borne fruit, and increasing therapeutic skills in the treatment of character difficulties are witness to the close interrelations of theory and therapeutic technique.

In written reports this has not been true to the same extent. One might say that the art of case history writing has been lost, perhaps partly because of the lack of clarification of hypotheses. Again, the deficiency is greatest where the genetic aspects are concerned. At a time when a case history in the sense here postulated should include the growing up of the individual in all essential areas, the selection of data becomes an enormously difficult task, but its importance should be underlined. I am inclined to go a step further: the comparatively rare attempts to embody in case histories genetic reconstructions which embrace that series of functions which we attribute to the ego as an organization tend to produce a high coincidence of concrete therapeutic suggestions and of concrete suggestions on reformulations of hypotheses.

In this area, as in all others, the sociological position of psychoanalytic research accounts for its present stage of development. To a considerable extent it is being carried on as a leisuretime occupation by psychiatrists in private practice. Only to a small extent has it been institutionalized. In this respect, psychoanalysis is still in the earliest stages of a science.

SUMMARY

Clinical observation, especially the psychoanalytic interview, is still the most important source of our knowledge. While the psychoanalytic interview is uniquely suited for the double purpose of therapy and research, the hypotheses established by it are ambiguous in many areas. They should be verified by more rigorous methods; other types of observation and better checks on the interview procedure itself will have to be combined. The need for verification is greatest where genetic propositions are concerned. At the present time we still have many more hunches than tested hypotheses.

3: Training in Psychoanalysis and the Development of Theoretical Concepts of Clinical Psychology

(1947)

During the first day of this Conference, psychoanalysis was mentioned only in one context. The personal analysis, it was said, constituted a highly desirable, if not essential, part of the training of clinical psychologists. I should like to take this opportunity to state briefly that I prefer the term didactic analysis; that a didactic analysis, to my mind, should be distinguished from a therapeutic analysis. In stating that difference, I am aware of being at variance with the views expressed by many psychoanalytically trained psychiatrists, psychoanalysts, and with some, though not all, references to the subject in Freud's writings: I believe that the didactic analysis should not be less thorough or "complete" than the therapeutic analysis, but definitely more so. It should give the analysand an insight into the dynamics of his behavior and personal conflicts and, insofar as possible, into their origin. It should enable him to use this insight under the changing circumstances of life in the continuous process of adjustment, which includes his reaction to the pathological material to which he will be exposed.

In the present context I use the word *psychoanalysis* to designate a body of propositions. The term *clinical psychology* is, for the purpose of this communication, defined as referring to diagnostic procedures based on a variety of tests, no specific definition of "test" being implied.

First published in *Training in Clinical Psychology*, ed. M. R. Harrower. New York: Josiah Macy, Jr. Foundation, 1947, pp. 61–64.

There seems to be no need to establish the value of psycho-analysis for clinical psychology since at least two of the most important projective tests—the Rorschach Test and the The-matic Apperception Test—have been devised by psychiatrists deeply imbued with psychoanalytic thinking.

The first question which presents itself is a very general one. How can psychoanalysis be taught? Our experience is well founded as far as psychiatrists are concerned, who have been exposed to didactic analysis and practice the therapy under appropriate guidance. Their theoretical studies supplement not only their general psychiatric training but also both of these experiences; indeed, they are an essential part of their training.

In answering the question for the training of clinical psy-chologists we would have to assess in the first place to what ex-tent the didactic analysis is a precondition of any fruitful understanding of psychoanalytic concepts. This is an empirical question and the impressions available seem to me not deci-sive. There seems to be little doubt that the changes in cultural conditions and in the method of presenting psychoanalysis have somewhat affected some of the manifold phenomena which are traditionally lumped together under the heading of "resistance." I do believe—and here I am sure to be in agree-ment with most of you—that a didactic analysis is highly de-sirable, provided it does not mean "an abbreviated analysis." I am aware of the danger of being called a purist in this matter, but I consider this to be only a slight disadvantage.

However, those who wish to study psychoanalysis, whether analyzed or not, must have at least some firsthand experience with certain types of human behavior that can substitute to some extent for the clinical experience of the psychiatrist. To put it briefly: some close and prolonged contact with either psychotics or small children, or some group of human beings under mental stress, seems to be essential for any fruitful un-derstanding of psychoanalysis.

Psychoanalysis itself can today be presented in fairly rigor-ous formulation. The biological thinking and the constructs of psychoanalysis can be offered to the student by a discussion of clearly formulated propositions, which rest upon these constructs.

The appropriateness of the constructs themselves, i.e., the meaning of psychoanalytic terminology and thought as a whole, can thus be related to the question of the validity of these propositions. Some are verified to the satisfaction of many observers, some to that of few; some are considered to be still unverified; but we assume that all are empirically verifiable, by rules of procedure generally accepted in science; and that unverifiable propositions are being excluded.

Psychoanalytic propositions can be related continuously to the clinical and "objective" evidence to which they refer. I should like to stress on this occasion that I am using "objective" evidence here in order to designate two areas: "objective" evidence, gained by experimental procedures on the one hand and by systematic observation outside of the psychoanalytic interview on the other. In addition, many of the findings, which I refer to as "clinical," have experimental character. Psychoanalytic observation, one might say, approximates experimental procedure in many areas, but not in all. In any one case of psychoanalytic therapy a large number of verifications and invalidations of hypotheses is repeated; any interpretation given to the patient, whether it proves to be "correct" or "incorrect," is based on a hypothesis that has been put to the test.

When psychoanalysis is presented in terms of sharply formulated propositions related to empirical evidence, the teaching of psychoanalysis offers an added challenge; the semantic and systematic clarification upon which such a teaching is bound to be based will gradually reduce or eliminate some of the present controversies.

Psychoanalytic propositions tend to support each other. Through their relation to some basic assumptions, they form a system or a *theory* of psychology, both normal and abnormal; a theory that is subject to continuous change and is not equally well elaborated in all directions. This latter fact determines, to my mind, the relation of psychoanalysis to the concepts of clinical psychology.

When the clinical psychologist tests *performance* or *isolated functions* of thought, perception, or motility (in the sense of psychoanalysis, ego functions), he deals in an area that has only recently been subjected to psychoanalytic observation. Here psychoanalysis offers only a loose set of propositions, which may supply a frame of reference, but which is hardly apt to allow for hypothesis detailed enough to be useful to the clinical psychologist; this will be especially true if the continuum of abnormal and normal functions traditionally tested is extended to include supernormal functions or performance. In this vast area, then, psychoanalysis might gradually be able to adopt findings of clinical psychology. Many psychoanalysts are interested in estimating concretely what specific functions and performances of their patients have been influenced by the therapeutic process. Moreover, it seems that the various methods of quantification which clinical psychology is using and will develop may exercise a healthy influence on clinical psychoanalysis—thinking in terms of quantity, and comparing intensities being an essential part of any dynamic approach.

The situation changes when the functions tested by clinical psychology are seen as part of the total personality and its basic conflicts. Psychoanalysis is the psychology of human conflict, and the set of propositions dealing with this area is elaborated in considerable detail. However, the use of these propositions by clinical psychologists meets with various difficulties of which I shall refer to only one.

The material of clinical psychology yields access only to a cross-section of behavior. The clinical psychologist will therefore tend to focus his attention on dynamic propositions. This may tend to impoverish the structure of psychoanalytic propositions. In speaking of obsessional-compulsive symptom formation, for instance, the psychoanalyst has a set of both dynamic and genetic propositions in mind; he has certain expectations as to the formation of these symptoms in certain patterns of life history; the same is true of expressions such as oral or anal-erotic behavior patterns. The clinical psychologist is likely to disregard the connection between the cross-section to which he has access and the longitudinal expectations relevant to the psychoanalyst. Here lies a potential danger that might result in the growth of two separate kinds of languages and an increase in semantic confusion.

Didactic analysis of the clinical psychologist may afford a certain protection against this danger. However, it is questionable whether this protection will be lasting. It seems to me that it should be supplemented by an intense cooperation in research. Sooner or later, test records covering the critical phases in the life history of subjects at least from childhood to late adolescence, but possibly including even earliest childhood or infancy will be available. The clinical psychologist will then deal with the development of trends. At this stage the danger of a division between the dynamic and the genetic approach will be reduced. At the same time some lamentable gaps in the genetic propositions of psychoanalysis might be closed. We might finally learn in great detail how the development of ego functions, gifts and talents of an individual is related to the area of his conflict. Such a cooperation seems to me valuable particularly for one reason: I feel that our knowledge in the area of dynamic and genetic problems of psychology is in a stage in which too rigid a division between techniques, diagnostic or therapeutic, and research is, to say the least, premature.

4: On Psychoanalysis and Education

(1948)

The relationship of psychoanalysis to education is complex.[1] In a first approach the inclination may be to characterize it as one between a basic science and a field of application. Psychoanalytic propositions aim at indicating why human beings behave as they do under given conditions.[2] The educator may turn to these propositions in his attempts to influence human behavior. The propositions then become part of his scientific equipment, which naturally includes propositions from other "basic" sciences. In any relationship between a more general set of propositions and a field of application outside the area of experience from which these propositions were derived a number of factors must be taken into account. The more general propositions, in this instance those of psychoanalysis, must be formulated in a way that permits their operation in the new field, here that of education. The process of application is likely to act as a test of the validity of the propositions or of the usefulness of their formulation (chap. 1). Hence we are dealing not merely with a process of diffusion of knowledge from a "higher" to a "lower" level, from the more

This paper was presented at the 1948 Annual Meeting of the American Orthopsychiatric Association. It was first published in the *American Journal of Orthopsychiatry,* 18 : 622–635, 1948. Copyright 1948, the American Orthopsychiatric Association, Inc. Reproduced by permission.

1. The term *education* will here be used in a broad sense, designating all measures applied by adults, expert or nonexpert, teachers and parents, to influence the behavior of the growing child in a desirable way. When the context seems to offer safeguards against misunderstanding, education will also be used to designate principles upon which such measures may be based. *Psychoanalysis* is used as defined in earlier chapters.

2. For a more detailed statement see Hartmann and Kris (1945).

"general" to the "applied" field, but with a process of communication between experts trained in different skills in which cross-fertilization of approaches is likely to occur.

The relationship between psychoanalysis and education, however, is more complex than this schematic presentation would lead one to believe. The contact with psychoanalysis has modified and enriched not only the measures educators (whether experts or parents, and no parent is expert where his own children are concerned) use "in order to modify the child's behavior in a desired sense," but the direction of the desired modification of behavior has itself to some extent been influenced. The goals of education have come to include mental hygiene in a new and previously unknown sense.[3]

We are not dealing with an isolated phenomenon. Psychoanalysis started as an attempt at the scientific study of an area of life which had previously been dealt with by nonscientific means and in a nonscientific context. It had been in the domain of religious and philosophical systems and appeared in the works of those great intuitive masters in the understanding of human nature, the poets and writers. The scientific approach that in Freud's work has supplemented these traditional approaches to our knowledge of man has exercised considerable influence on general attitudes toward human life. Many things which "had been taken for granted" appeared to be *modifiable*. Psychiatry was enabled to link maladies of the body to those of the mind, or better, to reduce the danger of spurious differentiation between the two—psychosomatic medicine. Psychiatry began to extend therapy to types of behavior previously not considered related to illness, to items such as "character," "unhappiness," even "lack of luck." Similarly in public welfare, charitable organizations have extended the areas in which they help clients, from material support to that of aid in psychological adjustment. In practices of management and personnel selection, intuitive procedures are being supplemented by others aiming at improved predictions. The change in goals of education is part and parcel of

3. Another general direction in which principles of education have been influenced by psychoanalysis will be discussed later.

this development that extends from medicine to many areas of social control.

At the threshold of this brave new world it seems appropriate to halt and raise the question: how well is science equipped to meet the tasks with which it is confronted, tasks set by society, in an age of rapid social change? Let me anticipate what I think is the answer—I believe there is some danger that the demand may outgrow our supply of firmly established knowledge, and that inferior products may temporarily "swamp the market."

I shall not attempt to enumerate reasons for this state of affairs or to describe its manifestations. These problems were treated by Caroline Zachry (1941) in a paper in which she discussed not only the place of progressive education within the total contemporary educational scene, but also the special place of psychoanalysis within the larger setting of progressive education. Nor shall I attempt to describe how interactions and clashes of various principles of education practiced by different educators within one institution or by two parents in one home affect the child; nor how they affect the child when they manifest themselves as inconsistencies in the practices of one educator.[4] It is also out of place to present a survey of the relationship of psychoanalysis to education in its historical development and in its manifold implications, since such a presentation has been given with great completeness by Hoffer (1945).

I propose to focus on a discussion of some typical misunderstandings of psychoanalysis by educators and, more specifically, on misunderstandings concerning the use of indulgence and deprivation as a means of education. Both terms are used here in a very broad sense. Indulgence includes all actions of the educators which meet the child's demands. The range of these actions includes the mother's care and expressions of her love; parents' and teachers' participation in the child's play and daily life, understanding of his joys and sorrows, and tolerance for his unruliness. Deprivation includes all expression

---

4. Some of these problems were touched upon by Peller (1946).

of the educator's disapproval, from the denial of the smile to disciplinary methods of all degrees of severity. Indulgence and deprivation might be taken as synonymous with reward and punishment if it is clearly understood that in the present context these terms refer not only to isolated actions, but also to a general attitude of the educator toward the child. This attitude may respond to the child's behavior during long periods of time and cover a wide range of behavioral details.[5]

The discussion of the use of indulgence and deprivation as a means of education will, I hope, help to clarify some of the general problems which tend to impede cross-fertilization between psychoanalysis and education, and sharpen our eye for means that might enhance it in the future.

The contact between psychoanalysis and education was established when, in the progress of his work with the adult neurotic, Freud (1933) discovered that for an "understanding [of] the case or for producing a therapeutic effect" it was necessary to "trace the determinants of his symptoms . . . back to his early childhood" (p. 147). The gradual development of this insight forms a considerable part of the history of psychoanalysis. Well known in outline, its importance for an understanding of Freud's work is still underrated. There is a tendency to look upon Freud's writings as a unit and to quote his views without reference to the stage of development of his hypotheses from which the quotation was drawn. This misuse is favored by a number of factors. In many areas Freud's views remained relatively unchanged over long periods; in others, changes were at first imperceptible, consisting only in minor changes of wording. Moreover, Freud himself seems to have underrated the extent to which his later work reformulated and modified many of his earlier assumptions. Whenever his views were applied outside the closed circle of psychiatrists trained in psychoanalytic therapy, another element played its part: the time lag of diffusion and understanding. Hence Freud's earliest assumptions concerning the relationship of

5. Fenichel (1945) uses reward and punishment in such an extended sense.

childhood experiences to adult behavior, which have outlived their validity, were tenaciously retained in certain fields of application and are only gradually being abandoned.

Freud's first propositions assumed that neurotic illness in the adult was due to traumatic experiences as a child. In a literal sense Freud maintained this proposition only during a short period (1895 to 1897), when he believed that actual sexual seduction by adults could be considered the decisive etiological factor in the genesis of psychoneurosis. Later (1926) the concept of trauma was modified in various ways, until it referred to experiences of the child in crucial phases of typical development—experiences which, from the viewpoint of the adult, may show no unusual features and yet affect the whole of the child's psychic economy.

The persistence of the older concept of trauma invited the avoidance of educational measures which were thought likely to cause traumata in the sense of shock experiences. Let me give two examples. In restricting autoerotic activities of the child, explicit threats were avoided, since psychoanalytic case histories had repeatedly demonstrated the importance of castration anxiety in the structure of adult neuroses, and the relation of this anxiety to the threats to which the patient had been exposed as child. Similarly, corporal punishment was discredited largely because clinical material indicated that the erotization of corporal punishment experienced in childhood was among the factors contributing to the development of sexual perversions in the adult. On a similar pragmatic level arose the interest of the educator in explaining to the child "the facts of life."

The frequency with which symptom formation in adult neurosis could be connected with fantasies concerning the sexual behavior of adults (the so-called infantile sexual theories) seemed to make it desirable to give truthful information to the child on the sexual life of the adult, and even to anticipate the child's questions. Such isolated procedures could of course do little to pacify the demons, especially since this information tended to remain incomplete and to conceal the element of pleasure connected with adult sexual activity. Only gradually was a less specific concept of the trauma accepted. The avoidance of certain means of education was substituted by aiming at changes in the total relationship between the educator and the child.

These changes were not brought about by psychoanalysis alone. Many social and ideological factors which cannot be enumerated entered into the picture, but the name of John Dewey, one of the initiators of this movement, must be gratefully mentioned. The special contribution of psychoanalysis to the change of educational atmosphere in general was manifested in the tendency to avoid frustration and to increase indulgence in the child's life, an attitude which has rapidly expanded. In certain educational circles, it tends to pervade much of the life of family and school. The general principle on which this attitude is based is difficult to formulate. It seems to be assumed that any deprivation imposed upon the child is necessarily evil, since it creates tension and tension must in turn lead to undesirable behavior, to an increase of aggression or of manifest anxiety. It also seems to be assumed that any interference from the world of the adult damages the child's process of growth; that, left to the child, "things will take care of themselves." The clinical experience to which this attitude of educator or parent most likely refers, is the part played by frustration and anxiety in case histories of psychoneuroses, and the fact that some interpreters of "frustration" relate it to those who imposed it upon the child.

It is tempting to quote examples ridiculing extremes, and demonstrating how, in shifting the burden from the child to the parent whose endurance is visualized as inexhaustible, intolerable situations may arise. Such examples, however, are superfluous in a professional circle; moreover, they are likely to lead to misunderstandings.

In discussing the dangers of a too permissive attitude one may seem to advocate returning to an outdated method of dominance in handling the child. Nothing could be less desirable. We are, to quote Freud (1933, p. 149), dealing with the avoidance of two dangers, of Scylla *and* Charybdis. While indulgence and deprivation may both create unwanted effects, both are essential measures of education. Both meet with some of the child's needs; the question is one of modality and timing.

Modality is particularly difficult to assess; it is part of the most intimate interplay between educator and child. The child's receptive perception for the unconscious motivations of adult behavior has been repeatedly stressed. It is particularly great when the child reacts to the adult's aggressive proclivity that finds expression in the modality of imposed deprivations (Greenacre, 1944). The child's reaction is frequently counteraggression. Usually reactions and counterreactions follow each other in rapid sequence and the child may be provoking or may be provoked. His incentive to exploit the educator's aggression and start upon his own bout of aggressive behavior will be the greater, the more his economy of aggression is in a general state of imbalance.

While I touch only briefly upon the modality of deprivation, the second factor, timing, can be successfully approached if we take into account some psychoanalytic propositions based on Freud's structural concepts. Introduced during the early 1920s, these concepts were later amplified by Freud (1926), and have subsequently been gradually elaborated by others. The area covered by many of the propositions is frequently referred to as "psychoanalytic ego psychology."

These structural concepts of Freud's—the id, ego, and superego—used in psychoanalysis as *constructs,* are being used in every science. They lead to the formulation of a richer, more accurate, and more general set of propositions than could be formulated without them. These propositions are in turn subject to validation or disproof by methods used in science for this purpose. The constructs themselves can therefore be considered only from the point of view of their usefulness. In their formulation Freud followed the lead of a complex set of considerations; in defining them, he followed the lead of his biological training. The structural constructs are seen as psychic organizations and are defined by their functions, as physiologists define organ systems (Hartmann, Kris, and Loewenstein, 1946).

While many of the propositions of psychoanalysis are based on assumptions about the interaction of the three psychic organizations, a small but growing number refers to the formation of psychic structure in a process of gradual differentiation. Thus in considering the formation of the ego, the organized functions of which control motility, thought, and perception, one must take into account the maturation of the physiological and mental equipment of the child; i.e., the maturation of the apparatus of the ego (Hartmann, 1939a).

In relation to the earliest experiences of the child, the ego functions as an organization-delaying response. According to what Freud called the reality principle, the need for immediate discharge of tension is transformed into waiting for well-assured but postponed gratification. Understanding of the requirements that the environment, mainly the nursing mother, imposes is mediated by the first attachment of the child to the mother (Benedek, 1938). In the details of these intimate situations a high complexity of factors is at work. The equipment of the child and the attitude of the mother must be taken into account. While the most tangible part of the earliest mother-child relationship is linked to feeding, other bodily contacts exist in which the handling of the child and the amount of stimulation given can all be related to the general category of indulgence and deprivation.

Throughout the process of child development situations and experiences vary, but they can still be usefully described as processes in which the child strives for self-control of his needs. At first it is to satisfy his environment and retain its favors. Later, when the first steps in the formation of the ego have been taken, when processes of identification have constituted the child's "inner world," he may exercise self-control because he has accepted these demands of his environment and the control of his drives has become an essential goal of his ego functions. Control of drives does not always imply renunciation of gratification, but rather the assurance of gratification through the execution of *action*.

Freud subsumed a variety of impulses, the control and gratification of which are related to the child's needs, under two categories of instinctual drives of a sexual and an aggressive nature. The usefulness of this assumption is evidenced by a rich set of propositions (Hartmann, 1948). However, in many presentations derived from psychoanalysis, the difference between Freud's concept of drives and that of instinct has been obliterated.[6] Only in exceptional and ill-defined areas do drives show the capacity for self-regulation. They require the mediation of a special organization to guarantee adjustment and survival; this organization is the ego.

The problem to which I refer has frequently been approached from a somewhat different angle. When Freud points to the prolonged helplessness of the human child, in that the infant depends longer on support from the outside for his survival than do other mammals, he has the same set of data in mind. The duration of dependency and the fact that human behavior is self-regulatory only in marginal areas, thus differing from those animals whose behavior is predominantly regulated by instinct, are responsible not only for the importance of social learning, but also for the role of conflict in human development. Conflict itself gains a new dimension. Not only is there conflict between the child and the environment, and conflict between opposing needs or drives, but there is also conflict between the id and the ego, and later the superego. This "new" type of intrapersonal conflict has been adequately described as structural conflict (Alexander, 1933).

The appropriate or desirable function of indulgence and deprivation, gratification and discipline, in the child's education can now be described. Indulgence aims at the reduction of tension by satisfying the id impulses; it also helps to establish the child's dependence on and identification with the educating adult. In establishing and reinforcing the norms of desired behavior, deprivation (discipline) supports the ego in its attempt to gain control of id impulses. Were it possible to represent each of the typical conflicts between id and ego by means of a curve, points or stretches might be suggested on which increased indulgence or increased discipline might help

6. The confusion is due to a mistake by earlier translators of Freud's writings (Jones, 1946).

to improve the chances of successful conflict solution. This can clearly be considered only as a model intended to clarify our thinking. It implies a number of assumptions not all of which can here be made explicit. By successful conflict solution is implied the existence of an optimum of tension or an optimum of intensity of conflict in which the child achieves gratification and mastery of his impulses. The only measure at present is whether or not the child's development is favorably or unfavorably affected by the conflict which he has learned to resolve.

Before I comment on this point let me demonstrate the usefulness of the model by examples. Educational mistakes can in some instances be described as "missing the point on the curve."

Recent attempts to reduce the imposed feeding schedule of the neonate, and to entrust the establishment of the schedule to the periodicity of the infant's own needs, aim at reducing unnecessary tension at the time of the child's greatest helplessness; i.e., when no differentiation of psychic structure has as yet taken place. Those who advocate training to start "at once" do not take this fact into account. "Through training in regularity of feeding, sleeping, and elimination," they assume, "the tiny baby will receive his first lessons in character building . . . [and] begin to learn that he is part of a world bigger than his own desires." [7]

Such learning, however, as can be achieved under these conditions may at best be of the nature of a conditioned response, and though no exact data on the potential disadvantages of this type of training are available, the impressions of trained observers and students of child development seem to be well-founded. They indicate that too early training is likely to favor a number of undesirable consequences, foremost among them the increased probability of fixation at the level of development on which the premature training was imposed and hence the probability of regression to this level. This danger seems to be reduced when training is postponed to a

7. Quoted by Mowrer and Kluckhohn (1944, p. 89) from U.S. Government Children's Bureau Publication No. 8, 1942.

time when the child's cooperation has become possible. The recent tendency to postpone toilet training to the time when maturation of muscular equipment enables the child to control his sphincters and sit on the pot without undue effort is based on this assumption. But bowel training is dependent not only on the maturation of the "apparatus" which the ego uses, but also on the child's attitude toward the educator who is involved in the training process.

The observations of Anna Freud and Dorothy Burlingham (1944) in the Hampstead War Nurseries have conclusively demonstrated how the progress of the child in this and other areas involving control of his impulses are dependent on his relationship to one love object. Some of the complex factors in this dependency are referred to in psychoanalysis when we speak of the identification of the child with his love object. This identification in turn plays an essential part in the development of the ego.[8]

When the child has formed his first lasting object relationship, his need for the presence of that love object is maximized. The clinging to the mother at the end of the first and early in the second year of life is a typical manifestation of this need. The relationship is complicated by aggressive impulses in the child which arise especially in response to frustration. They threaten the stability of his attachment to the love object and make the presence of the mother even more imperative. Attempts to detach the child from the mother at an early stage of this conflict may heighten the conflict by mobilizing a circle of increased demands, subsequent aggression, and concomitant fear in the child. Similar attempts at a later time, when independence has been accepted and some pleasure from it derived both in the mastered dependency and in the activity which independence permits, may facilitate the conflict solution in the child's life. The educator then has something in the child on his side; he cooperates with parts of the child's ego.

This relationship becomes even clearer as we approach latency (A. Freud, 1930). The child of five is determined to

8. For a more detailed discussion of psychoanalytic propositions concerning ego formation, see (Hartmann, Kris, and Loewenstein, 1946).

fight against some regressive impulse in himself, for example, the impulse to suck his thumb. He is aware of the ridicule to which he exposes himself. At this point the appropriate help that education can offer may consist in the strengthening of the ego in the child's battle against the regressive impulse. This strengthening can take various forms, one being the imposing of discipline, preferably in agreement with the child, as external help to strengthen the inner forces. Other methods may aim at reducing the tension which impels the child toward regressive behavior by substitute gratifications and indulgences, or permissiveness in other areas. One may resort to psychotherapy or methods akin to it, and try to support the child by interpretations, which may give him insight into the reasons for his behavior. Such alternatives in turn tend to give rise to misunderstandings, especially when the choice between some form of discipline and some kind of interpretation is involved (S. Bornstein, 1937; E. Sterba, 1945).

To give an example: a boy of eight stole some money from his mother's purse. The mother noticed it, but did not discuss it with the child. The father, a prominent scientist, had himself just started psychoanalytic treatment. Instead of yielding to his original impulse and showing disappointment and anger, the father sat down with his son that evening and asked him what reasons he had for being unhappy. He intended thus to replace education by interpretation, much to the (unconscious) regret of the son. As it became apparent later, the boy wanted his father to set the standards and protect him against his own delinquent tendency, which resulted from envy of his father. The motivation of the father's behavior was easily traceable to his identification with his son. When he began psychoanalytic treatment, the father claimed a privilege in fee to which his academic position entitled him, but at the same time concealed considerable sources of private income. From this and similar observations one may deduce that in many instances where discipline is avoided, where pseudointerpretations are attempted and other educational mistakes occur, the educator identifies with the child in conflict and chooses the easier rather than the more appropriate way.

Appropriateness, I said, was to be defined by the child's progress. In establishing criteria for what is meant by progress, many problems arise, some of which will be mentioned briefly. First are the general proclivities in the educator, especially the parent, which barricade the way. Any contact with the child tends to mobilize impulses and desires of the parent's own childhood. We are well aware of the fact that the adult's aggressiveness toward the child, which may be manifested as discipline, may be due to experiences in the adult's own child-parent relationship, or that displaced ambitions may become an undesirable motive in education that tries to push the child to increased performance. Both these tendencies are, on the whole, being discouraged by current educational theory, or at least by that educational ideology which bears the hallmark of the influence of psychoanalysis. This ideology, however, encourages another displacement. The idealized image of childhood as a period of undisturbed happiness, really a projective fantasy in the mind of the adult, has been discarded. Insight into the frequency of childhood conflicts is opposed to so primitive a view. Yet it survives in a special disguise as a utopia of what childhood should be, a utopia in which the adult's suffering as a child should not be repeated.

I suspect that in this displaced ideal the hope is rooted that in maximizing indulgence, conflict will be eliminated. But even those who recognize the importance of these conflicts in the child's development are frequently tempted to consider anxiety in the child's life as symptomatic. There is a tendency to draw the line between normality and psychological illness in the child at the same point at which it is drawn in the symptomatology of the adult. This view has repeatedly been contested. Anxiety, it has been said, is part of the child's normal development; its appearance during critical periods is unavoidable. During the solution of the constellation in the child's life which we subsume under the oedipus complex, concomitant castration anxiety is the fertile ground out of which the child's moral energies grow. The integration of the superego has its roots in this anxiety; it lives on in the adult as fear of conscience. Similarly, it has been claimed that the appearance of what in the adult may be considered symptom formation may in the child appear as temporary compromise. Thus the moral rigidity which under many educational influences accompanies the years of early latency, sometimes supported by rituals and other manifestations of obsessional-compulsive behavior, need not become the basis of an obsessional neurosis or an obsessional character in the adult. It may be a transitory compromise, protecting the newly accepted standards of behavior against threatening impulses, and thus function as one of the reinforcement techniques frequently encountered during early phases of many learning processes.

The problems with which I am dealing here have been treated in the psychoanalytic literature as the ubiquity of infantile neurosis. According to Anna Freud (1945), diagnosis and treatment should be based not on the apparent severity of symptoms, but on other criteria, related to the flexibility of the ego in its relationship to the id, and to the development of the various functions of the ego. The appearance of infantile neurosis distorts this relationship and impedes some of these functions. It acts like a calcification in the middle of a living organism. The dynamics involved can be studied in relation to the mechanisms of defense utilized by the child in order to solve his conflicts. The excessive use of each of them may affect the child's control of his outer and inner world.

A more detailed examination of these problems may be based on a distinction that Hartmann (1939a) introduced. He points to the fact that not all of the childs' achievements are related to his conflicts; that in physical and intellectual life, and in growth and development, many steps are normally not affected by conflicts. The factual question arises: where in the development of each child does the area of conflict cease and the area free of conflict begin? Variations in this respect seem to be considerable. The endowment of the individual and his formed predispositions must be considered. Involvement in conflict need not necessarily act as a force which reduces ego functions. Obsessional proclivity may act as a stimulus to develop certain abilities in problem solution through thinking.

Such stimulation of ego functions in the conflictless sphere can be mediated by the mechanism of sublimation. The particular importance of this factor can be fully assessed only if we realize that, while ego functions genetically depend on their relationship to the child's original needs and tensions, this does not necessarily determine the extent and nature of their effectiveness. The original impulse may lose its importance with the disappearance of early needs and tensions and ego functions may become autonomous. The child's curiosity may become the scientists' bent for research, and the quest for the truth may be as distant from his peeping impulse as striving for social justice may be from the child's effort to protect himself against jealousy by a law of equity in the nursery. Briefly, the area where the function was first developed need no longer limit its scope.[9]

In attempting to establish a model condition under which indulgence or deprivation might be indicated as a means of education, I implied that it should be based on criteria that include concern for the child's development; the ego was to be prepared for its functions.[10] I have considered the extent and complexity of these functions. The control of impulses for purposes of socialization is only one element; the progressive capacity of the ego to detach itself from conflict and to enrich its autonomous functions introduces new elements. This multiplicity of factors may well remind us of the stage our knowledge has reached. Psychoanalytic study of the child started as a reconstructive method; during the last two or three decades it has been supplemented by observation of the growing child. Our approach has remained essentially clinical. The knowledge and insights of some observers are extraordinary and far-reaching, but attempts to enlarge the circle of experts must necessarily be based on a more systematic foundation.

Gaps in our knowledge are due not to a scarcity of studies

9. I do not here enter into the question of a distinction between "successful sublimation" and autonomous ego function. The latter concept was introduced independently by G. Allport (1937) and Hartmann (1939a).

10. For a similar view based on a somewhat different approach see M. Balint (1942) and Fries (1946).

on child development, but rather to the fact that these studies only exceptionally include attempts to verify or modify psychoanalytic hypotheses, perhaps in part because these hypotheses have not always been formulated with sufficient clarity. The admirable investigations of Gesell and his collaborators contain detailed and precise data on most areas of the child's maturation, but maturation is that part of growth which is least dependent on social influences. Far fewer and less precise data are available on personality development; i.e., that part of growth which is largely dependent on social influences. To give only one example: the use of indulgence and deprivation as a means of education is based on assumptions concerning the child's object relation, but systematic study of the genetic aspects of this area is still in its beginning. A comparatively small number of investigations has already yielded important data and opened new vistas. Thus the needs of the child during the first six months of life had erroneously been described before systematic observation could independently produce a correction of our views (A. Freud & D. Burlingham, 1944; Spitz, 1945).

The intensity of the child's need for love in this period is great, but relatively independent of the attachment to one individual. The need for the one and only mother grows as the child's ego develops and object relations gain in importance. On second thought, we may find that Freud's propositions in this area have prepared us for this finding; yet without the work of the last decade we could not distinguish between alternative possibilities.

Concerning the development of the child's ego functions, based on physical and intellectual maturation, extension of the area of observation suggested by psychoanalysis points mainly in one direction. We are interested in further elucidation of the specific relation of these functions to the child's typical conflicts—to the change from passivity to activity, from dependence to independence, to coping with libidinal and aggressive impulses which threaten the child's object relations. A new type of intensive observation by nursery and primary school teachers, who have been familiarized with the clinical aspects of the problem, promises to take the lead. It is an area in which the trained educator may well be able to increase the insight of the clinician and where cross-fertilization may become most fruitful. Systematic study of the child's ego functions can be facilitated where measurement procedures can be utilized. Projective and nonprojective tests may, under certain conditions, sharpen our eyes to discern conflict or autonomy in ego functions.

In outlining some gaps in our knowledge, and in pointing to some of the areas where systematic observation should prove useful, one difficulty has explicitly been omitted. Current studies on child development tend to be based on the isolated child. Wherever psychoanalysis is to guide child observation, the social environment in general, but mainly the person of the educator, must be taken into account. Psychotherapy of the child includes the mother—or rather, much of it starts with the mother and includes the child. Similarly, any study of education must include the educator. When enumerating the areas in which psychoanalysis has affected education, this relationship deserves special emphasis.

Psychoanalysis has taught us that education rests on interpersonal relationships. Clinically, we study the educator's influence, especially the parents'. We are aware of the impact of their own conflicts on those of the child (Fries, 1946) and of the chain formation in neuroses occurring in families (Spitz, 1937). Systematic study of a child's reaction to his educators, as they follow each other in his development, will have to take similar factors into account. It seems particularly important to stress this point since the psychoanalytic approach to child development and contemporary learning theory have many interests in common. One point at which understanding tends to turn into misunderstanding concerns the part played by the educator. Psychoanalytic observation aims at including the total field of the child's interpersonal relations, something very difficult for experimenters to reproduce. To put it briefly: every step of learning in early childhood is codetermined, as are many steps of learning in later life, by object relations and involve conscious and unconscious identification.

It is probable that only the teamwork of participant ob-servers will be able to cope with these factors. Similarly, cul-tural variations become tangible reality if the study of the child includes the educator and the total cultural environ-ment. Available studies have proceeded to describe these fac-tors and their influence by stressing what might be called patterns of deprivation and indulgence (Kris, 1949). Ob-servers have noted to what extent each of the child's basic demands were met by his environment, how long he was breast-fed, how suddenly or gradually he was toilet-trained. Much less attention, however, has been given by the same ob-servers to the child's ego development under culturally dif-ferent conditions, to his inner world, to his concern with reality versus fantasy, retained versus repressed memories, and many other factors.

Such are the manifold tasks which lie before us. They will be solvable if the trend toward cooperation of various ap-proaches in the study of child development continues, and if such cooperation gradually allows for an integration of con-cepts and hypotheses.

5: Notes on the Development and on Some Current Problems of Psychoanalytic Child Psychology

(1950)

The beginnings of psychoanalytic child psychology can be traced back to the period of 1890 to 1900 when clinical observations first suggested to Freud that childhood experiences constitute one of the etiological factors in neurotic symptom formation in the adult. Material made accessible recently (Freud, 1950) shows that from this starting point a set of generalizations arose, which enabled Freud to recognize the potentialities of his whole approach to psychopathology, to establish the relative independence of his findings from neurophysiology in the contemporary meaning of the word, and thus fully to realize the scope of his venture. We are justified in saying that it was the ontogenetic approach which helped Freud to realize that what had been initiated as an attempt to investigate etiological factors in hysteria led to nuclear parts of a new psychopathology and psychology (Kris, 1950). It would be a fascinating essay in the history of psychoanalysis and a worthwhile contribution to the history of science in general to investigate in some detail how Freud's views developed and how, based on data from the analysis of adult patients, insight into the psychosexual development of the child was gradually gained. We know in general terms that the reconstructive method had enabled him to recognize regular maturational sequences in the child's life; this unparalleled

Contribution to the Panel on Psychoanalysis and Developmental Psychology, held at the Meeting of the American Psychoanalytic Association in Detroit on April 29, 1950. First published in *The Psychoanalytic Study of the Child*, 5 : 24–46. New York: International Universities Press, 1950.

and uniquely successful procedure cannot be evaluated merely as an awe-inspiring feat of that one observer; it has at the same time established the fruitfulness of psychoanalytic observation as the method of ontogenetic inquiry. However, the individual steps by which Freud reached his conclusions have never been demonstrated. No such detailed investigation will be attempted here. I shall have to limit myself to tracing a number of trends in contemporary research to their initial stages. For this purpose I am introducing a somewhat arbitrary division in the history of psychoanalytic child psychology. I assume the existence of a chronological dividing line constituted by the early 1920s, when several important developments in psychoanalytic thinking occurred. Although they were closely interrelated it seems permissible to start with an enumeration. The formulations on psychic structure which replaced the assumptions on the topographic stratification of the psychic apparatus—i.e., the formulation of a psychoanalytic ego psychology—opened new vistas in the area of developmental psychology. The emphasis on aggressive impulses directed attention to hitherto less closely observed manifestations of behavior. Simultaneously, clinical data directed general attention to the part played by preoedipal experiences in the development of neuroses.

These theoretical and clinical developments, each in turn and all of them in their interdependence, were bound to influence the development of therapeutic technique, to enlarge the scope of psychoanalytic therapy, and consequently to encourage attempts to vary procedures in adjusting them to cases hitherto out of reach of analytic understanding. The most important, but not the only, instance of this tendency was the development of child analysis.[1] Its independent contribution to psychoanalytic thinking in general, and to the psychoanalytic knowledge of childhood in particular, strengthens the idea of

---

1. See Anna Freud (1927). One should not in this connection overlook the techniques developed to deal with delinquents, first by Aichhorn (1925) and later by Staub (1943). Experience with delinquents may well have been a formative element in the development of Alexander and French's (1946) views on technique, with their overemphasis on corrective experience.

the chronological dividing line—a device that in the course of this paper will not be justified any further. Rather, I shall operate with the idea of two phases in the history of psychoanalytic child psychology; moreover, for the sake of clarification, in pointing to differences I shall always imply and occasionally refer to "before" and "after" as means of characterization. The differences to be discussed will be related to three interdependent and overlapping areas of problems. I shall discuss first "the consideration of the environment" (or the development of psychonalysis as learning theory); second, a specific aspect of this general area, the problem of object relation; and third, child observation and trends in current research.

THE CONSIDERATION OF THE ENVIRONMENT

During the various phases of Freud's development, emphasis on the importance and interest in the effects of environmental conditions was subject to change, though fluctuations in emphasis were never extreme. At certain times of Freud's development the quest for an understanding of the mental apparatus and its propensity to react even under minimal external stimulation stood in the foreground, at others the external sources of stimulation were studied in great detail.

Shortly after Freud had become aware of the extreme importance of childhood experiences for the etiology of neuroses, he formulated a set of hypotheses which one might call "environmentalist" to the extreme. The seduction hypotheses of 1895/96 not only stated that hysteria in the adult was due to seduction of that adult during his childhood but went considerably further; they envisaged the interaction of familial influences. The best-elaborated part of these assumptions stated that perversion in the seducer produced hysteria in the seduced. This assumption, which postulated a high incidence of adult (parental) perversion, enabled Freud to recognize first the improbability and shortly thereafter the incorrectness of his assumption (1950, letter 69). He himself described the crisis in his life and the development that followed—the emergence of new insight which evolved from the initial failure. Since the reports of his patients did not describe real events but fantasies, the study of fantasy life became essential. The study of these phenomena led to the discovery of the oedipus complex and to that of the various manifestations of infantile sexuality, and hence to the development of a set of nuclear hypotheses of psychoanalytic child psychology.

If we try to comprehend these early vicissitudes in theory formation in more general terms, we may say that a shift had occurred: the seduction hypothesis maximized attention to concrete experiences to which the child had been exposed; the later orientation was implicitly based on the supposition that relatively minimal external stimulation would produce the reactions observed; and these reactions, the working of the mental apparatus rather than the concrete environmental conditions, were investigated in detail.

It would be misleading to take this description of a shift in Freud's interest at the turn of the century and during the subsequent decade too literally. It was not equally true of all parts of psychoanalytic work at the time, and the division of interest was at no time sharp; yet it existed.

Let us turn to an illustration. In the case history of Little Hans the child's mother and father are extensively characterized, but it is not their personalities or the interaction between their own and the child's proclivities which are mainly studied. They are primarily, though not consistently or exclusively, seen as agents from whom the stimuli to which the child reacts are coming or have come. The main considerations center on the sequence of these reactions, and on their economic and dynamic interrelations with other experiences of the child. Only when the problem of Little Hans's identification with the parental figures is envisaged, father and mother are treated more as individuals than as agents (Freud, 1909).[2]

Without a discussion of examples to the contrary which are not infrequent and clearly prepare the future, we may gener-

2. The distribution of interest is somewhat different in the case of Dora (Freud, 1905a). Yet, in spite of the unparalleled vividness with which the actors of the drama are presented, even in this case history attention is not fully focused on their individual traits.

alize and state that during the whole of what I here designate
as the first period of psychoanalytic child psychology the distribution of interest was approximately of the following kind:
it remained focused on typical reactions of the child; on their
sequence; and their genetic, economic, and dynamic interrelations. Environmental conditions, though recorded in detail,
were mainly considered as the source of such "required" experiences; there was something unavoidable about them.

The change in outlook occurred largely in relation to the
development of ego psychology. The way in which this change
was effected can best be illustrated if we turn to one of the
most crucial applications of ego psychology, to the problem of
anxiety. The older toxicological theory, which had assumed
that undischarged libidinal tension was transformed into anxiety, was abandoned in favor of one which considered the
danger situation as its center. Anxiety as a signal mobilizes
defense against danger; anxiety as a symptom may then, in
turn, be experienced as danger against which defenses are
being mobilized. The theoretical setup is no longer a physiological one but rather a biological one; organism and environment are seen in their interaction. At the same time, historical
factors gain an even greater relevance: the ontogenesis of the
reaction to danger, the history of danger experiences, and the
history of defenses against them are recognized as decisive.
The gain for the elaboration of psychoanalytic views on child
development was very great indeed.

The development of the child was no longer viewed only in
terms of crucial conflicts and typical danger situations related
to the maturational sequence of libidinal development. First
the contribution of aggressive proclivities to each of these
phases and conflicts was considered, and initial attempts were
made—which are being continued (Hartmann, Kris, and Loewenstein, 1949)—to view the interaction of libidinal and aggressive drives in each of the typical danger situations of
childhood. Soon, however, the study of typical danger situations gained in scope. It became possible to take the stages of
ego and superego development into account. In a number of
instances, at least, it was possible to correlate the use of certain

mechanisms of defense to certain situations and developmental phases and thus, however incompletely and tentatively, to establish certain facts in the "regular" development of the mechanisms of defense (A. Freud, 1936).

The decisive contribution to these questions came from a new source of clinical experience, from the analysis of the latency child. This is the age in which the intensity of defense is maximized, since the danger from which the child has escaped is particularly great. At the same time, the study of the latency child opened the way for a more meaningful understanding of the problem of defense. In speaking of danger and defense against it, I refer not only or not mainly to pathology but rather to conditions of tension which constitute normal growth. When Anna Freud (1936) describes how anxiety of a certain intensity stimulates intelligence, she aims at this area of problems which, particularly during the last decade, has considerably gained in importance. We have come to understand the extent to which conflict, danger, and defense are part and parcel of normal development not only in the sense of their being "innocuous occurrences," but as essential and necessary concomitants of growing up (Anna Freud, 1945). Phases of particularly intense conflict—such as prepuberty—have been shown to stimulate progressive trends (H. Deutsch, 1944/45). The adaptive function of defense in general has been stressed, and the assumption has been made that the prospectively favorable development of autonomous ego functions is closely related not to the absence of, but to an optimal distance from conflict (Hartmann, 1939a; Hartmann, Kris, and Loewenstein, 1946).

These then are some of the most general insights that our understanding of child psychology has gained, largely stimulated by the work of Anna Freud and her collaborators in child analysis, who took full account of "situational" factors and were inclined to relate their findings to the interaction between the concrete environment and the development of the child's capacities.

Up to this point I have referred only to the contribution of child analysis to the study of the mechanisms of defense and

have neglected other vistas that child analysis helped to open
up. A host of intimate data about the child's life, his fantasies
as well as his daily experiences, became accessible to observation. Not all of these data were "unique"; some, for instance,
had been familiar to open-minded and analytically oriented
educators, but the analytic interview with children and the information accessible only to the child analyst provided a setting in which daydreams and night fears, games and
productive expressions of the child became understandable in
their exact position in the texture of the child's daily experience in home and school, in a much more concrete sense than
the secret parts of a child's experiences, at least, had ever
before become accessible to adult understanding. These remarks do not by any means exhaust the contribution of child
analysis to the development of psychoanalytic child psychology. On the contrary, they still refer only to one of the two
schools of child analysis which developed during the 1920s,
the one initiated and guided by Anna Freud.

It is much more difficult to evaluate the contributions of
Melanie Klein's school of child analysis (1932, 1948). Its work
was centered on preoedipal conflicts and, although the theoretical and technical principles developed seemed at first to
allow direct therapeutic access to two-and-three-year-old children, the emphasis was placed almost exclusively on the use of
observed behavior for the purpose of reconstructing much
earlier experiences of the infant. However, of the various
techniques of reconstruction applied in psychoanalysis, one
was predominantly utilized by Klein; namely, the extrapolation from mechanisms known from adult psychoses. The controversy which arose between the two approaches to child
analysis (see Symposium on Child Analysis, (1927) was carried
on for well over a decade in this and other areas, since Klein's
hypotheses led to many generalizations which by some are
thought to represent an independent system of propositions,
constituting the so-called "British School of Psychoanalysis." It
seems superfluous to characterize this system anew, to polemicize against part of its hypotheses, and to suggest modifications of others since similar attempts have repeatedly been

undertaken (Waelder, 1936; Glover, 1945; E. Bibring, 1947). It seems, however, that during the decade which separates us from the climax of the controversy certain general prospects have become clearer than they seemed at the time. We have realized how much in our understanding of oral fantasies is due to some of Klein's elaborations of Abraham's views, how our appreciation of aggressive manifestations within orality has gained in scope, and how much more familiar we have become with certain typical fantasy contents of oral destructiveness than we formerly had been. The problem is different when the chronology and sequence of events described by Klein are at stake. While there are some who claim that they can establish irreconcilable contradictions between her chronological assertions and proven facts of child development (Spitz and Wolf, 1946), there are others who feel that any reprojection of mental content into earliest infancy (as attempted by Klein) is bound to be so vague that no single statement can actually be shown to contradict any purely observational data concerning behavioral manifestations or developmental gradients.[3]

But at the same time it seems to me that the experience gained in the decade of which I spoke has in one decisive area facilitated a decision in the controversy between the two schools of child analysis. That area concerns what I have previously called "the consideration for the environment." Anna Freud's approach derived its peculiar vividness from detailed scrutiny of the child's concrete situation; in Melanie Klein's reports, these elements play no comparable role. The psychic events which she describes as having taken place during the early months of the infant's life are cataclysmic. They seem, therefore, hardly touched by the ways in which stimuli from the outside reached the child through the mother's ministra-

---

3. I have little doubt that the Kleinian hypotheses are so formulated that not a single one can actually be disproved by child observation. In this respect, the Kleinian propositions would exaggerate certain features of general psychoanalytic propositions, some of which, it is true, are difficult to validate by observation. It also seems probable that the contributions of the late Susan Isaacs (1933, 1935) first to developmental academic psychology, and then to the school of M. Klein, established a guarantee of noncontradictory formulations.

tion. The drama between breast and mouth, visceral tract and muscular apparatus is enacted with little regard for external trappings.

It is here where the experience of a decade has facilitated the decision. From very many and independent sources we derive data that contradict the meaningfulness and fruitfulness of such an approach. Psychoanalytic child psychology has undoubtedly made a shift toward the environmentalist position. I shall not attempt to give in detail the evidence which brought this shift about. It was inherent in the developments initiating the second phase of psychoanalytic child psychology. Psychoanalytic ego psychology had, as I said, reemphasized the character of psychoanalysis as a psychology of adaptation, of learning,[4] and clinical data have implemented these general assumptions as far as the child's earliest experiences are concerned. In speaking, as I did before, of the importance of preoedipal conflicts, I really referred to the uniqueness of the mother in human life. While one might say that the discovery of the oedipal conflict was centered on the male child, the gradual but rapidly growing insight into the general importance of the preoedipal phase was initiated by renewed interest in the development of female sexuality (Brunswick, 1940);[5] and little more than a decade after the preoedipal development of girls had been discussed, a similar attempt, based on case material, was undertaken for the boy (Lampl-de Groot, 1946).

Next to this purely psychoanalytic material stands a vast array of data derived from analyses of mothers, various therapeutic techniques practiced with children in child guidance setups of different kinds; and last but not least, clinical impressions of child analysts and analytically oriented child psychiatrists that stress not only the general intimacy existing

4. See Hartmann (1939a). Both terms, adaptation and learning, require closer definitions. This has recently been emphasized for the term adaptation, particularly by P. Weiss (1949) and H. W. Smith (1949). As far as learning is concerned, a point of view that stresses complexity and warns against simplification has recently been presented by Beach (1950a).

5. For a historical survey see R. Fliess's introduction to the relevant section of his *Psychoanalytic Reader* (1948).

between mother and child, but also a particularly close relation between the behavior of the two. No better and more dramatic illustration of this insight could be quoted than the
universally accepted idea of treating a small child by treating
his mother, as if we were in fact still faced with one organism—an idea which G. Bibring expressed many years ago
(in a meeting of the Psychoanalytic Society in Vienna), when
she spoke of mother and child as a unified system.[6] At the
same time the various procedures of simultaneous treatment
of mother and child have produced a great deal of material
that illustrates the types of interaction that exist between
them. We are entering here into a vast area of recent research.
Its clearest manifestations may well be seen in some of the extreme hypotheses advanced. There are those who try to establish a definite relation between one type of maternal
behavior and a symptom or group of symptoms in the child:
children with a predominance of psychosomatic symptoms are
children of certain kinds of mothers (M. Sperling, 1949);
there is a mother of the child with eczema (Spitz, 1951); and
there is a mother whose children become stutterers (Glauber,
1951). Before I turn to a more detailed examination of this
trend in recent research, it seems appropriate to enlarge the
theoretical foundations from which this account started.

THE PROBLEM OF EARLY OBJECT RELATIONS

When late in 1943 Margaret Ribble's book *The Rights of Infants*
was published and the quest for "early psychological needs
and their satisfaction" was answered under the sloganized
heading "food is not enough," a trend of psychoanalytic thinking and investigations that had gradually developed over
many years suddenly reached the general public. Before we
turn our attention to these antecedents it seems appropriate to
state how much we owe to Margaret Ribble's own investigation, to those of Margaret Fries (1946) and to the long set of
investigations on the consequences of early institutionalization

6. For similar formulations see also Hoffmann (1935).

of the child, to which Spitz (1945, 1946) has contributed so decisively. These studies helped us fully to realize that in extreme cases the lack of adequate object relations in infancy may threaten the infant's life, may cause serious and even irreversible changes in areas of maturation, and create psychosomatic disturbances, the extent and impact of which are not yet fully known.

In these and similar inquiries the field of investigation was not limited to the child, it included and frequently was centered around the mother and the family setting. It is in this connection that the problems arose of how to investigate the mother's personality, which standards to apply, and what observations to recommend in order to establish a link between her behavior and the symptomatology of the child. The psychoanalyst or child psychiatrist who had to deal with similar problems in consultation was, it seems to me, never seriously in doubt as to how to proceed. The approach of the psychoanalytic clinician has guided a group of workers at the James Jackson Putnam Children's Center in Boston in formulating general assumptions in this area. Beata Rank, Marion Putnam, and their collaborators assume quite generally that the child's personality bears the imprint of the mother's personality. This general problem was and is being studied in a specific area, in cases in which the emotional detachment of the mother (in some cases the detachment of the psychotic mother) is viewed as an etiological factor in the condition of the child, of his psychotic, atypical, or arrested development. Several cases which were published give evidence of the application of these assumptions to therapeutic procedures. With the reestablishment of the emotional climate, in which maternal behavior is assumed not to have met the child's needs, not only considerable therapeutic progress could be demonstrated, but the type of processes in themselves, which were observed during treatment, carried confirmatory value (Rank, 1949a, 1949b; Rank, Putnam, and Rochlin, 1948; Rank and MacNaughton, 1950).

In my opinion, the decisive assumption in this area seems to be connected with the criteria used in assessing the mother's

attitude. I am not sure whether in what follows the opinions of
the workers at the Putnam Center, in particular the views of
Beata Rank, are correctly rendered or whether I have interpreted their views for my own purposes; I read them to
state that the overt behavior of a mother to her child can be
evaluated only with difficulty—i.e., cannot simply be measured
or rated—unless it is seen as expression of and in relation to
an unconscious fantasy. It therefore does not make much
sense to speak in general terms of maternal qualities; rather, it
is essential to study in detail a mother's attitude to a specific
child. The assumption that behavior is an expression of an unconscious fantasy—an assumption which the psychoanalytic
clinician is bound to stress—permits us partly to account for
the confusing differences in mother-child relations within one
family.

Hypotheses of this kind seem to me to represent a significant advance, since they effectively implement older theoretical assumptions, to the extent that some of these assumptions
seem to become fully meaningful only now. When in 1926
Freud entered into the discussion of typical danger situations
to which the human child is exposed, he distinguished two—
the two most archaic ones—which have a direct bearing on object relations: the danger of losing the love object and the
danger of losing the object's love.[7] The first represents the
anaclitic needs; the second, the more integrated relationship
to a permanent, personalized love object that can no longer
easily be replaced.

It might well be that this basic distinction will have to be
refined, that differentiations will have to be introduced, and
that, for instance, the question of the capacity to accept substitute objects will have to be correlated closely to the various
phases of the child's ego development. Quite obviously, what

7. A fairly large literature on the fringe of psychoanalysis consistently ignores
Freud's views in this area or manipulates his statements; to mention only the most
glaring examples, Suttie (1935) in England, and Fromm (1941) in this country. The
rapidly growing number of contributions on "separation anxiety" rarely stress that
they are simply variations of the theories of Freud, against whom they prefer to
polemicize. For psychoanalytic elaborations on the problem of separation anxiety, see
Odier (1948).

is true of any other division into phases in the child's life is also true of this distinction: there are not only fluctuations from one type of object relation to the other, older one, but the two types normally overlap. The fear of object loss never quite disappears; the fear of loss of love adds a new dimension to a child's life and with it a new vulnerability. Quite possibly, then, in studying child development further and in greater detail, we might find it convenient not only to introduce "subphases" but also to describe the simultaneous distribution of both types of object relation in one child, e.g., in terms of a ratio. But this does not detract from the value of the distinction established by Freud; on the contrary, it enhances its importance. His distinction between two types of attitudes to the object gains in significance by its relation to the child's ego development and describes a decisive step in this development (Hartmann, Kris, and Loewenstein, 1946). One might use as an illustration what at the same time was an unintended (and as yet unrecognized) experiment at validating Freud's distinction; i.e., an experience made at the Hampstead Nurseries in London. When their toddler population did not react in any way to educational pressures by the nurses dealing with them, the suggestion was made to substitute for the various nurses dealing with the whole group one nurse permanently or predominantly dealing with a smaller group. Anna Freud and Dorothy Burlingham (1944) describe the effectiveness of this device. We may say in Freud's terms that the anaclitic and transient object relation had been "outdated," and a more permanent attachment was needed in order to facilitate the control of impulses by identification. For the sake of pleasing *their own* nurse or of winning and retaining her love the toddlers became clean and quieted down. I have little doubt that a similar explanation applies to other types of behavior noticeable around the one-year limit—particularly in the details of the mother-child relationship. The increasing demands for the mother's presence, the clinging which extends to the bedtime rituals may well be connected with the new type of need arising at that time—the need for the object's love.[8]

8. Its (at least initially) insatiable character may indicate that novel needs may express themselves by older pathways, by archaic cravings. Even under normal cir-

It seems that the further study of object relations and their bearing on ego development may also prove its value for an understanding of the clinical problems of psychotic, arrested, or atypical development to which I previously referred. In some of these cases we find indications of a comparatively undisturbed development during the earlier phases of infancy, up to a point, during the second or third year of life, when the picture suddenly changed or a change became manifest. In a case in which, to some extent, a similar process was jointly observed by the Rooming-in-Service (Dr. Edith B. Jackson) and the Child Study Center (Dr. Milton J. Senn and staff) at Yale, a closer study of the data strongly suggested that the type of environment and care—overindulgent in a fanatical sense— was "appropriate" during the first year of life, but the very detachment, which is the corollary of a fanatical attitude, did not constitute an object relation that could meet the requirements of subsequent stages of the child's ego development.

Observations of this kind, tentative as they are, may become strategic in more than one sense, since they draw our attention to gaps in our knowledge which seem of considerable relevance. By what criteria, by what observational techniques, or by what testing procedures will we be enabled to recognize such and similar symptomatology before it becomes manifest; what are the methods to spot danger before it appears?

Without attempting an answer to these questions at this point, I believe that the stress on certain sectors of ego development rather than on others, on the social and learning sectors in the widest sense of the word, has proved to be useful (Spitz, 1950). A challenging formulation of a similar view I find in a statement by K. Wolf, according to which relationship to human objects has to be firmly established "to enable infants to form relations with inanimate objects." [9] This statement formulates more concretely a general impression

---

cumstances, this frequently sadistic and therefore often not fully satisfactory child-mother relation is many a time soon overshadowed by the concomitants of the training process; in such cases the anal expression of aggression is substituted for the oral one, a sequence familiar from reconstructions in analyses of adult patients.

9. See Spitz and Wolf (1949). In the text it is said that "libidinal" object relations have to be firmly established. I take this to be a shortcut for both libidinal and aggressive cathexes.

shared by many; namely, that during the earliest phases of childhood the development of many ego functions tends to be directly dependent on the nature of the object relation—an impression that fully satisfies and in turn justifies some of our metapsychological assumptions. To put them in briefest form: the assumption that the energy cathexis of the ego as an organization is derived from object cathexis is a necessary part of Freud's formulation concerning the nature of psychic structure; one further step, outlined by him and elaborated by Hartmann (1950a), assumes that the cathexis of the ego with neutralized energy (desexualized libido and deaggressivized aggression) is a guarantee of the autonomy of its functions (Hartmann, Kris, and Loewenstein, 1949). It seems only sensible to insert into this chain of propositions some formulations which take the nature of the object relation into account. Thus we might assume that the more satisfactory the object relation is, the higher is the chance of a successful neutralization of that energy which by identification becomes available to the ego. If we want to propositionalize further and thereby to contribute to a closer circumscription of what might be meant by "satisfactory object relation" in the context of these assumptions, we are, it seems, driven into one direction: the "better"—the more completely—aggressive and libidinal energies are fused in the cathexis of the object, the higher are the chances of a successful neutralization. At this point a possibility for verification seems to open up. We know from clinical experience of what significance the freedom to manifest aggression can be in childhood; might it not be that early manifestations of this kind in sucking or biting, in twisting or grasping the mother's body could supply indices of a freedom to attack an object or part object that is so securely invested with libido that no harm can reach it by its investment with aggression?

The attempts to establish interconnections between various Freudian hypotheses in the area of ego psychology with our developmental interests have led us far afield. Once more the question presents itself how similar problems had been dealt

with in what I have called the first phase of psychoanalytic
child psychology. At first there were, quite obviously, some or
even a good many problems that had not been considered at
all. Some others, such as the questions connected with the
conflict-free sphere or autonomous ego functions (IIartmann,
1939a), appeared out of context. Some of the data pertaining
to the problems raised by Hartmann formed in some instances
part of the qualitative descriptions given in case histories; they
were part of an area that contributed to the improvement of
our general understanding of the patient; but as far as psychoanalytic propositions were concerned, that area was at the
time "no-man's-land." [10] Other problems were naturally familiar, but the context in which they appeared was different.
Danger situations to which the child was exposed and his traumatic experiences were not seen mainly in their relation to the
behavior of love objects—they naturally were in extreme
cases—but were viewed primarily in connection with the
operation of "the means of education." We hear less of the
fact that mother's absence or the lack of her devotion left its
imprint, but we hear that weaning did. Next to the quantitative factors which are always stressed, very soon a second factor gained attention—the factor of phase specificity. Relevance
or irrelevance of an experience was thought to be determined
by the developmental phase in which it is experienced by the
child. A little girl's reaction to the sight of the male genital will
depend on whether or not she has reached the phallic phase;
some went further in saying that possibly the frequent exposure to similar experiences would accelerate the process of
reaching the phallic phase.

When similar problems were discussed during the "second
phase"—the change seems to have occurred gradually during
the '30s—a larger number of factors is taken into account.

10. There can be little doubt that one of the strongest incentives for Freud's reformulations was the desire to cultivate or conquer "no-man's-land"; his starting point
was frequently the notion that a certain type of behavior proved to have unsuspected
clinical relevance—and the attempts to elucidate this relevance determined, in part,
the selection of the next step in the formulation of his new propositions. The expansion of psychoanalytic propositions during the last decade, for instance, in Hartmann's contributions, followed, as far as I can see, similar principles.

The situation in a specific crucial period can no longer be described only in terms of psychosexual development; equal consideration has to be given to that of the aggressive impulses, to the development of the ego and to that of object relations—in addition, naturally, to historical factors, i.e., previous experiences that determine present behavior (Hartmann, 1950b). Thus the reaction of children to air raids (A. Freud and D. Burlingham, 1942) has been explained by taking a multitude of factors into account. The calmness or excitement of the mother with whom the child identifies, the question whether the child had lost a member of his family in a previous raid, the closeness of destructive id impulses to the ego, and finally the closeness or distance from the castration complex. Only in taking account of such a multitude of factors did it seem possible to account for the fact that children in certain age groups seemed frequently less afraid of air raids than adults expected them to be.

In a similar sense, the problem concerning the means of education has become more complex during the second phase of analytic child psychology than during the first. Few if any clear-cut rules can be established: rather, every discussion of the handling of the means of education must take into account a multitude of developmental factors. As far as the alternatives between indulgence and deprivation (discipline) are concerned, a formulation can at least be attempted (see chap. 4).

Thus every step we take and every formulation we achieve implies one connection: that between our set of data and a clear and detailed notion of what constitutes normal child development. Is this not the very area, one might ask, which a host of investigators in academic child psychology has pursued; are there not data assembled which could satisfy all needs? However rich these data, their bearing is limited; they are more useful where mere maturation is concerned, or the development of motility and intelligence is at stake; in other words, they are more useful for certain ego functions than for others. The capacity of the ego to cope with conflict and anxiety, the chances of achieving positive synthesis of tensions—briefly, the development of all those functions of the ego that have a direct bearing on the structure of personality is known only in unreliable outline. There seems to be wide agreement that the psychoanalytic study of child development would fill an urgent need, might usefully function as a center of integration of various approaches, and promises the only way to answer the questions with which we all are occupied, questions in which the problem of prevention is omnipresent. Let me here list some of them. How soon can we, from observational data, predict that pathology exists in a given child; how soon can we spot it from the child's behavior, from that of the family unit, or from the history of mother and child? Which therapeutic steps are appropriate to each age level and its disturbance, or to each typical group of disturbances? The problem of diagnosis and indication requires constant refinement; the severity of one isolated symptom does not lend itself as indication for therapy (ubiquity of infantile neurosis). The self-healing qualities of further development are little known. How much can latency, prepuberty, or adolescence do to mitigate earlier deviation or to make the predisposition to such disturbances manifest?

CHILD OBSERVATION AND TRENDS IN CURRENT RESEARCH

Psychoanalytic views on child psychology are based on two sets of data, on data gained by the method of reconstruction in psychoanalysis and on those gained by direct observation of children. The relationship of these two sets of data to each other is of considerable importance for any discussion of problems of research. First we have to stress that the relationship has not remained stable throughout the development of psychoanalytic child psychology. During its first phase, observational data largely provided confirmation or supplementation of insight gained by reconstruction. During the first two decades of the century, the psychoanalytic periodicals carried frequent collections of accidental observations which fulfilled these requirements. During the second phase, observational data were collected more systematically and used for other purposes. They were expected to provide decisions where al-

turnative hypotheses had been advanced by reconstructive
methods (Waelder, 1936) and to contribute to an understanding of areas of behavior to which reconstructive hypotheses had not been able to gain access; e.g., to the details of
infant development during the preverbal stage. However, the
main difference between the first and the second phase of psychoanalytic child psychology lies elsewhere. During the first
phase, the data based on child observation seemed to form an
isolated and marginal field of interest, more closely related to
psychoanalytic education or pedagogics than to any other part
of psychoanalytic thinking (Hoffer, 1945). During the second
phase, the tendency developed to integrate observational data
into the general flow of psychoanalytic thought and to relate
them also to the therapeutic technique of psychoanalysis.

The value of observational data has never been in question
in Freud's mind. When he wrote the *Three Essays on the Theory
of Sexuality* (1905b), he deplored that he had not been able
fully to utilize observational data, though even at that time
they supplied some "isolated hints" and some valuable pieces
of information (p. 193, footnote added 1910).[11] Freud's interest in this problem area extended over many years; it led him
to develop many aspects of psychoanalytic interpretations in
considerable detail and was subject to that same change in emphasis which the development of ego psychology brought
about in many other areas. Freud's starting point was the traumatic experience to which I previously referred; i.e., the inability early in his work to distinguish between the fantasies of
his patients concerning their childhood and the recollections
of events that had really taken place. There are ways to establish a decision, but none, he argued later, is more decisive
than the study of the disturbances of the child during childhood. While we might, at the present stage of our knowledge,
doubt to what extent the neurotic disturbances of childhood
(at least of later childhood) can be understood without reference to older experiences—to a past that would have to be
reconstructed—there can be no doubt that, in speaking of

11. In view of such explicitness it is hardly understandable how it could have been
said that it never occurred to Freud to study the vicissitudes of childhood while they
happened (Gorer, 1949).

childhood neuroses, Freud does not refer mainly to the psychoanalytic technique of study but has in mind observational procedures (1916/17, p. 358ff.). He develops his ideas even further and stresses the direct impact of the child's experiences on the etiology of neurotic illness; he does so, however, with some hesitation and in a polemic vein:

> The significance of the infantile experiences should not be totally neglected as people like doing, in comparison with the experiences of the subject's ancestors and of his own maturity; on the contrary, they call for particular consideration. They are all the more momentous because they occur in times of incomplete development and are for that very reason liable to have traumatic effects. The studies on developmental mechanics by Roux and others have shown that the prick of a needle into an embryonic germinal layer in the act of cell-division results in a severe disturbance of development. The same injury inflicted on a larval or a fully grown animal would do no damage [1916/17, p. 361].

The actual study of childhood experience seemed to Freud at the time particularly important in order to decide how much of the emphasis on some past event which is recalled or reexperienced in analysis is due to regressive cathexis and how much to the reaction to the original event. He kept the two conditions apart and never lost sight of the fact that this question was one which required investigation in each case. Others did not share in this view and this caution. Thus Ferenczi and Rank (1924) not only stress—correctly—the fact that what appears in analysis as experience related to the past need not actually have been experienced before; but in writing their treatise they behave as if it could not have been experienced before; reconstruction then has nothing to do with what had once occurred.[12]

12. The confusion of their point of view reveals itself in their wording: "In the phase of transference—in contrast to that of resistance—it is always a question of making conscious the tendency of the libido, operating in the transference, to reproduce situations which mostly were never conscious at all, but resulted from those tendencies and impulses which were partly experienced in the infantile development, but were at once repressed" (p. 10). One might well say that their discussion, no less than Otto Rank's subsequent *The Trauma of Birth* (1924), represents a caricaturelike exaggeration of Freud's view on "psychic reality."

When after a time lag of two decades Freud returned to a discussion of the problem of reconstruction of the past, his position had further developed. He not only discusses the criteria upon which such reconstructions have to be based, but, in comparing the advantages of the reconstruction in archaeology to those in analytic work, he points to the special difficulty of the latter: "psychical objects," he says, "are incomparably more complicated than the excavator's material . . . and we have insufficient knowledge of what we may expect to find" (1937b, p. 260).

It seems permissible to argue that some of this knowledge can be supplied by child observation. In fact, there can be little doubt that the more detailed and concrete our knowledge of infancy and childhood is, the more knowledge we have to draw on, the higher will our chances be to present the patient with reconstructions that, in covering a large set of details, stimulate those displacements of cathexes which are part of the therapeutic process (M. Katan, 1939) and may ultimately lead to the experience of recall.

There is little doubt that contributions from child observation to reconstructions in psychoanalysis have become more frequent since concentrated efforts of many workers have contributed in various ways to the study of the child; the frequency of interpretations in terms of the types of defenses initiated by the child, e.g., in reaction to the absence of the mother, has probably increased considerably. So have undoubtedly many reconstructive interpretations in which the type of behavior one has reason to expect from a specific adult is taken into account; briefly, it is, I believe, possible to show that the integration of all that we have learned of childhood and infancy into psychoanalytic thinking is taking place and that this integration is generally filling gaps in our knowledge and drawing our attention to less well appreciated types of conflict situations.

All this, however, characterizes only one aspect of the problem area. The other aspect concerns the contribution of data derived from reconstruction to the observation of the child. Briefly stated it is my impression that however rich the data are that observational techniques supply, all that concerns their organization, the coherence of phenomena—i.e., all steps that we take in establishing hypotheses to be tested by what we observe—are directly dependent upon what we have learned and are learning from reconstructions in psychoanalysis. This can be stated only as an impression because there are, no doubt, considerable differences between various observers and their equipment. What may remain meaningless to one can very well gain meaning for another. However, as far as I can see, the history of recent research seems to confirm this impression. Let us turn to the area in which observational techniques have contributed most during recent decades—the early features of the mother-child relationship. As stated earlier, stimulus for intense observation in this area came from the analysis of women in whose early history the preoedipal mother attachment played a decisive part. But even the further hypothesis concerning the relationship of severe personality disturbances to lack of warmth in the earliest object relationship was not gained by observation, but only confirmed by it. The hypothesis itself was first formulated in relation to analytic work with schizoid personalities, in whose early childhood the attachment to parental figures had never fully developed (H. Deutsch, 1934, 1944/45).

It would be erroneous to generalize from such impressions that all that the observational study of infant and child will ever be able to provide is a test of psychoanalytic hypotheses, their confirmation or their refutation in defined but limited areas. It is certainly true that this function exists; that as far as many questions are concerned, the analyst's knowledge gained from reconstructions offers neither a correct nor a sufficiently detailed picture of child development but at best only an approximate one; a picture that needs to be implemented and supplemented, controlled and enlarged. But this is undoubtedly not the sole and dominant function of child observation, if its relation to psychoanalysis is fully utilized. Optimal conditions seem to require that the observational and reconstructive data be comparable. Such conditions would exist if observations were not limited to cross-sections but organized in a longitudinal sense; if observations supplied data on life history (Sears, 1943; Hartmann and Kris, 1945; Hoffer, 1945). Such data would certainly not replace those supplied by psychoanalytic reconstruction, but would supplement them in at least two ways. Data obtained by psychoanalysis are naturally selective. They not only contain more precise information on areas of conflict involvement than on areas free of conflict, but even within conflict involvement their selectivity has to be taken into account. They indicate what was important in an etiological sense and when it became important. Events that seemed not crucial while they happened may later become crucial; earlier—neutral—experience when regressively reinvested may become traumatic. The simple comparison between two sets of data, selective and weighted ones and the unselected ones, collected without reference to the dynamics that may suddenly change their importance to the individual—such a simple comparison might prove to be immensely instructive. Such comparative study of data would be particularly interesting (according to suggestions made independently by Hartmann and Anna Freud) if some of the subjects whose development would have been studied by observational techniques could then be studied under the condition of analysis. One might expect that investigations of this kind would not only elucidate a large number of problems that have hitherto never been studied adequately—such as the problem of the development of memory—but there is a chance that the function of psychoanalytic theory as a potential point of integration of various approaches in the study of child development might here become of practical importance. Integration of knowledge in child development can at the present moment not be seen as detached from another problem to which I have previously referred: the problem of prevention. Only the systematic longitudinal study of life histories, combined with attempts to predict at each point all that can be predicted about future development, seems to meet the requirements of the moment. This is not the place for detailed discussions of the question how general or how specialized such predictions should be; a question that Benjamin (1950) discussed very lucidly.

It is probably best to assume that we will have to learn not only how to observe but also how and what to predict. That both observation and prediction can derive their rationale from the coherent dynamic picture which psychoanalytic theory has to offer seems to me obvious. The two approaches, the one by reconstruction, the other by observation, are bound to overlap, but cannot be made to substitute for each other. No observation and no longitudinal study has replaced or, I believe, will replace the value of psychoanalytic observation proper for the study of child development. It is not only the method which provides relevant data otherwise not obtainable; it is not only, at least frequently, the one way to establish the etiological relevance of experience in the child's life; but it also is the method to show how various phases of the past were interrelated; to see the life history as a whole, as it is organized by the personality and in turn has organized the personality. But this factor in itself establishes its limitations. It is that factor with which Freud was engaged in a lifelong struggle. The telescopic character of human memory—to use an expression of Phyllis Greenacre—suggests the necessity of the study of the very elements which constituted the unified picture. One may at this point raise the question which kind of observational setup is most suited to serve our purpose. Is it the study of the normal or that of the sick child, the study within the family or that within an institution? Every setup, every observational technique can provide us only with a partial answer, can make accessible only part of the problems.

There are those who want the burden to be shifted to most exact, most continuous observations of the family setup. To state an extreme: the shadowy observers who live with the family would obviously, in the opinion of some writers, disrupt the family; and even the most shielded home visit has its temporal or situational limitations (Dollard, 1949). The advantages of the residential nurseries to which we owe so much as compared to obversation in nurseries and kindergarten are obvious. Yet the artificiality of the extrafamilial setup has its natural limitations. Limitations of observational methods are by no means accidental: they are partly inherent in the nature of the child. A large number of observers are inclined to draw

conclusions from spot observations; i.e., from short-term intensive observation in home or nursery. The limitations of this
method, well known to these observers, can be illustrated by
mentioning two problems—the problem of *behavior constancy*
and the problem of the child's *regression rate*. The constancy of
behavior under various situations is limited in the adult. It is
not only more limited in the child, and infinitely so, but subject to extraordinary variations according to the child's state of
development and a large number of individual factors; e.g.,
fear of the new, shyness, ease or difficulty in forming substitute object relationships, in fitting into the group. The questions which children, and under what conditions, show a high
or a low constancy of behavior and what constancy distribution is "normal"—questions related to ego development—will
be accessible only if large quantities of observations are combined and probably if various observational setups can supplement each other. The behavior to which I refer as regression
rate may prove useful as an indicator in a similar sense. How
far does a child regress under stress, fatigue, or in response to
any one specific or many unspecified frustrations? In two-
year-olds the end of a nursery period looks strikingly different
from its beginning, and in some children more markedly so
than in others. It is not only the expectation of the mother,
but, as some details indicate, the very duration of the nursery
period that has instigated regressive behavior.

Advantages and disadvantages of each setup in which investigation is being carried out can be evaluated only if we take
the working hypothesis of the investigators into account; in
each such case, the awareness of the limitations is part of both
planning of research and evaluation of results. In conclusion,
I want to return to a point at which I interrupted my presentation. I referred to several hypotheses which related certain
types of behavior in the mother to certain types of symptoms
observed in the child: some of these correlations seemed plausible, but all seemed questionable to the extent to which the
problem of specificity of causation was involved. It seems that
in each of the areas further research is required; and in each
the test of the hypotheses advanced could best be reached by a

convergence of two sets of data—those gained in analysis and those assembled over many years and tested by predicting short-term steps.

Moreover, once we have decided on such coordination of data we shall sooner or later have to include the problem of hereditary factors in our investigation.[13] Again if the double approach, psychoanalytic and observational, were systematically directed toward a study of identical twins, in both similarities and differences that according to some preliminary impressions seem not unrelated to parental preferences—we would have advanced further toward what we take to be our goal: the integration of data and approaches in developmental psychology around a center rooted in the thought of Freud.[14]

13. [In an unpublished Progress Report of the Yale Longitudinal Study (see chaps. 8, 9, and 10), which was written in 1953, Ernst Kris stated a related hypothesis: "We are interested in establishing *in what way* the 'sameness' of personality manifests itself. . . . This requires at least two different steps: first an attempt at greater precision in describing the equipment of the child, and secondly an assessment of the interaction of the child with the environment. . . . At this point a large number of difficult problems open up. To emphasize only two extreme possibilities as an illustration: the environment's influence may reinforce the equipment or predisposition, or it may act in the opposite direction. The child will, we believe, have different personality characteristics and adaptations if his predispositions are reinforced than if they are 'toned down' by the environment. We do not underestimate the complexity of evaluating the forces."]

14. [The implications of the ideas first expressed in this paper were discussed in detail by Anna Freud (1958).]

6: Opening Remarks on Psychoanalytic Child Psychology

(1951)

The increased interest in the psychoanalytic study of the child since the early 1920s coincided with a decisive phase in the development of psychoanalysis. Two aspects of this development are: first, the transition from the topographic stratification of the psychic apparatus to structural concepts—the beginning of ego psychology; second, the increased understanding of the preoedipal experiences of the child and their etiological importance. Child analysis has made early contributions to both problems. The contributions to ego psychology proper consisted at first in a refinement of systematization of our knowledge of defense mechanisms, largely based on the analytic study of the child during the latency period. Freud had pointed to the special importance of typical danger situations against which defenses are mobilized; hence the special position of the latency child, who has just escaped the dangers of the oedipal phase.

To the more detailed knowledge of the preoedipal phase child analysis supplied a large mass of data. They were, however, less conclusive since, as far as the early phases of development are concerned, even the child analyst works by reconstruction. In this specific area reconstructions had to be

First published in *The Psychoanalytic Study of the Child*, 6 : 9–17. New York: International Universities Press, 1951. [This brief, historically oriented survey was meant "to stimulate discussion and controversy" at a two-day discussion meeting on Problems of Child Development, which was held at the Austen Riggs Foundation in Stockbridge, Massachusetts, on April 23, 24, 1950. The meeting was chaired by Robert P. Knight, who had invited Anna Freud, her former collaborators, and a selected group of child analysts.]

based largely on extrapolation. By extrapolating from psychotic mechanism to early childhood the Kleinian theories were formulated and an area of controversy arose. The last ten years have, I believe, contributed much to clarify this controversy. The valuable thoughts of the Kleinian school and its shortcomings have both become evident.

This controversy was one of the factors which stimulated more consistent attempts to supplement data gathered through analysis of children and adults by data of direct observation of the child during the early stages of development. Not that the contribution of observation had started at this point; it had been postulated by Freud as early as in *The Three Essays on the Theory of Sexuality* (1905b), but through this controversy the importance of observations became more obvious. They were carried out in a large number of setups and confirmed the view of those who stressed the importance of the child's concrete environment for his development, a point underrated by the Kleinian school. The observational approach was in part facilitated by the conceptual clarification initiated by Freud in 1926.

Psychoanalytic ego psychology with its central concept of the *danger situation* and its distinction of typical danger situations for each phase of development was formulated as a theory of learning. Adjustment and learning are processes which refer to the interaction between organism and environment.

Psychoanalytic ego psychology has set out to embrace a wide field. It deals not only with those ego functions which mediate between conflicting demands of id, superego, and environment, but also with the wide area of functions which are not, or only in a minimal way, involved in conflict; or, to put it differently, functions that at an early stage of development emerge from conflict and become autonomous (Hartmann, 1939a). It is with these functions that other approaches to the study of child development had been mainly preoccupied. It seems appropriate at this point briefly to comment on the relation of psychoanalytic child psychology to other approaches to developmental psychology.

The question how far the data collected by nonanalytic ob-

servers can be used by those who study the child with a psychoanalytic orientation has been with us for some time. There
seems little doubt that where growth and maturational processes are concerned their value is considerable, and that
where the social behavior of the child is at stake they tend to
become useless. One might say that these two areas are to
some extent roughly correlated to the relative absence or presence of conflict involvement. It seems therefore that tests and
measurements can approximately establish the level of the
child's development as far as the maturation of the ego apparatus and the autonomous ego functions are concerned; a distinction between the two is easier the more we approach the
later phases of childhood. One may therefore feel that tests
and measurements could in the future become useful aides in
diagnosis and in the attempt to approach a crucial area to
which so little has been contributed—the quest for the conditions under which special aptitudes and talents develop.

The data relating to developmental psychology appear in a
different light where psychologists use psychoanalytic thinking. This is happening to an ever-increasing extent. Up to the
present, investigations of this kind have formalized certain
problem areas. Moreover, they have facilitated the demonstration of psychoanalytic tenets to those to whom psychoanalytic data were inaccessible. They also serve the function of
intrascientific communication. But they are still scant and have
not yet produced new insight. Estimates of the chances that
they may do so in the future vary according to the training of
the investigators, the methods they employ, the goal they have
in mind, and a number of other factors.

Even in the ideal case the difference between psychoanalytic
and academic investigations does not rest only on a difference
of emphasis. It is not only one of much "scientific rigor"
versus less of it, of artificial laboratory problems versus the
richness of life. Some of these differences, I believe, can be
traced back to the dichotomy between what I should like to
characterize as *action research* and "pure" research. In order to
avoid misunderstandings, let me say that here we are not dealing with methodology of science but with procedures in re-

search with the procurement of data.[1] The traditional view that "pure" research establishes the general laws, while action research is limited to the preparation of action, seems applicable only in a limited number of cases. It certainly is not applicable to the science of human behavior in the broadest sense, and the very fact that this is gradually being recognized may at least in part be due to the influence of psychoanalysis (e.g., on the late Kurt Lewin).

In general studies of child development, this view still tends to be neglected. It is still assumed that the less the observer interferes, the more significant, i.e., the more reliable, will be his findings. To this we oppose the view that in many—or better, in most—problem areas the growing infant and child can be studied only in his environment, of which an adult (his mother) is part. We may have a third person reporting about the two—but there are two to report about.

Attempts to isolate factors are to be viewed with some distrust. Much in our knowledge of speech development is based on Gesell, and Gesell's data are in turn to a considerable extent based on twin observations. How were some of these data gained? At the age of one and three quarter years, one twin was "taught" to speak, i.e., his speech development was stimulated, the other twin's development was not stimulated. For the purpose of the experiment they had not only been separated from each other for five weeks but had also been separated from their families. This in itself creates a very specific situation. The "not-stimulated" twin was, during the period of training of the other, i.e., during five weeks, kept in a speechless environment: nurses and psychologists pretended muteness. When after five weeks the language development of this child was being studied, what did the observers obtain? Did they gain evidence on the influence of maturation on learning (Gesell) or evidence on maturation under the particular conditions of a specific and frustrating situation?

Psychoanalysis has grown up as action research. We have

1. The difference between them has been discussed in various contexts: see, for example, the discussion in *The Journal of Social Issues*, Vol. II, No. 4, 1946, on "Action and Research—A Challenge."

learned to investigate as part of the therapeutic procedure and have been trained to take our own actions into account. It seems plausible that in our future work we should not discard this tradition. It has served us well.

As a method of investigation, action research is naturally not limited to psychoanalysis. It characterizes many situations in which the observer takes part; these include in particular the functions of pediatrician, nurse, and teacher. It also determines the attitude of the psychoanalytically trained observer to this subject. This attitude is decisively influenced by the therapeutic and preventive intention.

Such an intention naturally harbors dangers. Therapeutic and preventive enthusiasm tend to distort the observer's attitude. The history of analysis is replete with instances that could be used to illustrate this point. Let us therefore say that the intention of which I speak has to be controlled, and that some aspects of this problem are sometimes overlooked. It is this intention that creates the situations in which new data become accessible. The historical basis of psychoanalytic child psychology is Freud's finding concerning the stages of psychosexual development, discovered in the course of psychoanalytic therapy of adults. A quarter of a century later, based on insight into psychoanalytic ego psychology and the nature of preoedipal attachments, Freud outlined two stages in the development of object relations; the need for gratifying objects—the anaclitic object relation—and the later need for the permanent love object. The study of these two overlapping phases, which cover a large variety of phenomena, has proved immensely stimulating and fruitful in every sense.

In studying differences between institutionalized and noninstitutionalized children, the extent to which even maturational processes depend on environmental factors has recently been investigated. The hypotheses which the observers had in mind were derived from Freud's formulation on object relations, originally gained in psychoanalytic work with adults. The insight into the degree to which the child's immediate physical dependence on the mother, his anaclitic object relation, is supplemented and paralleled by his psychological dependence on her, the recognition of the traumatic effect of separations, has been elaborated and consolidated over two decades. And yet, at every point our knowledge is fragmentary; details are missing and the specific interconnections are uncertain.

One of the difficulties that deserve to be mentioned concerns the connection between the development of object relation and ego formation on the one side, and the psychosexual development of the child on the other. In reading some recent publications, one feels as if two sets of problems were kept apart, or as if the closeness of the interconnection was not always or not sufficiently evident. This may have several reasons. One of them seems to be obvious: while our theory is refined and our observational skills are considerable in questions pertaining to the libidinal development, we still feel a far lesser degree of familiarity when we are confronted with studying the economy of aggression. And yet the development and socialization of both groups of instinctual impulses can not, as we know, be separated from each other. They cannot be separated from the study of object relation; nor can that area be separated from the study of the development of the ego functions of the child. Freud's conception of the role and the transformation of psychic energy provides the link between these areas of problems—in the assumptions that the love object is cathected with libido and aggression, that the early identification with the love object leads to the cathexis of the ego with energy, neutralized, or at least in part neutralized. As a consequence of these assumptions one might expect that the permanent cathexis of the ego with neutralized energy—one of the surmised conditions of ego autonomy—is dependent on the quality of the preceding object relation.

It could easily be demonstrated that a large number of concrete observations and investigations in the details of the early mother-child relationship are directly related to these assumptions—although both the recent investigations and Freud's assumptions cover much independent ground.

In view of these experiences we may well state with some confidence that psychoanalytic theory has offered a useful framework even in most recent phases of work. In fact, it seems to me that in a not too distant future the attempt may well be made to describe, explicitly and in detail, the relation between these recent interests and our theoretical assumptions. Such explicitness would permit us to establish not only what we know but also to ascertain the most glaring and painful gaps in our knowledge. The leading trends in most investigations of psychoanalytic child psychology could be characterized as the study of the child's personality development during the sequence of typical danger or stress situations and as the study of the typical methods of adjustment in the development of psychic structure and defense. But the question how this "personality formation" takes place is in many respects an open one. The more we know, the less we feel that we know the essential. Not only does every piece of new insight pose new questions—a natural process in science—our own demands also are growing. New questions are being suggested by the very goals that explicitly or implicitly determine so much of our research.

The driving power is the quest for prevention. This quest not only impinges from the outside upon our work, reflecting the needs of the community. It is not only firmly rooted in the personality of investigators who have grown up in therapeutic work; the quest for prevention also supplies the basic questions that further investigation should clarify.

Which method of child care, which distribution of indulgence and deprivation, seems most promising? In response to these questions, doctrines of child care and education tend to arise; advocacy of maximal indulgence, avoidance of all restrictions, etc. Some of these thoughts have led to organized research of a semiexperimental kind in the study of early feeding procedures, particularly in relation to self-regulation. The idea is highly suggestive, but the difficulties are obvious. How rarely is it possible to rely on the change one type of procedure of child care has introduced, since that procedure is embedded in the infinite complexity of the environment?

In therapeutic practice the simultaneous treatment of mother and child, and the therapy of the child through treatment of the mother have proved useful. These therapeutic procedures clearly derived from the theoretical assumptions stated above. At the same time our views and data have been decisively enriched by the experience of the clinician.

Without further insisting on the interaction of therapeutic and preventive orientation and theoretical assumptions, I repeat (see chap. 5) some leading questions which seem to be omnipresent: How soon can we, from observational data, predict that pathology exists in a given child; how soon can we spot it from the child's behavior, from the child-family unit, or the history of mother and child? Which therapeutic steps are appropriate to each age level and its disturbance, or to each typical group of disturbances?

Our criteria of diagnosis and indication require constant refinement; the severity of one isolated symptom does not lend itself as an indication for therapy. The self-healing qualities of further development are little known. How much can latency, can prepuberty, can adolescence do to mitigate earlier deviation or to make the predisposition to such disturbances manifest? These are questions that also tend to be discussed in various types of follow-up studies.

These and other questions not mentioned here are bound to direct us into an area which, though never abandoned, has of necessity been left underdeveloped. This distressed area of psychoanalysis is the study of the normal, and we are directed to it by many considerations. It has been said that the study of the neurotic cannot be separated from that of the normal (Hartmann); if this is true for the adult, how much more relevant is that point for the problems of child development? Briefly, I believe that with or without our avowed intention, we are forced to postulate that psychoanalytic child psychology embraces the total field of normal and abnormal development, that it be the center around which other approaches should be organized, and that it gradually develop methods for such integration. Much ground will have to be covered before this goal can be reached, and here we are concerned with some of the steps leading toward it. Which type of setup, which kind of observational facilities are most appropriate to our purposes? In chapter 5 I stated my views on this matter.

Every such setup, every observational technique can provide us only with partial answers, makes only a part of the field visible. Advantages and disadvantages of each setup in which investigation is being carried out can be evaluated only if we take the hypothesis into account which the investigators have in mind, and in each such case the awareness of the limitations in part of both planning of research and evaluation of results.

One of the suggestions for future investigation that some of us consider essential and promising can briefly be stated. Most of our hypotheses—and many that have not been mentioned here—require prolonged patient observation of individual children in various observational setups over many years. In this connection one could speak of a study population that can be followed from the prenatal period into later life. If the suggestion of such longitudinal studies needed to be justified at all, it could be done by saying that such studies would supply data that are to some extent similar to those we are used to in psychoanalysis. To some extent they would be dissimilar and supplement the data to which we are used. The ideal combination might exist if an individual known by such studies would at a later date be observed in psychoanalytic treatment.[2] Only then would the data gained by observation attain their full significance. It remains the prerogative of the reconstructive method to establish the etiological relevance of experiences in the child's life, to show how various phases of the past were interrelated, to see the life history as a whole as it is organized by the personality and in turn has organized it.

2. [The "suggestions for future research" outlined here formed the basis of the longitudinal study in child development which the author (together with Milton J. E. Senn) initiated at the Yale Child Study Center in 1949. An additional assumption, not mentioned in this paper, but frequently expressed in research conferences, was that meaningful observations could be made only in a service-oriented setting—in the context of the child's and the mother's developing relationship to pediatrician, nursery school teacher, social worker, and subsequently to child analyst. (See also chaps. 8 and 10.)]

7: Some Comments and Observations on Early Autoerotic Activities

(1951)

I

The reader of the 1912 symposium on masturbation—on which Annie Reich's comments (1951) have thrown new light—may well feel humble in front of the wealth of clinical observations and the breadth of vision of pioneers joining in enviable teamwork under Freud's guidance. The cooperative effort no less than the frankness of controversy constitutes a model for inquiries into an area where clinical data of some general significance are not likely to be assembled by isolated observers. The need for such procedures has, if anything, increased with our growing insight into the complexity of psychoanalytic research, which seems greatest where early phases of childhood are concerned; in the specific framework of this contribution, the study of early autoerotic activities. It is at the same time the area where our understanding, however fragmentary, has advanced most during the last decades, particularly through the comparison of data gained in various fields of work. These cooperative efforts had been postulated by Freud (1905b) and there is little that need be added to his reasoning: "The direct observation of children has the disadvantage of working upon data which are easily misunderstandable; psycho-analysis is made difficult by the fact that it

Presented at the discussion on Masturbation, held at the New York Psychoanalytic Society on February 13, 1951. First published in *The Psychoanalytic Study of the Child*, 6 : 95–116. New York: International Universities Press, 1951.

can only reach its data, we well as its conclusions, after long detours. But by co-operation the two methods can attain a satisfactory degree of certainty in their findings" (p. 201). This certainty has not been reached and even the discussion of methods and concrete procedures to be used in research is comparatively new.[1] But the goal indicated by Freud, an integrated approach to the study of infancy and childhood, is likely to stimulate research over a long time to come. In what follows I propose to discuss and to illustrate some problems arising in connection with the comparatively recent advances in our understanding in the hope of directing attention to concrete questions which might be clarified by further and if possible systematically oriented inquiries.

The psychoanalytic approach to an understanding of early autoerotic activities is bound to relate these activities to various overlapping aspects of the problem of growth, particularly to the sequence of maturational processes, the development of the ego as a psychic organization, and to the development and vicissitudes in the infant's and child's relation to his love objects. In studying any concrete phenomenon, we are faced with a merging or interacting of these and other factors. The division in aspects tends to present them in isolation. I shall not attempt to distinguish sharply between maturational and developmental factors, i.e., to discuss the problem of learning.[2] All I can attempt is to exemplify the assumed relation between the two in a schematic fashion. Some movements of the mouth, some activities which resemble parts of the (later) sucking activity—a reflex-controlled physiological mechanism (Peiper, 1936) no less complex than the psychological meaning which it is gradually to gain in the infant's life—are present in the fetus and in the neonate before his contact with breast, bottle and mother. There are considerable individual variations in the extent and intensity of these activities.[3] The value

1. For more detailed discussions of these problems, see Hartmann (1950a, 1950b), Spitz (1950), Anna Freud (1951), Anna Freud and Dann (1951), and chapter 5.

2. See Carmichael (1951) and similar attempts in animal psychology (Beach, 1949, 1950b). Maturation and development are used as defined in chapter 1, note 8.

3. Here, as in other instances, the complexity of factors even during the earliest postnatal periods is great indeed; for example, the possibility of pre- or postmaturity

of these variations as indicators of "potentialities" has, as far as I know, never been studied in sufficient detail. It would obviously be extremely difficult to assess their impact even on the earliest feeding experiences of infants. They might, however, constitute one of the large number of factors which determine the initial postnatal interplay of mother and child, of the "nursing couple" in the felicitous expression of Middlemore (1941). In the present context, the very presence of these earliest pre- and postnatal "oral" activities—be they limited to the repeated (and sometimes rhythmical) lip-tongue contact or express themselves in finger sucking—is merely taken to indicate that the sensory experience produced satisfies a need not stimulated from outside. However, after the feeding experience has set in the meaning and impact of similar oral activities can be fully evaluated only if we realize that the sensory experience produced by the child himself, i.e., initially by reflectory reactions, is likely gradually to be colored at least to some extent by his experience with the mother.[4] The slowly increasing number of detailed observations on early feeding behavior—rare and insufficiently or irrelevantly focused as they still tend to be—supply some indications on the gradual merging of the two components. The type of memory trace which we assume to be formed, the type of learning experience which the infant undergoes, is naturally dependent upon the general process of maturation; its specific manifestations in feeding behavior and the postulated concomitant psychological processes are known only in outline, at least up to a time in the infant's life when many developmental data suggested by various criteria indicate the existence of a "gradient." However hesitant we may have become in our

---

at birth has to be taken into account. Furthermore, only systematic and detailed descriptions of behavior promise to supply a reliable basis for subsequent evaluation.

4. Hendrick (1942, 1951) stresses that identification begins when the desire for repetition of pleasure has come to be an emotional demand mentally experienced by the infant for these mother-emanating stimuli. If the feeding experience is unsatisfactory, this "coloring" may never gain the intensity which it presumably gains if satisfaction is maximal. I do not in what follows take such differences into account. This is not meant to imply that they are unimportant or that no methods could be devised for a more detailed study of these and similar factors.

endeavor at setting such gradients, it seems that at the age of twelve weeks or three months previously imperceptible or less well perceptible functions become on the average integrated and can be established by observation.[5] The most spectacular of these developments concerns a definite change in the relation to need satisfaction, a step in ego development. The infant learns to anticipate the imminent feeding situation and under optimal conditions to wait for it.[6] In the apt word of Therese Benedek (1938), the infant has gained confidence in his mother. We may assume that at this point, if not earlier, the sensory experience elicited by oral activities which the infant undertakes before—and under certain conditions after— feeding time will have been merged to some extent with some sort of recall of the need-satisfying situations. What I here postulate as recall and try to imagine in terms of mental processes on a more adult level is undoubtedly a compound of various experiences; we may assume that the "situation" recalled is constituted by an amalgamation of sensory imprints which contain next to specific experiences many of a general nature. Some of them may be comprehended as the experience of being handled. The autoerotic activity of finger or thumb sucking then may be supposed to gain a new dimension; it can be viewed as the active repetition of the passively experienced. In producing the sensory experience by the insertion of finger or thumb into the mouth, the child takes over from the mother.[7] This step is clearly dependent upon (or bet-

5. See, e.g., Hoffer (1950) and his apt summary of Gesell's findings. In speaking of gradient I refer to "expected" developmental processes. Not only are they subject to changes by alterations in child care procedures, such as those suggested by current trends in parent education, but any systematic observation is likely to heighten the sensitivity of observers; this may in turn not only lead to greater refinement in distinctions but direct attention to formerly neglected details of behavior as indicators of developmental processes.

6. No detailed observations on circumstances attending this step in development nor on the spread of individual differences and their value for predicting subsequent steps are available, though such observations seem particularly promising and may constitute one of the instances where psychoanalysis can indicate areas for future investigations; see Hartmann's comments (1950a, 1950b) on this function of psychoanalysis.

7. It should be noted that this does not contradict the assumption that through his autoerotic activity the child also supplements a not sufficiently "saturated" need, e.g.,

ter: synchronized with) various maturational processes, particularly with the growing capacity for purposeful motor activity. The ability to lead the hand to the mouth is an indispensable condition for and element in the sequence of processes which are relevant in the present context. In a significant discussion of detailed observations of these steps in maturation and development Hoffer (1949) pointed to the vicissitudes encountered by the child in establishing a reliable hand-mouth contact and to the postulated importance of these events. The gradual emancipation of the hand from the mouth, its independence, may be supposed to initiate progressing redistribution of psychic energies. We are wont to assume that originally mainly the mouth region serves the purpose of tension discharge, possibly neglecting that other areas of the body, particularly the viscera, participate in this function. Our assumption implies in metapsychological terms that we imagine the mouth at this time to be invested with particularly large quantities of energy both libidinal and aggressive. The emancipation of the hand from the mouth may then contribute to a redistribution of energy which presumably invests the whole body and facilitates not only further steps in the differentiation between self and environment (Hoffer, 1950) but also steps in the development of the ego as an organization,[8] which is at this point largely, though not solely inhibitory. In saying that this hand-mouth contact facilitates the redistrib-

---

if in feeding no sufficient opportunity for sucking was offered (Levy, 1928). The experimental reproduction of this situation by Levy (1934) has been confirmed by Ross (1951). The data presented by Davis, Sears, Miller, and Brodbeck (1948) on the behavior of infants who were cup-fed and did not later in their development manifest increased sucking of fingers or thumb do not invalidate these findings. Should they prove to be reliable I am inclined to assume that they may well indicate that a certain degree of stimulation deficit does not necessarily lead to supplementary stimulation but leads to other substitutive steps. Analysts are familiar with similar substitutions later in life. There seems no reason to doubt that similar processes may occur very early. Nor is sucking satisfaction isolated in the child's life; it is neither the only need for stimulation, nor the only need whose "deficit" can be substituted or supplemented by self-stimulation.

8. For older psychoanalytic hypotheses concerning this redistribution of energy and the grasping stage of motor development, see the stimulating discussion by Bernfeld (1925).

ution of energy, rather than saying (as Hoffer does) that it initiates it, I have in mind the multitude of other types of contact
between the child and the environment; particularly the tactile
contact with the mother, which seems to play an important
part in establishing certain aspects of the body image and
other ego functions. One is, as it were, naturally tempted to
establish a connection between these assumptions and the first
discernible steps in ego development, to which Benedek's
views referred, but also to the finding reported by Kunst
(1948). According to her observations, the frequency and intensity of finger sucking maintain a plateau after the third
month and are subject to change only after the sixth month, at
an age level to which other observations have related important changes in the child's object relation.

In the present context it is not my purpose to discuss further interdependences of various areas of maturation and development. The formulation that finger or thumb sucking can
be viewed as in part determined by the active repetition of a
passive experience deserves further comment. This formula
was first applied by Freud (1920) to an explanation of a crucial
aspect of the child's play—to the attempt to overcome the separation from the mother by a self-engineered peek-a-boo performance—and later used to explain the turning from
dependence to independence in a general sense; it is in this
form that it constitutes a general principle of ego development
in its relation to the mechanism of identification. This generalization occurred when Freud (1931) gained the conviction that
the distribution of masculinity and femininity in the later development of child and man must be seen in relation to, and
ontogenetically connected with, an earliest phase of identification in which the active repetition of nursing experiences
dominates future steps in development.[9] Freud's reformula-

9. Freud himself has elaborated this thought only in part in his 1931 paper on
"Female Sexuality" and left it to the late Ruth Mack Brunswick to treat the problem in
a larger context in her paper on the preoedipal phase, published 1940, but based on
discussions with Freud conducted in 1930. Through the courtesy of Miss Mathilde
Brunswick I was able to see the draft which Ruth Mack Brunswick submitted to
Freud. It contains all essential thoughts of her subsequently published paper and two
marginal notes by Freud, one of which is of immediate bearing on our subject. It

tion was stimulated by the growing familiarity with the impact of the preoedipal development in psychoanalytic work, hence predominantly by material gained by reconstruction. Though data from direct and systematic observation of children have never been viewed in the light of the specific mechanism which Freud pointed out, impressions based on the evaluation of random observations available at present seem to indicate the fruitfulness of the general principle.

II

Those who had an opportunity to study earliest developmental retardations report in many instances a paucity of autoerotic practices during the first year of life, and even a flattening out of finger sucking—a picture that seems limited to cases in which the absence of stimulation is extreme (Rabinovitch, 1950). According to Spitz and Wolf (1949), the reverse occurs in children raised under particularly favorable, and, as I would add, permissive care, i.e., in environments which do not overtly object to some kind of handling of the genitalia. Spitz and Wolf argue against the presumably widely accepted view that stimulation by maternal care in these children acted as seduction. They compare cases in which genital play occurs with those of actually genitally seduced children in whom they did not observe genital play and draw the conclusion that not any specific traumatization by seduction but satisfactory maternal care and attention are responsible for the freedom and moderate enjoyment children may derive from the handling of their genitalia during the later part of the first and during the early part of the first and during the early part of the second year of life. It is, they conclude, the mother's love which

---

reads: "Events during the preoedipal phase should not be described in terms of 'masculine and feminine' but in terms of 'active and passive.' It is the time of the sole phallic genital. The new era starts with the discovery of castration, with the influence of the castration complex. Then a new contrast is added; not yet the contrast of masculine and feminine, but the one of phallic and castrated. The opposing pairs (are to be) followed through the development of sexuality: A.) active—passive, B.) phallic—castrated, C.) masculine—feminine. It is to be shown how they follow each other, overlap, and combine."

stimulated this development. Lampl-de Groot (1950) showed that there is no contradiction between this assumption and traditional views in psychoanalysis and that it actually confirms Freud's earliest expectations, formulated in the *Three Essays on the Theory of Sexuality:* "What we call affection will unfailingly show its effect one day on the genital zone as well" (1905b, p. 223).

The transfer from general affection to the genital zone itself is a complex process; it need not come about only by the direct contact of the mother with the genital region of the child during her ministrations, an experience the child would repeat by self-stimulation. It may also arise as a consequence of the general bodily closeness to which, we assume, the child tends to react with sensation in the genital region. No detailed data on these reactions are available, since the investigations of Halverson (1940) on penile tumescence in male infants cover only the neonate period and no similar observations for later phases of development have been made available.[10] The genital self-stimulation could then replace the more general stimulation which had produced the pleasurable sensation in the genital region. The scarcity of observational data and their unavoidable lack of precision are well known to all investigators of similar problems. No observation for short periods of time can guarantee that the essential events have come to the observer's attention. The very fact that his presence "alters" the field, influences mother and child (in spite of protestation to the contrary), need hardly be mentioned. It seems more relevant to stress that the very presence of the mother may already at this early age determine the child's behavior. Therefore, no one isolated technique of observation, least of all spot observations in family or nursery school and not even those infinitely richer ones from Residential Nurseries (see Anna Freud and D. Burlingham, 1944), can tell the whole story or a particularly relevant part of it. The main reason for the limitation of the scope and value of observational methods, however, seems to rest in the fact that it is not the au-

10. Contradictions between Halverson's interpretation of his observations and psychoanalysis have been discussed and clarified by Stone (1954a).

toerotic practice itself but the fantasy content which proves to be of decisive importance, and our interest in the practices is to a large extent stimulated by their relation to fantasy life. The question as to the link between autoerotic practices and concomitant fantasies has repeatedly attracted Freud's attention. He was originally inclined to stress the existence of two phases, and to assume that fantasy and autoerotic activity have to be "welded together." Later he emphasized the existence of a third earlier phase. He stressed that in the act of sucking for its own sake the erotic component is itself independent from the nutritional act; the child gives up the mother's breast, the object in an external person and replaces it by a part of his own person: "the sexual instinct then *becomes* auto-erotic" (1905b, p. 222; italics added). If we add that the exchange of activity for passivity enters into this relationship, we gain firmer ground for the assumption that even during the autoerotic activity the former relationship to the object need not—or better: cannot—be fully in abeyance.

To illustrate what is meant by this assumption I turn to fantasies pertaining to early experiences in the genital zone; clearly, the reconstructive method alone can lead us. Certain masturbation fantasies of boys during the phallic phase, uncovered or reconstructed in analysis, have in common the sexual aim to be touched and handled by the mother. In the later development of these masturbation fantasies this wish tends naturally to appear in condensation with other wishes and various defenses against them.[11] Loewenstein (1935), who drew attention to fantasies of this kind in adults, speaks of a passive part of the phallic phase in the male. It seems that alternatively we may assume that within each phase of maturation and development the distribution of "activity" and "passivity" may fluctuate, that after an attempt at "activity" the "passive" component may tend to gain renewed importance. The decisive factor, however, seems to be that within each phase the meaning of the passive tendency changes, in the sense indicated by Freud and Brunswick. The question to

---

11. For the general dynamics of masturbation fantasies see Eidelberg (1945).

what extent the passive strivings during the phallic phase are "regressive" or to what extent they have survived from the past without or with little alteration seems at the present stage of our knowledge difficult to answer and quite possibly not meaningfully posed. The wish to be handled by the mother may, for example, express the thought, "If I don't touch myself, I need be less afraid, I am not guilty"; it may replace other phallic fantasies concerning the mother. Yet I would assume that whatever component drives are gratified by the fantasy, or whatever conflicts solved by it, its content is simultaneously colored by the reenactment of the earliest preoedipal passivity, the period of total dependency on the mother.[12]

The conscious masturbation fantasy of a young man proves in analysis to be in part determined by the attempt to ward off the wish that his mother should handle his genitalia, as she was handling those of his eighteen-month-younger sibling. A memory represents the mother as examining the younger boy's testicles, a regular occurrence in the care of this sickly boy during the patient's earliest latency years. The repressed fantasy aims at sexual contact with the mother, and various clinical data indicate that they reawaken the original and never quite mastered wish for direct dependence. The birth of the sibling resulted in an overintense attempt to be active and independent, instead of passive and dependent. Naturally, other elements overdetermined the fantasy itself; being passive had at that age gained the meaning not only of being castrated but also of being feminine.[13] At the time into which memory leads, a third sibling, a boy, was born instead of the expected girl. The feminine fantasy was at this point not only stimulated by the negative component of the oedipal conflict in its relation to castration anxiety but also by the strongly repressed thought: "If I had been the little girl, whom my

12. In the masturbation discussion of 1912 Sadger reported case material which he was inclined to relate to the later development of latent or overt male homosexuality; the finding which he stresses is the identification of the masturbator with the "active" mother. The image of this activity is naturally merged with that of the phallic mother.

13. In other screen memories of this patient these two components could be more clearly distinguished.

parents desired in vain, I would be the favorite of mother and father; I would have remained the privileged, the only child." Following the lead of jealousy, the experience of the original closeness to the mother is linked to, and becomes transparent behind, later developmental layers.

The observations of Spitz and Wolf (1949), and to some extent the insight supplied by similar examples, draw our attention to a number of problems which at the present time must remain unanswered. Early self-stimulation of the genitalia ("genital play") need not coincide even with the most liberal chronological assumption concerning the onset of the phallic phase. Our views on chronology in zonal sexuality are rapidly shifting. We are unable to indicate conditions responsible for any given type of overlapping of phases and displacement of stimuli. Attempts to elaborate in a systematic way the ideas developed by Abraham combined with Alexander's vectorial tendencies have been undertaken by Erikson (1950); they seem not to have been found useful by clinicians or have not yet been sufficiently absorbed by them. Any attempt to look at the manifestations of zonal behavior in isolation is bound to prove disappointing. Hartmann (1950a) pointed to the fact that certain behavior details, previously closely linked to the anal phase, for instance, certain traits of orderliness, may appear as reactions of a particularly early development of the ego. It seems that such accelerated development is closely related to the patterns of present-day child care among progressive and psychoanalytically oriented parents.

Similar explanations may be appropriate as far as the early manifestations of behavior are concerned, which we are or were inclined to link solely to the development of the phallic phase; the acceleration may, according to tentative impressions, be due to the fact that the dominant climate of child care facilitates not only the close relationship with the mother in general terms, but specifically the identification with her activity. In the case of the patient mentioned above, this relationship determined even later in life the tie between the mother and her oldest son. The two shared within the family the characteristics of active, driving personalities, a unity pre-

sumably established at a time when, after the birth of the second and weak sibling, activity and grownupness of the little
boy represented an incentive to winning mother's attention. It
is in line with our general expectation that the acceleration of
this development facilitated a later regressive tendency, somewhat stronger than normal: at the height of the phallic phase
and castration anxiety, after the birth of the third child, the
boy planned as a girl, feminine fantasies developed in my patient.

The opposite, but not totally contradictory picture is familiar from cases described by Phyllis Greenacre (1952) in which
either general traumatization or specific violent overstimulation affect the maturational sequence; in these more or less
severely impaired patients we sometimes find a prematurity of
phallic attitudes, but not the concomitant steps in ego development; the zonal reactions have, at least for some time, as it
were, remained isolated.[14]

III

The idea that autoerotic self-stimulation arises in part as a
substitute for the stimulation by the mother has been taken
for granted in analysis, since case histories reported by child
analysts established the link between excessive frequency and
intensity of masturbation and the absence of satisfactory ties to
the principal love object. Since then experience with deprived
children, particularly of the toddler age reported from the
material in the Hampstead Nurseries (Anna Freud and
Dorothy Burlingham, 1944), has shown that the increase in

14. The existence of early phallic tendencies have naturally been repeatedly
stressed by analysts. M. Klein's theories bear upon this point; however, in her view,
maturation has mainly a defensive function and serves the escape from the dangers of
oral aggression. It seems appropriate at least briefly to refer to Ernest Jones's (1933)
concept of the "proto-phallic" phase, during which before the full awareness of sex
differences phallic strivings are ascribed to the infant. In combining Freud's later
thought with Jones's earlier views, we would come to consider the proto-phallic phase
as one in which the phallic strivings are dominated not by the dichotomy phallic-
castrated, which would correspond to the maturational peak of phallic development,
but by the dichotomy active-passive: at this stage not the fear of castration, but the
fear of the loss of the love object seems prominent.

autoerotic activities appears in a context of a general withdrawal of libido and aggression from objects, and can be reversed when permanent or even semipermanent substitute
objects are offered to the child: the energies of his instinctual
drives are, as it were, in search of the object. Observations of
this kind seem to have led some investigators to assume that a
radical dichotomy exists between the investment of the self
and that of the object, a view expressed particularly in the
writings of Maloney (1949): "If the child cannot reinstitute the
positive relationship between himself and his mother, he en-
lists some other means of allaying anxiety. Often, he will retreat into a plastic phantasy—a fixed unconscious phantasy. In
this phantasy he, himself, replaces the unpredictable mother.
He sucks himself, fondles his ear or his nose or any part of the
body. He sucks on something. He scratches or tickles himself.
He wallows in warm feces or urine. He tickles his nose with a
feather or fuzz. The possibilities at playing mother to himself
are legion. Once introduced it is not easy to rob him of the unsuspected substitutes for the delinquent parent" (p. 340).

In Maloney's view—or better, in the suggestive but incomplete formulation here quoted—masturbation appears as
pathological, caused by a deficit of object love. Some such deficit, it seems, is unavoidable, however devoted the mother; or
to put it more correctly, "total gratification" seems to be a fig-
ment of our imagination. The instinctual desires prepare the
ground for a magnitude of demands,[15] which makes a certain
degree of deprivational experience an unavoidable and, we
believe, a necessary factor (Hartmann, Kris, and Loewenstein,
1946). While in the practice of child care much depends on
timing, extent, and nature of deprivational experiences, the
periodic shifts and reversals of investment between self and
object, caused, or at least in part stimulated, by deprivation,
constitute a necessary element in normal development, first in
differentiating the self from the environment, then in the variety of steps by which the bridge between self and the human

15. The absence of an ego organization may cause these demands to be experienced as particularly "great," quite apart from what attempts at measurement of individual differences may one day be able to reveal.

object is established by identification. Shifts in cathexis between the self and the human object frequently imply a tendency toward regression. However, the fact that such behavior
may constitute adequate problem solution, that for this purpose temporary regressive mechanisms may be utilized, is in
full agreement with the views on ego functions, particularly
with Hartmann's formulations on this subject (1939a, 1950b).
Not the isolated mechanism but the context in which it occurs
decides on its meaning. In the following I shall attempt to
compare a number of observations under this contrasting
aspect.

Alex, whose family history and development have been discussed in some detail by Jackson and Klatskin (1950) and
whose development was followed in their presentation to the
time of the birth of a sibling (twenty-seven months), was a
child who was rarely seen to suck.[16] His oral activities in the
nursery school were limited to mouthing of objects. In the
course of observations, I suggested that this served the function of testing new objects rather than of retaining or incorporating them. Such tentativeness seemed in line with his
difficulties in establishing contact, which were as great as his
desire for situations in which such contact could be established
without danger of the interference from aggression. In Jackson and Klatskin's presentation, these attitudes of Alex could
tentatively but plausibly be related to similar mechanisms operative in his mother. There also seemed little doubt that
more energetic finger or thumb sucking had met with considerable disapproval in his home environment. The tentative
mouthing represented a compromise between a reduced or
inhibited sucking and a specific function which this activity
had retained; namely, the oral exploration overdetermined as
it was by early restrictions on other exploratory functions, particularly by the prohibition to touch.

On the day when Alex's mother went to the hospital for the
delivery of a sibling and on subsequent days a change in the
pattern of Alex's mouthing was seen to take place. He was visi-

16. See my summary of Alex's behavior in nursery school (Yale University, Child
Study Center) quoted by Jackson and Klatskin (1950, p. 254f.).

bly depressed, and even more prone to isolate himself from the group than at any other time. Under the impact of this mood the generalized mouthing not only was more frequent than ever, but turned at least for part of the time into finger and occasional thumb sucking, into object-directed pleasure sucking; it was physiognomically speaking, "autoerotic." The impression to an observer was that a definite "image" was connected with this activity: the sucking replaced the lost object, the mother, whom he would not or did not find at home.

A different picture was offered by John who, at the age of three years and ten months sexualized his object relationship. The brilliant description of his behavior by Putnam, Rank, and Kaplan (1951) can here be summarized in the light of observations which I was privileged to make on repeated occasions at the James Jackson Putnam Children's Center in Boston.[17]

After an initially favorable development John withdrew from attempts at verbal communication around eighteen months of age. He impressed observers as a desultory child, almost constantly engaged in some oral or other autoerotic activity. Many factors contributed to this extent of oral fixation. From the case history we note that during his early infancy bottles were on many occasions almost literally pushed into his mouth. The invitation to sucking was used to pacify all his demands. Sucking with John was a complex activity, in which the lips were less engaged than the anatomical structure of the mouth, at an age when such participation is normally no longer prominent (Peiper, 1936). John's upper jaw, the region of the palate close to the front teeth, seemed to have become a preferred locus of self-stimulation and discharge. There cannot be any doubt as to the destructive quality of this oral activity and none as to its function as a general avenue of tension discharge. The particular type of behavior on which I should

17. I should like to take this opportunity to express my warm appreciation to the directors of the Center, M. C. Putnam and B. Rank, and to their collaborators for much stimulation during regularly repeated discussions and many shared clinical impressions. I am particularly grateful to Beata Rank, who initiated my contact with her institution and thus a cooperation which she continued in valuable comments on the present paper.

like to focus attention concerns John's contact with his mother. From time to time he was readily taken into her lap and cuddled, but such close bodily contact was often of only limited duration. John tended to react to it with marked sexual excitement, could not maintain the tender contact, and started to masturbate violently. Only during masturbation, mostly at the peak of excitement, did his facial expression resume a child-like expression. On other occasions the face was dominated and disrupted by the almost square-shaped opening of the ever-active mouth, which stigmatized his appearance. The mother found his often violent gyrations at times unbearable and tried to break off contact; on one occasion she was seen to distract his attention by pushing a plastic dish into John's mouth.

This type of behavior illustrates the fact that in cases in which the normal object relation has not developed or could not be maintained, a sexual relation can still survive. There exist infinite variations between John's behavior and the normal child. Case material from child analysis informs us about many types of intermediary conditions, and in reconstructions from the analysis of adult patients one gets insight into others. In the analysis of "schizoid" individuals, one sometimes gains the impression not only that the absence of an adequate latency period, the continued predominance of masturbation through the total course of childhood, can be viewed in terms of the incompleteness of their involvement with love objects, but also that a narcissistic element predominated in their masturbation fantasies. In two cases of male patients which fit into this broad picture, these fantasies were of an exhibitionistic nature. Both men, who had achieved potency in adult life, the one excellent, the other satisfactory, retained the imprint of passive demands—to be admired in their performance—the one under the disguise of the demand for total inactivity of the partner, the other in rigidly limiting or prescribing her modes of participation. In both cases, intercourse itself was the exclusive or main anchor in their object relationship. In both cases, the more accessible layer was the passivity toward the male, but hidden behind the repressed identification with the mother was the wish to be passive in relation to her. Both men had been exposed to rather severe deprivation, the one by the fact that very early his mother had concentrated her attention on a fourteen-month-younger sibling and subsequently on other children, the other by the fact that his mother had prided herself in constantly stimulating his maleness to the extent of hardly veiled sexual advances during prepuberty. In reconstructions it was suggested that similar plays may have occurred even during the nursing situation, and members of the family confirmed the teasing characters of the mothers' earliest handling of the infants. The point of resemblance of these cases with John's might be underlined; they show in a very much more adapted form a similar, though less exclusive, limitation of object relations to the sexual sphere; the factor of early deprivational experiences, stressed by Putnam, Rank, and Kaplan in John's case, also plays a similar part. Possibly even the area of deprivation may have been a similar one—that is, the unsatisfied need to be the object of mother's ministration and attention. However, it should be stressed, as it was on previous occasions (chap. 5), that we do not at present know how large the part played by such deprivations is.[18]

Cases such as John's are particularly apt to confirm our belief in the fruitfulness of recent reformulation of psychoanalytic theory by Hartmann (1950b). We usually viewed the substitution of object contact by autoerotic activity in general terms as a narcissistic procedure; Hartmann pointed out that in such connections we should speak of an investment of the self. In earliest infancy we assume that shifts of this kind occur incessantly or very frequently. In later development, once the permanent relation to the object is established, or at least some of its relevant antecedents, not all of this energy can be as-

18. Among the factors which tend to be neglected is one in which a mother shows marked lack of warmth toward one but not toward another child. This may not only be due to a specific unconscious fantasy concerning this child—a view stressed by B. Rank and her collaborators—but might conceivably be connected and/or combined with her earliest perceptions of some trait in the infant to which she reacts. In other contexts this reaction of the mother to the child's predispositions has been investigated and stressed by Bender and mentioned by Erikson (1950).

sumed to be fluid. Part of it presumably remains vested in the object, part of it in the self, and part of it is neutralized and used as permanent cathexis of the ego as an organization.[19] The profound disturbance in John's development, whatever its etiology or diagnosis, is characterized by the fact that no higher ego development has taken place. Few ego functions could develop, and no relevant part of his actions reach into a sphere free from urgent conflict. We assume a deficit in the neutralization of psychic energy, an absence of (secondary) ego autonomy. In John's case, the self and the object are related to each other by constant shifts of nonneutralized energies, of libido and aggression. The mother is on the whole an object used for immediate tension discharge. It is an exquisitely infantile object relation enacted with a more mature body.

We have as yet no experience in assessing the stages and modalities of the development of ego autonomy in the sense defined by Hartmann. Conventional measurements of isolated ego functions by testing procedures of various kinds supply, in spite of their obvious limitations during infancy and early childhood, data that may prove useful. However, at least in many instances, they seem to measure, not the autonomy of the ego, but stages in the maturation of its apparatus and other developmental processes in isolation. One might take the view that the time has not yet come to establish too close a relationship between the data of observation and theoretical concepts in this area. Though I realize these uncertainties I should like tentatively to indicate at least one area of observation, which may prove pertinent and permit an approximation—little is known about the development of the sense of rhythm in the child.[20] Its relation to many and general functions of the organism (Schilder), the fact that "the brain is so organized as to offer a physiological substratum for automatic repetitiveness both of fragments of behavior and of more

19. This summary of the theory formulated originally by Freud and reformulated by Hartmann (1950b) is rendered in considerable simplification, since it serves here the purpose of establishing connections between the various observations reported.

20. For a survey of the older literature see Ruckmick (1924).

complete patterns of behavior" (Kubie, 1941, p. 29) form the broad background for discussion of the problem, recently surveyed by R. S. Lourie (1949). Only a segment of the problems to which Lourie has pointed gains importance: the link of rhythm to autoerotic activities.[21] This segment permits a view of the gradual control which the ego gains over various types of automatic motor discharge processes, some of them rhythmic ones. Several years ago (1939) I suggested that we may speak of the control of rhythmic, automatic motor discharges and their transformation into the melody of movement as one of the important functions of the ego. As far as early autoerotic activities are concerned, several areas in which manifestations of rhythm occur gain particular importance. It is less the heartbeat, "the general pacemaker of rhythm," which seems relevant, but rather the occurrence of rhythm in sucking, its relation to respiration and peristalsis, and particularly the focal role which the mother plays in response to these experiences or by new stimuli she tends to set. The physical contact between mother and child seems many a time to adopt patterns of rhythm as if the unity of the two could best be restored by their sharing in it. On this basis rhythm gains its importance in child care and its value as a "relaxational expedient" (Gesell).[22] Clearly, not all manifestations of rhythm in the child's life can meaningfully be linked to autoeroticity: rhythmic repetitiveness in motion may lead to learning, particularly in the area of motor control (Isaacs). The existence of this nexus plays its part in attempts to come to an understanding of rocking, the most conspicuous rhythmic autoerotic activity of early infancy. Lourie reports that in an unselected sample of pediatric clinic population one form or another of rocking or swaying was observed in 15–20 percent of children, in private practice in about 10 percent. The frequency of oc-

21. In what follows I remain aware of the high complexity of the subject matter, and of the fact that I am presenting simplifications by stressing one aspect only.

22. I should like gratefully to acknowledge stimulation by a memorandum of S. Margolin's on the ontogenesis of rhythm, in which a wealth of suggestions derived from various areas of research is combined with case material from psychoanalytic observation.

currence drops after the child has achieved coordinated activity in new areas, particularly after he has learned to walk. Lourie also points out that "the most common time for the use of rhythmic motor patterns is when an infant is in the transition between one stage of growth and development and the next." The transitions from sitting to standing and standing to walking are instances in point. The lag between one maturational step and the next can also be viewed as a frustrating experience to the child. At any rate, the occurrence of rocking (as that of other autoerotic activities) in face of and in reaction to frustration is well established. That rocking movements of some kind occur in some children in the course of maturational processes seems to contradict observations by Spitz and Wolf (1949). They found rocking behavior frequent in children living in an institution with their mothers, whom they describe as impulsive characters. In the developmental profiles of these children they note retardation in social contact and in the manipulation of objects. Since, according to Wolf's opinion, the manipulation of inanimate objects reflects the relation to the child's primary objects, the authors argue that rocking children are arrested "at the level of primary narcissistic discharge of the libidinal drive in the form of rocking." Although the impression that rocking behavior per se is pathological is not shared by others, I shall later refer to some of the implications of these findings.[23]

The early relation between the occurrence of rocking and the maturation of the child's motor development should not blind our interest in the part played by rhythmic discharge patterns later in the child's development. I refer here to two such representative modes of discharge observed during a nursery school day of the three-year-old. A record is being played and around the stimulus supplied by music rhythmic

23. For a different evaluation of rocking, see, e.g., Lampl-de Groot (1950). In a discussion of the paper by Spitz and Wolf (1949) in the New York Psychoanalytic Society M. Kris pointed to the possibility that the frequency of rocking behavior in the population studied by the authors may have to do with the various restrictions imposed by life and care in a penal institution on child and mother. This suggestion is in agreement with Levy's observation (1947), according to which rocking occurs in reaction to restraint.

stamping develops, sometimes initiated spontaneously by one or two children and taken up by others, sometimes initiated by the nursery school teachers beating the rhythm by hand clapping. In many instances the rhythm of music is followed only for a short while, the stamping becomes independent, outgrows and outlasts it, but retains the character of a group activity of a more or less organized and shared discharge. Different in nature are manifestations of rhythm which seem to appear the more frequently the younger the child is—in the group discussed here, the closer he is to the two-year limit. A child plays with wooden trains and is trying to connect engines and cars. At one point, mostly but not regularly when a difficulty appears or failure is feared, the attempt is gradually—in rarer cases suddenly—dropped for the sake of rhythmic movement: engine and car are pushed against each other, one of them is pushed forward and backward on the floor, against another object or along part of the child's body. Neither details nor variations of similar processes can here be reported. I can only state that rhythm here interrupts purposeful action, motor impulse disrupts constructive playing.[24] That this happens frequently in response to a frustrating experience coincides with our expectation. This emergence of rhythm can be viewed in connection with many frequently discussed problems, with the child's attention span, with the disorganization of ego functions described by Anna Freud, as a consequence of overtiredness, or with what I suggested to call the child's regression rate (chap. 5). In the present context I am concerned only with the evident closeness of this emergence to autoeroticity; in some of the observed children, rhythmic movements, such as those described and other similar ones, tended to lead to rubbing of the genital area. The regressive character of the breakthrough of rhythm can in these cases ac-

24. Similar observations concerning children at a somewhat later stage of development have been made long ago and repeatedly since by students of children's drawings. Thus Krötzsch (1917) assumes that "continuous rhythmic movements without attempting formation or continuous sliding back into rhythmic movements are indicative of mental disturbance"; see also Prinzhorn (1923) and Elkisch (1945, 1947) who considers rhythm and rule (Klages) to be contrasting tendencies between which the ego has to mediate.

tually be viewed as a sexualization (and in other instances as an aggressivization) of energy, which in other activities—problem solving or organized playing—has presumably been to some extent neutralized.[25] During the later part of the third and during the fourth year of life sudden discharges of this kind seem to become less obvious. We might speak of the growing attention span, of progress in ego development, and consequently of the growing distance between ego and id. Autoerotic and other activities seem gradually to be better differentiated from each other and transitions from one mode of discharge to the other become less easily observable and possibly on the whole rarer.

If we turn from the average nursery school child to a group of severely disturbed children (psychotic children, children with arrested or atypical development), we gain a different impression. The separation and delimitation of which I spoke has not taken place. One of the very disturbed six-year-old patients at the James Jackson Putnam Children's Center showed interest in the observer's cigarette lighter and wished to play with it. Attempts to explain its function did not succeed, but when the short-lived attempt to operate it had failed, the little boy grasped it and performed a frantic rubbing motion with it along the edge of the telephone switchboard. While in this instance what I call frantic is meant to convey the impression of a general state of excitement with a predominantly libidinal discharge function, in other no less frequent instances one gains the impression of the primacy of aggressive discharge. A six-year-old inmate of a state hospital, under observation at the James Jackson Putnam Center, suddenly broke away from the contact with a therapist with whom he had been intimately familiar for a long time, turned to an old telephone directory, and started systematically, but with marked excitement, to tear page after page carefully through the middle. Whatever the organic and/or psychological etiology of similar conditions may be, we are justified to speak of archaic (arrested or regressed) behavior in a double sense. The contact with the in-

25. The terms sublimation and neutralization are discussed in chapter 9.

animate object is not meaningful, it is treated without regard to its function,[26] and the uncontrolled rhythmic discharge impresses the observer physiognomically as sexual or aggressive. This is what I have in mind when I speak of lack of neutralization. The ego is, as it were, not organized, and the disturbance can well be described in terms of the lack of cathexis with which it is endowed.[27]

The full impression of the usefulness of these concepts can be illustrated by observations concerning Ellen, a little girl of eight, who at the time of observation was hospitalized; she had for several years been under treatment at the James Jackson Putnam Center. At first sight she offered the typical picture of an adolescent catatonic, reduced in size: slender and extremely attractive, with long blonde hair, and with what appeared to the casual visitor a searching look in her blue eyes, and seemed to connote meaningful and soulful vagueness. This impression changed within a few minutes into one of complete emptiness. It seemed never to leave the child, neither when she played with a baby doll and chanted to herself, soon moving from coordinated into rhythmic motor patterns, nor when cuddling in the lap of her therapist, or this observer, when the rhythmic movements soon grew into masturbatory patterns. Her face seemed to revive only in three situations: when she drank unusually large quantities of orange juice or ate highly salted raw tomatoes; when she reached orgasm during genital masturbation; and during defecation. It was as if cathexis had been left only for the zonal organization; "the ego was empty." In a very detailed case history, the gradual loss of ego functions, not without several transitory or apparent remissions within a general trend of deterioration, has been traced by the workers at the James Jackson Putnam Center. Only one aspect seems relevant here: the exclusiveness with which all other experiences were replaced

26. K. M. Wolf's assumption (referred to earlier) that the treatment of the inanimate object is causally related to that of the human object appears, in view of some of these cases at least, to be incomplete: the possibility that both relationships are manifestations of the same disturbance should be kept in mind.

27. In a similar connection Beata Rank (1949b) speaks of ego fragmentation.

by extensive zonal gratification, provoked by prolonged or massive stimuli, by something of the nature of violence. It is an impression with which we are familiar from many instances in the autoerotic behavior of severely disturbed children and from cases of compulsive masturbation in child and adult. In psychoanalytic observations of such cases we are used to discover resentment directed against love objects for their true or alleged frustration turned into self-destructiveness. This leads me to point to a more general problem: as far as autoerotic activities represent an impediment to normal development—and they do so naturally only under special conditions—we are used to pointing to the dangers inherent in the withdrawal of libidinal cathexis from the world as one of the causes leading to excessive narcissistic cathexis of the self, i.e., to its cathexis with nonneutralized energy. Only recently have we become aware of the parallel danger in the economy of aggression,[28] i.e., of the cathexis of the self with aggression. The manifestations of compulsive masturbation are one, but surely not the only or the most important, manifestation of this danger. I do not intend to enumerate others, but should like to point only to one relevant problem. Hartmann's suggestion (1950b) that neutralized aggressive energy is mobilized for the purpose of anticathexis must here be taken into account. A deficit in the neutralization of aggression—whether or not it arises in consequence of impaired object relation (Anna Freud, 1949a, 1951; Anna Freud and Dann, 1951; and chap. 5) or for other reasons—may result in a variety of disturbances in the development of mechanisms of defense. Such defectiveness in defense is typical of severe disturbances in childhood and of considerable importance in the structure of most psychoses,[29] and hence related to a wide area of problems which invite further clarification.

28. I intend to deal with some of these problems in another context, in connection with a discussion of problems of anal erotism. This might explain some of the more obvious omissions in this paper.

29. Hartmann, who had this point in mind, when he commented on the economy of aggression and the problem of defense, will elaborate it in greater detail in another context [see Hartmann, 1953].

The observations here presented have led the way from attempts to clarify our views on some early autoerotic activities to inquiries into some problems of ego development. The circuitous route leads back to the familiar, to opposing tendencies, never neglected in psychoanalysis, i.e., to the relation of the tendency to immediate discharge to one which accepts delayed and differentiated discharge processes. In this connection, the question as to the function of autoerotic activities as part and instigator, but also as impediment, of child development poses itself anew. It is a question which renews our interest in the memorable controversy of 1912.

8: The Study of Variations of Early Parental Attitudes

A Preliminary Report
(Written with Rose W. Coleman and Sally Provence)

(1953)

CULTURAL AND INDIVIDUAL VARIATIONS: THE APPROACH OF APPLIED PSYCHOANALYSIS

During the last three decades, largely under the influence of psychoanalysis, the study of variations of parental attitudes has gained in scope. The most extensive contributions have come from social scientists who study variations of parental attitudes in their cultural distribution. Most of these investigations deal with preliterate societies and only a few more recent ones with literate Asiatic cultures or subcultures of the Western world.[1] In none of these studies could data from psychoanalytic observations be used and few offer individual case histories of any kind. It is assumed in these investigations that the study of parental attitudes will lead to a better understanding of the development of the individual as a member of a specific group or culture. The studies in question deal essentially only with the methods of child care and education prescribed by social code. Hence parental attitudes are viewed not as reflecting an individual parent's sentiment concerning the child but as part of institutionalized behavior.[2]

First published in *The Psychoanalytic Study of the Child,* 8 : 20–47. New York: International Universities Press, 1953.

1. For a bibliography of these studies see, for instance, M. Mead (1946).
2. For this term see Hartmann, Kris, and Loewenstein (1951).

For some time a similar focus of attention has been shared by the various skill-groups and professions concerned with the study and the provision of optimal conditions for the growing child, by educators, pediatricians, psychologists, and psychiatrists interested in children or in preventive medicine and mental health. It has been repeatedly shown that the changing views and fashions in child care and education reflect a large number of influences, some derived from the changes in social climate, others related to current interest or recent advances in various areas of investigation (see also Wolfenstein, 1953). Among the latter the influence of psychoanalysis finds its place. Some early clinical impressions of psychoanalysis were generalized and in the course of this process some were misinterpreted. Thus the tendency to "humanize" child care and to avoid traumatization of the child reflects the influence of psychoanalysis in a fruitful sense, while the frequent exaggeration of this principle reflects a misinterpretation. We refer to the tendency to maximize indulgence, to minimize deprivation at all costs, and thus to withdraw support from the child in his battle against his own instinctual forces.[3]

The crucial misunderstandings can readily be traced to the difficulties in communication between psychoanalysts and those who apply their findings. The time lag which arises in the course of "translation" adds to the difficulty since the progress in psychoanalytic insight is only gradually channeled into the various fields of application. During the last decade this time lag has tended to be reduced. The cooperation between psychoanalysts and students of child development and child care has become closer and as a consequence a decisive shift has occurred. Interest is no longer exclusively or predominantly focused on evaluating procedures in child care. The relationship between a specific parent and his child finds consideration.

In any case history in social work or dynamic psychiatry in the broadest sense and in many pediatric case histories, a characterization of the parent-child relationship has come to find a

3. For a more detailed discussion see S. Bornstein (1937), Hoffer (1945), and chap. 4.

place. For special research studies a number of typologies or ratings were developed by groups of psychological investigators,[4] but none of them seems to have been acceptable to other groups and none has entered clinical practice. However, a number of standard designations have become accepted, which, close to everyday language, differ from it by one connotation. In speaking of a "warm," "seductive," "cold," or "rejecting" mother, one refers not only to the gestures but also to their meaning, not only to the surface of behavior but also to unconscious motivations which color this behavior and determine its nuances. The broader professional public has apparently been introduced to this approach by Levy (1943) who chose the term "overprotective mother" to characterize mothers who rely predominantly on overcompensation as defense against their hostility.

Psychoanalysts, even when they use designations of this kind, tend to remain aware of the fact that any descriptive typology oversimplifies the highly intricate picture that psychoanalytic observation itself offers. Some simplifications are unavoidable; without them no general principles could be established and no applications of psychoanalysis would become possible. Moreover, the usefulness of the current designations of parental—or in this instance, more specifically maternal—attitudes cannot be doubted. They have a firm place in dynamic psychiatry and serve as a means of communication between the various skilled groups which constitute the psychiatric team.

However, the more widely simplifications are used and the more firmly a vernacular is entrenched, the more essential does it become to restate from time to time the more complex aspects of a problem. The present paper attempts a restatement of this kind: we shall point to some aspects of parent-child relationship which the psychoanalyst is accustomed to include in his thinking and which tend to be neglected by those who apply psychoanalysis. From such a restatement one might expect a modification of traditional connotations at-

4. For an example of the most consistent attempt in this direction, see Nowlis (1952), who reports on work stimulated by Sears.

tached to the vernacular and an enlargement of the vista with which the study of parent-child relationship may be approached.

We feel that current studies of variations of parental attitudes, whether they deal with "intercultural" or "interindividual" variations, tend to view parental attitudes as "fixed" or "static." While it is often stressed that one parent may have different attitudes to various children, variations in his attitude to one and the same child are often overlooked. In contrast to this, we shall emphasize here the variability of this attitude and the importance which adaptation plays in this connection.

UNCONSCIOUS FANTASIES AND THE PROBLEM OF ADAPTATION

The psychoanalytic understanding of parental attitudes has a natural center in the unconscious meaning which having children or a specific child has for the parent. We shall refer in this paper to the varieties of these unsconscious meanings as "unconscious fantasies."

No analytic observer believes that unconscious fantasies alone determine parental attitudes. There are factors of reality which dominate the picture: there is the wanted and the unwanted child; the child born as seal to a happy and satisfactory union or born to cement a dissolving one, the child born into a firmly rooted family where the sacrifices of child care are readily accepted or that born to parents who in the midst of the struggle for independence or existence resent the burden imposed upon them. The influence of these or similar conditions on parental attitudes is viewed in analysis not only in the light of the individual's current conscious and unconscious conflicts. These reality factors also prove as a rule to be connected with specific unconscious fantasies concerning parenthood and children which are of different importance in the lives of mothers and fathers. To the woman the birth of the child is part of the biological cycle of her sexual function. Labor and delivery are vaguely anticipated in many kinds of sexual experiences, more regularly and concretely in the sensations attending menstruation. Throughout pregnancy an apparently new and yet unconsciously prepared network of fantasies tends to develop—or more correctly, older fantasies tend to be refocused or reactivated. These fantasies, however different from individual to individual, are impressively grouped around well-known common themes (H. Klein et al., 1950).

> The biologic process [of pregnancy] has created a unity of mother and child in which the bodily substance of one flows into the other, and thus a larger unit is formed out of two units. The same thing takes place on the psychic level . . . by perceiving the fruit of her body as part of herself the pregnant woman is able to transform the "parasite" in her into a beloved being [Vol. 2, p. 139].

Helene Deutsch (1944/45), whose thought we have followed and from whose writing we quote, feels that this love will reestablish the oneness between mother and child when the child is born. In the transition from separation to reunion she finds the roots of the universal striving of the human for contact with others and for union with them.

No comparable biological link connects the father and his child. His wife's pregnancy may revive oedipal fantasies of bearing a child to his own father, but the revived fantasy is different in nature. It is elicited by the mechanism of the revival of his own past and is not rooted in biological functions.

This mechanism of revival of the past is operative in the mother as well and for both parents constitutes a central point in the experience of parenthood. The relation to one's own parents is repeatedly reenacted by repetition or by avoidance. In parenthood the psychological life cycles of two generations overlap and a third one is regularly involved (Freud, 1933).

Parents as analytic patients find access to repressed experiences of their own childhood by living with their own children, by observing them, and by reacting to them. Among the reactions the tendency to identify with their own parents is paramount. This identification may manifest itself in behavior ranging from compliance with the parental model to protest

against it, and these tendencies may range from complete una-
wareness to full consciousness.

It is this experience of analytic observation which suggests a
general approach to the function of unconscious fantasies concerning the expected and the growing child. They are not, as
the literature sometimes seems to suggest, mere elements intruding into the "real" parent-child relationship; they are its
ferment. They are part of the equipment of man for parenthood and probably its essence as far as the psychological
equipment is concerned.

Analytic case histories, it is true, tend to stress the opposite
aspect. It is pointed out to the patient that his child is not his
sibling and rival, to be envied or pitied—the most frequent initial reaction of fathers; he is not meant to fulfill what was
missed, is not the patient reborn anew as male or female; he is
an independent being. While this is the way—admittedly simplified—in which in analytic observation unconscious fantasies
attached to the child tend to reveal themselves, psychoanalytic
material viewed in a broader sense illustrates the progressive
and adaptive nature of the unconscious fantasies to which
Helene Deutsch has drawn attention.

The classical instance of a progressive fantasy concerns the
equation penis = child. Universal in the development of the
female, its transformation corresponds to the sequence of
maturation and development. The wish for the child merges
with and follows that for the penis, and this transition initiates
or consolidates the forming of the woman's mind in the small
girl. This process is strengthened later when the sister's or the
neighbor's child may take the place assigned to the doll. But it
is not the reality of the external experience which determines
its importance. The dynamically essential step toward feminity
can be made only during adolescence under the impact of its
physical and physiological changes.

Similar progressive steps in fantasy production become observable during pregnancy itself. Material from analytic observation and some data from the study to which we shall refer
later suggest that in many instances a change in focus of the
fears of pregnant women can be noted. The anxiety tends to

shift from damage to the own body to damage to body or
mind of the child. There are women in whom the child is
from the beginning included in the dark apprehension which
feeds on many reactivated fantasies—on the fear of retaliation
for the ancient wish of a child from father, on the fear of
mutilation arising in consequence of guilt over masturbation,
and on a deeper layer of fears connected with the ambivalence
to the mother. In many women the first movements of the
child stimulate a new focus of apprehension, a "more realistic
one," as we usually put it. And yet it appears at times that
what has changed is frequently only the content of the fear.
Instead of the safety and integrity of the self, it is that of the
child as part of the self that is endangered.

The process of adaptation gains a powerful impetus by the
contact with the newborn when the infant "responds" to the
mother's stimulation. This is the first in a continuous chain of
experiences which extends over time. Before we turn to some
more detailed comments on these earliest phases of mother-
child or parent-child contact it seems necessary briefly to
round out the position we take—a position implied in psychoanalytic writings but rarely made explicit. Parental attitudes to
the child are continuously influenced by the child's growth
and development. With the changing needs and demands of
the child different reactions of the parents are stimulated,
since changing demands tend to mobilize different unconscious material in the parent (chap. 4). In principle this is
equally true of both parents. The interaction between the
child's development and the unconscious material which it
mobilizes in the parent suggests that "fixed" and "static" designation of parental attitudes are unsatisfactory or incomplete.
Parental attitudes are subject to variations in accordance with
the varying needs and demands of the child. The mother who
genuinely delights in or can tolerate all of the infant's demands may react with irritation when the child becomes "independent," when early in his second year he can move away
and at the same time may develop an intolerance against separation at bedtime. And again the reverse occurs: the child that
has become independent may gain admiration from a mother

who did not gain satisfaction from her care of the infant.[5] In the later course of development, bowel training, the first manifestations of negativism, or the first signs of phallic and oedipal strivings may elicit previously dormant reactions in the parent. The more frequent and probably best known intolerance concerns the parental reaction to the child who shows sibling rivalry. Therefore, no study of parental attitudes seems to us complete so long as it neglects the variations arising in the course of those changing characteristics of infant and child.[6]

This problem also has a bearing on the approach in psychoanalytic therapy. In the course of most analytic treatments adult patients recall a variety of their experiences with their parents. We know that these changing versions reflect dynamic changes in the patient and may call upon related memory material. But changing images of parental figures may also be related to some extent to the actual variations that occurred in the attitudes of parents. In some instances, analytic material definitely supports this assumption; in others, the changing images of the parents which the patient offers seem only to be related to the development of the conflict pattern during the analytic process. However, it seems that in the expectation with which the analyst approaches the task of reconstruction insufficient emphasis has been placed upon the actual changes in parental attitudes that may have occurred.

From the study to which we refer later our impression is

5. Much of this has become general knowledge. Child placement agencies are accustomed to take into account that certain foster mothers do better with infants, others with toddlers or older children of a specific age group.

6. In the life history of an obsessional male patient, who in his forties had the long-awaited child, similar reactions became apparent. During the first months and years of the little girl's life, the father, a tall, fair man with blue eyes, was beset with fears that his baby would smother in her bed. He had to get up at night to check on the position of her pillows. At the same time he was unable to recall whether she had blue eyes like himself or brown ones like his younger sister. The fear for the child's welfare repeated the early aggressive impulses against his sibling. Fears and doubts vanished simultaneously when the little girl, some time during her third year of life, spontaneously developed a new relationship to her father, demanded his attention, and prescribed what he should do with and to her. Under the impact of this powerful experience, i.e., the daughter's love, different responses were stimulated in the father and the shadow of the sister was banished.

that such changes are more frequent during the first months or years of the child's life than has been generally assumed.

Before we try to illustrate the variations of parental attitudes which we have in mind, it is once more essential to enlarge our vista. In speaking of the parents' reactions to the sequence of demands as they arise during the child's development we refer to "the child" as an abstraction, but the child who manifests the needs of which we speak is an individual and the parents' reactions will be influenced by this individuality. His individual traits determine in part which unconscious material in the parent is being stimulated and thus which conflicts may arise.

"Individuality," as we use the term here in a general sense, reflects the part that fate plays in human affairs: whether boy or girl, a well child or a sick one, an attractive or less attractive baby. In a more specific sense we refer to a complex set of differences between children. This includes not only the infinite series of differences in behavior and reaction which strike trained observers as present in newborn infants, but also traits due to the interaction between the child and his environment.[7]

The child who readily accepts the cuddling of the mother will elicit different responses in her than the child who refuses such intimacy, is difficult to comfort, and does not adapt to the mother's body. Observations which would take such differences into account are few; they have to cope with a large number of variables. To illustrate opposites we refer only to two approaches in current child psychiatry: the one considers severe childhood disturbances largely, if not solely, a product of the behavior of certain mothers and here the term "schizophrenogenic mother" has arisen; the other also views the

7. Psychoanalytic literature, and for that matter any other kind of scientific literature, has so far contributed little to the question of how to study the properties of inborn equipment. Margaret Fries's pioneer work (1953) has proved extremely stimulating and there is little doubt that the distinction of activity patterns which she introduced describes certain observable differences. The question arises to what extent this distinction is adequate, since it does not take into account the difference in thresholds for certain sensory stimuli (Bergman and Escalona, 1949), the difference in general responsiveness to stimuli, and some of the other differences in the neonate which have impressed observers.

mother's behavior as response to a child who does not or cannot adequately respond to her. Obviously, both factors interact and their interaction has to be studied. The general
characterization of parental attitudes has, we suggest, to take
such interaction into account. The characterization of the
parent should include an attempt to indicate the adaptability
of his attitude to the varying demands of the child and to his
developing individuality. Unconscious fantasies play an important role in the nature of this interaction. They may reinforce
the mother's ability to respond to the stimuli which the situation offers, i.e., may enable her to react even to minimal clues,
or they may limit this responsiveness in various ways. Parental
attitudes may be or may become fixed, outdated, or not in
tune with the child with whom they are concerned. The child
has not become an individual; he remains a projective screen.[8]

Before we attempt to reformulate these statements in a way
which is more in line with current analytic concepts, we turn
to a presentation of some data concerning early variations of
parental attitudes.

CASE HISTORIES

A Longitudinal Study As Observational Setup

The subtleties of interactions between parents and child
have been first observed in child analysis. Instances when both
parent and child were under treatment by different or by the
same analyst have proved instructive, and the practice of therapy of the small child via therapy of the mother has become
accepted procedure. These clinical procedures are potent as
instruments of observation, but they only rarely throw adequate light on the earliest interaction between mother and

8. In the study about which we briefly report, this aspect of parent-child relationship is represented by a paradoxical question: When we discuss the attitude of
pregnant mothers, we ask ourselves: "How old is the expected baby in the mother's
mind? Does she expect a smiling or babbling infant, a toddler or even an older child?"
Similar examples in the behavior of fathers are well known: the urge to give the electric train or the football to a two- or three-year-old is all too familiar.

child. Child analysts too have to rely on the method of reconstruction.

The relation of reconstruction of the past to observation of the present in the study of child development has been discussed repeatedly (Hartmann, 1950a; chap. 5). While reconstructive procedures serve as signposts, focus attention, and pose problems, direct observation plays a limited but essential role. Such observation is included in the traditional approach of psychoanalysis; in the *Three Essays on the Theory of Sexuality* Freud stated that he relied on both sources, on material from analysis and the direct observation of the child.[9]

The data derived from observation are clearly limited. They lack almost all the features upon which analysts tend to rely; what they offer will largely depend on the context in which they are made and on the nature of the selection of data.

At the Child Study Center of Yale University a project has been under way which uses an observational approach in the study of mother-child relationship and of certain aspects of child development.[10] It is intended as a pilot investigation in the organization of longitudinal studies, and wishes to pose problems and develop hypotheses which will require validation in studies dealing with larger numbers of subjects.

The study is service-centered. The families under observation join the study as subsidiary to hospital services. The selection is limited to a small number of families which intend to stay in New Haven indefinitely, and referral for participation was left to the obstetrical service of the Grace-New Haven Community Hospital. The study offers complete well-and sick-baby care and, later, nursery school participation. Participant parents are interviewed in the antepartum period by a social worker who remains attached to the family and continues the contact by home visits after the birth of the child. During delivery and the lying-in period intensive observation of mothers and children is undertaken. At frequent intervals

9. It tends to be overlooked that Freud was in charge of an outpatient service in child neurology when he prepared *The Interpretation of Dreams* and the *Three Essays on the Theory of Sexuality*.

10. This study was supported by the Commonwealth Fund.

in well-baby clinics developmental tests are administered by the pediatrician in addition to regular pediatric examinations. Additional observations of mother and child are made through the one-way vision screen by trained observers. Since both social worker and pediatrician are in constant touch with the home, a fairly clear picture can be gained.

We neither intend at this point to enter into a detailed description of the procedures used nor to evaluate these procedures in any way. We also do not propose to discuss the advantages which it seems to offer that the study is service-centered and the pediatrician is conversant with psychoanalysis. We intend only to report briefly on some principles used in the collection and evaluation of data. Contact with the parents is kept spontaneous, i.e., a minimum of questions is asked. The topics of discussion are largely determined by their urgency to the parent. We start, therefore, with a limited set of data on the parent and watch the growth of these data over time. Hence presence or absence of data at any given time becomes significant in itself. The contact with the parents is viewed as a dynamic and unfolding experience.

The pediatrician's role with the family is essentially that of the authority on child care, and no advice or instruction is withheld which the doctor feels would enhance the health of the child and the parent-child relationship. This advice is, of course, modified in accordance with the individual situation. The pediatrician advises not in terms of what is theoretically optimal in child care, but in terms of what seems best for this mother and her child. It should be added that the physician-family relationship remains child-centered. Perhaps the only important variation of the pediatrician's role in this study from that of the pediatrician in private practice is in the enlargement of her responsibilities for observation of the child's environment, and the efforts to distinguish as clearly as possible between subjective and objective data.

A further point concerns the evaluation of data: meetings of the research staff try to view the data presented in terms of their use for prediction. What can be predicted at any given time, i.e., the range of predictable events, is to us more signifi-

cant than the correctness or incorrectness of any specific prediction.[11] Past predictions become part of the material for
retrospective evaluation: in rediscussing a case we turn to the
past material in search for clues which would have suggested a
different or a more specific prediction. Thus predictive and
retrospective evaluation interact.[12] In addition, we try to remain aware of the fact that we study processes and to include
in our data the changes in our own insight.

The four case histories from which we can present only very
abbreviated abstracts have one factor in common: they describe dramatic events in early mother-child relationship,
events which may be viewed as crises. They are presented with
frequent reference to the predictive viewpoint. We were
throughout concerned with the question at which point we
could have anticipated the turn in the relationship. We concentrate in this report on *earliest* changes in parental attitudes.
Wherever possible, we have stressed the importance of the interaction of the attitudes of the parents with the development
of the child.[13]

11. This technique had been adopted before we were familiar with Benjamin's
views (1950). We find ourselves in full agreement with his methodological discussion.

12. [In an unpublished Progress Report written in 1953, Ernst Kris stated: "It is
our contention that we understand the three-year-old infinitely better because we
knew him as a three-week-old and as a three-month-old. We expect every new impression and observation thus to add to our understanding of the past."]

13. We are aware of defects of the data we use; for instance, that many details on
parental sex life which are routinely part of psychiatric material are missing. This is
an unavoidable shortcoming of our setup. The parents are not psychiatric patients;
they consider themselves normal parents and hope that their children will be normal
children. The extent to which the fact that they joined a study in "child development"
has influenced the sample cannot be discussed in this context. We also—and for obvious reasons—do not use in this paper either diagnostic psychiatric terms or evalua-
tions of Rorschach tests by F. Weil, which have been important to us. In the case
reports no attempt was made to present in each case the same set of data. We had to
leave out anything that could have led to an identification of the families involved,
e.g., we purposefully omitted the description of their social background. We have
reduced the speculative element as far as possible and therefore refer to such things
as the relationship of mothers to their own parents only where we felt we were on
solid ground.

Case Reports

The first two cases concern mothers whose initially close relationship to the child was negatively influenced by his growth and development.

Mrs. A., an attractive, energetic twenty-three-year-old girl, one of twelve children, joined the study during the fourth month of her first pregnancy. She continued her work as a semiskilled factory worker until the sixth month. Although she and her husband of two years had not planned to have their baby until later because they were living in the home of Mr. A.'s parents, she seemed accepting of this alteration of their original plan, felt "wonderful" during her pregnancy, and eagerly anticipated the arrival of the baby.

Billy was born after a labor of six and a half hours which Mrs. A. experienced as being much less painful than she had anticipated from the stories she had heard from her older sisters and friends. From the very beginning in her handling of the baby—a boy—she not only was surprisingly technically skillful and competent, but she seemed particularly responsive to clues from him related to his needs and had great success in making him comfortable and happy. For example, by the time he was four days of age, she noted that he had particular objections to being wet, was able to change his diaper competently, and was exceedingly pleased that she was able to comfort him. In the first visit of the pediatrician to the home when Billy was three weeks of age, a note was made that Mrs. A.'s way of comforting him, once she picked him up and once when she patted him in his bassinet, seemed to be "all he needed and not more."

During the first nine to ten months she was described by all members of the research team who saw her as a particularly warm and skillful mother and the impression of unity and understanding between her and Billy was repeatedly commented upon. This came up not only in relation to her ability to persuade Billy to respond as she wished him to in the areas of his eating, sleeping, and toileting, but also in the definite but indirect and subtle ways of prohibiting things of which she did not approve. It was noted, for example, that she interrupted the thumb sucking which she did not like not by pulling his thumb out, but by enticing him to become busy with something else— playing with her or with a toy. Her prohibition of masturbation was recorded in detail by the physician when Billy was slightly under ten months of age; he reached for his penis while on the potty and she took his hand away, said in a not unpleasant tone, "That's not to play with," and thereafter supported him on the pot in such a way that although she did not appear to be restraining him, he could not again reach the genital area and turned his attention to her vocal stimulation. She seemed to set her limits in a way that aroused a minimum of protest from the baby. She anticipated no difficulty and seemed to feel perfectly sure that everything would go well between them. The only area in which it might be said that there was a limit to her competence was in relation to illness. Billy had his first illness at five and a half months—a severe cold and cough. Not only did she prove to be a surprisingly poor reporter of his symptoms, but she needed considerable help in giving him his medication. It has remained a consistent finding that Mrs. A.'s success in meeting Billy's needs and in interpreting clues from him is much less when he is sick than when well.

Some time must here be given to a description of Billy who showed surprising adaptability and smoothness in many of his physiological and maturational patterns from the beginning. As a newborn he was described as well developed, moderately active and mature. There was a specificity about his way of expressing his discomfort or wishes which seemed to make comforting him quite easy (i.e., not just by his mother but by others as well). One might say he gave clues which could easily be interpreted. His parents found him attractive, entertaining, and easy to live with.

Some of the smoothness and adaptability in his behavior patterns can be illustrated by the story of his sleep. From the first, Billy was an infant who when he was asleep, slept deeply. By age twelve days he was already sleeping seven to eight hours consecutively during the night and by six weeks was sleeping ten hours. At four months he had a period of about ten days of being wakeful intermittently at night at a time when he had grown too large to sleep comfortably in his bassinet. He returned to his uninterrupted twelve hours when placed in a large crib. When he was five and a half months old his father took a new job in which he worked from late afternoon to midnight. Billy very obligingly fit into the new family schedule by being perfectly amiable about going to bed slightly later and sleeping until 9 A.M. In the four illnesses which he had before he was eleven months of age his sleep would be temporarily disturbed (two or three days) while he was ill, but return to normal when he was well.

His rate of skeletal growth was rapid during the first months. He weighed 7 lbs. at birth and at the age of four months was at the 75th percentile in weight and the 60th percentile in length. He was described as well nourished and solid, but not fat. He took large amounts of solid foods and formula eagerly, a fact which manifestly pleased Mrs. A. His caloric needs during the first months were greater than those of many infants whose early growth pattern is slower, and thus his mother found him wonderful in still another area. We do not for a moment suggest that her way of feeding did not influence his intake and the pleasure of this experience for both of them. We do suggest that it was a happy and important coincidence that he needed more food than many babies do. Mrs. A. never had to cope with a baby whose appetite was small; his point of satiation unquestionably met her standards of adequate intake and he could usually be persuaded to "take one more bite for mommy" if she wished it.

He was responsive to every adult, both friend and stranger, and most of all to his mother. He smiled readily, babbled freely, and gave observers the impression of great amiability and enjoyment of life, and that he expected the world would be good to him. As K. Wolf (1953) said in her report, "It is not easy to explain the impression he created. He seemed so well put together, so smoothly integrated, and so completely unaware of the hardships of life [he was by no means a hand-

some baby, but] he enchanted every person . . . who saw
him" (p. 135). There was no trace of anxiety toward the
stranger, though he clearly was discriminating in the quality of
his positive responses. He was physically active, and his motor
development during the first nine months was consistently
four to six weeks advanced. His developmental profile showed
unusually small scatter in the various areas measured by the
infant tests—another demonstration of his steady, well-in-
tegrated way of developing.

Thus, those first nine to ten months gave us the impression
of such an untroubled, conflict-free, mutually satisfying and
stimulating mother-child relationship that the period of the
"crisis" which became apparent during the tenth month was
impossible to overlook. The first indication of this came on the
occasion of Mrs. A's and Billy's visit to the clinic for his regularly scheduled checkup. It was both reported by Mrs. A. and
observed that Billy was more difficult to dress. He did not "cooperate" in this as he had previously, and it looked as if his
mother's usual ways of restraining him by distraction or touch
could no longer control his drive toward activity. At this time
he was creeping and cruising. He walked with two hands held.
When his mother tried to hold him on her lap, he tried to get
down. He was reaching out and scratching at her neck or face
in a provocative way and she was scolding him with a new
sharpness in her tone. She looked more harassed and tired at
that visit than the pediatrician had ever seen her and said
about Billy, "I really work up a sweat trying to figure out what
he wants now." She reported that Billy was now so active that
he seemed to want to be down on the floor, out of his crib, or
chair, or the previously satisfactory laps of his elders. She
spoke with much more feeling than ever before about how
much she wanted a "place of our own"—and added, "Big families are nice in a way, but I'm tired of crowds." Such a move
seemed impossible at that time as they had just bought a car
which Mr. A. had to have for his work. At that point Billy
would permit no one except his mother to feed him his meals
and she was both pleased and irritated by this behavior. He

also was making persistent grabs for the spoon during feeding and she found this annoying.

During the next three months Mrs. A. indicated her irritation at certain continuing aspects of her environment which had previously seemed less important to her. She complained about her husband's doing things for his mother. There was distinct displeasure expressed for the first time at Billy's enjoyment of his paternal grandmother, and the need to say, "But she [paternal grandmother] can't *really* take care of him," and an ever increasing determination to have a place of her own as soon as possible. She talked about Billy's behavior in a different way. For example, his activity and impatience with the lap were often spoken of as though they were primarily aimed at irritating her. His wish for certain objects to play with was seen as "everything he shouldn't have he wants." She was bothered by the fact that Billy could no longer be so easily persuaded to comply with her wishes. She summarized her difficulty in saying: "I can't figure him out anymore."

Under the pressure of the dissatisfaction Mrs. A. returned to work and left the part-time care of the child to her sister. This does not mean that her relationship to Billy had deteriorated, that she had become a "rejecting mother." The relationship has remained close, but has lost one impressive component—the full unity of mother and child. The relationship between mother and child now bears more resemblance to her relationship with other people. She is a woman who tries gently but firmly to dominate every situation. This is apparent in her relationship with her husband, and could be studied in some detail in her relationship with interviewer and pediatrician.

Retrospectively we find from this material that her reaction to the child's growing independence might have been anticipated, but we missed an even more significant clue. When the pediatrician discussed with her the giving of solid foods and in enumerating mentioned that he might not like the taste of some of them, Mrs. A. quickly responded, "Oh, he'll like spinach; I like it." What we saw in this was the unity; what we

missed was the germ of discord since what she implied was
that Billy was not thought of as having a taste of his own.

Mrs. B., a twenty-four-year-old, dark-haired, dark-eyed,
heavy-set, attractive young woman, was the youngest of several children. After completing high school she had done un-
skilled factory work. It was here that she met her husband to
whom she was attracted from the beginning, although she did
not go out with him until after he terminated a relationship
with another girl.

Mr. B., two years older than Mrs. B., was the only living
child of his parents. Mr. B. had always lived at home except
for a three-year period in the armed forces, and the young
couple moved into the family home with his parents. The
house, located in an isolated spot on the outskirts of the community, was large enough for two separate living quarters,
and prior to the marriage it was planned that the two families
would live separately. This arrangement was denied the B's
because the mother-in-law became angry at them. This characterizes both the domination of the mother-in-law and the inability of the young couple to assert themselves. The
mother-in-law insisted upon doing all the cooking for the entire family.

Mrs. B. conceived three months after marriage and seemed
to have been delighted about her pregnancy. They were both
surprised at the early conception; Mr. B. had had mumps
orchitis while in the armed services and had been told that he
might be sterile. Pregnancy was uneventful; the first movements of the baby were experienced with great pleasure. This
made Mrs. B. know that the baby was alive while prior to this
it had not seemed real.

Labor and delivery were medically uneventful. Jimmy, a
large, blue-eyed, blond boy, was characterized as a newborn as
moderately active, and easily comforted by touch and position
changes. Breast feeding was easily established with a large
supply of milk. In the handling and breast feeding of the newborn baby Mrs. B. appeared competent and comfortable. He
was entirely breast-fed for the first three months and weaned

only at eleven months. Solids were begun in the third month and taken well. We consider now the first part of this period: milk supply was ample; only one breast was used per feeding; a bottle of breast milk was given on the one occasion when Mrs. B. was away for her postpartal checkup. She continued manual expression far beyond the usual period. The intimacy between mother and child extended beyond the feeding. He was held or carried either by mother or paternal grandmother for most of his waking and many of his sleeping hours. The mother took him into her bed, how frequently we do not know.

When the child was six weeks of age the staff's impression of Mrs. B. was uncrystallized. Out of the group of mothers studied in this project it was felt that she could either be the most "normal" or belong among the most disturbed ones. There were only slight reasons for the latter view: there was her general difficulty in giving expression to anxiety and her hesitancy to ask for or accept advice generally. While her skill in handling Jimmy was noted from the beginning, she later told of her concern in her first contacts with the infant (would he eat enough? would he stay awake long enough for eating? would he go back to the nursery hungry? etc.). The first clue to some of her unexpressed concern came to the pediatrician on the second postpartum day, when out of her anxiety about feeding she asked for the rooming-in service, which she had previously refused. Other clues slowly accumulated in the early months. We heard that Jimmy was not taken outside "because we have no carriage." He was given only sponge baths until seven months of age "because he would be afraid" of a tub bath. In spite of repeated explanations, the startling of the baby was interpreted by her as fright.

The relationship of Mrs. B. with her baby can be fully appreciated only if we take a number of factors into account. Living on the outskirts of town with poor transportation available, contacts with her own family were infrequent and she felt a stranger in the house of her in-laws where she had few household responsibilities. Thus the baby gained the importance of an exclusive possession.

In the center of the relationship with the baby stands the experience of breast feeding for both mother and child.[14]

Some of its meaning can tentatively be illustrated by a number of facts: it was something the mother alone could give the child; the child often went to sleep with the nipple in his mouth; around three months, when his hunger was satisfied, he played with the nipple and held the breast between his hands (Mrs. B. reported this with obvious pleasure and added it made her "feel funny").

Jimmy's development and appearance reflected his experiences in child care. For the first four months he was universally described as attractive, handsome, the classical "fine bouncing baby." After four months he was less attractive, appeared flabby with poor muscle tone, and a relative delay in gross motor development was noted. Observation and the mother's information revealed that some of the situations which are generally thought to enhance gross motor development (e.g., opportunity for play on firm surfaces, freedom and stimulation to move about) were significantly reduced by the kind of care Jimmy received.

Jimmy's growing up was in itself a threat to the mother. When his first tooth erupted at three and a half months, she feared this would threaten the breast feeding. Difficulties due to his biting started at that time.[15] At eight months a certain decrease in his tendency to bite was noted. Mrs. B. permitted

14. This has to be seen in the context of a pervasive atmosphere of "orality." The environment seemed charged with it. The rationalization for her inability to try to persuade Mr. B. to separate from the in-laws is the fear that Mr. B. would "stop eating if he left his mother's house" (a rationalization which wears thin when one heard that in the armed services he gained 15 pounds).

Before pregnancy Mrs. B. herself gained 20 pounds on the mother-in-law's cooking, which she could not refuse to eat for fear of hurting her feelings.

Her own mother has a comparable diet problem; as a diabetic she finds it difficult to adjust to her diabetic diet. The consistency of the preoccupation with food goes into details: while in the hospital Mrs. B. is given a large basket of fruit by her husband instead of flowers.

15. We tentatively gained the impression that the interference with Jimmy's biting may have stimulated his "angry and prolonged biting of toys" (the cubes in the testing materials) which was accompanied by a vocalization variously described as grumbling, grunting, or scolding. A possible connection between this and the poor speech development is inferred.

him to bite her face, her arms or fingers, but forced his jaws apart to remove the nipple when he would bite the breast, in order to safeguard the feeding which was the center of her relationship with the child.

The decision to wean crystallized only gradually. Mrs. B. seems to have envisaged a period of nine months. The pediatrician at six and a half months suggested that she prepare for weaning. She did not follow the suggestion and was obviously torn by conflicting feelings—on the one hand feeling that she should now wean him directly to the cup and on the other hand not wanting to lose him.

She was not able to follow the recommendation to wean gradually. It made her feel guilty and depriving to give milk by cup instead of the breast. During an upper respiratory infection at nine and a half months when he had refused a feeding, Mrs. B. said that she was unable to wean gradually and asked if she could stop all breast feedings at once. When the pediatrician suggested that this be postponed until Jimmy recovered from his infection, a new period of exclusive breast feeding was initiated. Weaning took place abruptly at eleven months. At this time two events coincided: he bit the nipple until it bled, and a visit to the pediatrician was imminent. Two days before his visit, breast feeding was discontinued, and when Mrs. B. was asked how she felt about it, she replied, "I live it a day and then a night at a time and guess I'll get through it somehow."

The mother's reaction to weaning became manifest in many ways. She was depressed, found life at her in-laws increasingly intolerable, spoke of taking a job, but abandoned the idea because it would mean leaving Jimmy with the mother-in-law.

She was still skillful in her physical handling of him at the end of his first year, but what was meaningful to the young infant whose needs and moods she could anticipate was no longer of equal importance to the growing child. The physical intimacy continued in many ways, but the ways were not adaptive. Mrs. B. was inflexible and did not respond to his need to be given and allowed to play with toys, nor did she provide opportunities to move and explore the world about him.

A new reason was found for the restriction of his motility. The mother-in-law's furniture could not be pushed around. This in turn made it easier to explain the physical closeness between mother and child, which was reinforced by the mother-in-law's statement, "Babies need to be held."

To what extent the attitude of the mother-in-law who dominates the young couple supplied a model which could easily be adapted to Mrs. B.'s own purposes is difficult to say, but it seems possible that some ambivalent feelings of considerable intensity are stimulated by the child's attempts to grow with his months.

Concurrently with weaning there was an increase of upper respiratory infections; he impressed observers more and more as a disagreeable and dissatisfied child. His lack of initiative became apparent and was closely linked with intense anxiety of the stranger. Language production remains retarded, but in all other sectors of development which can be measured by tests he functions at a normal level. He wears long hair, and the decision to cut it now bothers his mother. A new situation has arisen in which she would have to part with something linked to his infancy.

In the following two cases we are concerned with a transition in the mothers' attitudes which at first were more negative and became more positive as time passed.

The first of these two, Mrs. C., was described in the initial contact as being a moderately attractive, pleasant young woman in the fifth month of pregnancy, who seemed eager to please the interviewer and glad to become a part of the study. As time passed there seemed to be little reason to doubt that her attachment to the study was based on her belief that it was the best available means of insuring optimum care for her child and help for herself in caring for the infant about whom she expressed much concern during the antepartum period. She read numerous books and articles about child care and asked many questions. She expressed far more than the usual amount of concern about whether or not the baby would be all right, particularly as this was related to mental development.

Pregnancy was complicated by nausea and vomiting from the third through the seventh months, and this necessitated one period of hospitalization for a few days. She worried about the effect of this vomiting on her baby, and expressed concern about her own ability to be the "right kind" of mother.

The last two months of pregnancy were infinitely more pleasant for Mrs. C.—her vomiting disappeared and she expressed eagerness and pleasure, mingled with anxiety about her adequacy, over the prospect of becoming a mother. She delivered at term after a prolonged and exhausting labor necessitating spinal anesthesia and low forceps delivery. The infant, a well-formed, vigorous little girl, was in good condition at birth and weighed 7 lbs. Twelve hours later she looked less good: she had a high-pitched cry of poor quality, reacted minimally to stimulation, had poor sucking and rooting responses and some degree of stupor. There was a mild peripheral facial weakness. Over the period of the next three days she became more wakeful and alert, the facial palsy disappeared, and the above-mentioned sucking and rooting responses became quite active and normal.

By the time she was six days old she was described as an attractive, well-formed, vigorous infant who was active, hypertonic, easily startled and sensitive to external stimuli (touch, position change, temperature change). She cried loudly for her feedings, could not be quieted by holding at such times for the few minutes needed to prepare the breast or bottle, and was characterized by the nurse in the newborn nursery as a "screamer." It was only slightly easier for the experienced nurse to comfort her than for the inexperienced mother. It was felt at that time that because of her physiological makeup, Margaret was going to be a difficult baby to live with, and it seemed unfortunate that this infant whose needs seemed to overwhelm her was to be cared for by such an anxious and inept mother. In this assumption we were eminently correct. The first few months of Margaret's life were a trial and tribulation. Mrs. C. described this period as the "worst three months of my life," a period in which she lost all confidence in herself, was not able to make decisions, was not able

to feel good about what she did for the baby, and was repeatedly confused by suggestions from neighbors and relatives.
She was encouraged to call the pediatrician whenever she
needed to and did this with impressive frequency. It was discovered quite early in the contact (by the time Margaret was
two weeks of age) that it was not possible for Mrs. C. to choose
between two acceptable methods of child care. She had to be
given very specific instructions with the admonition that there
was more than one way to do this, and if the suggested one
did not work with Margaret she should call the doctor. This
seemed to be the only way in which she could be helped during those first three months, and she was not ready for many
months to assume real responsibility in relation to the baby's
care. She could not carry over the reasoning behind one situation in child care to another. She had to ask separately about
hundreds of small—but, to her, vital—points.

The baby grew and developed well, but she was physiolog-
ically unstable and difficult to satisfy. She was partially breast-
fed for six weeks, but the mother finally gave this up because,
although "the books had said breast feeding was best for babies," Margaret spit up her mother's breast milk more
frequently than she did the complementary bottle feeding. On
the occasion of Margaret's first visit to the clinic at the age of
six weeks the pediatrician characterized her as being hypertonic, very sensitive to loud or sudden sounds or sudden
changes in movement, a very easy startler and difficult to comfort when crying. Although the pediatrician felt that these
findings were not beyond the range of normal, it was not possible to exclude some degree of central nervous system damage at this time—in view of the already mentioned reactions
during the first two days of life. This concern was not made
known to the mother. Additionally, Margaret had a laryngeal
stridor which, though of no medical significance in this instance, seemed to give Mrs. C. further cause for her fear that
she was not a normal infant.

At the three-month visit Margaret looked good, had grown
well, and was performing at or above her chronological age on
the infant tests, and particular efforts were made to explain to

Mrs. C. how well she was doing in the various areas in which infants can be tested.

During the first three months the pediatrician tried to emphasize several things with the mother; one was that the pediatrician realized and was sympathetic that this baby was very difficult to live with—that she was not placid by nature and obviously had more discomfort than many infants do; the other was that these characteristics were not a sign of defectiveness or of abnormality. Though temporarily relieved by the pediatrician's statements, Mrs. C. could show no pleasure in this baby, could not accept her individuality, and could not feel all right about Margaret's not being just like the baby described in the baby book or the child next door.

During the fourth and fifth months things went on pretty much as before, with Mrs. C. continuing to need much support and reassurance. By this time Margaret had very beautiful fair skin and rosy cheeks and it was quite easy and natural to comment on her attractiveness. She became increasingly responsive socially and it was hoped that this smiling, laughing, and reaching out toward her mother could be recognized by Mrs. C. as favorable signs. This was a period when Mrs. C. accepted momentarily the evidences of Margaret's good development and then reminisced about how terrible the first three months had been and how inadequate she had. felt as a mother. At the five-month visit, however, the concerns about Margaret's normalcy were still present. At that time it became apparent that Mrs. C. (evidently in an effort to reduce the necessity to make decisions) had become extremely rigid about feeding, placed great dependence upon its mechanical aspects, and failed to notice or disregarded the clues the baby gave her. For example, it was revealed that she always waited until the baby became loud and insistent in her crying for food before she fed her (and by this time the infant was expressing her needs by slight crying, followed only later by vigorous crying); she was stopping the feeding *exactly* after each 2 oz., to wait for an *exact* number of bubbles regardless of the baby's state of hunger or satiation. The pediatrician felt at that time that mother and child were caught in a mutually hazardous situation, that the mother was relying upon mechanistic devices to insure that she could function as a mother, and that she was still concerned, anxious, and preoccupied with her own inadequacy. It was therefore decided that the pediatrician must interrupt the mother's self-imposed mechanistic regime and for another period take away as much as possible some of the necessity to make decisions regarding the baby's care. Mrs. C. was therefore given very exact, specific instructions which she was told to follow without variation for the next ten days, at which time she was to report to the doctor.

The baby at that visit (age five months) was continuing to do well developmentally. She was able to roll from supine to prone, would support a large fraction of her weight when placed in standing position, and was (as expected at this age) more interested than before in sitting and in moving about. She gave her usual good performance in relation to her interest and drive to exploit the test materials. The most striking change to the staff at that visit was her discrimination of strangers and her marked preference for her mother. She was sufficiently apprehensive of the pediatrician and the room that it was necessary for the *first* time to permit her to sit on her mother's lap for the developmental and physical examinations. Mrs. C. confirmed that this had also been present in other situations for about two weeks.

Five days after this visit, Mrs. C. called the doctor to report with great pleasure how well things were going and to tell about what she termed "little Margaret's advance." The "advance" she was seeing was described by her as much the same behavior the pediatrician had seen five days before: Margaret's increased activity, her moving about, her social responsiveness and reaching out, behavior which had been pointed out to her at that time.

There was no doubt that after this visit *something* had enabled Mrs. C. for the first time to look at Margaret in a different way. Her developmental level as compared to her age had been excellent for months; her physical growth had been good from the first, and she had become infinitely less irritable and demanding, but Mrs. C. had derived only meager comfort from these things. The nature of the help being given by the pediatrician seemed no different from that of the earlier months. What did change was the kind of developmental steps taken by the infant: she was entering the period of turning more active in motor development, demonstrating her progress in ways usually more easily recognized by parents than some other aspects of development. She also developed a distinct preference for her mother and apprehensiveness about strange people and places. It might be said that she gave to her mother at this time unmistakable evidence of responding in a specific and flattering way, which Mrs. C. seems to have interpreted not as a demand upon her, but as a preference for her company in much more adult terms. This is in contrast to the attitude of some mothers who interpret the child's "fear of the stranger" as a defect in the child or as an increased demand upon themselves. During the next few months there were continued evidences of Mrs. C.'s growing pleasure in Margaret, her recognition and appreciation of her as an individual, and a disappearance of the expressions of her fear that Margaret would be retarded. Moreover, she was increasingly able to make many everyday decisions which came up in relation to Margaret's care. As she expressed it to the interviewer, "Things are so much better now. I can talk to Margaret and see that she understands what I mean."

In summarizing we may add that for several months before the change in attitude, the staff had observed that in spite of her difficulties Mrs. C. could comfort Margaret better than anyone else and had devised ways of handling her which were adapted to the specific requirements of this baby. For example, Margaret was a baby who was often more upset than comforted when her skin was stroked or she was patted, so that this common avenue of giving comfort to a baby was closed to her. Mrs. C., without realizing her own wisdom, learned to talk to Margaret before touching her, and to introduce a toy for her to look at or hold as an effective means of comforting her. The pediatrician felt certain and stressed to Mrs. C. that she was doing better than she realized. And yet the change in Mrs. C.'s attitude came only after five months.

It seemed to have been due to the two factors which we mentioned before. The specific developmental advance ("turning active") banished the fear that the child was damaged or defective. This fear verbalized during pregnancy by Mrs. C., as by so many mothers, was in this case presumably related to the fear of having damaged the unborn child by excessive vomiting, and by the mother's excessive dissatisfaction with herself as a person, which dated back to her own childhood. The second factor which produced a change in the mother's attitude, the personal response of the child to her ministrations and her presence, strengthened the reassurance.

Mrs. D. was an attractive woman in her late twenties who prior to her pregnancy had combined a full-time career with marriage. She had been married for four years to her husband who worked in a profession and described these years as the happiest of her life. While they had planned to have children, the pregnancy at this time was unplanned and it meant for her a radical change in their mode of living. As a couple they would no longer be able to enjoy frequent trips and excursions, and more specifically it meant that Mrs. D. would have to abandon her career just as she was about to achieve a long sought-for position, because she had firm convictions that a child should be cared for by his own mother and not left to the care of others.

The physical aspects of the pregnancy were uneventful. An increased need to sleep and a difficulty in regulating the diet were the only complaints. She found it hard to restrict her consumption of candy. Not only was the child unwanted at this time, but she stated that the rearing of children was something "to get over with." She was frightened by the idea of having a child as "there is in it something final—a new responsibility is added and how can I bear it?" She had had no experience with infants under three years. She characterized herself as an impatient, restless, and quick-tempered person, who would spank the child when she becomes angry. She felt her husband was more likely to do things correctly than she. She believed in strictness for children and not in babying or spoiling.

She was afraid of having a child with cerebral palsy or mongolism as she hated the thought of being a mother who would be pitied by others. Even her positive plans seemed determined by competitive thoughts. She would breast-feed as she had been fed herself; her brother's wife was unable to do so.

The child was to be a boy and while she thought her husband would not care, she would be disappointed if it were not a boy. From her own past she later recalled that she always felt her father wanted her to be a boy. She remembered his intense desire for her to excel academically and if the grades were not satisfactory to him, he would not talk to her for several days and tutoring would be instituted. During her childhood she often was dressed as a boy and was mistaken for a boy by strangers, which hurt and angered her.

Mrs. D. was admitted to the obstetrical ward with mild vaginal bleeding followed by a slowly proceeding labor of about twelve hours; contractions increased in intensity and as she was about to be taken to the delivery room, she delivered in bed, the husband cheering at the bedside. The obstetrician's impression was that this was a gratifying experience for both parents. She reported the following day that the delivery was a satisfying event and talked of both the terrific speed of the delivery and the surprise of the obstetrician as minor triumphs. Though the baby was small (5½ lbs.), she added, "but she tore me apart," thus referring to a minor vaginal tear.

The baby, a girl, impressed all observers as a small, slightly immature infant, who was attractive, pretty and doll-like, and healthy in every way. The attitude of the mother to the infant became manifest through innumerable details. Anne was outstandingly attractive and elicited many spontaneous remarks to that effect from the staff, which the mother negated. Even in the baby's third month of life the mother said to the admiring interviewer, "Let me show you a really pretty baby" and produced pictures of herself in infancy, adding, "Since she won't be pretty, she had better be clever," a statement which in its brevity sets the tone of the mother's verbalized attitude toward the child. A similar attitude characterized the details of her physical care of the baby.

As a newborn, Anne was easily comforted by holding and yet the mother reported after a few weeks that the child preferred not to be held. She expressed disapproval of picking up the infant, and the impression was gained that all handling was as much restricted as possible.

Breast feeding was abandoned in the hospital period because of Mrs. D.'s repeated questioning as to whether she could manage it at home alone. The milk supply was adequate, but she felt the breasts were so large they might smother the baby.

Formula feeding was easily instituted, but Mrs. D. soon found it too time-consuming. By observation it was noted to be mechanical and hurried. While Mrs. D. availed herself of the best literature and advice on child care practices and followed "the letter of the law," it was repeatedly observed that in these procedures she gave little of herself.

At six weeks of age certain predictions were made concerning the mother-child relationship. It was felt that there was little evidence that she enjoyed the baby; she would be unable to invest much in the infant; and she would have little tolerance if the baby disturbed her. It was also predicted that she would manage efficiently and that explicit directions in child care would be helpful to her. She possibly would be better able to respond to a latency child. The predictions did not extend to the time of onset and specific areas of development that might be affected.

Anne was healthy, and feeding and sleeping difficulties were absent. She continued to be a small, attractive infant who showed normal developmental progress until six months of age. At six months of age her total developmental picture was within normal limits, but she was noted to have poor control of the trunk and poor mastery of large body movements. This was evidenced by her inability to roll to prone from supine, not lifting the head in supine position, not maintaining the trunk in an erect position even when propped, and inability to support more than a fraction of her weight when held in the standing position. Her grasping patterns with both large and small objects were slightly above her age; in the absence of any illness or evidence of neurological difficulty, it was felt that the slight lag in the gross motor area was not alarming.

By eight months of age the clinical picture gave rise to serious apprehension from the staff. Anne could not yet sit alone except momentarily and could not support her full weight on her feet when supported. All gross motor functions were significantly retarded. Fine motor functions were not retarded. Her interest in toys was considerably less than expected for her age. In addition to the gross motor delay, there was also delayed language development. She was observed to react to the mother's approach with vigorous crying, which was the reverse of her reaction to the stranger (no anxiety for the stranger was noted).

Mrs. D. expressed concern about Anne's progress and reported that the child had episodes of crying for no reason apparent to the mother. These episodes were more frequent on days when Mrs. D. felt lonely and depressed. Consciously she related her depression to the feeling that being a wife and mother were insufficient and she longed to work again at her career.

The mother's attitude to the lag in development showed two sides. Initially she was predominantly depressed and hopeless and seemed ready to abandon the child by having another with whom she could have more success. Later she tended to deny the situation and bring forth evidence to support her denial.

Therapeutic aims were directed chiefly toward the mother in helping her obtain psychotherapy. However, a return to her career and outside help with the child's care were additional aims toward improving the situation for both mother and infant.

Neither the pediatrician nor interviewer were able to help Mrs. D. accept any of these measures. A consultant of wide pediatric and psychiatric experience and high professional competence had a similar experience. Pediatric contacts were increased in frequency in an attempt to help Mrs. D. increase the amount of physical handling and stimulation given the child, in the hope that this would help the child.

It may well be that during this period the mother followed some of the advice concerning the care and stimulation, detailed nutritional advice, and general intimations of the child's needs. The atmosphere prevailing during the contacts with the mother was so tense that details were difficult to elicit.

At thirteen months of age Mrs. D. reported that Anne was now much more of a person; she was able to talk to her and believed that the child was beginning to understand her. While Anne was not yet walking alone, Mrs. D. seemed confident that she was a normal child. The mother-child contacts as observed at home had taken on many aspects of a teacher-pupil relationship. Anne was able to stand alone momentarily, had two words, comprehended a few objects by name, and showed interest in the picture book. Development appeared to be up to her age level in all areas for the first time in many months.

During the interval between eight and thirteen months certain external events are known to have taken place which may have influenced this change. Both mother and child had a mild respiratory illness during which the father took over the child's care. Immediately following their illness, mother and child spent several weeks with relatives, a visit the mother enjoyed and where both adults and children were interested in playing with Anne. Subsequently, the family spent several weeks in a resort area where the contacts between father and child were possibly more frequent.

It seems no single factor can be assumed to be solely responsible for the change in the child's development. We assume the interaction of more favorable external conditions with the forces of maturation. As far as the father is concerned, the child around the end of the first year established a new type of relationship. Earlier he had been charmed by her attractiveness and denied that there might be anything wrong with her developmental progress but apparently had little actual contact with her. The illness of the mother may have initiated a more intense relationship between father and child. By eighteen months she was known to have turned to the father with obvious eagerness.

The mother's contribution to the child's developmental spurt is unclear. We know only that the mother felt less discontent with her lot during the visit with relatives and the vacation period. However, her response to the child's spurt was clearer. She expressed pleasure that Anne could understand her and was now teachable, and she began a program of coaching and tutoring to which the child was able to respond. Teaching and the value of performance had been one of the main themes in Mrs. D.'s relation to her own father. It now dominated her attitude to her child. Another factor also was evident. She expressed pride in the child's developing aggression toward other children. It may have meant to her that the child was now less helpless in relation to the mother's own aggression.

Mrs. D. found it possible to adapt more positively to the child as a toddler than as a helpless infant.[16]

DISCUSSION

The four cases here reported have some elements in common: in each of them the attitude of the mother to the child underwent an early and marked change. We point here only to some salient aspects.

The simplest case seems to be that of Mrs. B. The child-lover on the breast is her exclusive possession. A skillful mother, she fails when the toddler strives for independence. She cannot effect the separation from the infant and remains unaware of the requirements of the growing child.

The case of Mrs. A. illustrates an initially somewhat similar relationship with different further development. A mother who experiences the child as part of herself and reacts to minimal clues finds it difficult to accept even the first signs of independence. When she says that she no longer understands what the little boy wants, she describes her initial reaction to this change. Out of a loving couple develops a fighting one. A new type of object relation—the one which seems to pervade

16. [Other aspects of Anne's development are discussed in chapters 9 and 10.]

Mrs. A.'s life— develops. She finds it possible to adjust in returning to work and in sharing child care with her sister.

The change in attitude was observed earliest in the case of Mrs. C. From birth on the child had been unsatisfactory to her. The actual peculiarities of equipment, the difficulties which the child offered to any approach seem to have reinforced the tendency to project her dissatisfaction with herself onto the child. Moreover, the pregnancy with its disturbing events apparently reinforced the feeling that she had inflicted damage on the child. With the help of the pediatrician and with the progressing development of the child, a change in attitude occurred. The decisive factor seems to have been that the child turned actively toward the mother. The mother became able to "understand" the child's very specific needs, to react to clues hitherto missed or ignored, and she became more skillful in her approach to the child. We assume that a change in the working of identification had occurred: the child, no longer so much a part of herself and thus subject to attack, could be understood.

The positive impact of the child's development on the mother can also be seen in the case of Mrs. D., a woman who never desired to have this child and felt unable to handle the infant. The infant was at first a rival; it might have been different if it had been a boy instead of a girl. The change of attitude occurred when the growing development of the little girl made her independent, when she could be "taught" and thus the relation between mother and child could elicit the memory of the mother's own past—when her father had taken active interest in her scholastic progress.

The material presented is in various respects inconclusive. We are unable to evaluate the extent and effects of the variations in attitude here described. We report on one small aspect of a larger picture. We are concerned with processes in progress and propose on a later occasion to present the case material in greater detail and in longer time perspectives.

The relationship of the variations in parental attitudes here ascribed to underlying unconscious fantasies can only be postulated; in certain instances we have by implication assumed the predominance of the one or of the other of such fantasies. We feel, however, that the material presented invites some comments on points of psychoanalytic theory which have a bearing on similar problems. These points concern the relationship of identification to object relationship. We start from an apparent contradiction in formulation. We know from Freud that identification may take the place of object relationship; the lost object may be replaced by a transformation of the self. On the other hand, identification opens the way for an understanding of the object and is therefore part of object relationship.

The apparent contradiction can be resolved when we more sharply distinguish between archaic and higher, id and ego aspects of identification. Identification rests on the mechanisms of projection and introjection. In its extreme form: I am (in the) other, he is (in) me. The opposition is one of being incorporated and incorporating (Lewin, 1950). In these terms the dynamics and actually the behavior of certain psychotics can adequately be described (Lewin, 1950; Jacobson, 1954a). Many aspects in the development of the small child seem better understandable if we postulate the existence of such mechanisms. The cases here discussed show a reversed picture: the child, once part of the mother, becomes a person. The earliest variations in maternal attitudes suggest that much of the ability of the mother to handle the small child and much in the difficulty to adjust to his growth depends on the capacity to shift from one type of identification to another. In more accurate—but still somewhat simplified—theoretical terms, we would say it depends on the extent to which the mechanism of identification has become autonomous, the energies used in it have become neutralized (Hartmann, 1950b). Quite obviously the archaic forms of identification never disappear fully and remain the source which feeds parent-child relationships in general.

In psychoanalytic writings similar problems are frequently dealt with in terms of the opposition between "narcissistic" and "true" object relationship. The point which we should like to make in this context is that identification as a mechanism used by the ego permits the understanding of the child as an individual and enables parents to react to his changing needs.

CONCLUSION

In this paper emphasis is laid on the adaptive element in parent-child relationship. It is shown that even during early infancy variations in parental attitudes can be noted. It is postulated that these variations play a part, at present difficult to estimate, in the development of the child's personality.

Variations in parental attitude are viewed as normal reactions of the parent to growth and development of their children. It is suggested that in the study of parental attitudes in general this problem deserves more attention than it has hitherto found. In describing parental attitudes the capacity of the parent to adapt to the changes in the child and to his individuality as it manifests itself over time should be taken into account. Adaptability of the parent, it is implied, may prove a factor which may throw light on some neglected aspects of parent-child relationship and its impairment may possibly gain importance in early diagnosis of expected difficulties.

9: Neutralization and Sublimation

Observations on Young Children

(1955)

The problems with which Hartmann (1955) found himself confronted in surveying the concept of sublimation, its history and its vicissitudes, are familiar to me from a similar, but much more restricted attempt which I undertook some years ago (Kris, 1952).

In this publication my attention was focused on art and creative activity. I was at the time faced with the fact that sublimation was being used to designate both transformations of energy and displacements of goal; that is, activities in which this transformed energy was being discharged. In any discussion I suggested that the term *neutralization could be conveniently used to designate the relevant energy transformations,* and that the term *sublimation* might be reserved for *the displacements of goal.* This terminological division, I thought, would help to avoid misunderstandings which tend to arise because of the fact that displacements of goal can take place without the energy used in the activity having been neutralized, or because these activities can be continued when the formerly neutralized energy has become deneutralized (i.e., "instinctualized," "sexualized" or "aggressivized"). The use of the terms neutralization and sublimation as two relatively independent variables seems useful for the following reasons: the division preserves the term sublimation and attaches it to its original meaning. However, my attention was centered on the study of a specific activity,

Presented as a contribution to the Symposium on Sublimation at the Midwinter Meeting of the American Psychoanalytic Association, in New York City on December 4, 1954. First published in *The Psychoanalytic Study of the Child,* 10 : 30–46. New York: International Universities Press, 1955.

i.e., "art," and I believe that the study of specific activities represents an important subject for future psychoanalytic investigations. "It seems possible not only to organize the structural characteristics of various types of activity according to the opportunities they offer for more or less direct discharge of instinctual energy, but also to organize them according to the degrees of neutralization of libidinal and aggressive energies which they 'require' " (Kris, 1952, p. 27). A further reason which led me to suggest the distinction of terms leads thus to a specific problem. I feel that many problems of neutralization, and particularly some ontogenetic aspects of it, can best be investigated if viewed in conjunction with the influence that certain activities exert on the process itself. In the course of this presentation this point will be illustrated by examples.

The relationship between goal displacement and energy transformation is naturally that of a circular interdependence. However, as the child grows, so does complexity, so that the choice of activity is increasingly determined by the interaction of many factors. Some concern the influence of endowment; others are more specifically related to the problem of discharge of id impulses, the aspect which is best known from our clinical experience.

> . . . expectations are significantly limited when we hear that a certain patient is an actor, a dancer, a cartoonist, or a dress designer. They are less limited but still significant when we hear that he is a writer, painter, architect, or poet. In all these cases—in the first instances more definitely—we expect that certain typical conflict constellations will more likely occur than others: The problem of rapidly changing identification may be crucial in the actor, that of coping with exhibition in the dancer, the wish to distort others in the cartoonist, and to adorn them in the dress designer; but each of these dominant wishes—which we here have mentioned only in order to characterize one direction of our expectations—is clearly merged with innumerable other tendencies in the individual, and each of them is rooted in his history. According to clinical experience, success or failure in these professions depends, among other factors, on the extent to which the activity itself has for any particular individual be-

come autonomous, *i.e., detached from the original conflict* which may have turned interest and proclivity into the specific direction [Kris, 1952, p. 29].

To the psychoanalytic study of what is commonly called creative activity the relation of ego and id is of particular importance. It is a powerful factor not only in the experience of the creator but also in the reaction of his audience. The specific functions of ego autonomy in this connection have certainly not been sufficiently explored. Our guidepost is still Freud's suggestive hint, when he spoke of a peculiar "flexibility of repression" as distinctive feature. As implementation of this thought, I proposed, many years ago (1934, 1936) that the control of the primary process and generally the control of regression by the ego may have a specific significance for the creative process. Only recently two observations suggested to me an additional approach. The first of these observations started out from analytic experience with professional "creators." In the analysis of one such individual, a particularly successful man, it became evident that a sharp cleavage existed between routine work and work in which he was fully, one might say, personally engaged. The first type followed a formula; the second was deeply and, as it were, inextricably interwoven with his present and hence also with his past conflicts: the process was a painful one and accompanied (preceded or followed) by a more or less intensive acting out of the same conflicts in the transference or in his life situations. It later appeared that the cleavage between the two types of creative activity was one of degree only; that in routine or formula work the experiences of the "true" or "great" creative process appear reduced to signals and that it is justified to say that "in every process of creation the gradual emergence from conflict plays a part" (chap. 24). This then led to the following assumption: it may be useful to distinguish between "the permanent or relatively permanent investment of the ego with neutralized aggressive or libidinal energies" on which secondary autonomy in ego functions mainly depends, and "the energy flux, i.e., transitory changes in energy distribution and

redistribution such as the temporary and shifting reinforcement of sexual, aggressive, and netural energy as it may occur
in the course of any type of activity" (Kris, 1952, p. 27). The
first, the permanent investment of the ego, represents what
Hartmann (1955) describes as the reservoir; the second, the
transitory changes in energy distribution and redistribution,
the flux, represents instinctual energy which may or may not
be added. The capacity to neutralize can then be viewed as determined by both the reservoir and the flux. Creative individuals may be characterized by a particular span between the
two.[1] However, the usefulness of similar distinctions seems
somewhat limited, their relation to observable phenomena
tenuous, unless other factors are taken into account, factors
related to the individual's endowment. While one part of
them, those connected with the strength of instinctual forces,
remains in the area of those necessary assumptions which at
the present time cannot be specified, another factor has become somewhat more tangible through one of Hartmann's
suggestions (1955). He points to the possibility that the permanent investment of the ego may in part consist of energy of
noninstinctual origin.[2] When Freud hinted at the existence of
such energy sources, it seemed difficult to find a place for
them in psychoanalytic thinking. Now this assumption seems
to have become eminently useful. The energy might be
thought to stem from the apparatus of the ego, and we might
add that by its quantitative variations it may influence the investment of the ego with neutralized energy. To put the vista
which this opens into a highly condensed example: the endowment of the gifted facilitates the development of his capacity
for successful activity.

The suggestion that a sharper distinction between energy
reservoir and energy flux might throw some light on the vicissitudes of creative processes was, as I said before, brought to
my attention by two kinds of observation. While I mentioned
that the first was gained in analytic work, I did not refer to the

1. A more detailed typology of creativeness would obviously have to take a larger
number of variables into account.

2. For a similar suggestion see Jacobson (1954b).

second: it is of a different nature and connected with the study of nursery school children.[3]

I shall briefly report on three types of observation. The first will deal with the relationship of neutralization of drive energy to a specific type of activity; the second is meant to illustrate in even more aphoristic form two contrasting ways in which identification may influence the process of neutralization; the third tries to illustrate the possible influence of earliest object relations on the development of the capacity for neutralization.

THE EASEL IN THE NURSERY SCHOOL

There is an easel in every well-run nursery school; on the ledge there are pots neatly set apart, in each one color and one brush. Why is the easel there? How do the two- to fours- or fives who use it behave? What can we learn from watching them?

The literature has no systematic answer to these questions. The few who have studied the problem have been attracted by the product:[4] the masses of more or less well-organized colors distributed over white sheets of paper, out of which in the later years configurations and even representations emerge. In recent years the easel paintings of nursery children have been largely viewed as projective material and used for diagnostic purposes. This particular viewpoint will be neglected here. I turn, at least initially, not to the product but to the process of production.

The two- to three-year-old child in front of the easel finds himself in a situation which as a rule does not satisfy one of his

3. The impressions I am going to report have been obtained in the course of my participation in various research projects in the Child Study Center at Yale University. They owe their focus to the fact that I have had the privilege to organize some psychoanalytically oriented investigations in creative activity under a grant from the Arthur Davison Ficke Foundation of New York. Some of this work deals with creative sublimation in early childhood. For data from other studies I feel particularly indebted to Dr. Rose W. Coleman, Miss Eveline Omwake, Drs. Sally A. Provence, Samuel Ritvo, and Albert J. Solnit.

4. I found the comprehensive material presented by Alschuler and Hattwick (1947) very useful; see also Friess (1952).

most urgent demands: the situation does not allow for imitative role play. Hence there are many who use the easel only as a starting point for other activities; their interest focuses on the apron which has to be put on before painting, on washing of brushes, on the cleaning of pots, or more generally on cleaning of what has been soiled for this purpose.

But let us leave this longlasting and time and again repeated cycle of playful housewifery and turn to the child who stays at least for some time before the easel. There are significant and typical moments: there is the first stroke and its result. The transposition of the kinesthetic experience of the arm movement with the big brush onto the trace on the sheet is to some two-and-a-halves a significant experience. It is not a totally new experience; the principle is familiar from the handling of pencil or crayon. But the broader scope of the movement, the larger and brighter result on the sheet, is bound to attract interest. There something has been done; dare we say "created"?

Some children are, as it were, soon captured by the expansiveness of the movement; the hesitancy of others is gradually overcome—and in some instances the motor pattern alone can serve as the child's signature.

These and similar individual differences offer a promising field for study. I shall neglect many alluring sideroads and concentrate on the problem with which almost all those who stay with the easel for their nursery years meet at one point: the battle against the impulse to smear which the medium itself stimulates. (I do not here enter into the problem how easel and finger painting compare in the opportunities for discharge which they offer.) That battle apparently sets in without a clear temporal relation to the stage of bowel training, i.e., irrespective of the fact whether bowel training has been completed or not and, if completed, whether it was a light or a bitter, a short or a protracted experience.

The battle against smearing starts not at once and its intensity is subject to great variations. There are children who start to mix colors in the pot, others who change the brushes and by putting the green brush in the blue pot achieve their first

result. There are children who for some time produce mono-
chromes, then add a second and third color kept strictly apart;
then a slight shading starts until the mixing becomes wilder
and wilder. At one point the sheet will look like a cauldron. In
any one painting the whole process of defense and eruption
may be repeated. The smearing may start after ten or more
minutes of work, and then an explosive process may take over,
sometimes supplemented by excited stamping, clutching of
the genitals, and rhythmic rubbing of the brush against the
sheet—briefly, by a passionate outburst.

There is the four-year-old who has sensed the danger.
When in the nursery school much interest had been focused
on easel painting, Rick, a highly verbal gentleman with a great
capacity for a dry but gentle kind of what might be called
"prehumor," was suddenly heard to say: "I wish I would like
to paint." And when he finally yielded to the (slight) pressure
of the group and the temptation itself, his apprehension
seemed justified. He was one of those whose temper carried
him finally into an outbreak of violent excitement.

Let me turn to another example: this time I start from the
product. A brown mass irregularly shaped but placed approximately in the center of the sheet; not dirty but somewhat
repulsive. The painting of the three-and-and-half-year-old is
almost unambiguously representative: he has painted fecal
matter and calls it "a big one."

A study of the *process* of painting reveals that the result at
first was not easily or painlessly achieved, that the first sheets
in brown were not covered in a wild discharge. He went to
great length to mix on the sheet out of pure yellow, pure blue,
and shining red the right shade of brown. The effort involved
in achieving this mixture could be studied "experimentally."
The teacher added green to the colors previously available.
Now the mixing became more arduous. For some weeks it
seemed as if green would prevail, but then Tommy learned
the trick and once more he was able to produce the desired
brown masses.

Tommy's interest in "brown" was highly overdetermined.
He was under psychiatric treatment for a stool retention of

unusual severity and long duration. The symptom itself, closely linked to his struggle with his mother, who actually—not figuratively—provoked it, represented at the same time an identification with her. Tommy had been aware of his mother's pregnancy, and of the birth of a baby that died a few days after birth when Tommy was sixteen months old, and of a second pregnancy which had started when he was twenty-six months old.

Tommy's painting in the nursery school had in the past not shown unusual features. He turned to the series of brown themes after he had been witness to a dramatic spontaneous abortion of the mother. (He simultaneously developed stuttering.) Under the influence of this experience and his rising anxiety, the goal of displacement was lowered, and after this lowered goal had first been achieved by a well-coordinated production process, deneutralization became noticeable in his painting behavior; he learned to mix the brown in the painting pots and filled the sheets with it while stamping and masturbating in trembling excitement.

How do other children try to cope with impulses which, activated by the medium, become threatening? Some retreat after more or less bold attempts at color mixing into monochromatic drawing, others interrupt their work when temptation approaches: they ask the teacher to remove the sheet, start on a new one, and interrupt once more when the point comes at which the tension rises. (This naturally is not the only reason for their wish to complete their work at a given point. The sheet may satisfy some of their intentions and they may feel that to continue might mean to destroy it. Only in careful analysis of individual cases is it sometimes possible to determine what "completion" signifies to the child at any given moment in his development.)

Defenses against the danger may appear in strange combination: a particularly illustrative one was displayed by a four-and-a-half-year-old boy who has obsessional-compulsive mechanisms of various sorts at his disposal. He is intellectually far advanced, and intellectualization has become his preferred tool in coping with conflicts. His colors tend at first to be simply isolated, in bandlike configurations. But then he turns from bands to shapes, squares and rectangles, outlined in one, filled in another color; seen over the course of a nursery year, his work conveys the impression of a sequence of solutions of the problem of balance in shape and color—so consistently that observers are able to establish the chronological sequence of the paintings, as they might do it in viewing the work of say Cezanne. And yet there is little thrill in looking at this boy's achievements; only when he borders the danger zone, the attraction to the observer seems to increase. During two phases of the year's work his paintings are flooded with red: shortly after a suddenly performed tonsillectomy, and six months later when in an organized play situation the operation was reenacted.

With those children who stay at easel painting and do not abandon it at one point of the conflicted period, other less dramatic but no less significant methods of conquest of the danger can be studied. At an early stage the pleasure in mixing and smearing already may appear combined with pleasure in interesting color contrasts, rare shading, balanced shapes and fantastic configurations. During the fourth and fifth year these configurations tend to be named, and gradually (typically during the fifth year) the representational elements take charge. Fantasies become attached to shapes. An early stage shows similarity to adult doodling: the brush produces and the child names the configurations. He plays at rendering and combining recognizable or not so recognizable shapes and at developing and combining fantasies. The primary process is at work, but while it emerges, first attempts at control—or at pretense of control—can be noticed. At later stages the fantasy content becomes elaborate, stories may be expanded, and some of those faithful to the easel achieve what seemed to attract them when the first stroke of the broad brush created that bright trace on paper: but now their product is "organized," they "make" a world of things. This progress requires renunciation of direct discharge. The neutralization of energy can, as it were, be watched. There always is initially a defensive move to ward off the temptation. There comes in every child's painting development the moment when the dripping paint is resented, when the disorder it produces disturbs the child, when mixing of colors is done with particular care, and when out of the cauldron some signs of a tasteful arrangement emerge—all this with individual differences for which we can account only rarely.

The easel painting of nursery school children is here being used to illustrate the interdependence of drive discharge and goal displacement, of neutralization and sublimation. The point I should like to make is that as maturation proceeds, as the inner world grows, as new pleasures in fantasy and mastery become accessible, the structure of the activity itself influences the process of neutralization.

The easel then stands in the nursery because it is thought that instead of the sudden and "total" suppression by reaction formation of a component drive of anal satisfaction, the child should be offered an activity which as catalyst stimulates further neutralization. In the course of this process the easel painting of the nursery years comes into being. It is difficult to account for the attraction many of these paintings exercise on adult observers. The most plausible explanation may well be that some of the conflicts which the child experienced, some of the intensity of the struggle between id and ego, some pleasure at compromise, some triumphs are shared by their adult admirers. The transparence of the id, the charm of the infantile, may have led educators and artistically inclined people to lift the color scribbles in loose designation into the category of the sublime: they do so when we speak of children's art.

THE ROLE OF IDENTIFICATION AND OBJECT RELATION

The experience of the children who perform as easel painters has here been viewed in the light of one problem: I tried aphoristically to illustrate how during a given phase of development one component drive, stimulated by the medium, breaks through neutralization, how deneutralization and reneutralization follow each other. The processes described can be viewed as exemplary: most activities of two- to three-year-old's (and sometimes those of older children), are constantly threatened by a regressive trend; the breakthrough of immediate instinctual gratification is almost at any time a possibility, depending on the amount of stress and direct stimulation to which the child is exposed (see chap. 5). The structure of the activity, pure or constructive play as the case may be, supplies an incentive for increased neutralization; on the other hand, the capacity to neutralize codetermines the preference for any one activity. But the general aspect of what is here being viewed as childhood behavior is, I believe, of less interest than the place of these vicissitudes in the development of the individual. Macroscopic observation itself suggests the problem, since individual differences seem to be most significant where attitudes of children to organized activity are concerned. Preference for any one activity, the range of such preferences, the degree to which the child can endure difficulties, solve problems, elaborate fantasies, and at the same time discharge instinctual tension, have to be taken into account.

A whole range of problems for the study of initial steps in ego functioning opens itself before our eyes. But only where a large set of data on any individual child is available, where influences of the various figures in his home and environment are accessible, and the child's history is known in some detail can such questions gain full meaning. The two cases which I shall report are part of a longitudinal study, which supplies the required data.[5] It is a single episode in the life of a charmingly smiling girl of two and a half which I should like to choose as starting point. One day in November, four weeks after she had first learned to handle the brush on the easel, Evelyne sets to work. As usual the young lady, at the time a painter in monochrome blue, selects her brush and color. She carefully drives it over the paper and a circle emerges. She looks at it for a while, then sets in it eyes, nose, and mouth, and clearly says, "Halloween."

The achievement is an extraordinarily advanced one. The elaborateness of the performance leaves no doubt about the

5. This study was supported by the Commonwealth Fund.

intention, and circumstances before the painting throw light on the motivation. Evelyne is a fearless child; her courage and independence are outstanding, but a few days before the painting she had an attack of prolonged terror and fright. She reacted to children with Halloween masks.

The painting reproduces this impression. The active repetition of the passively experienced terror is here not entrusted to play. Evelyne can represent what she wants, and she wants to represent what frightened her. Active repetition is entrusted to a higher level of imagination and action: Evelyne herself, unaided as always, produces the mask in a painting.[6] We may describe the step she has taken from three aspects: the drawing requires an unusual degree of skill, which cannot be achieved without neutralization; the goal, a reproductive painting, is very highly set for her age, at least a year or a year and a half ahead of others; and this capacity is mobilized by a painful experience and serves to cope with it. The model of similar behavior, familiar from latency age, and there described by Anna Freud (1936), is extremely rare at Evelyn's age. Can we determine some of the factors which enabled Evelyne to act on a level which is not only out of the range of her peers, but which even much older children will reach only rarely?

Evelyne is highly advanced in all her intellectual achievements. She is not very sociable, but determined and resolute even if alone. When she came to nursery school she impressed the teacher as the most mature and best predictable of the children, as the one who sought least help, was least dependent, and least forlorn when the mother left. In fact, her independence is demonstrative and energetic. Nothing in her behavior indicates disturbance; all seems smooth and even. However, there are differences in her skill. She has less ability in motor achievements than in others; and during a whole

6. Evelyne was at the time a master in role and fantasy play, an ability which, like that of representational painting, has stayed with her. We find her at three and a half enacting Alice's adventures in Disney's version. The problem of why the active repetition of what seemed to have been her first fearful experience was entrusted to painting rather than to role playing raises many intriguing questions, which are reserved for a more detailed report on Evelyne's personality development.

year at the nursery she sets to work on this area, purposefully determined, and yet full of high spirit, she learns to ride a bike. And in her very independence and courage she is a striking simile of her mother.

During the very period in which she drew the Halloween mask she was engaged in a bitter fight with her mother, in the battle for toilet training. In this battle, induced and fostered by the mother, the child tortured the mother by a highly complex sequence of behavior, best described as aggressive sweetness. The singularly interesting fact is that trait by trait the child's handling of her mother could be transposed a generation backward: Evelyne's mother had used similar techniques when she struggled against her own mother's impositions. A long and detailed story of the interaction between mother and child starting from birth and largely based on observations by Dr. Sally Provence will present answers to the question on how such a closeness of identification came about. Here it suffices to say that Evelyne's mother is a gifted, highly introspective, and, according to all clinical criteria, normal woman who devoted to her child a maximum of attention. It was less in the area of intimate physical contact that this intensity became manifest; there is some reason to believe that the lack of motor skill in Evelyne may have to do with this. But no opportunity for mental stimulation was missed. Imagination seemed to mold every contact with the child. The very history of feeding is one of which mental stimulation was communicated jointly with an almost puritanical scale of values by a skillful combination of indulgence and deprivation. The control of impulses, e.g., the distraction from masturbation by thigh pressure at seven months, was entrusted to stimulation by play and later by fantasy. At fourteen months the child was able to recognize in a cookie into which she had twice bitten the shape of a dog; at nineteen months her play with imaginary companions started; she is one of the children whose infantile "fetishes," the transitional objects of Winnicott (1953), soon became fantasy beings in their own rights.

The creation of an inner world and the ability to produce the Halloween mask are connected in various ways. Visual stimulation played a decisive part in the contact of mother and child—and then there is the crucial fact that the mother herself was a drawing teacher and drew for her child. The child was never "taught" to draw. There was never explicitly a premium set on her achievements, and yet every one of Evelyne's achievements meant much to the mother. The skill which Evelyne displayed is only one in a broad picture of a relationship in which learning by imitation becomes part of the molding of personality.

This is one example out of several which I might have chosen to illustrate the point that the activity to which neutralized energy can be directed, is likely to be the most significant to the child, and the choice of sublimation most successful when this activity at the same time represents a bond with the love object.

This is only a special instance of a more general principle; the richness of needs simultaneously satisfied by any sublimation, the overdetermination of the activity, or the multiple functions which it fulfills have always been considered to be of decisive importance. When the activity satisfies the most important need of the child, the wish for cloeseness to the parent, we may expect it to be of great significance indeed.

Evelyne was thirty months old when she painted the Halloween mask. It is not her skill or what it means prospectively which is likely to interest us most, but rather the factor behind it: the extraordinary capacity to neutralize, the extent of her secondary ego autonomy.

I now turn to an example meant to illustrate a different and, in some sense, opposite aspect of the problem:

The relationship of Anne to her mother had gone through dramatic vicissitudes.[7] The normally born and originally active little girl soon showed signs of decline in her development under the care of a mother whose unconscious makeup revolted against the double narcissistic mortification of having to give up her career and of having to devote her attention to a girl. The developmental picture of the child between six

---

7. Anne's development is also described in chapters 8 and 10.

months and twelve months resembled that of children in institutions. Under the influence of a variety of circumstances the picture changed around one year, when a particular developmental spurt of the child enabled the mother to find an outlet for a fantasy: she became the child's devoted teacher, as her own father had been her teacher. The ambivalence in the relationship did not subside, but a complex interaction—one in which aggressive elements played a part comparable to that which more frequently libidinal elements play between the small child and his mother—opened the way for a workable and even satisfactory relationship. Anne developed into an anxious but active and gradually sociable two-and-a-half-year-old whose behavior was compounded out of friendliness tempered by a "be-a-nice-girl" comportment and a genuine "touch-me-not" attitude. She had some outstanding achievements to her credit: her vocabulary and language development were extraordinary, her pronunciation immaculate, and her ability to name and recognize pictures was above that of her age group. These were the areas in which the mother's ambitions were most marked.

Initially the interest in picture books facilitated the separation from the mother in nursery school, and was the bridge on which Anne moved to a closer attachment to one of the teachers. During a brief period, when the relationship of mother and child was once more obscured, two of Anne's achievements were subjected to a slight regressive trend. The mother was pregnant and could not decide to let her child know about her pregnancy. During this period Anne's speech became excited and somewhat more infantile, its use defensive. At the same time her handling of books changed in character: she would anxiously go from one picture to the other in restless search for what she needed.[8] No other symptoms of

---

8. Anne's behavior with the picture book supplies a further example for the relationship of neutralization to sublimation. On the first level, the picture-book activity serves to alleviate the anxiety. When connected with the separation from the mother, it has a defensive quality. We therefore assume that neutralization has been carried to a given point. In the mother's absence the shared activity is simply repeated with a substitute. This defensive performance breaks down when difficulties between mother and child arise. Though the activity with the picture book, i.e., the sublimation, con-

regression were noted: in the rigorous atmosphere in which she was brought up a regression in cleanliness or sleep might have been too dangerous. But the area which she chose for regressive behavior was the one in which she had established the relationship with her mother. She had acquired mother's attention by performance, and performance deteriorated first: the energy was clearly deneutralized. No similar regression affected Evelyne's development. Her reaction to the birth of a sibling at two was reinforced resistance to bowel training, whereas her ego functions, "her character" remained unaffected. The areas in which neutralization had been achieved remained autonomous. Anne's choice of sublimation, the mastery of language, never reached the freedom and scope of Evelyne's achievements, but the fundamental difference between the two children is best characterized if we make a very general assumption: in Evelyne, the capacity to neutralize was developed early; in Anne, this general capacity did not reach a comparable stage. Most areas of her behavior were free from instinctual outbreaks, but in none was neutralization carried as far as in Evelyne. While Evelyne soiled at two and a half, in those activities in which neutralization had been achieved the degree of neutralization seemed extraordinary. It is a difference which can be well expressed, I believe, in terms of the "reservoir" and the "flux."

We may assume that in Evelyne the permanent investment of the ego is far advanced, but the flux is left relatively free. In Anne, the flux is well controlled, but the degree of neutralization is not comparable; there is something reactive and defensive about her achievements. Though these differences must have many roots, some, we may assume, are likely to be connected with the quality of the early relationship of the two mothers to their children.[9]

---

tinues, the energy neutralization seems lowered. On a third level the activity is used in a new context. Instead of mere repetition, initiative and problem solving can be noticed. After the mother had been able to tell Anne about her pregnancy, their relationship improved. When Anne sees a sad child, she now comes over to him with a picture book, sits down, and suggests that she would "read to him a story." (These and similar instances in Anne's behavior were noted by Lottie M. Newman.)

9. They are naturally also related to the personalities of the mothers themselves.

Object Relation and Initial Steps in Neutralization

Since the early 1930s the influence of early object relations on ego development has been a much-discussed topic of psycho-analytic work in various areas. If we view this work from the vantage point of neutralization and sublimation, it seems obvious that emotional deficit in child care affects specifically the capacity to neutralize—so obvious, in fact, that it is scarcely necessary to review the evidence in detail.

A word needs to be said first about one group of clinical pictures in which the corroborating impressions are highly suggestive but ambiguous—the psychotic children. There the interaction between the defect in the child and in the mother, the reaction of the mother to an unsatisfactory "receiver," and the reactions of the child to an initially or reactively unsatisfactory "sender" of stimuli lead to a large number of puzzling phenomena repeatedly discussed and clarified particularly in Mahler's contributions (1952). The deficient neutralization of libidinal drives has been repeatedly implied in the literature. It is my impression, however, that the deficient neutralization of aggression is equally pathognomonic (and this may sharpen our eye for the lack of synchronization in the neutralization of aggressive and libidinal drive energy in other children, thus pointing to an area in which even variations of normal behavior could be fruitfully studied from a new vantage point). But the complexity of the clinical pictures in this area excludes them from more detailed discussion on this occasion.

I now turn to another group of data. They concern the developmental deficit in institutionalized children. The findings reported are derived from an ongoing, detailed, longitudinal study of individual children by Drs. R. W. Coleman and S. Provence [see Provence and Lipton, 1962]. The study confirms in a general way previously established knowledge (Spitz, 1945) but presents more detailed and in many instances unexpected findings. However, I bear sole responsibility for the selection of data here mentioned and the conclusions drawn.

The decline in the general response and developmental picture of these children, some of whom were institutionalized shortly after birth, starts even with apparently well-endowed individuals at five months. It does not affect all areas measured by tests with equal intensity. Motor functions are on the whole at first (up to six months) less affected than others, and fine motor activity less than gross motor activity. (One might say the body needs a mother to stimulate it; the self-stimulation of the hands is more effective.) That language development or response to human contact should be more severely affected, needs hardly an explanation. In our context, however, it is particularly interesting that no activity that involves higher organization of discharge, problem solving, and thinking as related to action develops as it does in normals. Individual variations as to the degree of maturity at birth play a decisive part, and the investigators gained the impression that the resistance to deprivational experience constitutes some sort of measure for intactness or for some other total factor of endowment. Moreover, the maturational processes themselves change the picture. Maturation proceeds, as it were, in spite of impediment. During the second half of the first year rocking dominates the picture. But, though mostly delayed, the institionalized children here studied "learn" to walk. These and similar steps in maturation initiate around one year a shift in the total picture. It seems that some substitutions and restitutions are being attempted; yet the total achievement level (as measured by developmental tests) does not rise. Much more impressive than the quantitative data are the clinical impressions. The investigators feel the absence of "driving power." The children lack initiative. Imitation comes easier than self-initiation of action; and though equipment facilities brought about by growth are at the child's disposal, they are not being used. It should be added that none of the children studied showed the depressive reaction to the separation from the mother described by Spitz and Wolf (1946), since the separation had taken place at a very early stage. In certain areas, the impression arises that one can actually differentiate purely maturational forces from those which show influences of the environment. The area where this differentiation is clearest is that of early language development.

Seen in conjunction with the assumption concerning the existence of two kinds of energy at the disposal of the ego, the following hypothesis becomes feasible: one might assume that maturational processes are more closely connected with noninstinctual energies and that the organization of action and problem solving is more dependent on the neutralization of instinctual energy. If this neutralization does not occur to a sufficient extent and/or degree, even the flow of noninstinctual energy tends to tarry. Only the combination of both energies in the investment of the ego leads to the normally expected developmental steps during the later part of the first and the second year of life.[10] Such an assumption encroaches, as Hartmann (1955) said, on the competence of the physiologist. I therefore continue on lines more familiar in psychoanalytic theory. The neutralization of instinctual energy presumably does not occur or does not become effective in institutionalized children because a central love object is absent. We have learned from Freud (1931) that the child's development is largely determined by the general tendency to repeat actively what has been and is being passively experienced in infant and child care; Freud speaks of the child's identification with the active mother. I assume that through this identification the child develops certain action units, which seem to include some more complex motor performances and adaptive movements as they occur in the contact between mother and infant. These action units, I assume, require and stimulate neutralization.[11]

10. A separate set of assumptions might naturally envisage the possibility that the conditions of institutional care affect the quantity of available instinctual energy itself.

11. [In an unpublished Progress Report written in 1953, Ernst Kris stated a hypothesis which is relevant in this context: "Traditionally motor development has been viewed as a manifestation of maturation; links to the development of personality have rarely been made and, when made, have almost exclusively been connected with the development of the body image. This development in turn has been successfully related to the closeness of the child's relationship to his primary objects. Our experience points to the possibility of additional and more immediate connections. The ability for motoric discharge is rooted in the child's equipment; hence it is not likely to play

The study of two interacting processes, of maturation and adaptive patterning in response to the mother's ministrations, might enable us to approach the question of how specific types and modalities of maternal care can be related to the development of the capacity for neutralization of instinctual energy in the child.

In my own mind, I have viewed the opportunity for simultaneous discharge of libidinal and aggressive energies, their earliest fusion in discharge, as a favorable factor. But it can be no more than one among many.

A more comprehensive approach can be suggested if we generalize some of the assumptions made by Winnicott (1953) in the study of transitional objects. To put his thought in briefest outline: Grossly defective maternal care fails to stimulate the child's earliest mental processes. These earliest mental processes tend to supplement whatever satisfaction the child obtains by the illusion of complete satisfaction. The "ordinarily devoted mother" gratifies the child's needs at any given time only to some extent; there is always some slight deficit, some discontent. This discontent, Winnicott argues, is filled by the child's capacity to imagine full satisfaction. Not only extreme deprivation but also extreme indulgence eliminates the incentive for mental activity (Hartmann, Kris, and Loewenstein, 1946). In this setup, mental activity, which is related by Winnicott to an equipment factor (he chooses, I believe erroneously, the IQ), stands, as it were, at the beginning of what might be called initiative for independence. The assumption of a hallucinatory state (Ferenczi) can thus be related to specific experiences of the infant; it can be integrated with other assumptions, for instance, those concerning the relation to the

---

the same part in one child that it does in another. We assume that motoric discharge is directly linked to the handling of the child's aggressive impulses. Hence, the particular reaction of the child to newly acquired gross motor skills during the second and third year seems to throw a light on hitherto neglected patterns of discharge of aggression. Children in whom this motoric discharge plays a minor part (by virtue of their inborn equipment) may be inclined to internalize aggression earlier. This may find expression both in their behavior and in their fantasies. Briefly, the assumed correlation leads to a hitherto neglected approach to the understanding of ego development."]

mother and the growth of the apparatus itself. The capacity for appropriate illusion seems to constitute one of the earliest stages in neutralization. It would be the one which predominantly and typically depends on the interaction between mother and child, and prepares the way for identification.

10: Decline and Recovery in the Life of a Three-Year-Old

or

Data in Psychoanalytic Perspective on the Mother-Child Relationship

(Alternately, subtitle as major title)

(1962 [1956])

[PART I]

INTRODUCTION

The Problem

It is late in spring, close to the end of the school year, and the nursery school group is playing in the yard. The morning is well advanced, and the first of the parents come to take their children home. They have been expected. The ten three-year-olds who form the group have been together since September, twice a week for three morning hours, which seemed long at first and have become shorter as the months progressed. The children have formed something more than fleeting attachments to each other and distinct relationships to the teachers, and to the psychiatrists acting as helpers in the

[Ernst Kris started writing this essay in 1956. It was unfinished at the time of his death in February of the following year. He had revised the first part once; the second part is a first draft; the section on "Anxiety and Despair" is clearly incomplete.] The paper was published posthumously in *The Psychoanalytic Study of the Child*, 7 : 175–215. New York: International Universities Press, 1962.

group, each of whom had devoted special attention to one of the children throughout the school year. And yet leaving the group comes easily. The call of the home has not lost its unique power. There are few who display their pleasure; most seem proud to have been found in the midst of some activity, which the parent is supposed to watch for a moment or two before the child surrenders the world (of his own) in which he had been living for the past few hours. This is the average picture that mirrors the conflict of the age between growing independence and old attachment. Even in this clearly structured situation variations are infinite. The intensity with which the parent is welcomed, the speed with which the activity is abandoned, the way of parting depend on a large number of obvious factors: what sort of a morning it has been; how successful it was in terms of social experience; whether or not the preferred teacher or playmate and the preferred toy have been readily available; whether it is one of the rare mornings when father comes, or whether the mother comes alone or with the baby on her arm; what had happened earlier that morning at home, before they left for school. But these circumstances or experiences do not account for the full extent of the variations that strike observers who have learned to perceive individual demeanor within the typical behavior patterns of three-year-olds. The attempt to contribute to an undertanding of the nature, extent, and sources of such individual differences stands as an impressive and, in a sense, intimidating problem in the background of this report and of some others, more detailed and richer ones, which are to deal with other children of this group of ten.

Anne's reaction to the going-home situation differs in a few elements from that of others. She seems pleasantly surprised at her mother's arrival, but there is no stormy welcome. Is it that the mother, a woman with clear green eyes and a friendly though somewhat stereotyped smile, has taught her to avoid intensive bodily contacts, since she is well advanced in her pregnancy—or is it a more general trait of Anne's behavior? The latter it must be, since even with teachers and playmates the short good-by procedure is more like that of an adult than that of a young child. There is also the clear and well-enunciated speech, appropriately used, with noticeable pride in achievement. Anne's graceful small body moves once more down the slide; she was one in a row of three who had been waiting for their turn, and she wanted to take her turn once more before she leaves. She is fully alert to the pleasure, but her hands grasp the edge of the slide perhaps somewhat more firmly than those of other children; her sharp, almost shrieking laughter may also be somewhat more excited. But after this interlude she easily adapts to the mother's request, straightens her hair with a furtive gesture—a gesture obviously borrowed from the mother—and is ready to leave. Hand in hand the two walk through the gate of the yard, a contented pair.

No description of Anne's behavior during a short time span, however subtle, can convey satisfactorily the multitude of impressions which constitute the "individual traits of behavior." Only if we extend the time span do our chances of capturing the specific in the general increase. But it is not this pathway which I here intend to follow: I shall try to present Anne's life history and to trace a number of factors which, through their interaction, have presumably contributed to make her what she is. This life history has been a particularly dramatic one; Anne has gone through experiences of most pronounced and shaking deprivations during her first year. When we meet her at three, she has recovered from physical retardation and developmental arrest, is a friendly and mostly smiling child, and her physical status is satisfactory.

The central question with which this study deals is thus laid out: How have decline and recovery come about, and how lasting does the recovery promise to be? While the second of these questions will be left to inference and speculation, I hope to be able to specify in some detail that decline and recovery can both be viewed as related to the interplay of parents and child.[1]

---

1. A preliminary and partial presentation of some of these questions was offered by M. Kris in a paper delivered at Arden House (1954). The report has not been published. For some remarks of A. Freud on this report, see *The Psychoanalytic Study of the Child*, 9 : 70–71, 1954.

The Nature of the Data

The data which I shall use in this presentation differ from those usually available to psychoanalysts. The observations of this child were not gleaned in psychoanalytic or psychiatric treatment situations. They were gathered in interviews with the mother centered around development and care of the child, in numerous observations of home life, and of the child in a variety of settings, which a longitudinal study conducted at the Child Study Center of Yale University offered.

Families participating in the study had been referred to the Child Study Center by the Obstetrical Clinic of the Grace-New Haven Community Hospital. In the mind of the patients the institutions were closely affiliated as part of the Yale University Medical Center.

Three criteria crystallized and guided our selections: (1) The mothers had to be "normal" primiparas. (2) There should be some reasonable prospect that the families would remain in New Haven for the subsequent five years. (3) The parents had to be ready to cooperate with the staff in a study "of the development of the child's personality in his family setting." They had to agree to regular interviews with the social worker, starting during pregnancy; [2] to regular and, during the first year, frequent well-baby clinics and developmental examinations. In exchange the study offered complete well- and sick-baby care, and later the prospect of free school attendance at the nursery school of the Child Study Center.

The influence of these facilities on the readiness of young couples to participate is difficult to evaluate. It stands to reason that parents feeling a need of institutional support for economic or psychological reasons were more likely to be attracted by the plan than others.[3] In the case of Anne's mother, these and other incentives seem to have been at work. The contact with "the University," i.e., with the staff of specialists

2. In Anne's case, the professional status of the interviewer was characterized in terms of her special interest in problems of pregnant women and young mothers.

3. See also K. Wolf (1953).

of considerable educational status, satisfied some of her own intellectual aspirations; the participation gave her a special position among the expectant mothers of the community; it promised to alleviate economic pressure and be of some help in the bewilderment and conflict into which her pregnancy had thrown her, and of which she seemed to have been aware without initially fully admitting it to herself.

Compared to other longitudinal studies on which reports are available in the literature, this one was different in various respects. The contacts were strictly "service-centered." Participants were not seen without a direct relation to the current situation in which they lived, and the focus of contact was always derived from one aspect or another of child care in the broadest sense of the word. This included much of the family interaction, the life and problems of parents and siblings; the latter were given comparable, though not as extensive, attention as the original study child.

While the character of the contact imposed, at least initially, had certain limitations, it proved beneficial as time progressed since the information we gained appeared in a dynamically structured context. Thus the "history" of the childhood of Anne's mother was not elicited in a structured interview by systematic questioning; all we know came to light during the vicissitudes of her relation with Anne.[4] Moreover, the length of the contact itself proved fruitful: the attitude of the mother to her first infant appeared in a much clearer profile when certain of its peculiarities could be studied when her second and third child were born. By the same token, the strict relation to the service purpose allowed for intimate observations of the parent-child relationship, which otherwise would not have been available:[5] the mother was seen not only with the child in well-baby clinic during medical and developmental examinations, during the social worker's home visit, but also

4. In our conferences much care was taken to assess in which context any information was gained.

5. [In research conferences Ernst Kris stressed another advantage of the service orientation: he expected that at times of crisis, the family would turn to the members of the research team and thus provide another dimension to the data—an expectation that was repeatedly fulfilled.]

during day and night home calls by the pediatrician when the child had an illness. As the child grew up and joined the nursery school, the opportunities for observation multiplied, and the number of observers reporting on mother and child (or contributing accidental observations) grew.

From the beginning of our work a considerable number of individuals had occasion to observe the child in one situation or another. During the well-baby clinics opportunities for observation were provided through a one-way vision screen; and later the nursery school was regularly visited by some, and intermittently visited by others, of those who attended the numerous research meetings in which the material was currently discussed. When mother and child visited the Child Study Center, Mrs. D. was casually seen by many staff members, and some of the "nodding acquaintances" soon developed into more familiar contacts.

In addition to its assets, the multiplicity of observers might have contained certain dangers had we not succeeded in combining it with a continuity of observing personnel. A number of the observers, particularly the pediatrician who combined the function of physician and developmental examiner (in addition to other more complex functions about which a word will be said later), have remained the same throughout the course of the study and have in their understanding grown with the child. However, even those, who for external reasons had to be added to the team and to replace members who dropped out, profited from the total duration of the study contact: a "transference to the institution" (Reider, 1953b) had developed. A familiarity with its staff, reciprocated in varying degrees by the individual workers, could comparatively easily be extended to new staff members. This became particularly clear in the contact of this family with the social worker. In Anne's case over the years of the study it happened that three social workers had to be assigned to the family. In others there was no change. It was the length of contact and the increase of trust in the venture of which the family was a part that seemed to be mainly responsible for the fact that information tended to become more personal and relevant as time proceeded.

Much that concerned the earliest reactions of the mother to the child gained its meaning in the light of information which she volunteered years later, when under the pressure of some family crisis the social worker could offer help and guidance (McCollum, 1956). Those who joined the staff at a later date had the opportunity to study the record which contained not only the observational material itself, but also the large set of prognostications, ruminations, and hunches, some apt, some far afield, which seem to present themselves when a multidisciplinary team and a vast variety of data are constantly brought in relation to new clinical impressions and theoretical expectations. However, the specificity of the study rests in the fact that these expectations were based on psychoanalysis. All members of the staff had for some time been familiar with psychoanalysis and all who had direct contact with the family had been analyzed.

There is no doubt that the hypotheses of psychoanalysis have infiltrated into the observations themselves. No observer, I believe, can or should be seen as being a blank screen. A wisely moderated and continuously checked relation of observation to expectation seemed to us on the whole to guarantee satisfactory procedures. The fact that the team was a multidisciplinary one, that many participants came from long and independent training in their special area of work seemed to provide for checks and balances in each instance when the reported observations were discussed and their meaning tentatively evaluated. The effect of this cooperative venture was highly stimulating. To the psychoanalysts of the team in particular it was full of challenge. While there will be opportunities to give instances of this in the course of this paper, it may be appropriate to mention some aspects on which this challenge became focused.

The absence of the kind of material with which the analysts were familiar imposed upon them the need to translate what they had learned from the study data into the context of their analytic experience. Analysts are used to discover the past in the present. The discussions of the current experiences of mother and child were geared to the future. Whenever advice or guidance—medical or educational—is offered, the future has our attention. This then implies that on many occasions the possibility existed to compare views held and recorded at one time with "the outcome"—an experience which can be stimulating or humiliating, depending on one's personal reaction when faced with clear-cut limitations of our knowledge.

The task of the analyst during the work of the study and the report on some of the material is to direct our attention to the nature of these limitations. Much of the data here used, e.g., those on the development of the child during her first year, not only have little resemblance to what analysts learn from their patients, they have also only a limited resemblance to the striking and fundamental work of analysts who observed large groups of children during shorter time periods in different settings (Spitz, Bowlby) or with less intensive observations over many years (Fries).

Our interest is focused on the individual child in his family surrounding. Our material on Anne is presented with an avowed intent: to draw attention to one of the ways in which a critical and traumatic earliest childhood may come about, and how it appears when studied while it develops.[6] I hope by this report to stimulate interest in further similar studies which might add materials to psychoanalytic work in reconstruction by detailed and, as it were, naturalistic recording. However, in selecting the way in which data are to be presented, I once more follow the lead of experience that psychoanalytic work supplies: the starting point of our thinking was Anne at age

---

6. [In an unpublished Progress Report written in 1953, Ernst Kris formulated a related hypothesis: "Psychoanalysis has introduced the notion that disturbances in the adult are rooted in childhood. Hence a tendency has developed to view crises in child development as roots or bases for adult neuroses. A variety of observations we have made suggests an alternative. We are led to assume—more firmly even than other observers—not only that "crises" may be concomitants of *every* developmental process, but more specifically that even intense and severe early crises in the child's life may not be *directly* related to later personality difficulties. We rather assume that the relation is indirect; i.e., a crisis in the child's life may constitute an important phase of his ego development, may put at the disposal of the personality certain aptitudes and abilities as well as certain susceptibilities. *In other words, crises lead to both assets and liabilities.* The vast area of crises in the mother-child relationship deserves to be observed from this angle."]

three. In order to keep the two time perspectives apart—the one we had followed when the data were collected, i.e., the perspective of the future, and the other from which we are working while reporting on these data, i.e., scrutiny of the past—I shall endeavor at crucial points to indicate divergences which their comparison reveals.

The presentation of a biographical picture based on data supplied by multiple observations affords an opportunity of contributing to psychoanalysis in another sense. Though we cannot aim at validating or invalidating propositions, a survey of those propositions which prove useful in the present context is suggestive: they form a unit, in the sense of an implied hierarchical organization, and more than once will it be possible to select preferred alternative propositions within this unit.

THE PARENTS: SOME BIOGRAPHICAL INFORMATION

Although in our research project contacts with mothers are infinitely more frequent and more intensive than those with fathers, in hardly any case has it proved so difficult to draw the image of the father as in the case of Mr. D. He is by nature a retiring young man, with a rare but friendly smile, which may blossom into laughter when Anne, the three-year-old, greets him enthusiastically. His precise New England manner covers a somewhat diffident deportment. He always seems hard pressed for time and working against odds. During most of the period of our contacts he was working in a law firm and concerned with completing work for an advanced degree at an early date in order to achieve full financial independence.

He had come successfully through a hard life, as far as we know without severe psychological impairment. He had lost his father at six or seven, and had been sent to an Episcopalian boarding school whose headmaster had apparently become a friendly mentor and an important ideal in the secular, though not in the religious, conduct of life. Anne's brother was later to be named after this man and Mr. D.'s father. Drafted shortly after the completion of school, Mr. D. was a prisoner of war for part of his military service. He started studies after the war in Boston, where he met his wife.

Mr. D. describes his mother as severe and determined; when she appeared on the scene of Anne's life, her interventions seemed to confirm this impression. Stern, resolute, with Victorian standards, presumably frozen by a hard life, she had supported her four children after her husband's death by independent business activities. She remarried late in life and moved with her second husband to another country. Little is known about Mr. D.'s relation to his siblings with whom, at the time of our study, he maintained contact by correspondence only.

Mrs. D.'s appearance stands in marked contrast to her husband. Somewhat full in build, of medium height, she has a ready and outgoing smile at her command, which enlivens the attractive features of a roundish face. Simply but tastefully dressed, neat without obvious effort, there is also frequently a tinge of artificiality about her. Most noticeable is the precision in speech and accent of the foreign-born girl whose speech has to come up to the standards of her well-educated husband. Her attempts to cast her own behavior into the mold of the rigid New England pattern in which her husband grew up are generally noticeable. At times when she is preoccupied or involved in conflict those slightly forced adaptations seem to disintegrate and it is as if her behavior became somewhat amorphous. In good times, however, her determined, well-organized demeanor and her purposeful attempts at empathy tend to impress favorably those with whom she is about to establish contact.

The only child of her parents' marriage, she grew up in her South American homeland under favorable economic conditions. Her father held an important administrative position in industry and the family lived in considerable comfort. During the summer they went to the maternal grandmother's house in a mountainous and forested area nostalgically recalled by Mrs. D. When she was nine years old, the financial decline of the family started. The industry in which her father was active closed down and within five years both parents died. After a short stay with an aunt, to whom she had been sent before her father's death, Mrs. D., in early adolescence, was made to follow a ten-year-older half brother, who had emigrated to the United States and held at the time a position in Boston. He fully accepted parental authority and obligations, which he later shared with his wife. They have remained dominant figures in Mrs. D.'s life, and observers who have seen the two families living together confirm the impression that Mrs. D. conveys. Throughout the years of our acquaintance with her, contact with the half brother and his wife seemed to restore her confidence, and yet there is some evidence that closeness to and separation from the brother play a more complex role. It seems that she could gain independence better when she was on her own; and yet she would be driven back to him with great force. She herself, however, is barely aware of her attachment. Under the half brother's guidance she completed her schooling in Boston, which led her away from intellectual pursuits and toward artistic pursuits. This was apparently in opposition to what her parents might have expected, but was in fact unconsciously tied to the memory of her father, who had dabbled in the arts though he considered art an "unmanly" occupation. Mrs. D. made her father's hobby into her profession in which she achieved some success early in adult life. In the years of her professional training she experienced some platonic infatuations, but after a short while the interest died down. She met her husband through the boyfriend of a roommate, was astonished when she discovered that he was interested in her. She was initially hesitant about marriage, but decided to accept, possibly influenced by the fact that her half brother had moved away from Boston. Mrs. D. continued with her work and her husband with his studies. Life was happy and gay, with much chance for travel and relaxation. They had no intention of settling down when they moved to New Haven. Shortly after they had moved, Mrs. D. discovered that she was pregnant.[7]

While information about Mrs. D.'s life during her adoles-

7. Three months after Anne's birth the fact that Anne's birth had not been planned is already vigorously disclaimed; later there is evidence that the memory of it is actually repressed.

cent and later years was comparatively difficult to obtain and had here and there to be implemented by direct questions, information concerning the years of Mrs. D.'s childhood and her relation to her parents appeared spontaneously and in manifold variations. It was in these childhood years that the stage was set for her later life—and for Anne's earliest experiences.

I put at the beginning a tale about her parents' marriage. The first husband of Mrs. D.'s mother had died when their little boy was six years of age. Mrs. D.'s father saw the widow playing with the boy and fell in love with her. Shortly thereafter they married. Tales of this kind have a peculiar impact which makes them worth remembering, quite apart from the possibility that the tradition itself may have been molded into shape by the teller of the tale. To Mrs. D., the story is part of the evidence that her father, who at the time of his marriage was a man in his middle thirties, wanted a boy child. Whatever she reports on her early experiences with her father—and in a contact of four years' duration there were many occasions when one item or another appeared—were elaborations on this theme. She is at times aware of the connection in which she presents the material; and often seems to heap evidence upon evidence as if trying to prove the case.

Stocky, muscular, and vigorous, a mountain climber and horseman, her father was interested in sports and physical exercise. When a physical handicap of the stepson thwarted attempts to make him into an athlete, his interest focused upon the little girl. She was made to wear boys' clothes and haircut, and at five years of age she was started on a course of weight lifting and systematic exercise. She was to be "brave" and a "big" girl and was to overcome her fear of animals. In her schoolwork, if things did not come easily enough, she was tutored in order to shine. The demand for perfection was both unrelenting and insistent. When the report card was less good than expected, the father would refuse to speak to her. There are early recollections about some strong reactions to this: she longed to be the little girl that could hide behind her mother's skirt. Her feeling of being physically inferior is linked to the father's training, which her mother seemed to have viewed as "foolish." As a baby she had been beautiful, but later she felt she had become unattractive. There is no doubt that the way in which she views her body is in part derived from the way in which she views these early experiences. She dislikes her stocky, overweight figure, her short fingers, her varicose veins, her enormous breasts—a derogatory self image which contrasts sharply with her present appearance. Similarly, she thinks of herself as "nonintellectual" with a mind "like a sieve," at times as stupid, and believes that she is a "down-to-earth" person. And yet she enjoys at times impressing people with her intellectual gifts, attempts somewhat marred by even higher aspirations.[8]

The self-derogatory picture obviously clusters around her role as a woman and is supplemented by a variety of psychosomatic symptoms. She has conflicts about being a wife and mother, and at least throughout the first years of Anne's life she repeatedly thinks about returning to work. In this she consciously follows the example of her own mother, who as a widow had supported herself and her son and relinquished work only under the pressure of sickness.

Mrs. D. has the impression that her mother led an unhappy and frustrated life. She was "terrifically in love with her husband, but they were not compatible." She was idle and dissatisfied. Housework was done by servants, and care of the child was entrusted to various hands, e.g., even to the maternal grandmother. She breast-fed the baby, but she obviously did not know how to bring up a daughter. In later years this relationship was not a close one, and not one that we might expect between mother and daughter; rather they were close to each other primarily as friends. The mother was not able to relate the facts of life to the child. However, already as a child, she was made to share in many important decisions concerning the family.

There is ample evidence of Mrs. D.'s deep resentment of her parents, but whenever this resentment appears, she will deny its existence in the same breath. Thus, when she ex-

8. Mrs. D. rates on intelligence tests as superior.

presses her resentment of her father's training, she will add
how delighted the father was with her, how they adored each
other, how he brought her candy and cakes.[9]

When she refers to her mother's lack of interest in her and
recalls times when she felt lonely as a child, she counters this
with the idea that "we were friends after all." When on rare
occasions she criticizes her husband, the criticism is soon balanced and smoothed out. The reproaches she levels against
him are in many ways similar to those that she levels against
her father: too many demands, too little understanding. In almost the same breath she observes that Mr. D. is often absorbed in his thoughts and that she must help organize his
life. While Mr. D. shares his wife's interest in art and literature—the "higher things in life"—he is unbendingly, though
not always optimistically, independent where his work and his
career are concerned. Mrs. D. seems to resent this attitude.

The conflict of which we gained some glimpses on the surface reaches deep into her personal life. While the apprehension about libidinal manifestations, the turning away from too
much instinctual gratification, and an attempt at control are
conscious, the conflict with the instinctual life concerns aggression. I have mentioned how the defense against ambivalent
feelings characterizes Mrs. D.'s utterances. These instances
render only a feeble impression of her constant and hard
struggle against her own aggressive impulses. While she mentions only an occasional obsessional-compulsive symptom (for
instance, the urge to recheck on the gas jets when leaving her
home), the dynamics of an obsessional-compulsive pattern
permeate her behavior. When she appears dissatisfied or depressed, one gains the impression that she had devaluated
herself instead of devaluating or attacking an outside person.

A diagnostic study of her Rorschach record, independent of
our clinical evaluation of Mrs. D.'s personality, supplied a similar impression.

---

9. One of the most marked patterns of Mrs. D.'s behavior during the years of our
contact seems directly related to this experience. Whenever threatened by disappointment in herself and others, whenever she merges into a depressed mood, she turns to
sweets. Her weight curve becomes a reliable indicator of her mood; in peace she is not
overweight, but burdened she grows heavier.

While the information which Mrs. D. supplies is scanty compared to the set of data with which analysts are wont to work,
an evaluation of this information must take one particular feature into account; we are not dealing with a set of anamnestic
data or with a life chronicle. Our information concerning Mrs.
D.'s early years has appeared spontaneously in a dynamic context in which the present in which she has been living led her
mind back to the past. Her recollections were stimulated by
the experience of pregnancy and delivery and by the care of
the child with all its traumatic vicissitudes. In addition, the
general setup of the study (more than any specific inquiries by
interviewer or pediatrician) may have encouraged her reminiscing. The relation between past and present is in some instances particularly dramatic: Mrs. D.'s recollections of her
parents in childhood seem item by item related to her own experiences with Anne. During her pregnancy only a boy is expected; her disappointment in the birth of a girl was evident;
she feels unable to handle a small child, but when she can
become a teacher and the procedures of developmental testing supply a yardstick for the measure of performance, the
relationship to the child changes: a teacher-pupil pattern and
a "companionable" relationship in which mother and child appear as "equals" give her some chance to establish closer contact. I shall in various places of the paper advance tentative
subsidiary hypotheses on the dynamics of this relationship. At
this point it must suffice to stress that Mrs. D., largely identified with her parents, reenacts actively what she recalls of her
own experiences. While she consciously disapproves of the
way she has been raised, she is driven to repeat what she views
as her own experience, thus illustrating one of the ways in
which the cycle of generations affects parent-child relationship
[see also chaps. 8 and 9].

PREGNANCY, DELIVERY, AND EARLY CHILD CARE

The course of Mrs. D.'s pregnancy was uneventful in every
clinical sense of the word. Physical discomfort was slight during the first few weeks and returned only toward the end,

when Mrs. D. felt tense and sleepless in part due to some mild urinary tract involvement.

Except for this last period she felt cheerful and determined. Her apprehensions and anxieties seemed not particularly intense; they were well focused, centered on definite problems, and by this very fact revealing of the intensity with which denial operated: the baby was expected to be a boy, and only for a boy a name had been provided.[10]

When she heard that a relative had had a stillborn child, she did not show any undue anxiety, but when she saw a Mongoloid child and read about the frequency of cerebral palsy, her apprehension became manifest: the thought of being pitied because of a defect in the child seemed unbearable. The impending delivery itself seemed to her a fearful experience; she was definitely afraid of the pain involved and described in detail her low tolerance for physical stress, particularly in relation to experiences with dentists. Her most definite and articulate apprehension concerned the handling of the infant. In order to illustrate the dynamics of this apprehension I here present the gist of an interview during the seventh month of pregnancy, in our third contact with Mrs. D.

> Mrs. D. feels that once the baby is born everything will be different and that it is a very final kind of change. She believes that they will always be responsible for this youngster, even when it gets to be quite a bit older. Granted that she wants the responsibility, she realizes that they will never be free again. Mrs. D. believes that part of her fear and apprehension at taking care of the baby comes from the fact that she was babied for so long and that this has something to do with her feeling now. She thinks her husband would be better with the baby than she. She said that she has a terrifically quick temper, that she flares up suddenly and then it's past, but that she is extremely impatient.

This sequence of thoughts, which starts at the conscious level, with the fear of the disruptions of the plans for her life,

---

10. A few weeks before delivery, in a conversation with the pediatrician, who explained that part of her role would be to help Mrs. D. to enjoy being a mother, Mrs. D., who had previously stated that she was not "one of these women who just have to have children around, just for the sake of having children," added, "I don't know why I want a boy, but I just do."

leads from unfamiliarity with infants and the competition with the baby [11] to the fear of her attacks against the baby, stimulated by her "impatience."

At a time when we were still unfamiliar with Mrs. D.'s conflict, the pediatrician who saw her during the eighth month of pregnancy was impressed that she was eager to be instructed about the baby's care so that she would feel better equipped to manage, but that she did not seem to anticipate pleasure or enjoyment of the baby. The thought of this burden seems to have grown during the last weeks of pregnancy. Mrs. D. found it difficult to relax: "If your mind is going a mile a minute, then you can't really relax, and how does one go about thinking about nothing?"

The delivery was easy, and its last phase proceeded rapidly. The obstetrician had not anticipated that she would do so well during labor and the postpartum period. At the same time another physician was impressed by the many questions Mrs. D. had about her physical condition, indicating an underlying anxiety that overshadowed her interest in the baby at that time.

She seemed rather detached from the baby during the lying-in period and was not perceptive of the infant's attractiveness or of the discomfort expressed by the crying. She was happy to be supported in her wish to give up breast feeding after a disappointing attempt. She felt that her breasts might smother the infant.

During the first months of Anne's life Mrs. D.'s handling of the child was repeatedly observed: she did not seem tense, had a good control of the situation, and handled the baby's body without difficulty, but she had a way of holding the infant at quite a distance from her, rarely cuddling Anne. There was annoyance about the fact that after four weeks Anne, who took only twenty or thirty minutes for a feeding during the daytime, wanted to spend an hour and a half at night taking the bottle. A month later Mrs. D. told us she did not pick up Anne very much as the baby did not seem to need it and she

11. When Anne was two months old and was admired by the interviewer, Mrs. D. produced a photograph of herself at age one year which had always been admired.

did not want to spoil her. The child, the mother thought, seemed to like to be talked to best of all and to be talked to in her crib without being handled. While Mrs. D. seemed initially mainly concerned with her own performance as mother, soon the baby's developmental progress became important to her. Later, when she became aware of the fact that other—even younger—infants had developed more rapidly, she started to be depressed; she feared that the child was abnormal and she asked for reassurance from the pediatrician, which was offered in a carefully guarded way in order to impress upon the mother the necessity for changes in the handling of the child.

The interest in the child's performance was clearly linked to her fear of being pitied as the mother of a defective child. At the same time it was linked to another trend of thought. Mrs. D. found the baby not so attractive long before the child showed symptoms of developmental retardation and at a time when others felt that the child had great appeal. Mrs. D. expressed the hope that Anne would be clever since in her eyes she was not so pretty. She felt that the infant resembled her husband's family and not so much her own. In this way she expressed some feeling of strangeness toward the baby. Feeding and care were a duty, and at seven months the feeding problem was aggravated by the child's unmistakably growing interest in her environment—an interest which deprived Mrs. D. of the possibility to read whiie feeding her.

Of the data which might illustrate the environment in which Anne grew up, those which concern the lack of contact between the mother and her child are numerous and impressive. There was a disability of the mother to understand the baby's needs, and a problem in perceiving cues which came from the child. Some examples concern the feeding situation. Mrs. D. would start to prepare the bottle not when the child woke up but only when the child began to cry. She often felt upset and helpless when the intensity of the baby's crying mounted; then she was apt to react strongly and in ways that did not alleviate the situation. The mother, especially when depressed, was often unaware of the time that had elapsed between feedings. At other times there was an insistence upon rationed quantities of food which were unrelated to the infant's needs of the moment. When the child was almost one year of age, the mother expressed concern about her decrease in appetite. At the same time a feeding was observed in which Mrs. D. was unable, for inner reasons, to permit the child to have more milk when she obviously wanted it. Our observer added that Anne, who had been happy until the moment of refusal, became very quiet and subdued.

The impression that both the absence of physical contact and the difficulty in understanding the child's needs are only part and parcel of deeper ambivalent feelings which have become centered upon the infant is well substantiated. Especially when the child was fussy or crying, the mother's inner aggressive excitement increased. While this fluctuated in intensity, it seemed to have been mounting when Anne was around six months of age. In such states when attempts to calm the child by feeding or picking her up had failed, Mrs. D. was prone to adopt punitive measures. These measures ranged from leaving the infant to her own resources, to shouting and even to spanking the child. The more excited the child's crying grew, the stronger grew the mother's urge to hit. Reporting about her actions, Mrs. D. expressed feelings of guilt, but at the same time she would add, perhaps in an attempt to justify herself, that though she hits hard she also loves hard.[12]

Mrs. D.'s attitude to Anne as neonate and small infant could be enlarged considerably without enriching the picture. There is a consistency about this material, and our records do not contain any observation which would deepen the impression conveyed by those here reported or referred to.

Conjectures on the dynamics of this attitude can start from Mrs. D.'s own statement. The infant is experienced without awareness as a rival in appearance, a competitor for attention, and as an intruder into her life. She is disappointed at having given birth to a girl. Three years later, when her son is born

12. The intensity and nature of the conflict which beset Mrs. D. during the early months of Anne's life was illustrated by a number of episodes in which she called the pediatrician to determine whether some aspect of her care of the infant had done irreparable harm.

and a dense layer of repression will cover all reminiscences of her experiences with Anne, she will remember this initial disappointment.[13] And yet this disappointment—presumably related to Mrs. D.'s own masculine wishes—which may have set the tone for the subsequent experiences between Mrs. D. and her infant daughter cannot explain the extent and nature of the difficulties in perception to which I have referred. Three years later in the care of her boy some of the attitudes here noted will reappear. The setting then is different: Mrs. D. has found a new balance in life, motherhood and marriage, and yet she will express a certain lack of understanding for her second newborn.[14] There is no doubt that a small infant's helplessness and total demandingness stimulate in her responses of which distraction and casualness are the most moderate expressions. The assumption that her own repressed wishes of a passive and infantile nature and her envy of the infant play a decisive role seems well supported. We are reminded of the facts that the complaints against her mother describe a feeling of deep dissatisfaction possibly surviving from, but very surely projected into, her own infancy.[15]

I have up to this point referred to two unconscious themes which seem powerfully to determine Mrs. D.'s behavior to her infant daughter. The one, presumably more deeply buried, concerns the reproachfully harbored longing for a true mother, the wish to be and not to have the infant. It reverberates throughout the history of our observation in Mrs. D.'s struggle for an adequate diet for herself and may have supplied important components to the feeding struggle between mother and daughter. Interconnected with it is the wish for a male child with whom to identify—the wish for the penis.

13. At this point a distortion of memory occurs, apparently to ward off guilt feelings; she believes she remembers that when the obstetrician, to whom she remained attached, first spoke to her, he said in his excitement, "It is a boy."

14. See below for speculations about the reasons for the infinitely greater intensity of Mrs. D.'s ambivalent feelings toward her small daughter, compared to those toward her son as an infant; one might assume that in her disappointment she also feels identified with her father's disappointment at having "only" a daughter.

15. For the role of the rivalrous attitude in mothers after delivery and during early infancy of their children, see Escalona (1949) and Benedek (1949).

Derivatives of this wish color Mrs. D.'s ambition for Anne who remains, as it were, "part of herself." The interest in her progress and intellectual achievement, the emphasis on appearance and manners impress us more when we meet Anne at age two and three. And yet to point to these plausibly interconnected wishes in the makeup of Mrs. D. seems far from satisfactory. In naming deeply rooted impulses active in every woman, we have not reached anything which seems specific. However, we cannot be satisfied to utilize in a general way our knowledge of psychological dynamics, but are forced to attempt a more detailed reconstruction of unconscious impulses and fantasies.

Rivalry with the infant can only be one of the themes in Mrs. D.'s conflict. There are deeper conflicts at work which we can only tentatively reconstruct. Such reconstructions naturally lack the richness and the precision of its models in analytic work where they are gradually developed in constant interaction with the patient's response. Yet we find no way of avoiding these reconstructions since these or similar assumptions give us a chance to connect various apparently unconnected data of behavior. Moreover, without such assumptions, we would be left with a cliché: the rejecting or hostile mother who damages her child because she cannot control her own selfishness or hostility.[16]

Mrs. D.'s conflict is infinitely more complex: it is fraught with many vicissitudes. To put in outline form what will later be reported in detail: when the harmful effects of her attitude became apparent and the baby developed crying spells, a mounting rage soon became uncontrollable and she hit the infant. We infer that she has perhaps become aware of some guilt feeling and, in turning against the "naughty" child, she tried to shift the responsibility away from herself, but the balance is precarious and Anne's condition deteriorates further and serious developmental arrest appears. At the time of the severe crying spells and the retardation of the child Mrs. D. shows unmistakable signs of an increase in her depressive re-

16. For the variety of these clichés, see reports of the First International Congress of Child Psychiatry by E. Kris.

action. Later when she can become a teacher to the child, the relationship to Anne changes: the teacher-pupil pattern and a companionable relationship in which mother and child appear as equal give her some chance to establish closer contact.

It seems obvious that in the second of these phases when she becomes Anne's teacher she reenacts her own recollections about her father's relationship to her. It is our impression that next to this repetition of what persists in her memory as a possibly idealized, screened image of her own childhood, another unconscious version of this relationship exists in a fantasy. This fantasy would contain a struggle between a little girl and her father, a "battle of wills" in which the girl is beaten by the father. These assumptions are derived from many items of observation spread over the years of our contact with Mrs. D.

We suggest that her lack of understanding of the infant is due to the fact that in her mind the infant daughter is overshadowed by the image of an older child; the nursing situation is devalued in favor of a fantasy relation (the beating fantasy). The feeding relation, for instance, is not only characterized by deficits: there is also a clearly provocative element in it, an attempt to heighten the child's tension and to build up a scene which may lead to spanking.

A similarly set scene is observed one year later when mother and child glare at each other furiously with "tigerlike" looks. But now the situation is eased by the fact that Anne can respond, that she is no longer the "helpless" infant; and we will have occasion to report in detail how the interaction of mother and child in these later scenes has its impact on both. Even Anne, the four-year-old, and her mother are interlocked in a peculiarly poignant battle of wills—complicated by the fact that the fantasy of the mother has molded the child, and that the child repeats in her relation to the mother some of the experiences which the mother inflicted upon her much earlier. The choice of Anne's mechanisms of defense seems determined by these experiences. It is a process that illustrates how in the cycle of generations unconscious determinants of the parent-child relationship are transmitted.

The content analysis of the mother's attitudes through the

first three years of life compiled by the social worker shows that it is possible to distinguish between types of the child's behavior which aroused sharply negative reactions in the mother and stimulate anxiety and/or aggression from those types of behavior which she tolerates or appreciates.

During the first year the crying and other insistent demands for attention stimulate outbursts in the mother; messiness is borne with suppressed anger; poor food intake or evidence of the child's retardation in the motor area is connected with the thought of later intellectual deficit and seems mainly anxiety provoking. Positively valued are the opposite attitudes: the child's lack of demand, quietness, and progress as manifested mainly during the first two months. There is not enough, or not conclusive enough, evidence concerning autoerotic behavior. It seems that rocking and thumb sucking were tolerated, but that mouthing of other objects tended to be prohibited.

During the second year messiness, particularly in eating, and resistance to bowel training seemed intolerable; the child's opposition to and aggression against the mother, the latter frequently manifested in wild, tigerlike looks, are equally intolerable. The child's demand for the mother through crying is less disturbing since the bottle is offered as a substitute. The mother appreciates compliance in all areas, particularly in bowel training (accomplished toward the end of the second year) and the progress the child makes under her instruction.

During the third year the mother tends to be intensely angered by messiness with food or water, by the child's clinging to the bottle, which the mother had earlier promoted, and by demands for the mother's attention as they particularly recur during weaning. She is made anxious through the insufficient food intake and through what she experienced as Anne's physical defects, each of them matched by defects which she recalls from her own childhood. She reacts to the child's attachment to a transitional object and to the father with jealousy and denial. Anne's masturbatory activity makes the mother anxious and she denies it at the same time. She appreciates the child's independence when it gives her time for herself, but later shows growing annoyance when in the four-year-old the independence becomes assertive and aggressive. She values highly the well-mannered little girl's social compliance and cooperativeness. Most striking, however, is one difference: she can now use physical contact to comfort Anne, and hence the child's crying tends to arouse her anger only when the crying becomes uncontrollable.

[PART II]

ANNE'S HISTORY

The Period of Decline

The First Nine Months

As a newborn, Anne was characterized as a very attractive, small, and beautifully proportioned infant. She was alert looking when awake and fully normal with a suggestion of slight immaturity. She was easy to hold, in no way stiff or hypertonic, and settled down easily in one's arms. She moved vigorously. The holding had a marked comforting effect and so had the changing of positions. When held she looked around without crying for several minutes.

This description presents a composite picture of the pediatrician's experience with Anne during her first days of life when the child was seen daily in the hospital. During the first two months of Anne's life, our contact with the family was less close than at any later time. The D.s left town immediately after the return from the hospital, and Mrs. D. and the baby stayed for several weeks with her half brother, a period during which contact with the pediatrician was continued by mail. After their return, the baby was seen at home for a checkup. She seemed to develop well, and the pediatrician's attention was at that time focused on understanding the mother's attitude and on establishing effective contact with her in dealing with the immediate problems of child care. On this occasion Mrs. D. complained about the length of the feeding period at night compared with the period during the daytime. When the pediatrician expressed the expectation that night feeding could be discontinued sometime in the near future, the mother seemed relieved.[17] Later, during the second month of Anne's life, the parents took a week's vacation, leaving the baby with the half brother's family. Shortly thereafter, when Anne was nine weeks old, she was seen in her first well-baby clinic. The physical and developmental examinations did not reveal any striking features. The baby seemed to get along well; the tests were interpreted as indicating that the slight immaturity in motor development was still noticeable. Moreover, the baby's "language," i.e., the vocalizations which constitute the most characteristic part of the infant's social responsiveness, was considerably in advance of her chronological age. The profile was viewed as typical of a well-endowed, but slightly immature infant.[18]

And yet, at this well-baby clinic the pediatrician already felt uneasy about the mother's approach and about the adequacy of the stimulation offered. When Mrs. D. reported that she did not pick up the baby frequently, that she was afraid of spoiling Anne, and when she revealed her reluctance for close physical contact offering various rationalizations, the pediatrician pointed out that Anne might be asking more in the way of attention from the adult now that she was two months of age and beginning to be quite responsive socially.

The mother reacted immediately: she expected that this was true and that giving Anne more attention would make her develop faster. I do not intend in the further course of this presentation to reproduce the exchange between mother and pediatrician or social worker in any detail. It seems worth reporting that at that time the pediatrician was in no position fully to appreciate the bearing of Mrs. D.'s remarks. The pediatrician saw that Mrs. D. would consider it now "legitimate" to play more with Anne or to handle her more because this

17. Shortly thereafter Anne developed into an excellent sleeper.

18. These impressions founded on the Gesell tests were corroborated by those of the Hetzer-Wolf test, evaluated by K. Wolf two years later. The evaluation speaks of a "very advanced child," with "an excellent balance of receptivity and reactivity," and "unusual facility to discriminate," of an infant with the potentiality "to develop into a gifted child."

would make her develop faster. The pediatrician noted that the idea that this might also be fun for the mother did not come up. Later it was easy to reinterpret this in a different light, but at the time we were not yet familiar with Mrs. D. and though some of the prognostications which were made had already pointed in the right direction, we were not ready to follow consistently the lead of our own interpretations. The child was well and, in speaking of her future demands, the pediatrician had only drawn the mother's attention to the problems she might normally expect to encounter. A number of factors contributed to strengthen denial among the observers and among the research group. There was the mother's "interest" in speaking about her child, and it was for some time not evident that this interest was centered exclusively on her own and on the child's performance. There was the efficiency of her management which concealed its more damaging features. Thus, in all observations of the feeding situation it was stressed how firmly the baby was held, and only gradually was it noted how little physical and emotional contact there was between mother and child. In one of the descriptions of the feeding situation at home when Anne was two months old, it was mentioned that Mrs. D. held the baby at quite a distance from her, not cuddling her. The pediatrician who observed this feeding felt that it looked uncomfortable for mother and child, but the mother did not appear tense. It was particularly emphasized that the lower limbs, for instance, were left dangling or stiffly stretched without ever touching the mother's body. The same strange postural configurations were seen again when three years later Mrs. D. was observed feeding her boy.[19] When it was brought to Mrs. D.'s attention how well she seemed able to perform all her duties in spite of the apprehensions she had felt during pregnancy, her reply indicated

19. Three years later, observers in the well-baby clinic noted that the mother overlooked the growing restlessness of the infant boy; when the pediatrician brought it to her attention, the mother offered the baby a pacifier, pensively adding that she would not have done this with Anne. When the pediatrician suggested that she feed the baby, she put him across her knee and once more there was minimal contact between her own body and that of the child. As the child fed the mother continued to talk to the pediatrician.

that she never doubted herself, but wondered about Anne's ability to manage.

A further factor which may have delayed the realization of the specific qualities of the environment in which Anne developed was that after the first well-baby clinic a new pediatrician, who had just joined the group, was assigned to the case. In retrospect, the earliest signs of the later, more extensive disturbance in Anne's development was perceivable in her second well-baby clinic when Anne was fifteen weeks old.

At fifteen weeks, her neuromuscular maturation was fully age-adequate, and the immaturity of the motor system in the neurophysiological sense was no longer present. The continued acuteness of visual perception and discrimination was reflected in her visual recognition of the bottle and her early awareness of strangers (eight weeks in advance of the usual age). Inanimate objects were of little interest to her. They had not become invested for her to the extent that one usually sees in babies of this age, and it was almost impossible to induce her to accept them. She was more visually preoccupied with the adult than most infants of her age who have had adequate social stimulation. Language as revealed in cooing, babbling, and socially linked vocalizing at which she had been advanced on the nine-week examination was now slightly below normal for her age.

Anne's performance reflects certain deficiencies of stimulation in the environment. Low investment in the toys and the depressed language and intense visual preoccupation with the adult are common findings in the institutional infants at this age. One way in which Anne differs from the institutional infant of this age is in her discrimination of strangers.

Two months later, at twenty-six weeks of age, the signs of insufficient social and physical stimulation were clearly evident. Her neuromuscular maturation as reflected in the character of the grasping patterns was slightly above age, but this equipment was put to minimal use. Gross motor development was below age with no evidence of organic disorder—either physical or neurological. Interest in toys was still low, although the toys were of slightly more interest than on the fifteen-week examination. She showed no displeasure when they were removed. There was less preoccupation with the examiner, although Anne did initiate social contact by smiling and more interest in play with her own body (mouthing of hands and feet, looking at hands). Language was delayed both in output and in level of development. She preferred the handling of a single toy rather than one in each hand, although she was quite capable of holding two. It was suggested that she found two stimuli too intense, but there was no way to confirm this. Language and gross motor development were her lowest areas.

When Anne was thirty-four weeks old, her general developmental quotient had dropped below 100 for the first time. Gross motor skills and language were now six weeks behind. There was brief interest in the toys which she picked up and dropped, often as though they were hot. There was wide scatter in her adaptive performance, with some successes as high as forty weeks. An interesting observation will illustrate some of the discrepancies between her basic equipment for functioning and the way she looked in relation to her contact with people. She was able to "match" two cubes holding one in each hand and approximating them in the midline. This activity with the toy reflects the maturation of a particular pattern of adaptation, which is also demonstrated in the average infant by the ability at the same age to play pat-a-cake. The pat-a-cake game, however, is much more dependent upon social stimulation. Anne matched cubes and did not play pat-a-cake. An interesting observation was the negative reaction to the mother's approach as contrasted with the positive reaction to the examiner's approach. At fifteen weeks there had been fearfulness of the examiner's approach which was alleviated by the mother; at twenty-six weeks there was no differential reaction between the two; at thirty-four weeks there was negative response to the mother and positive response to the examiner. Five weeks later, at thirty-nine weeks, some anxiety to the stranger was present which was minimized by being on the mother's lap. Fine motor development was the only age-adequate sector. Adaptive functions which had previously shown wide scatter but had averaged at age now showed even wider scatter. There were a few adaptive successes at forty weeks described as being of poor quality. Some attempts to crawl on her belly were noted, but she could not yet creep. Language was her lowest performance, seven weeks below her age.

She would retrieve a toy she had dropped within reach, but would not change position to get it if the toy was out of reach, nor could she solve the problem of uncovering it if it was hidden within reach. Thus both interest in the toy and ability to remember the disappeared object were below age.

By this time Anne's condition gave rise to intense concern from the study staff. Her crying spells, her extreme fearfulness, her poor nutritional condition, and some similarities of her developmental profile to that of children in institutions suggested the need for immediate measures. Before I proceed with this account, I have to supplement the developmental picture of the first nine months by further observations which I prefer to present in the context of some more general considerations.

Discussion and Further Observation

Deficit and Provocation in Mother-Child Contact

The state of retardation and distress in which we find Anne at nine and a half months invites some further comment. I mentioned that her developmental status as measured by test performance reminds us of that of children brought up in institutions; and yet the conditions under which Anne grew up show in a superficial sense no similarity with those in orphanages or children's homes.[20] The deprivation suffered by in-

20. See Rheingold (1956) who reviewed the literature on children's homes. In the following I utilize data, observations, and inferences from a longitudinal study of individual cases of children living in an institution since early infancy by R. W. Coleman Lipton and S. A. Provence, which is being prepared for publication [see Provence and Lipton, 1962]. (On some preliminary comparisons of these children with Anne, see Coleman and Provence (1957). The interpretation of these findings was the subject of many consultations and discussions between Lipton, Provence, and myself. I have offered some preliminary comments on this material in chapter 9.

fants in institutions has often been related to two factors: it has been thought to be due to the multiplicity of individuals who shared in the care of these infants in the absence of *one* mother with all that this entails, and to the shortness of the time spent in the care of these children. Neither of these factors applies to the case of Anne; her mother was the only person who took care of her (with the one exception of the parents' vacation trip) and did not call upon a baby sitter until Anne was in her second year. We have no measure of the time devoted to the child's care, but it seems unlikely that Anne and her mother were less in each other's company "together in one room" than other infants and their mothers. Nor was Mrs. D.'s handling of the child in any gross sense negligent. There was, as I indicated, a dry competence about the care Anne received, and before the decline started to become manifest, during the earliest months of her life, the mother occasionally noticed, for instance, some of Anne's enjoyments during her daily bath. Moreover, there was always the father's interest in Anne; though he is rarely mentioned in our observations, he is described as adoring toward the one-month-old baby by an observer, and we hear from the mother that he likes to "roughhouse" with the infant. But such contact must have been rare. When he came home from work, the infant was mostly asleep and since he had the feeling of working against time, he seems to have felt that this was unavoidable. Later, when the child was disturbed and retarded in many functions, he was the one who refused to show concern, not out of lack of attachment to Anne, but, according to his statements, the baby seemed to him to be at all times fully satisfactory.

The environmental deficit, then, to which we may attribute the similarity of Anne's developmental profile to that of children in institutions cannot be explained by the similarity of general conditions. Anne was reared as a family child in the ordinary sense of the word. The deficit to which we attribute her retardation can be traced to a specific set of elements in the care she received: both physical and play contacts between mother and child were kept at a limit. There was little or no free interaction or emotional interplay between the two. In this specific sense we may speak of a marked lack of stimulation.

But it is only Anne's developmental profile that reminds us of children in institutions. Her behavior differs from them in several essential respects. Her bad nutritional status, the frantic crying spells, and the marked, at times hardly controllable, fear of the stranger are not part of the syndrome of children in the institutions mentioned before (Provence and Lipton). Though at times a normal tendency toward crying or tearfulness will appear, we see features in Anne's behavior which reach an intensity that forces us to consider them as symptoms. These symptoms are, we suggest, not due to lack of stimulation, but rather to a specific kind of provocative overstimulation which was bound to produce mounting tension in the child without offering appropriate avenues of discharge. The distinction between lack of interactional stimulation and an abundance of provocative, irritating stimulation in the child's care may at first seem artificial. In the unconscious motivation of the mother those tendencies must have been closely interrelated. The "reason" why she avoids handling and cuddling of her baby can hardly be isolated from the other reasons that lead her to postpone feeding until the baby was crying, and to approach the crib but not to comfort the infant by lifting her out. In both these instances the double attitude leads to or is expressed in the same action. What starts as avoidance of physical contact leads to the infant's desperate crying and the crying in turn to mounting excitement in the mother.[21] At least in the feeding situation, the mounting tension can be clearly followed in the sequence of our data. In

21. The assumption that the handling of the baby has an intensely stimulating effect on the mother, as the pediatrician had sensed, suggests a tentative expansion of our reconstruction of an unconscious fantasy of Mrs. D.; the child, one might postulate, also represents a female phallus and it is the phallus which is being beaten. It is claimed (Bonaparte, 1953) that this fantasy in which the phallus replaces the clitoris not only occurs frequently in female patients but represents a regular phase of normal female development. Be this as it may, even without the assumption that the unconscious drive derivative should be crystallized in and derived from this fantasy, the dovetailing and interlocking of each, of the lack of physical contact and the provocation of the infant's irritation, are, psychologically speaking, plausible. Some members

Anne as a newborn the pressure of physiological need seems to be moderate.[22] She could easily wait for feeding and was promptly comforted by holding. As if in response to remarks of the pediatrician who earlier stressed Anne's capacities in this direction, we hear the mother saying of the three-month-old that her capacity to wait does not "impress" her. Somewhat later, when under the impact of frustration and irritation Anne tends to cry for long periods and the mother tries to wait until the crying stops, Mrs. D. compares the crying to that of a cat, but, she adds, with a cat one knows what to do. . . . And finally, at the time before she can admit to the fact that she is spanking the infant, she describes Anne's crying and indicates that it makes her feel wild inside.[23] Though no curve of the mounting crying spells can be charted, their increase after two months and their gradually rising intensity after three months are apparent. This trend, which is duplicated in several other areas of Anne's period of decline, is in full agreement with the findings of other investigators who date an important change in the mental functioning of the infant between two and three months.[24] Up to this point growth was, as it were, relatively independent of the personal nature of infant care. From this moment on, the human contact becomes

of the research staff suggest that some influence from the superego might prompt the mother to keep a distance: namely, a protective attitude of the mother to shield the child from damage from the aggressive impulses.

22. At the present stage of our knowledge, such comparative estimates of individual characteristics existing at birth seems unavoidable as long as exact measurements are not available. It is our experience that such estimates can be validated by judges with comparable professional experience.

23. It should be kept in mind that we do not know exactly how frequently the child was spanked. Our data stem from the mother, and her confessions are always proffered with deep guilt, though they rarely go into great detail.

24. See Gesell, Spitz (1954), and Hoffer. What those observers of growth processes describe as a growing capacity of the child to perceive and react to humans around him fits into the setting of psychoanalytic theory as a highly invested function that serves important meanings. The fact that the developmental status of children in institutions tends to show the beginning of dysfunction and retardation sometime shortly after three months is impressive evidence of the nature of these meanings. It should, however, be stressed that usually developmental decline becomes fully noticeable only after five months. A certain lack of precision of these date lines is due to the large number of factors; for instance, to the variation in the length of the preceding institutional life of the child and to the completeness of the tests and observational data, and also apparently to differences in individual "vulnerability."

essential. A further discussion of these findings seems aided
by the use of two terminological distinctions. We distinguish
between development and maturation (Hartmann and Kris,
1945) and distinguish between the ego and the apparatus it
uses (Hartmann, 1939a). Maturation here designates growth
processes relatively independent from environmental influence, from "learning" in the broadest sense; development designates those growth processes which are characterized by this
dependence. Psychic structure in the individual arises in a
process of differentiation. During the neonatal period, when
differentiation plays little part, the distinction between the ego
as a however rudimentary central organization and the physiological apparatus it uses will be of little help in organizing
data of infant observation. Later that distinction will seem to
be essential. The two terminological distinctions obviously in-
terlock. Maturation would be largely concerned with the
growth in apparatus function, the ego with the growth of processes in which experiences of the nature of learning and contact with the environment play an essential part.

The observation on Anne, as far as it is parallel to that of
children in institutions, suggests that up to two or three
months maturation proceeded, as it were, on its own accord.
After that period in some instances the effects of maturation
on Anne's growth can be clearly discerned and differentiated
from the normal development of which they are an essential
part. In my description of Anne's development I spoke of the
fact that a function had matured, but was not being used. The
grasping pattern was available to her, but the two cues were
not coordinated. She could clap her hands, but she did not
succeed in a pat-a-cake. This latest instance is clearly of a
special order since it concerns communication between child
and mother, the developmental area where retardation is most
related to the restricted interaction of mother and child. The
developmental examinations permit us to follow the retardation in Anne particularly clearly. From active babbling at two
months, the decline leads to clear retardation after four
months of age. As in many instances of institutionalized children, the relation between maturation and development can

in this area be indicated clearly: the child is able to pronounce consonants, but they do not merge with vowels to form first syllables and later designations with multiple meanings (Provence and Lipton [1962]).

However, these are the simple instances. Other more complex ones remind us of the fact of how much detailed investigation will be required in order to clarify even fundamental issues. At the present stage of our knowledge, the simple formula of growth of the neuromuscular apparatus vs. its use, of maturation vs. development, does not satisfactorily describe the bulk of observations pertaining to the first half year of life. Moreover, in later months this distinction becomes more and more difficult to handle since soon the environmental deficit may lead to some impairment of the maturational pattern itself.

One of the test findings in which Anne's case fully resembles that of children in institutions concerns the discrepancy between the normal functioning of hands and arms compared to the poorer functioning of lower limbs: when held in a standing position at six to eight months, Anne would not extend her lĕgs to support her weight while her hands and arms functioned well. As we shall see in the further progress of this report, the development of her fine motor functions (i.e., the fingers and their interaction) will remain more advanced than other (gross) motor functions. Since no physiological data seem to account for this difference, psychoanalytic considerations gain a more than subsidiary function. They concern the specific position of the infant's hands through their capacity to release oral tension or to regulate its discharge. Hoffer (1949), who has advanced this view and surveyed his own observations in the light of the general knowledge on early phases of growth (Gesell and Ilg, 1937, 1943), suggests that throughout the first year of life the child is building up through the help of the hand-mouth contact "an oral-tactile concept of his own body and the world around him and regulates to a certain extent by this means his erotic and aggressive (active) drives" (p. 55). Early stages of this sequence can be observed during the third and fourth months: "from intra-uterine life onward" the hand is "closely allied to the mouth for the sake of relieving tension and within this alliance leads to the first achievement of the primitive ego. . . . [The hand] becomes the most useful and versatile servant of the ego . . . [through its] function of relieving tension" (p. 50). In the terminology I have adopted, I would stress the advance of the apparatus which in Hoffer's presentation seems to be enhanced by the finger play of the child. This finger play, typical for the age of sixteen weeks, was reported of Anne by her mother, but was less than that of other infants. When the child's fingers finger his fingers, a simultaneous experience of touching and being touched is carried out in the one act, sometimes in an experimental sense or with an experimental zest, as one might imagine, a study of the limits of the self.

The intimate connection of hands, and secondarily of arms, with the mouth and with the self-gratification during the sucking activities might then in part account for the fact that the growth of this function is relatively more independent of stimulation by the mother than that of other parts of the body. These other parts, we might say, purposefully introducing a metaphor, are "energized" only by the mother's handling of the infant.

Since the exposition of Ribble (1943), it is generally accepted as an empirical fact that the mother of the infant fulfills important functions through the stimulations normally connected with infant care. For example, there is constant interaction between mother and child during the feeding situation; the ministrations of the mother supply a wide range of sensory experiences, tactile, visual, and kinesthetic, without which satisfactory development would be difficult to achieve. Little is known about the effect of specific deficits in child care, though attempts to delineate their effects in one area or another are not missing. None of the numerous studies, neither those dealing with the difference between breast-fed and bottle-fed infants nor with the advantages of cradling, to mention only extremes, seem at this stage of our knowledge to offer convincing insight.[25] The prevailing impression indicates

25. See Goldman-Eisler (1951) and the paper in French on cradling. More promising material in the clinical studies seem to stem from longitudinal observations.

that any specific deficit in child care is frequently or mostly no more than the expression of the general attitude of the mother which may have affected other areas of experience in the child besides the one on which the specific investigation has focused. Nor have anthropological studies on the effect of specific child care methods in certain cultures thrown light on problems here under discussion.

From clinical experience with more severely disturbed, somewhat older children who sometimes become accessible to therapy only if the therapeutic contact is introduced by substitute mothering, one gains once more the impression that the total experience of closeness in a physical and emotional sense between mother and child can only in exceptional cases be viewed in terms of specific partial gratifications and deprivations. This then suggests the assumption as adequate to our present transient stage of knowledge that a state of general comfort, a certain level of comfort, is of essential importance. According to the infant's equipment and his specific needs, this level can be achieved by varying intensities of actual maternal attention, understanding, and ministrations.

In applying the conceptual model of psychoanalytic thinking to the balance between comfort and discomfort in the infant's experience, I formulate the following hypothesis: *comfort serves to build object relationships, discomfort stimulates the differentiation, i.e., structure formation in the psychic apparatus.* No comfort situation can be permanent. Few are likely to be fully satisfactory. The memory of food satisfaction derived from the model of satiation substitutes for the missing elements in actual satisfaction in any concrete situation. I assume that when the actual satisfaction originally was regularly "too low," the imprint of the memory image related to satiation would not be of the kind to serve as an adequate supplement to the actual experience.[26]

This formula, compressed as it is, concerns a wide range of processes. The investment of the maternal object promotes a sharp distinction between the self and the outer world; its correlate is the capacity of the at first hallucinatory recall of the

---

26. [This hypothesis was further discussed by Provence and Ritvo (1961).]

missed object or part object from whom satisfaction was derived. These first steps in formation of structure are coinci-
dental with change in the child's processes. To remain in the
area of our example: the memory trace of the object is now
permanently invested, psychic energy now exists, and from
now on continues to exist in two kinds, mobile and bound.
The gradual enrichment of memory traces of the object and
of the self proceeds through an interchange between object
and self which one may assume follows a functional pattern
which only gradually unfolds. At this point, however, our assumptions have to be left in considerable vagueness since any
precision would distort the complexity of simultaneous and interacting processes. Moreover, the specific danger of adul-
tomorphic connotation is great. When we speak of the fact
that the child acquires the ability to use his own motor apparatus from the mother, we have no learning by imitation in
mind, though such learning may in selected areas play a subsidiary part from the early months of life.[27] It is subsidiary to
processes in which perception and memory of the need-gra-
tifying object are merged with the first notions of the self. We
may assume that at an early age any contact with the mother is
experienced by the child as the reinforcement of merging,
particularly of the feeding situation itself, and only gradually
the differentiation between self and nonself comes about in a
close interaction of maturational and developmental processes. One might, furthermore, assume that as far as motor development is concerned, the maturational spurts act as sharp
incentives to progress, possibly as a sharper incentive than in
other areas of development.

   The division of the child's person from that of the mother
proceeds with various speeds in various areas of function. Our
observations seem to indicate that all the areas are affected,
and that tension between comfort and discomfort has origi-

27. One notion as to the ways in which the child acquires abilities, of the ways in
which the child learns, may be usefully compared with those of Hebb (1949) and his
theory of behavior with the sharp distinction between early (fundamental) and later
phases of learning. It must suffice here to point in a general way to the possibility that
we may gain advantages in utilizing Hebb's model.

nally, in the newborn, been extraordinarily great and cannot
be reached by the hallucinatory imagination of the child. Normally, already at three months, this hallucinatory imagination
is in certain situations clearly structured by the experience.
Perception and memory interact to produce an anticipation of
the future when the child learns to wait for his feeding and
registers in the mother's preparation the cues for the forth-
coming satisfaction. Benedek (1949), who was the first to stress
the prospective importance of this stage of development,
speaks here of the stage of confidence.[28] We believe that concomitant with the more structured experience in the interaction between mother and child, the capacity to accept and
invest substitutes for the maternal figure develops. The interest of the child in experiences with toys is derived from here.

In Anne's development the low investment of the comfort
situation, the inadequate structure of the experience with the
mother, seems to be paralleled by her inability to take interest
in toys or to play with other inanimate objects which might
substitute for the human object,[29] a retardation which will last
for a long time. It will persist in the inability to perform independent problem solving. The test situation in which this
problem solving is first studied is one in which a toy is hidden
by a cloth or screen (in the last quarter of the first year). The
child is to retrieve the toy. The observations of Anne and of
institutional children give the impression that at first the hidden toy is not important enough to be recovered. Soon, however, it appears that initiative to evaluate the situation, the
activity necessary to retrieve the toy, is blocked: a deficit in
thinking seems to be operating.

Anxiety and Despair

The decline of Anne's nutritional status can be traced to the
period between six and seven months. She had always been a
small baby. Her birth weight (5½ lbs.) put her in the 25th per-

28. See also Erikson (1950) on trust.
29. The idea of the investment of the inanimate object as derived from the mother-
child relationship was first expressed by K. Wolf (1948).

centile of normal infant girls. At three months she had
dropped to the 10th percentile, but in view of her appearance
and other physical findings this seemed not alarming. She still
maintained an adequate nutritional status at six months. Then
the weight curve dropped below the 3rd percentile.[30] At this
point she looked very thin. It was not the thinness of a bony
baby but rather a thinness of a limp unmuscular kind. The
unhappiness of her facial expression was described by all
those who saw her at this time; though the observers varied in
the words they chose, all were impressed by both lack of vital-
ity and sadness in her appearance. The impressions gained at
well-baby clinics were undoubtedly more marked than those
found in the home environment. The child seemed to react to
her mother's tension, which had been steadily growing since
Anne's mother had become aware of the fact that younger
babies were further advanced in their development than
Anne. But this mortification fitted in with a desolate mood,
evidenced by the mother's increase in weight and a growing
discontent. When later this mood was discussed with her, she
spoke of her loneliness during the day, her lack of occupation,
as contributory factors, but was herself aware of the fact that
she could not fully understand the nature of her mood. The
care of the infant imposed upon Mrs. D. very great strain.
One gains the impression that the previously mentioned
scenes between mother and baby have played a decisive, and
possibly a trigger role in her depressive reaction. The lack of
precision of our information at this point is part of the limitations which the setup of the study imposed.

The interaction between the mood of the child and that of
the mother could thus be traced only in a general way. The
clearest specific instance was the crying of the infant, and this
crying soon grew into spells of tantrumlike violence, first reported when the child was nine months of age. On this oc-

30. The lowest point was reached at nine months, she passed above the 3rd percentile at one year, dropped again between twelve and fifteen months, reached the 3rd
percentile once more at fifteen months. From then on it continued to rise. Her weight
in her second year of life continued on the 10th percentile of the curve. During her
third year her weight was somewhat lower.

casion the mother described in a diary she had been asked to keep that the child cried to exhaustion, was inconsolable until she fell asleep, and though she had cried in a similar fashion earlier, she had never cried to such a degree. The few reported occasions on which such spells occurred seemed related to two factors: the strangeness of the environment and physical exhaustion. One of these conditions was observed by the staff during a well-baby clinic (Anne was one year old) when mother and child had come from a vacation resort after a bus ride of an hour and a half, the first in the child's life.[31] The effect of the child's crying on all observers was lasting, as if they had witnessed a tragic experience. They found themselves watching a child that could not be reached or comforted, but was left to her own uncontrollable despair. On this occasion all observers professed that they had never seen a condition of the same character. It might well be that the regularity of the impressions was due to one crucial circumstance: while the crying was of the greatest intensity, all observers agreed that Anne looked considerably younger than her age.

Neither the nutritional deficiency nor the role of crying and despair in Anne's life between three and twelve months are in line with the behavior of children in institutions. We relate them to the special conditions of her upbringing, to the initially overstimulating and provocatively understimulating attitude of the mother, to the situation which possibly with some extravagance might be described as tantalizing: there was the human object, there was some contact, but not the comfort which was expected of it.

In order to attempt an understanding of this conflict I turn to the most significant symptom in which Anne's behavior differs from that of children in institutions, to her excessive fear of the stranger:

The fear of stranger as normal phenomenon.

Rheingold.

The antecedents in Anne.

31. The mother had refused help that had been offered in bringing the child to the well-baby clinic. She did not want to "impose" on the study staff.

The smile at the neighbor.
The reversal of the fear.
The relation to the father:

The good object can't reach her (highly speculative).

The sole position of the mother. *She, only she, can comfort. Assumption of two images sharply divided from each other.*

Frustration brings the negative image up.

The normal character of this.

Psychoanalytic speculation on the relation between self-love and object love.

Grief and depression, love (?) duress as leading to the extreme condition.

Appendix
Papers Deriving from the
Longitudinal Study

COLEMAN [LIPTON], R. W. & PROVENCE, S. A. (1953), Environmental Retardation (Hospitalism) in Infants Living in Families. *Pediatrics,1* **11 : 285**–292

KRIS, M. (1957), The Use of Prediction in a Longitudinal Study. *The Psychoanalytic Study of the Child,* 12 : 175–189.

——— (1972), Some Aspects of Family Interaction: A Psychoanalytic Study. Freud Anniversary Lecture, New York Academy of Medicine.

LUSTMAN, S. L. (1962), Defense, Symptom, and Character. *The Psychoanalytic Study of the Child,* 17 : 216–244.

MCCOLLUM, A. T. (1956), A Clinical Caseworker in Interdisciplinary Research. *Social Work,* 1 : 88–102.

PROVENCE, S. A. & RITVO, S. (1961), Effects of Deprivation on Institutionalized Infants: Disturbances in Development of Relationship to Inanimate Objects. *The Psychoanalytic Study of the Child,* 16 : 189–205.

RITVO, S. (1972), Outcome of Prediction on Superego Formation. In: *Moral Values and the Superego Concept in Psychoanalysis,* ed. S. C. Post. New York: International Universities Press, pp. 74–86.

——— (1974), Current Status of the Concept of Infantile Neurosis: Implications for Diagnosis and Technique. *The Psychoanalytic Study of the Child,* 29 : 159–181.

——— MCCOLLUM, A. T., OMWAKE, E., PROVENCE, S. A., & SOLNIT, A. J. (1963), Some Relations of Constitution, Environment, and Personality As Observed in a Longitudinal Study of Child Development. In: *Modern Perspectives in Child Development,* ed. A. J. Solnit & S. A. Provence. New York: International Universities Press, pp. 107–143.

——— & SOLNIT, A. J. (1958), Influences of Early Mother-Child Interaction on Identification Processes. *The Psychoanalytic Study of the Child,* 13 : 64–91.

——— ——— (1960), Relationship of Early Ego Identifications to Superego Formation. *International Journal of Psycho-Analysis,* 41 : 295–300.

[These papers are listed here because they provide further descriptive details of the research project. In addition, many of them develop hypotheses first suggested by Ernst Kris.]

SOLNIT, A. J. & KRIS, M. (1967), Trauma and Infantile Experiences: A Longitudinal Perspective. In: *Psychic Trauma,* ed. S. S. Furst. New York: Basic Books, pp. 175–220.

WOLF, K. M. (1953), Observation of Individual Tendencies in the First Year of Life. In: *Problems of Infancy and Childhood,* ed. M. J. E. Senn. New York: Josiah Macy, Jr. Foundation, pp. 97–137.

———— (1954), Observation of Individual Tendencies in the Second Year of Life. In: *Problems of Infancy and Childhood,* ed. M. J. E. Senn. New York: Josiah Macy, Jr. Foundation, pp. 121–146.

Part II
PROBLEMS OF MEMORY

11: On Preconscious
Mental Processes

(1950)

In recent psychoanalytic writings preconscious mental processes are rarely mentioned, even when fundamentals are discussed (Alexander, 1948). In publications further removed from psychoanalytic experience, the psychoanalytic connotations of the term "preconscious" are entirely lost.[1] This would not be remarkable or invite comment were it not that, in the area of ego psychology, certain aspects of preconscious mental activity have been studied with greater care and by a larger number of investigators than ever before in the history of psychoanalysis: to quote Freud's last formulation on the subject, "The inside of the ego, which comprises above all the thought processes, has the quality of being preconscious" (1940, p. 162).

The reciprocal relationship between the development of ego psychology and therapeutic technique has led not only to an

Presented at the Panel on Theories of Psychoanalysis at the Annual Meeting of the American Psychoanalytic Association in Montreal, May 1949. First published in the *Psychoanalytic Quarterly*, 19 : 540–560, 1950: also in *The Yearbook of Psychoanalysis*, 7 : 100–116. New York: International Universities Press, 1951; as chapter 14 in *Psychoanalytic Explorations in Art.* New York: International Universities Press, 1952, pp. 303–318; (condensed) in *Organization and Pathology of Thought*, ed. D. Rapaport. New York: Columbia University Press, 1951, pp. 474–493; and as "Considerazioni sui processi psichici del preconscio." *Rivista di Psicoanalisi*, 7 : 83–100, 1961.

[Even though this paper was published in *Psychoanalytic Explorations in Art*, it is also included here because it forms a vital link to the four subsequent papers (chaps. 12–15) and, together with them, contains the author's main contributions to a psychoanalytic theory of memory. He intended to include these papers, as well as the unfinished chapter 10, which was to be focused on memory, in a monograph on problems of memory.]

1. Murray (1938) distinguishes between preconscious and unconscious processes, without using the term preconscious; Murphy (1947) speaks of unconscious and preconscious processes without distinction.

increased concern with the "psychic surface" and many details of behavior, but also to specific advice as to the handling of the relationship of preconscious to unconscious material in therapy, advice that is sometimes too rigidly formulated, and yet eminently important. Briefly stated, this advice is to wait until what you wish to interpret is close to consciousness, until it is preconscious (Freud, 1940). One may object that this example from psychoanalytic technique proves that our interest in preconscious processes is not "genuine" or independent, but that these processes seem important only insofar as they facilitate access to an understanding of unconscious processes, the "real" subject matter of psychoanalysis. This objection is reminiscent of a period in psychoanalysis when interest was centered on the id, when only the repressed was considered as "real" psychic material, when defense was seen as a screen, resistance was considered a force of evil, and when what was a phase in the development of psychoanalysis was declared to be the only legitimate and relevant field of psychoanalytic investigation. Anna Freud's felicitous formulation (1936) of the equal distribution of interest between the id, the ego, the superego, and reality stimulated and enhanced the attitude of clinical psychoanalysis. This equal distribution of interest most definitely embraces rational thought and fantasy in their interrelations with conflict and—at least recently—in their significance as manifestations of the individual's capacity to act in a sphere free from conflict (Hartmann, 1939a). I therefore conclude that not preconscious mental processes generally, but only certain aspects of these processes have recently been less explicitly discussed. The term, rather than the phenomena, and certain of the theoretical connotations of the term have become unpopular.

It seems to me that in reexamining some of the theoretical problems connected with preconscious mental processes in the context of current knowledge, we may gain access to implications of psychoanalytic theory that deserve increased attention. Before us lies the project which Freud started when in the 1890s he planned a treatise of which a draft has recently come to light (Freud, 1950): a psychoanalytic psychology, normal and abnormal.

PROBLEMS AND MAIN ASSUMPTIONS

One of the immediate reasons for the relative neglect of preconscious mental processes may well lie in the history of psychoanalytic theory. Freud's ideas were constantly developing, his writings represent a sequence of reformulations, and one might therefore well take the view that the systematic cohesion of psychoanalytic propositions is only, or at least best, accessible through their history. The clearest instance of such a reformulation was the gradual introduction of structural concepts. The introduction of these new concepts has never fully been integrated with the broad set of propositions developed earlier. Many of Freud's views on preconscious mental processes are contained in writings (1915–1917) in which he discusses functions of the system *Pcs.*, later attributed to the ego. In sharp contrast to these early formulations stands Freud's later consideration of "preconscious" merely as a "mental quality" (1933, 1940).

In defining the quality of the preconscious, Freud follows Breuer: preconscious is what is "capable of becoming conscious," and he adds, "easily, under frequently occurring circumstances." It is different from unconscious processes for "which this transformation is difficult and takes place only subject to a considerable expenditure of effort or possibly never at all" (1933, p. 71). However, this general differentiation is a somewhat simplified rendering of complex problems which Freud discussed in other of his writings. Three of these problems have here been selected for brief discussion.

First, not all preconscious processes reach consciousness with equal ease. Some can be recaptured only with considerable effort. What differences exist between the former and the latter?

Second, preconscious mental processes differ widely both in content and in the kind of thought processes used; they cover continua reaching from purposeful reflection to fantasy, and from logical formulation to dreamlike imagery. How can these differences be accounted for?

Third, when preconscious material emerges into consciousness, the reaction varies greatly. The process may not be noticed—the usual reaction if the preconscious process is readily available to consciousness. But emergence into consciousness can be accompanied by strong emotional reactions. How can we account for these reactions?

The theoretical assumptions made to differentiate preconscious from unconscious mental processes have varied considerably. At a time when Freud still characterized the preconscious as a functional system, he considered verbalization as one of its functions.[2] Unconscious thoughts, he believed, had to pass through the stage of verbalization on their way to consciousness; feelings could reach consciousness "directly" (1915b, 1915c). Freud later avoided the obvious pitfalls of this assumption: "The presence of . . . [speech] makes it safe to infer the preconscious nature of a process. . . . It would not be correct, however, to think that connection with the mnemic residues of speech is a necessary precondition" (1940, p. 162). The difference between preconscious and unconscious mental processes, however, is explained by assumptions concerning the nature of the prevalent psychic energy: unconscious processes use mobile psychic energy; preconscious processes bound energy. The two degrees of mobility correspond to two types of discharge characterized as the primary and secondary processes. We are thus faced with the delimitation between the id and the ego. Two sets of assumptions are here suggested by Freud (the types of energy, free and bound, and the types of discharge, the primary and secondary processes) to account for the same events; the formulation in terms of energy permits differentiations in degree, in shading; the formulation in terms of process states extremes. Hypotheses of transitions between extremes seem to me, to Hartmann (1950b) and, possibly for other reasons, to Rapaport (1950), preferable.[3]

The assumption that the ego directs countercathexes against the id is essential to any study of preconscious mental pro-

2. See Nunberg (1932), who treats the system *Pcs.* and the ego as parallel concepts.

3. Freud was naturally aware of this problem. He explicitly stated (1916/17) that the primary process is unknown to preconscious thinking, or rarely admissible.

cesses; also essential is the assumption that a preconscious process from which the ego withdraws cathexis becomes subject to
cathexis with id (mobile) energy and will be drawn into the
primary process (the basic assumption of the psychoanalytic
theory of dream formation). The reverse (unconscious material becomes preconscious) occurs when id derivatives are
cathected with ego energy and become part of preconscous
mental processes at a considerable distance from the original
impulse. They may do so if changes in the distribution of
countercathexis have taken place, e.g., if the level of conflict
has been reduced and the id impulse has become more acceptable; they may sometimes enter preconscious mental processes
at a considerable price in terms of symptoms. Id contents may
also reach consciousness without ever becoming preconscious.
Metaphorically speaking, they may become accessible to the
ego not from within but from outside. They then appear as
percepts, acquiring at once, as it were, the hypercathexis
required for consciousness. This is an abnormal (or rare)
pathway to consciousness, the pathway of hallucination. We
consider it by contrast as normal when preconscious material
reaches consciousness by a further increase in cathexis, the
hypercathexis mediated by attention. In some cases, however,
this hypercathexis cannot become effective without considerable effort. This is the reason why we assume the working—at
the passage into consciousness—of countercathetic energies
that would prevent what is, to some extent, ego-dystonic from
entering full awareness.

Recognition, Recall, and Integration

The conditions under which ego-dystonic preconscious material may reach consciousness have in psychoanalysis been studied in many contexts, mainly in relation to lapses of memory,
and in psychoanalytic therapy when a dream, a thought, or a
fantasy is about to elude recall or has done so. It is well known
that in these instances voluntary effort or concentration of attention does not always succeed in recapturing elusory
thought. But when such an attempt fails, self-observation may

be successful in pitting one ego function against another and
achieve its end by reestablishing links that have been lost: the
various stages of the preconscious thought process are repeated, until, so to speak, the chain again hangs firmly
together. This process can best be studied in situations in
which the thought process and the self-observation occur in
distinct phases; for instance, when subjects, preferably analyzed, interpret their own "doodling." [4] The report of such
an instance permitted insight into the stages of recapture.

A woman of forty, successfully psychoanalyzed, reported at
the end of treatment that though she had never had any training in drawing, she was in the habit of "doodling," particularly
when concentrating on some external stimulus. During a concert she was "doodling" on the program—one of her preferred patterns, a flower with three leaves. This time,
however, she drew only two; then the "drawing hand became
independent" and when later she looked at the product, she
found a variety of ornaments all varying the theme of two or
three leaves. The external circumference of the leaves formed
a semicircle, but their tips never touched each other. The patient was able to interpret its meaning. After an interruption
of many months she had had a menstrual period. She had
been worried, and treatment with hormones had had no effect. The "doodling" revealed the reaction to the reappearance of menstruation. The absence of the third leaf
represented lack of intercourse during menstruation. The
leaves that almost touched each other represented "the egg
cell that is about to burst open." The patient now recalled that
the thought whether or not to have a third child disturbed her
during the initial phases of the concert. She reported that
soon after having started to "doodle" she was able to listen
with great ease and pleasure. This seemed to indicate a
frequent if not a regular circumstance: the ideas hidden in
"doodles" are often ideas of which the ego wants to liberate itself.

While in this case the attempts at recapturing a trend of

4. See Kris (1952, pp. 90ff.).

thought by recapitulation of its stages proceeded consciously, this process frequently remains preconscious and only its results reach awareness. Without any further instances, many analysts are likely to share the impression that what we describe as concatenation of free associations leading to a missing link in the patient's thoughts frequently—though perhaps not regularly—indicates that the patient's ego preconsciously has already established a unity of context, or reestablished its control over an ego-dystonic impulse or area of thought.[5] Frequently this control can be established only by analytic interpretation that indicates the context which, in other structurally simpler cases, was established by self-observation. The psychic concatenation, or the establishing of the unity of context, is due to the synthetic function of the ego; [6] we are thus faced with a general principle that may well deserve to be reemphasized. It is valid for the analytic process as a whole, not only for its parts. Cases in which during analysis material recurs that requires interpretation at repeated intervals are attributed to a lack of assimilation of the interpretation, or of the material, and indicate that the synthetic function of the ego is insufficiently established. Conversely, progress in analysis can frequently be described as successful assimilation preventing renewed repression.[7]

The preconscious process that is under the control of the synthetic function of the ego is safe against withdrawal of preconscious cathexis and hence against repression; as a rule it has effortless access to consciousness.

This hypothesis is not limited to the dynamics prevailing in psychological lapses of memory or tongue; it applies to the dynamics of the wider field of analytic observation. One aspect of psychoanalytic therapy is best described by focusing on the patient's ability to recall the past. In chapter 1, I said that if

5. For the general theory of free associations in psychoanalysis see Hartmann (1927), Bernfeld (1934).

6. Nunberg (1931). For a distinction between synthetic and organizing (integrative) function see Hartmann (1939a, 1947) [and chap. 13].

7. See Nunberg (1937); French (1936, 1945). The later repression of phases of a successful analysis, while little investigated, does not contradict this view.

"the interpretation has removed obstacles to recall; the forgotten memory can take its place within awareness. It is naturally not assumed that in such cases the interpretation 'produced' recall; rather the situation existing previous to the interpretation, the one which 'suggested' the interpretation, must be described as incomplete recall (and, therefore, as in some measure similar to the situation in which the memory trace was laid down). Interpretation, therefore, acts here as a help in completion. Incomplete recall had announced itself by a variety of signs in the individual's behavior"—which the interpretation uses to reconstruct the original event from which the behavioral pattern was derived. The aim of similar steps in interpretation can be accurately described by the term "recognition," frequently used in the study of memory. When recall is not yet possible, recognition may already be accomplished. The vicissitudes of the relationship between recognition and recall are particularly familiar in reconstructions of infantile experiences. While few, if any, case histories go to the length to which Freud went when, in the case of the Wolf-Man, he studied the reactions of the patient to various alternative reconstructions (1918), it seems to be the general experience that in many instances reconstructions must be varied and modified until they are correct. These various steps may all be described in terms of stages in the interaction of recognition and recall.

The suggestion that historical interpretations in analysis stimulate memory to recognition leading to recall is in accord with experimental findings. These experiments show how recognition improves recall or guarantees retention.[8] The theoretical, psychoanalytic explanation of the relationship between recognition and recall is that the synthetic function of the ego, establishing a context, is in the case of recognition facilitated by the help of perception (in our example, the analyst's interpretation). Recall then fills a gap, fits into a pattern.

8. The unfortunate limitation of these investigations to nonsense syllables makes it difficult to establish closer links between the laboratory findings and psychoanalytic observations (Postman et al., 1948). [For a comparison of preconscious memories as they arise in analysis and electrically stimulated memories, see Kris (1953a).]

If we examine the function of recognition in relation to mental qualities, an initial formulation suggests itself: what can be mobilized in recognition must have been preconscious. I should like to stress this formulation and to consider it as well established; and yet, it might be advantageous not to apply it too rigidly. We are familiar with cases in which a historical interpretation gradually—sometimes over extended periods of treatment—opens the way to the recall of repressed material. The complexity of the interdependent factors during the psychoanalytic process is such that we can surely not assume that any one single operation is responsible for major dynamic changes; thus any release from repression depends on the strength of defenses used for the purposes of counter-cathexis, which in turn depends on the ego's capacity to cope with the prevailing intensity of conflict. It seems therefore reasonable to assume that facilitation of the ego's integrative or synthetic function by recognition is one of the dynamic factors leading to recall.[9]

The relation of recognition to recall of the repressed can be tentatively described in these terms: since the "original" situation has been recognized, previously not sufficiently invested id derivatives can be integrated into the pattern indicated by the reconstruction; this in turn strengthens the ego's position, permits a reduction of countercathexes and the gradual infiltration of further material—a result in the end not dissimilar to sudden recall, in cases in which the interpretation has led to the spectacular revival of repressed traumata. In both types of cases the full investment by the ego, the syntonicity of the event with superego and id strivings, may then lead to the feeling of certainty, to the change from "I know of" to "I believe." With such expressions Lewin (1939) contrasts two levels of analytic experience. He links the second, that of certitude, to the reestablishment of infantile omniscience. From

---

9. When Alexander and French claim that recall of the repressed is not the reason for an increase in the integrative function of the ego but a consequence of it (1946, p. 287ff.), they have not improved the view they contradict; the two factors are better described as dependent variables. They constitute what modern theory of logic terms circular causality.

the point of view of the present deliberation, I attribute the triumph of believing to the complete investment by the ego, to what in Freud's terms might well be described as essential progress in the individual's mental organization.

DISCHARGE AND REGRESSION

It is a strange fact that in spite of all varieties of clinical experience which throw light on preconscious mental processes, the main source of reference for many of these processes should have remained for almost thirty years a book by the Belgian psychologist Varendonck, entitled *The Psychology of Daydreams* (1921), which reports a great variety of self-observed thought processes.[10] There are obvious and admitted gaps in Varendonck's reports. Upon closer inspection we discover a number of contradictions and suspect the influence of his character traits, a fact to which Rapaport has drawn my attention. The few theoretical views Varendonck develops are centered on two thoughts: the relation of all preconscious activity to wish fulfillment—mostly to the fulfillment of conscious wishes—and the assumption that preconscious mental processes follow laws of their own, sharply separated from the laws of conscious thinking.

The value of Varendonck's material consists in the fact that his reports cover a wide range of phenomena. We read of deliberations on the question of whom to choose as faculty reporter for his doctoral dissertation; of self-punitive fantasies in which he loses both legs in the attempt to escape from military service; of castles in Spain of a more conventional type. Many of Varendonck's fantasies are verbal only; others are full of imagery, and some replete with condensations and symbols that are to some degree reminiscent of dreams.

This variety cannot be ascribed to the personal qualities of one observer. Material from certain patients in psychoanalysis confirms such a variety in preconscious thinking. Unpublished

10. For a systematic survey of the literature see Seeman (1951). Among the older writings a most stimulating paper by G. H. Mead (1925/26) should be mentioned which opened new and wide perspectives.

experimental investigations (Rudel, 1949) show that when asked to report their daydreams, college students record a variety of phenomena that represent what might be called the "stream of preconsciousness" in highly varied expressions of highly varied contents. These are the impressions that justify my introductory remarks on the existence of two continua, one reaching from solving problems to dreamlike fantasy, and one reaching from logical cohesive verbal statements to dreamlike imagery. Both continua, I believe, occur with some frequency in preconscious mental processes.

The first and up to now only relevant critical evaluation of Varendonck's book, from the psychoanalytic point of view, is Freud's introduction to it (1921b). It has rarely, if ever, been quoted, and in the German translation of Varendonck's book it was not fully reproduced. In studying "the mode of thought-activity to which one abandons oneself during the state of distraction into which we readily pass before sleep or upon incomplete awakening," Varendonck has rendered a valuable service. While Freud appreciates confirmation found for his views on the psychology of dreams and "defective acts," he sharply opposes Varendonck's central thesis. Freud asserts that there is no difference between preconscious and conscious mental processes. What Varendonck calls daydreaming "does not owe its peculiarities to the circumstances that it proceeds mostly fore-consciously. . . . For that reason I think it is advisable, when establishing a distinction between the different modes of thought-activity, not to utilize the relation to consciousness in the first instance." Freud suggests that one should distinguish in daydreams, as well as in the chain of thoughts studied by Varendonck, "freely wandering or phantastic thinking, in opposition to intentionally directed reflection," since it is known "that even strictly directed reflection may be achieved without the co-operation of consciousness" (p. 271f.).

If we take this distinction as our starting point and remember that the economic and structural approach, the study of cathexes and ego function, has proved its value in discussing problems in the psychology of preconscious mental processes, we are easily led to one area of deliberation. The ego, we assume, has two kinds of bound energy at its disposal: neutralized energy, and libido and aggression in their non-neutralized form (Hartmann, Kris, and Loewenstein, 1949). Fantastic, freely wandering thought processes tend to discharge more libido and aggression and less neutralized energy; purposeful reflection and solving problems, more neutralized energy. In fantasy, the processes of the ego are largely in the service of the id. Not only the id, however, is involved. Naturally, the superego and "narcissistic" strivings play their part. The content of freely wandering fantasies is extended over the pleasure-unpleasure continuum; hence the probability that in this kind of process, the discharge of non-neutralized libido and aggression will be maximized. In reflective thinking the contrary is likely. Reflective thinking, according to Freud (problem solving, as I would prefer to say), serves to a higher degree the autonomous ego interests. Discharge of libido and aggression is therefore likely to be minimized, and that of neutralized ego energy to be of greater relevance.[11]

I now turn to a brief discussion of the second continuum of preconscious thought processes, that which extends between logical verbalization and fantastic imagery; the hypnagogic fantasies to which Freud refers in the passage quoted above, some of Varendonck's wandering fantasies, and fantasies of the more fanciful patients in psychoanalysis designate the area of the phenomena in question. We are clearly dealing with problems of ego regression.

The very fact that such phenomena of ego regression are infinitely more frequent in fantasy than in deliberative preconscious processes suggests that in fantasy the discharge of libido and aggression may have in general a greater proximity to the id—to mobile energy discharges. The id, as it were, intrudes upon ego functions.

Topographically, ego regression (primitivization of ego functions) occurs not only when the ego is weak—in sleep, in falling asleep, in fantasy, in intoxication, and in the psy-

11. Alternatively one might speak here of "degrees of neutralization" of the energy discharged; see Hartmann (1950b).

choses—but also during many types of creative processes. This suggested to me years ago (1938) that the ego may use the primary process and not be overwhelmed by it. This idea was rooted in Freud's explanation of wit (1905c), according to which "a preconscious thought is given over for a moment to unconscious revision" (p. 166), and seemed to account for a variety of creative and other inventive processes. However, the problem of ego regression during creative processes represents only a special problem in a more general area. The general assumption is that under certain conditions the ego regulates regression, and that the integrative functions of the ego include voluntary and temporary withdrawal of cathexis from one area or another to regain improved control (Hartmann, 1939a, 1939b, 1947). Our theory of sleep is based upon the assumption of such a withdrawal of cathexis. Sexual functions presuppose similar regressive patterns, and the inability to suspend ego control constitutes one of the well-known symptoms of obsessional-compulsive characters.

The clinical observation of creators and the study of introspective reports of experiences during creative activity tend to show that we are faced with a shift in the cathexis of certain ego functions. Thus a frequent distinction is made between an inspirational and an "elaborational" phase in creation (Kris, 1939). The inspirational phase is characterized by the facility with which id impulses, or their closer derivatives, are received. One might say that countercathectic energies to some extent are withdrawn, and added to the speed, force, or intensity with which the preconscious thoughts are formed. During the "elaborational" phase, the countercathectic barrier may be reinforced, work proceeds slowly, cathexis is directed to other ego functions such as reality testing, formulation, or general purposes of communication. Alternations between the two phases may be rapid, oscillating, or distributed over long stretches of time.

In ascribing to the ego the control of regression in terms of shifts in the cathexis of ego functions, which can be related to or pitted against each other in various ways, we gain a frame of reference that might in the present tentative state of our knowledge prove useful in various ways. Consider, for example, the shift of cathexis between the ego function of perception (the system *Pcpt.*) and preconscious thought. The individual, immersed in preconscious thought, takes less notice of his environment. Idle fantasies are given such a pejorative description as decrease of attention or, with Freud, of being distracted by fantasy. At this point we seem to gain a further and improved understanding of one problem. It is generally assumed that preconscious thought processes become conscious by hypercathexis. We now realize that there are various degrees of hypercathexis. If energy is diverted from the perceiving function of the ego to fantasy, this in itself may not lead to consciousness but simply result in an intensification of the preconscious process. Emergence into consciousness would still be dependent on other conditions.

The automatic functions of the ego are commonly considered to include a special kind of preconscious processes which become conscious only in the case of danger or under other special requirements (Hartmann, 1939a). Consciousness in these instances is no guarantee of improved function; on the contrary, automatic (habit) responses in driving automobiles or the use of tools, for instance, seem to have undoubted advantages. Similarly, the shift from consciousness to preconsciousness may account for the experience of clarification that occurs when after intense concentration the solution to an insoluble problem suddenly presents itself following a period of rest. Briefly, I suggest that the hypercathexis of preconscious mental activity with some quantity of energy withdrawn from the object world to the ego—from the system *Pcpt.* to preconscious thinking—accounts for some of the extraordinary achievements of mentation.[12]

REACTIONS TO REACHING CONSCIOUSNESS

The appropriateness of describing thought processes in terms of cathexis and discharge is further supported by a study of

12. For a good descriptive summary of these achievements see Delacroix (1939). The recent literature has added particularly striking observations in the field of mathematical inventions; see Hadamard (1949) and McCulloch (1949).

the reactions that some individuals exhibit upon becoming conscious of their preconscious fantasies or of the result of their preconscious productive deliberation.[13]

The privileges of fantasy are manifold. When fantasy has taken us far afield we do not as a rule experience shame or guilt—shame, for instance, for having arrogated some of the properties of infantile onmipotence; guilt, because the fantasy may have been ruthless and antisocial. Patients may feel ashamed or guilty in reporting such fantasies, although they did not feel so while they were engaged in them or when they recalled them. There is a feeling of not being responsible for one's fantasies.

Tentatively, I assume that in preoccupation with fantasy the ego withdraws cathexis from some functions of the superego. Our knowledge does not permit us to be more specific. One gains the impression that while the ego ideal loses its importance for the individual, the punitive tendencies of the superego are enforced [14] in some for whom self-punitive measures are part of the fantasy. In others, the hypercathexis of the ego ideal is predominant, while the function of critical self-observation seems reduced.

The absolution from guilt for fantasy is complete if the fantasy one follows is not one's own. This accounts for the role of the bard in primitive society and, in part, for the function of fiction, drama, etc., in our society. Opportunity for discharge or catharsis is guiltlessly borrowed. A close study of the phenomenology of the subjective experiences connected with fantasy, autogenous or borrowed, tends to confirm the opinion that feelings of relief (temporary or protracted), or of saturation (and final disgust), can all easily be explained by well-known psychodynamics.

A feeling of relief and discharge, similar to that provided by fantasy, can also be gained when the successful solution of a problem has been achieved—when a piece of preconscious de-

13. Not all reactions to "becoming conscious" are here considered; "negation" and the "feeling of uncanniness," for instance, are purposely omitted.

14. Alternatively, one might say neutralized energy is withdrawn from the superego; aggressive energy remains vested in it and leads to unpleasure in fantasy.

liberation has come to a satisfactory conscious conclusion. The indisputable satisfaction which attends the solution of a problem is usually described in terms of the gratification of a sense of mastery, feelings of triumph from achievements related to ego interests (Hartmann, 1950b), feelings of self-esteem which reduce intrapsychic tension as between superego and ego. It seems useful to consider in addition the possibility that the solution of problems—including all areas of creativity—affords pleasure through the discharge of neutral energy used in the pursuit of creative thinking.[15] This consideration is new neither in psychoanalysis nor elsewhere in psychology. It is frequently referred to as functional pleasure.[16] When Freud's interest was still close to the investigation of the psychology of thinking, he stated (1905c), "If we do not require our mental apparatus at the moment for supplying one of our indispensable satisfactions, we allow it itself to work in the direction of pleasure and we seek to derive pleasure from its own activity" (p. 95f.). There can be little doubt that the activity to which Freud refers is chiefly the discharge of quantities of neutralized energy. An elaboration of this theory seemed to lead to improved understanding of aesthetic experience (Kris, 1952, p. 63).

The gradual steps in the slow maturation of solving a problem sometimes extend over years. There is a considerable similarity or analogy between some aspects of this problem of thought formation and the problem of preconscious lapses. A solution once found may be forgotten, return after some time and be fitted into its frame of reference, or it may never again be recaptured. Undoubtedly, combinations of all psychodynamic factors may interact to produce such results; and yet such forgetting, such selectivity of memory, may also be due to a lack of integration necessary for the solution of the problem.

The appropriate material for the study of these phenomena

---

15. In speaking of the pleasurable discharge of neutral energy we assume that this energy need not be ideally—i.e., fully—bound and that the degree of immobility and neutralization of energy may be to some extent independent variables (Hartmann, 1950b).

16. For other aspects of functional pleasure, see Kris (1938, p. 210f.).

is the history of science, and what gestalt psychology can contribute has recently been tested in describing the development of Einstein's theory (Wertheimer, 1945).

Freud's recently published *Origins of Psychoanalysis* (1950) provides an opportunity to study some of these problems in relation to psychoanalysis itself. This book consists of a series of intimate letters, notes, essays, and drafts written by Freud between 1887 and 1902. During these years Freud reports to a correspondent the emergence of new ideas and their subsequent slipping away, about premonitions of hypotheses to come, and a large set of related phenomena. In 1895 Freud became aware of the main psychological mechanism of dream formation and established a link between the dream mechanism and symptom formation. But his theory of symptom formation was then incomplete and in large part unusable, and the link between the two was dropped. For two years Freud forgot that he had once seen this connection, and he treated dream and neurosis as disconnected and alternative fields of his interest until, in 1897, he temporarily reestablished the connection, forgot it again, and only one year later fully established it, experiencing what in fact was a rediscovery as a great and triumphant revelation. It took three years to safeguard this finding against lapses of memory, as it was only at the end of this period that the theory was integrated, infantile sexuality was discovered, and the problem of regression made accessible to closer investigation.

Examples of this kind indicate that only when the ego has completed its synthetic function by eliminating contradictions within the theory are the parts of the theory protected against slipping from conscious awareness. We may now revise and amplify the conditions required to eliminate the counter-cathexis between preconsciousness and consciousness. To the two conditions stated—ego syntonicity and full cathexis with neutral energy as prerequisites and consequences of integration [17]—I now add that ego syntonicity consists not only of freedom from conflict in the intersystemic sense (id and su-

17. The degree of cathexis with libido or aggression is clearly variable and related to ego syntonicity.

perego), but also in the intrasystemic sense (Hartmann, 1950b) in relation to the various ego functions. In solving problems, the feeling of fitting propositions together satisfies the requirement of the synthetic function; critical examination of the context satisfies the requirements of reality testing in an extended sense.[18]

Returning from this detour to the central question of reactions to the reaching of awareness of preconscious thought processes, I repeat that normally there is an absence of reactions. In many instances of both fantasy and creativity, discharge and satisfaction can be experienced. The mere feeling of relief is more manifest in fantasy, a mixture of relief and satisfaction more evident in creativity and solving problems. But there are instances in which these same experiences appear in a special form, in which the feeling exists that awareness comes from the outside world. This is obviously true of hallucinations, but it is also true of revelation and inspiration (Kris, 1939). In revelation and inspiration a preconscious thought is attributed to an outside agent from which it has been passively received. The literal and the attenuated meanings of the term form a continuum; we also speak of inspiration when a percept stimulates thought. Newton, who attributed the discovery of the law of gravity to the observation of a falling apple, is an example. The perception acted as a factor precipitating previously organized preconscious ideas waiting for the stimulus.[19]

Why do creators of all kinds so often prefer to attribute their achievements to the influence of such external agents as chance, fate, or a divine providence? One motivation is avoidance of the wrath and envy of the gods; but there are other more significant and deeper motivations. The feeling of full control and discharge of tension in the state of becoming

18. In this direction lies the further psychoanalytic exploration of reactions to completed tasks and incompleted ones, i.e., to a topic which has been treated with great insistence by experimental psychologists.

19. In a delightful chapter of his autobiography, Walter B. Cannon (1945) has described phenomena of this order under the heading "Gains from Serendipity."

aware of significant ideas or achievements mobilizes deep layers of the personality. In the case of ecstatic revelation, the hallucinatory character of the experience is manifest.

I believe that in the process of becoming conscious the preconsciously prepared thought is sexualized, which accounts for the experiences accompanying revelation. Id energies suddenly combine with ego energies, mobile with bound and neutralized cathexes, to produce the unique experience of inspiration which is felt to reach consciousness from the outside. Unconscious fantasies at work in some specific instances of these experiences can be reconstructed, and in 1939 I tried to demonstrate the variety of experiences that are derived from the repressed fantasy of being impregnated and particularly of incorporating the paternal phallus. It has since become plausible that additional fantasies are involved. The feeling of triumph and release from tension remind the individual of a phase in his development in which passivity was a precondition of total gratification, and in which the hallucinated wish fulfillment became reality—the period of nursing. We find here another approach to the full intensity of believing and its relation to infantile omniscience as described by Lewin: the analytic process and the insight it produces can be experienced in terms of an archaic wish fulfillment. Changes in cathexis during the working of the psychic apparatus tend, I suggest, to be generally experienced in terms of such an archetype. The maturing of thought, the entry into awareness from preconsciousness to consciousness, tends to be experienced as derived from outside, as passively received, not as actively produced. The tendency toward passive reception takes various shapes and forms, appears under the guise of various modalities, but the subjective experience remains one of reception. When, after the completion of his theory of dreams, Freud was urged to publish his theories of sexuality, he answered to his urging friend: "If the theory of sexuality comes, I will listen to it."

This relationship between creativity and passivity exemplifies once more one of the leading theses of this presentation: the integrative functions of the ego include self-regulated regression and permit a combination of the most daring intellectual activity with the experience of passive receptiveness.

12: Ego Psychology and Interpretation in Psychoanalytic Therapy

(1951)

While during half a century of its history the development of psychoanalysis has been comparatively little influenced by simultaneous discoveries in other fields of science, the various applications of psychoanalysis have almost continuously influenced each other. It is in this sense that the history of psychoanalysis can be viewed as a progressive integration of hypotheses. The clearest interrelationship exists between clinical observations and the development of both psychoanalytic technique and theory (Lorand, 1946, 1948). The development of the structural point of view in psychoanalysis, i.e., the development of psychoanalytic ego psychology, can profitably be traced in terms of such an interdependence. Freud was at one point influenced by his collaborators in Zürich who impelled him to an intensified interest in the psychoses. This led him to formulate the concept of narcissism and thus to approach the ego not as a series of isolated functions but as a psychic organization. The second group of clinical impressions that favored the development of a structural psychology was the observation by Freud of individuals motivated by an unconscious sense of guilt, and of patients whose response to treatment was a negative therapeutic reaction. These types of

Presented at the Panel on Technical Implications of Ego Psychology at the Midwinter Meeting of the American Psychoanalytic Association, New York, December 1948. First published in the *Psychoanalytic Quarterly*, 20 : 15–30; also in *The Yearbook of Psychoanalysis*, 8 : 158–171. New York: International Universities Press, 1952; and as "Ich-Psychologie und Deutung in der psychoanalytischen Therapie," *Psyche*, 22 : 173–186, 1968.

behavior reinforced his conception of the unconscious nature of self-reproaches and autopunitive tendencies, and thus contributed to the recognition of important characteristics of the superego. There is little doubt that other clinical impressions to which Freud referred during these years were derived from what we would today describe as "character neuroses"—cases in whose analyses the unconscious nature of resistance and defense became particularly clear and which, therefore, facilitated formulations of unconscious and preconscious functions of the ego.

However, these events were not fortuitous. Nobody can believe that the clinical impressions of which I speak reached Freud accidentally. Surely Freud did not turn to the study of psychoses merely to engage in polemics with Jung, or in response to suggestions of Abraham; nor can it be assumed that his interest in character neuroses was due only to an increase in the incidence of character neuroses among his patients during the early 1920s, and hence to a "psychosocial" event (Halliday, 1948)—though it is probable that such a change of frequency distribution occurred. It is obviously more sensible to assume that a readiness in the observer and a change in the objects observed were interacting.

Freud's readiness for new formulations is perhaps best attested by the fact that the principles of ego psychology had been anticipated in his papers on technique (Hartmann, 1951). Most of these papers were written contemporaneously with his first and never completed attempt at a reformulation of theory, which was to be achieved in the papers on metapsychology. The precedence of technical over theoretical formulations extended throughout Freud's development. It was evident during the 1890s when in the *Studies on Hysteria* Freud reserved for himself the section on therapy and not that on theory. Several years later, when his interest in dreams and neuroses was synthetized, and the importance of infantile sexuality gained ascendancy, he was first concerned with a modification of therapeutic procedure: the "concentration technique" was replaced by the technique of free association (Kris, 1950). Similarly, Freud's papers on technique during the second decade of the century anticipate by implication what a few years later he was to formulate in terms of ego psychology. His advice that analysis should start from the surface, and that resistance be analyzed before interpreting content, implies principles basic in ego psychology. This accounts for the status of Freud's papers on technique in psychoanalytic literature: they have retained a pivotal position and most treatises on technique have illustrated or confirmed rather than modified his rare fundamental precepts. If one rereads Freud's address to the Psychoanalytic Congress in Budapest in 1918, one becomes aware of the fact that many current problems concerning the variation of technical precepts in certain types of cases, as well as the whole trend of the development that at present tries to link psychoanalytic therapy to psychotherapy in the broader sense, were accurately predicted by Freud (1919). The development which he predicted became possible, however, through the new vistas that ego psychology opened to the earliest and probably best systematized modifications of psychoanalytic techniques, the development of child analysis by Anna Freud, the psychoanalysis of delinquents by Aichhorn, and later to some of the various modifications of technique in the psychoanalytic treatment of borderline cases and psychoses.

Not only did ego psychology extensively enlarge the scope of psychoanalytic therapy, but the technique of psychoanalysis of the neuroses underwent definite changes under its impact. These changes are part of the slow and at times almost imperceptible process of development of psychoanalytic technique. Isolated changes which constitute this development are difficult to study because what one may describe as *change* can also be viewed as *difference,* and differences in technique among analysts who share approximately the same fundamental views may be due to many factors; however, if we study the trends of changing attitudes, we are in a more favorable position.

Neither all nor most of the changes in psychoanalytic technique are consequences of the development of some aspect of psychoanalytic theory. If we reread Freud's older case histories, we find, for example, that the conspicuous intellectual indoctrination of the Rat-Man was soon replaced by a greater emphasis on reliving in the transference, a shift which has no apparent direct relation to definite theoretical views. Similarly, better understanding and management of transference were probably not initially connected with any new theoretical insight. It was a process of increasing skill, of improved ability, in which Freud and his early collaborators shared,[1] not dissimilar to that process of a gradual acquisition of assurance in therapy which characterizes the formative decade in every analyst's development. But other changes in psychoanalytic therapy can, I believe, clearly be traced to the influence of theoretical insight.[2] Every new discovery in psychoanalysis is bound to influence to some extent therapeutic procedure. The value of clinical presentations is that in listening to them we are stimulated to review our own clinical experiences, revise our methods, and to profit—in what we may have overlooked or underrated—from the experience of others. To assess this influence of ego psychology it is necessary to recall the ideas which developed synchronously with or subsequent to the new structural orientation: the psychoanalytic theory of instinctual drives was extended to include aggression, and the series of ontogenetic experiences studied included in ever greater detail preoedipal conflicts deriving from the uniqueness of the mother-child relation. A historical survey of the psychoanalytic literature would, I believe, confirm that these new insights were having reverberations in therapy, influencing, however, mainly the content of interpretation and not the technique of therapy in a narrower sense. A gradual transformation of technique came about largely through better understanding and improvement in the handling of resistances. In

1. Such a view is not uncontested. In describing her own development as an analyst Ella Sharpe (1930, p. 74) stresses the fact that only familiarity with the structural concept, particularly the superego, enabled her to handle transference problems adequately. For a similar report of his early technical vicissitudes see also Abraham (1919).

2. This naturally does not apply to all individuals. The relation of theoretical insight to therapeutic procedure varies from analyst to analyst, and there is no evidence upon which to base an opinion as to which type of relation is optimal.

interpreting resistance we not only refer to its existence and determine its cause, but also seek its method of operation, which is then reviewed in the context of other similar types of behavior as part of the defensive activities of the ego. Resistance is no longer simply an "obstacle" to analysis, but part of the "psychic surface" which has to be explored.[3] The term resistance then loses the unpleasant connotation of a patient who "resists" a physician who is angry at the patient's opposition. This was the manifestation of a change in what may be described as the "climate" of analysis.

In one of his last papers Freud (1937b) defended analytic interpretations against the reproach of arbitrariness, especially in dealing with resistance; he discussed in detail the criteria according to which, by the patient's subsequent reaction, correctness of the interpretations can be verified. In doing so he stresses an area of cooperation between analyst and patient and implicitly warns against dictatorially imposed interpretations.[4] That does not mean that it is possible or desirable always to avoid opposition of the patient to any interpretation, but it means that through the development of ego psychology a number of changes in the technique of interpretation have come about—not "random" changes, characteristic of the work of some analysts and not of others, but changes that constitute a set of adjustments of psychoanalytic technique to psychoanalytic theory.

ILLUSTRATIONS

To clarify issues, I cite first a simplified version of an incident in the analysis of a six-year-old boy reported by Anna Freud (1936, p. 111). The visit to the dentist had been painful. Dur-

---

3. These or similar formulations of the analysis of resistance were achieved in two steps, in the writings of Wilhelm Reich (1928, 1933), and of Anna Freud (1936). The difference between them is significant. Reich regards the problem predominantly as one of technical "skill"; formulations tend to be oversimplified or exaggerated. They lead to the rigorous "resistance" or layer analysis, the shortcomings of which have been criticized by Hartmann (1951). By Anna Freud, resistance is fully seen as part of the defensive function of the ego.

4. Waelder (1939a) has further elaborated this point.

ing his analytic interview the little boy displayed a significant set of symptomatic actions related to this experience. He damaged or destroyed various objects belonging to the analyst, and finally repeatedly broke off the points and resharpened a set of pencils. How is this type of behavior to be interpreted?

The interpretation may point to retaliatory castration, may stress the turning of a passive experience into an active one, or may demonstrate that the little boy was identifying himself with the dentist and his aggression. All three interpretations can naturally be related to the anxiety which he had experienced. The choice between these and other possible interpretations will clearly depend on the phase of the analysis. The first interpretation, an "id interpretation," is directly aimed at the castration complex. The second and the third aim at mechanisms of defense. The second emphasizes that passivity is difficult to bear and that in assuming the active role danger is being mastered. The third interpretation implements the second by pointing out that identification can serve as a mechanism of defense. It might well prove to be a very general mechanism in the little boy's life. It may influence him not only to react aggressively,[5] but to achieve many goals, and may be the motivation of many aspects of his behavior. The interpretation that stresses the mechanism of identification is, therefore, not only the broadest, but it may also open up the largest number of new avenues, and be the one interpretation which the little boy can most easily apply in his self-observation. He might learn to experience certain of his own reactions as "not belonging" (i.e., as symptoms) and thus be led an important step on the way toward readiness for further psychoanalytic work.

I did not choose this example to demonstrate the potentialities of an interpretation aimed at making the use of a mechanism of defense conscious, but rather in order to demonstrate that the situation allows for and ultimately requires all three

5. This is probably what Anna Freud means when she says that the "child was identifying himself not with the person of the aggressor but with his aggression" (p. 112). [For an appreciation of the impact of Anna Freud's book (1936) on psychoanalytic technique, see chapter 16.]

interpretations. A relevant problem in technique consists in establishing the best way of communicating the full set of meanings to the patient. The attempt to restrict the interpretation to the id aspect only represents the older procedure, the one which I believe has on the whole been modified by the change of which I spoke. To restrict interpretation to the defense mechanism only may be justifiable by the assumption that the patient is not yet ready—a valuable piece of caution, though it seems that there is a tendency among some analysts to exaggerate such caution at times. It may also happen that though we carefully restrict the range of interpretation, the patient reacts as if we had not done so. While our interpretation points to the mechanism by which he wards off danger (e.g., identification), the next set of associations causes the patient to react as if we had interpreted his femininity. A sequence of this kind indicates normal progress: the interpretation concerns the warding-off device, the reaction reveals the impulse warded off.[6]

No truly experimental conditions can be achieved in which the effects of alternative interpretations can be studied. Comparisons of "similar cases" or comparisons of patients' reactions to "similar situations" help us to reach some useful generalizations. The occasional situation under which somewhat more precise comparisons can be made is the study of patients who have a second period of analysis with a different analyst. The need for a second analysis is no disparagement of the first analyst, nor does it imply that the first course of treatment was unsuccessful. In several instances of reanalysis in which I functioned as second analyst, the first analysis had been undertaken at a time when the problems of ego psychology had not yet influenced analytic technique, or by a colleague who (at the time) did not appreciate its importance. The initial treatment had produced considerable improve-

6. Another apparent discontinuity or "jump" in reaction, no less frequent and no less important, is designated by what Hartmann (1951) calls "the principle of multiple appeal" in interpretations. Examples of this kind make the idea of interpretation proceeding in layers, advocated by Wilhelm Reich, highly doubtful; see also in this connection Nunberg (1937) and Alexander (1935).

ments, but the very same problems appeared in a new light, or new relationships, when interpretations of a different kind, "closer to the surface," were "inserted." In a few of the cases in which these conditions existed, a published record of the first analysis was available and furnished some reliable comparison.

At the time of his second analysis a patient, who was a young scientist in his early thirties, successfully filled a respected academic position without being able to advance to higher rank because he was unable to publish any of his extensive researches. This, his chief complaint, led him to seek further analysis. He remembered with gratitude the previous treatment which had improved his potency, diminished social inhibitions, producing a marked change in his life, and he was anxious that his resumption of analysis should not come to the notice of his previous analyst (a woman) lest she feel in any way hurt by his not returning to her; but he was convinced that after a lapse of years he should now be analyzed by a man.

He had learned in his first analysis that fear and guilt prevented him from being productive, that he "always wanted to take, to steal, as he had done in puberty." He was under constant pressure of an impulse to use somebody else's ideas—frequently those of a distinguished young scholar, his intimate friend, whose office was adjacent to his own and with whom he engaged daily in long conversations.

Soon, a concrete plan for work and publication was about to materialize, when one day the patient reported he had just discovered in the library a treatise published years ago in which the same basic idea was developed. It was a treatise with which he had been familiar, since he had glanced at it some time ago. His paradoxical tone of satisfaction and excitement led me to inquire in very great detail about the text he was afraid to plagiarize. In a process of extended scrutiny it turned out the old publication contained useful support of his thesis but no hint of the thesis itself. The patient had made the author say what he wanted to say himself. Once this clue was secured, the whole problem of plagiarism appeared in a new light. The eminent colleague, it transpired, had repeatedly taken the patient's ideas, embellished and repeated them without acknowledgment. The patient was under the impression he was hearing for the first time a productive idea without which he could not hope to master his own subject, an idea which he felt he could not use because it was his colleague's property.

Among the factors determining the patient's inhibitions in his work, identification with his father played an important part. Unlike the grandfather, a distinguished scientist, the father had failed to leave his mark in his field of endeavor. The patient's striving to find sponsors, to borrow ideas, only to find that they were either unsuitable or could only be plagiarized, reproduced conflicts of his earlier relationship with his father. The projection of ideas to paternal figures was in part determined by the wish for a great and successful father (a *grand*father). In a dream the oedipal conflict with the father was represented as a battle in which books were weapons and conquered books were swallowed during combat. This was interpreted as the wish to incorporate the father's penis. It could be related to a definite phase of infancy when, aged four and five, the little boy was first taken as father's companion on fishing trips. "The wish for the bigger fish," the memory of exchanging and comparing fishes, was recalled with many details. The tendency to take, to bite, to steal was traced through many ramifications and disguises during latency and adolescence until it could be pointed out one day that the decisive displacement was to ideas. Only the ideas of others were truly interesting, only ideas one could take; hence the taking had to be engineered. At this point of the interpretation I was waiting for the patient's reaction. The patient was silent and the very length of the silence had a special significance. Then, as if reporting a sudden insight, he said: "Every noon, when I leave here, before luncheon, and before returning to my office, I walk through X Street [a street well known for its small but attractive restaurants] and I look at the menus in the windows. In one of the restaurants I usually find my preferred dish— fresh brains."

It is now possible to compare the two types of analytic ap-

proach. In his first analysis the connection between oral aggressiveness and the inhibition in his work had been
recognized: "A patient who during puberty had occasionally
stolen, mainly sweets or books, retained later a certain inclination to plagiarism. Since to him activity was connected with
stealing, scientific endeavor with plagiarism, he could escape
from these reprehensible impulses through a far-reaching inhibition of his activity and his intellectual ventures"
(Schmideberg, 1934). The point which the second analysis
clarified concerned the mechanism used in inhibiting activity.
The second set of interpretations, therefore, implemented the
first by its greater concreteness, by the fact that it covered a
large number of details of behavior and therefore opened the
way to linking present and past, adult symptomatology and infantile fantasy. The crucial point, however, was the "exploration of the surface." The problem was to establish how the
feeling, "I am in danger of plagiarizing," came about.

The procedure did not aim at direct or rapid access to the
id through interpretation; there was rather an initial exploratory period, during which various aspects of behavior were
carefully studied. This study started on a descriptive level and
proceeded gradually to establish typical patterns of behavior,
present and past.[7] Noted first were his critical and admiring
attitudes of other people's ideas; then the relation of these to
the patient's own ideas and intuitions. At this point the comparison between the patient's own productivity and that of
others had to be traced in great detail; then the part that such

7. The value of similar attempts at starting from careful descriptions has been
repeatedly discussed by Edward Bibring. I quote his views from a brief report given
by Waelder (1937, p. 471). "Bibring speaks of 'singling out' a patient's present patterns of behavior and arriving, by way of a large number of intermediate patterns, at
the original infantile pattern. The present pattern embodies the instinctual impulses
and anxieties now operative, as well as the ego's present methods of elaboration (some
of which are stereotyped responses to impulses and anxieties which have ceased to
exist). Only by means of the most careful phenomenology and by taking into consideration all the ego mechanisms now operative can the present pattern of behavior be
properly isolated out. If this is done imperfectly . . . or if all the earlier patterns are
not equally clearly isolated, there is a danger that we shall never arrive at a correct
knowledge of the infantile pattern and the result may well be an inexact interpretation of infantile material."

comparisons had played in his earlier development could be clarified. Finally, the distortion of imputing to others his own ideas could be analyzed and the mechanism of "give and take" made conscious. The exploratory description is aimed, therefore, mainly at uncovering a defense mechanism and not at an id content. The most potent interpretative weapon is naturally the link between this defense and the patient's resistance in analysis, an aspect which in the present context will not be discussed in any detail.

The exploratory steps in this analysis resemble those which Helene Deutsch (1939) describes in a strikingly similar case, in which the unconscious tendency to plagiarize ideas of an admired friend led to so severe a memory disturbance that the psychoanalytic method was used to eliminate fully the diagnosis of neurological disease. Had it been possible to obtain material from the childhood of Helene Deutsch's patient, we might have been able to link similarities and dissimilarities in the early history of both men to the later differences in the structure of their defenses and their symptomatology.[8] The mechanism described and made conscious in my patient's analysis, the id impulse, the impulse to devour, emerged into consciousness and further steps of interpretation led without constraint into the area which the first analysis had effectively analyzed. It is naturally not claimed that such procedures were altogether new at the time. There surely always have been analysts who approach a problem of interpreation approximately as outlined here. This type of approach has to some extent been systematized by the support and guidance of ego psychology. It seems that many more analysts now proceed similarly and that they have gained the impression that such a shift in emphasis is therapeutically rewarding.[9]

8. When analyzing the patient here discussed I was familiar with Deutsch's paper. Without being consciously aware of it, I followed her example when I entered into the detailed examination of the patient's intellectual pursuits.

9. In the case here discussed the analysis was interrupted by the Second World War. During its course the patient published at least one of the contributions he had for a long time planned to publish. He intended to resume analysis after the end of the war, but contact with him could not be reestablished at the time. I have since heard that he has found satisfaction in his home life and in his career.

PLANNING AND INTUITION

One difference between older and newer methods of analyzing defense mechanisms and linking "surface" and "depth" of
psychoanalytic findings to each other deserves a more detailed
discussion. The advance in theory has made the interrelations
of various steps in analytic work clearer and has thus facilitated communication about these problems. We can now teach
more accurately both the "hierarchy" and the "timing" of interpretations, and the "strategy" and "tactics" of therapy (Loewenstein, 1951a). We are, however, gradually becoming aware
of many uncertainties in this area. In speaking of hierarchy
and timing of interpretations, and of strategy or tactics in
technique, do we not refer to a plan of treatment, either to its
general outline or to one adapted to the specific type of case
and the specific prognosis? How general or specific are the
plans of treatment which individual analysts form? At what
point of the contact with the patient do the first elements of
such plans suggest themselves, and at what point do they tend
to merge? Under what conditions are we compelled to modify
such impressions and plans; when do they have to be abandoned or reshaped? These are some of the questions on which
a good deal of our teaching in psychoanalysis rests, and which
are inadequately represented in the literature.[10] The subject is
of considerable importance because in using checks and controls on prediction we could satisfy ourselves as to the validity
and reliability of tentative forecasts of those operations on
which analytic technique *partly* depends.[11]

10. See Fenichel (1941), Glover (1927/28, 1940), Sharpe (1930), and particularly
Lorand (1946), who discuss some of these problems. A group of colleagues has started
a highly promising method of investigation. Long after graduation from supervised
work, they continue regularly to consult with several others on some of their cases
over periods of years in order to make comparisons of the analytic "style" among the
consultants. It is to be hoped that this comparison will include the problem of *prediction* in analytic discussions.

11. The idea of small teams working over a number of years (with or without insti-
᾿utional backing) seems rapidly to be gaining ground among analysts. The comparison of technique in general and specifically the study of planning and predicting
might well be ideally suited to stimulate teamwork, which, if adequately recorded,
might prove to be of considerable documentary value.

The tendency to discuss "planning" and "intuition" as alternatives in analytic technique permeates psychoanalytic writings, though it has repeatedly been shown that such an antithesis is unwarranted.[12] Theodor Reik's and Wilhelm Reich's unprofitable polemics against each other are liberally quoted in such discussions. In my opinion, not only this controversy but the problem which it attempted to clarify is spurious. It is merely to be determined at what point preconscious thought processes in the analyst "take over" and determine his reaction, a question which touches upon every analyst's personal experience. There are some who are inhibited if they attempt consciously to formulate the steps to be taken, with whom full awareness acts as inhibition or distraction. There are those who at least from time to time wish to think over what they are doing or have done in a particular case, and others who almost incessantly wish to know "where they are." No optimal standard can be established. The idea, however, that the preconscious reactions of the analyst are necessarily opposed to "planning" seems, in the present stage of our knowledge about preconscious thought processes, to say the least, outdated (see chap. 11).

Once we assume that the optimal distance from full awareness is part of the "personal equation" of the analyst, the contribution of preconscious processes gains considerable importance.[13] For one thing, it guarantees the spontaneity that prompts an analyst to say to a patient who showed considerable apprehension on the eve of a holiday interruption of analysis: "Don't trouble, I shall be all right." Many may at first feel that Ella Sharpe (1930, p. 65), who reported this incident, had taken a daring step, and that her unpremeditated short cut went too far. But on second thought we may conclude that, provided the patient had been suitably prepared for the appearance of aggressive impulses within the transference, the wit of the interpretation may have struck home and created insight. Whether or not one approves of such surprise ef-

12. See Fenichel (1941), and particularly Herold (1939) and Grotjahn (1950), who make similar points.

13. See Freud's description of these relationships in various passages of his early writings (e.g., 1950, p. 311f.).

fects—and I confess my own hesitation—it is obvious that conscious premeditation could hardly bring them about. But even those of us who do not share the ebullient mastery of Ella Sharpe have reason to believe in the constructive contribution of intuition.

Let me briefly refer to a patient who had been analyzed as a child, and whom I saw fifteen years after his first analytic experience had been interrupted through the influence of a truly seductive mother who could no longer bear to share the child with the child analyst. I was familiar with certain aspects of the earlier analysis. Some of the symptoms had remained unchanged, some had returned, particularly prolonged states of sexual excitement, interrupted but hardly alleviated by compulsive masturbation or its equivalents, which on some occasions led to disguised impulses toward exhibitionism. Long stretches of the analysis were at first devoted to the details of these states of excitement. It became clear that they regularly were initiated and concluded by certain eating and drinking habits. The total condition was designated by the patient and myself as "greed." In a subsequent phase phallic fantasies about the seductive mother were gradually translated into oral terms; the violent demand for love became a key that opened up many repressed memories which had not been revealed during the child's analysis. At one point, however, the process began to stagnate, the analysis became sluggish, when suddenly a change occurred. During one interview the patient manifested vivid emotions; he left the interview considerably moved and reported the next day that "this time it had hit home." He now understood. And as evidence he quoted that when his wife had jokingly and mildly criticized him, he had started to cry and, greatly relieved, had continued to cry for many hours. What had happened? In repeating the interpretation I had without conscious premeditation used different terms. I did not speak of his *demand for love,* but of his *need for love* or expressions with a connotation which stressed not the aggressive but the passive craving in his oral wishes. Intuition had appropriately modified what conscious understanding had failed to grasp or, to be kinder to myself, had not yet grasped. This instance may serve to illustrate the necessary and regular interaction of planning and intuition, of conscious and preconscious stages of understanding psychoanalytic material. It is my impression that all advances in psychoanalysis have come about by such interactions, which have later become more or less codified in rules of technique.

Whenever we speak of the intuition of the analyst, we are touching upon a problem which tends to be treated in the psychoanalytic literature under various headings. I refer to the psychic equilibrium or the state of mind of the analyst. One part of this problem, however, is directly linked to the process of interpretation. Many times a brief glance in the direction of self-analysis is part and parcel of the analyst's intervention. The interconnection between attention, intuition, and self-analysis in the process of interpretation has been masterfully described by Ferenczi (1928, p. 96):

> He [the analyst] has to let the patient's free associations play upon him; simultaneously he lets his own fantasy get to work with the association material; from time to time he compares the new connexions that arise with earlier results of the analysis; and not for one moment must he relax the vigilance and criticism made necessary by his own subjective trends.
>
> One might say that his mind swings continuously between empathy, self-observation, and making judgements. The latter emerge spontaneously from time to time as mental signals, which at first, of course, have to be assessed only as such; only after the accumulation of further evidence is one entitled to make an interpretation.

13: On Some Vicissitudes of Insight in Psychoanalysis

(1956)

The complexity of current psychoanalytic discourse on technique suggests that I state what I take for granted before I attempt to come to the small area of problems that I propose to survey in some detail.

Psychoanalysis offers the theory applied in many if not all psychotherapeutic techniques, and supplies a rationale even where its application is not intended. Some procedures central to these psychotherapeutic techniques play at best a peripheral role in psychoanalytic therapy. Their use tends to be part of the introductory or critical phases of treatment, and some of these procedures have come to be considered as parameters, which adjust technical precepts to specific situations or afflictions (Loewenstein, 1951a; Eissler, 1953). Even when parameters can be avoided, the interventions of the analyst through interpretation may be taken by the patient as clarifying opinions or reassuring hints; and the nature of the treatment situation itself (e.g., when the analyst does not react to criticism and aggression) may gain the impact of a corrective experience.[1] The "valence" of these experiences is clearly established

Contribution to the Symposium on The Theory of Technique at the Centenary Scientific Meetings of the British Psycho-Analytical Society in London on May 5, 1956. First published in the *International Journal of Psycho-Analysis*, 37 : 445–455, 1956; also as "Acerca de algunas vicisitudes del 'insight' en psicoanálisis," *Revista Uruguaya Psicoanálisis*, 4 : 287–309, 1961/62.

1. See the thoughtful and detailed discussion of some of these problems by Bibring (1954), with whose succinct formulations some of my statements seem to be at variance. The differences, however, are probably due only to the different angles from which the field is viewed. To take instances: when Bibring emphasizes that clarification must precede interpretation I find myself in agreement, but inclined to stress

by the fact that sooner or later in the course of treatment most of the patient's reactions to them will have to be viewed in their relation to defense and resistance. With the term resistance and the temporal dimension, a "sooner" or a "later," I refer to a distinct property of psychoanalytic therapy: its character as a process, with a notion, however loosely defined, of progressive development over time in a definite direction. True, the time is long and the curve is not smooth, but if we use indices reasonably detached from fluctuations in symptomatology, allowing for transient pejorative phases in all areas—i.e., if we use proper indices, as we currently do in evaluating cases in clinical practice—the rising level of the curve can often be discerned; often, that is, whenever we are successful. It is not claimed that other psychotherapies may not have process character. It is claimed that this process character is less central to their procedure, that the "direction" is not dependent on the same criteria, and that the process tends altogether to be different in kind, though there are clear and noteworthy exceptions (Gill, 1954).

The analytic process with its inexhaustible complexities and vicissitudes is the core of psychoanalysis, of its therapeutic effectiveness and its investigative value. Most of our clinical statements refer, or should refer, to behavior during this process, and most of our theoretical formulations are derived from the need to account for its nature, as it is regulated by psychoanalytic technique—hence the twin character of theory and technique since the inception of Freud's work. It was in existence when, *einer dunklen Ahnung folgend,* he replaced hypnotic exploration by the analytic situation. It can, I believe, be shown beyond any reasonable doubt that in the various steps in which this transformation took place, a preconsciously existing notion was elaborated. To put it briefly: the analytic situation with its requirements and rules, including the reclining position and the "anonymity" of the analyst, is no conglomer-

---

the preparatory character of this step. When Bibring distinguishes two kinds of insight (for a similar distinction see Richfield, 1954), in response to clarification and one in response to interpretation, I am here interested in another problem—the relation of insight to its "infantile prototypes."

ation of random procedures, of accidental survivals of Freud's early steps in therapy or of his personal idiosyncrasies, but a setup (Loewenstein, 1951a, 1951b) designed for the double purpose of cure and quasi-experimental exploration.

Many examples of the constant interaction of theory and technique have been given. (For a fuller discussion see Hartmann, 1951; Lorand, 1948; and chap. 11.) It might be said that this interaction constitutes the history of psychoanalysis. At times, the instigation has apparently come from the one side, at times from the other, and the development was, I believe, often accelerated by access to new clinical pictures. From Freud's own development we have learned how decisive was the impact which fully analyzed obsessional neuroses left on psychoanalysis, or the contact—at the time lamentably loose—with psychoses; or later, in the years after the First World War, the access to character neuroses. The impact which child analysis made in the 1920s (A. Freud, 1927; M. Klein, 1932) and the treatment of borderline cases and the more regular contact with psychotic patients in the '40s and '50s is part of the current scene.

These changes in technique have as yet hardly been recorded. They are part and parcel of the developing patterns of clinical practice. While the attempts to study them through questionnaires have yielded challenging data, which remain difficult to evaluate, another source has not been used: the clinical literature and the writings on technique themselves. I hope (and I have expressed this hope on previous occasions [chap. 12]) that a percipient, historically minded, but clinically versed and interested group of colleagues will one day present us with an account based on these sources; an account not only of the range of variations of technique as practiced by analysts today—and the range is wide—but also of the development of these differences as they branch off from the standard procedure in which they all are rooted. In this connection we become aware of one of its additional functions: it provides a standard that makes differences in technique comparable.

A random survey would, I believe, support the impression

that in most recent writings on technique problems concerning the functions of the ego have been of increasing importance. However, within this broad area a shift of emphasis seems to be noticeable: while we were at first largely concerned with the intersystemic functions of the ego, i.e., the ego in its relation to id and superego, more recently interest in its intrasystemic functions (Hartmann, 1950b) has been added. Thus the interest in defense, as manifested in resistance, has been supplemented by some considerations concerning the integrative (synthetic) ego tendencies,[2] which are more regularly concerned with both inter- and intrasystemic conflicts. My own comments follow this direction. They do not attempt to supersede but to implement other approaches.

Let me start with a schematic example. It concerns an experience which, though not frequent, is familiar to all analysts. And it is one welcome to all. I mean "the good analytic hour." Its course is varied, and I offer only an abstraction from experiences with patients well advanced in analytic therapy. Many a time the "good hour" does not start propitiously. It may come gradually into its own, say after the first ten or fifteen minutes, when some recent experience has been recounted, which may or may not refer to yesterday's session. Then a dream may come, and associations, and all begins to make sense. In particularly fortunate instances a memory from the near or distant past, or, suddenly, one from the dark days, may present itself with varying degrees of affective charge. At times new elements are introduced as if they had always been familiar, so well do they seem to fit into the scheme of things. And when the analyst interprets, sometimes all he needs to say can be put into a question. The patient may well do the summing up by himself, and himself arrive at conclusions.

Such hours, naturally not all as smooth, eventful, and complete as the one here sketched, seem as if prepared in advance. And yet nothing in the awareness of the patient, nothing in his behavior in the early part of the hour had indicated what was to follow. We may have sensed what was going

2. A differentiation of these terms is suggested below.

on when the dream was recounted. But we may also have
remained blind to its meaning until one of the associations has
suddenly lifted the veil—often not even an early one, but
rather later ones, when associations suddenly "converge"
(Freud, 1923b, p. 110).

That here the integrative functions of the ego are at work
needs hardly a comment. So elaborate a configuration, a structure built out of so wide a choice of elements cannot be merely
the result of the tendency of the repressed to reach consciousness (Nunberg, 1932). This tendency, I believe, reveals itself
most clearly by the oscillating character of other analytic sessions, in which the battle of forces becomes first dimly perceivable, and then traceable, when over a stretch of time the
analyst can piece together some of the slight elevations in the
patient's productions, as they reveal outlines of a larger submerged formation. The very fact that in the "good hour" the
material comes as if prepared—or better, actually "prepared,"
but prepared outside awareness—seems only a confirmation
of the view that some and perhaps all significant intellectual
achievements are products or at least derivatives of preconscious mentation (see chap. 11). This assumption is further
supported by the fact that even the appearance of the dream
has acted as communication to the analyst (Kanzer, 1955).
Freud, who dealt first and in some detail with the problems
here involved, has explicitly stated that "if anyone wishes to
maintain that most of the dreams that can be made use of in
analysis are obliging dreams and owe their origin to suggestion, nothing can be said against that opinion from the point
of view of analytic theory" (1923b, p. 117). And from the further course of Freud's thinking in the paper quoted (supported recently by experimental evidence; see Alexander and
French, 1946; Fisher, 1953), one may even gain the impression that psychoanalytic theory accounts rather well for this
phenomenon.[3]

3. Freud himself elaborated these thoughts through the distinction of dreams
"from above" and dreams "from below" and the later formulation that "dreams may
arise either from the id or from the ego" (1940, p. 166); see also Blitzsten et al. (1950).

A better understanding of it came to me some years ago in the long and painful analysis of a reticent patient, in whose treatment solutions always came in dreams, ready-made, definite or with only little ambiguity. And dreams, I should add, were not frequent among his productions. We learned in his treatment to trace in the dreamwork the hidden relation to the set of preceding interpretations which had found their way into the patient's mind, and the dream combined many a time acceptance and specification or, one might say, correction.

One feature in this analysis deserves further mention. During the "good hours" when all seemed to click and material came flowing, the mood of the patient, the atmosphere in the room was heavy. The transference relation was a negative one, as if even the "spontaneously" offered productions had ultimately been forced out of him. A mood of skepticism and even defeatism mirrored the reluctance originally attached to the scene of which the good analytic hour was a belated reflection.

I am stressing this point since it has a bearing on the explanation of the dynamics of the "good hour." The point I wish to make is not only that the good hour has an "infantile prototype," more often an oral interchange than an anal one, as in my example; it seems also relevant to stress that this prototype determines the state of transference. It is not so that positive transference determines the successful integrative work of the ego. It can proceed, whatever the transference reaction may be (provided naturally that transference there was, and that it had operated at a certain intensity).

This seems at first not quite what one might expect. Do we not assume that the ego functions "in alliance with" the analyst? Do we not believe that the synthetic functions of the ego are set in motion by libidinal energies (Nunberg, 1931, 1932) set free by analytic work, and, as one writer (Riviere, 1952) puts it, what else should synthesize, should bring together but libido itself?

There is much that can be said in favor of this view, and it

has served us well.[4] It seems, however, that a more complex
set of assumptions may serve us even better and allow for
some further differentiation. I assume that the good hour is a
reaction to preceding analytic work. Through it countercathectic energies and energies attached to repressed material
have been set free. The reorganization which takes place is the
essence of the analytic process with its vicissitudes and changing facets. As part of this reorganization some of the energies
set free are (at least temporarily) at the disposal of the ego. I
further assume that this is true of both aggressive and libidinal
energies—both of which have to be transformed, sublimated,
or, to choose a term intended for both energy groups, neutralized (Hartmann, Kris, and Loewenstein, 1949). Clinical experience and theoretical considerations seem to converge in
supporting the view that transformed aggressive energy may
play a specific role in the integrative functions of the ego, as
far as they can be studied in reactions to analytic work. Clinical observations indicate that the good hour tends to follow
the crumbling of a resistant structure (not the random interpretation of an isolated evidence of resistance) and
theoretical assumptions suggest that all anticathexis may
predominantly be derived from aggression (Hartmann, 1953).
Schematically speaking we might then conclude that since libidinal drives can be discharged toward the object, since love
can be lived with lesser danger than destruction, the investment of the ego with neutralized energy as it comes about
during analytic therapy may be in some considerable propor-
tion a precipitate of aggression. This energy then enables the
ego to participate in analytic work by the production of the
good hour. It need not arise in compliance with the analyst,
but, in the ideal case, it also (or even mainly) may arive in
compliance with the meaning and structure of the treatment
process. This "compliance"—or, as one might say, this "tuning
in"—leads to the experience on which analytic therapy in its

4. Those who wish to adhere to this view might account for the example given in
the following way: the discharge of aggression in the transference facilitated the integrative work, leaving libidinal energy free for it.

ideal case rests, to the experience of *insight,* in which the cog-
nitive elements are merged with a particular kind of assurance. In this assurance the multiple elements which have led
to conviction or comprehension tend to reverberate. Many a
time we can watch the progressive establishment of this state
of mind, when what was at first "intellectual," "flat," "two-
dimensional," becomes "real," "concrete," "three-dimen-
sional," to use expressions we all have heard from patients;
expressions which seem all to refer to rather specific archaic
modes of experience. These experiences I here suggest considering as the id aspect of insight, or as its infantile prototype. They may be of varied kind, oral in nature, and
reproduce the experience of the nursing situation (or more
correctly fantasy derivatives of this situation), as, with minor
variations, more recently Lewin (1939, 1950) and I (chap. 11)
have assumed; or they may reproduce the tactile grasping
comprehension which Reik (1937) had in mind, views which as
Payne (1946) has shown need not be incompatible. But whatever the infantile prototype, all who have surveyed current analytic views on the meaning of insight (Richfield, 1954) seem to
agree on the point that we are faced with an effect of integrative ego tendencies (Zilboorg, 1952).

The advantage of focusing on the autonomous function of
the ego in the experience of insight, i.e., the reason that leads
me to supplement one set of theoretical assumptions by another, has still to be given. I therefore survey schematically
some views at present held. Freud's statements on the patient's
compliance with the analyst have been elaborated by Sterba
(1934, 1940) in describing the alliance between the analyst and
the patient's ego: [5] when interpretation of the transference
resistance has done its work, an analyzing part of the ego
emerges which is identified with the analyst (see also below).
On not quite dissimilar lines (but in focusing on phenomena
which I here characterize as the id aspects of insight or as

5. Loewenstein (1954) has pointed out that this alliance involves the autonomous
functions of the patient's ego. My own comments follow the line of thought indicated
by Loewenstein, but focus on a different aspect of the problem.

their infantile prototypes), Strachey (1934) refers to the influence which the introjection of the analyst has in modifying the patient's superego.

The approach I suggest here supplements these views in various ways [6]—and, I believe, allows for a sharper discernment of certain clinical phenomena. The phenomena which I have in mind are extraordinarily varied and stem from a wide range of syndromes. For purposes of this presentation, however, I accept limitations and return once more to the "good analytic hour." The very term is likely to stimulate apprehensive hesitation among analysts, who are, and rightly, a skeptical lot. Was it indeed simply a "good hour" or did we miss something? What was the patient up to after all?

Let us compare, then, the good analytic hour with one of its more common and more insidious relatives, with what I would call the deceptively good hour. There are many of them; and out of a wide continuum I shall choose some types for brief reference.

There is one which at first may look strikingly similar to its genuine counterpart. But there may be less labor involved; more and, one soon feels, too much lucidity. Also, the reference to the last set of interpretations comes too easily. In some cases one may gain the impression that insight does not emerge, does not crystallize, but had been there from the beginning, or it comes as illuminating experience, as a gift of the gods, of the analyst. In all these shades and gradations compliance is at work, but, compliance in the personal sense, which I tried before to distinguish from the "tuning in" into meaning and structure of the process. The integrative functions of the ego are at work, but their function is not fully autonomous; they serve the aim of winning the analyst's praise or love, or that of gaining union with him. But not only is the aim a libidinal one, the process itself is libidinized; the archaic prototype is not distanced enough. It overshadows, as it were, the experience of gaining insight. In one case, in which such deceptively good hours were particularly frequent, the infan-

6. Some apparent contradictions or some areas of incompatibility will in the course of this paper become self-evident.

tile fantasy was in fact one of primitive merging. The dangers of this variety of gaining insight are obvious. Insight will not outlast the positive phase of the transference attachment.

A second, apparently rarer case, needs less elaboration: it represents the opposite of the first. Insight is here in the service of gaining independence from the analyst. In the extreme the analysis is—we assume here, prematurely—replaced by self-analysis, and a by-and-large competitive attitude tinged by hostility holds the field.

The third group of manifestations, often not free from libidinal or aggressive overtones, goes further: it is a particularly unfortunate and irresistible reaction, familiar from certain borderline cases and best known to me in the misuse of historical reconstructions acquired during long exposure to analysis with various therapists. The integrative functions seem to proliferate; for intance, everything in the patient's life seems directly derived from *one* experience, *one* model, say one cataclysm early in infancy. When this tendency is at work, one soon notices a certain jiggling with data and facile transformations of what earlier had seemed an assured gain in understanding. If the process has been going on for some time, specific distorting mechanism may become apparent; all may seem meaningful to the patient, and meaning may seem, to him, hidden in every one of his manifestations.

The economic viewpoint, which I introduced when I spoke of the energy investments of the ego, seems to account well for an understanding of these varieties of insight: in all these cases the neutralization of the energy used in the integrative functions of the ego is "incomplete." In the third case the drive energy has been deneutralized to a considerable extent, and in its extreme manifestations insight has become a delusional experience. One might attempt to fix the level to which instinctualization has been carried in such extreme cases by the use of a terminological distinction: the synthetic functions, one might say, continue, but the integrative functions have ceased. Synthesis, as Nunberg (1931) has stressed, is at work in all kinds of symptom formation, and may reach a peak in the building of systematized delusions.

The first two schematic examples are of a simpler kind: libidinal energy in the one, aggressive energy in the other, has retained some or much of its instinctual character; the neutralization was only a partial one or, to take a wider range of clinical experience into account, the degree of neuralization may have been reduced after insight had been achieved. Insight is then being used for defense and resistance.[7] At this point we reach familiar ground and a problem in technique in the narrower sense: the analysis of miscarriages and partial misuses of analytic insight is part of analytic routines, and an all-important part. It also protects against the most common and insidious defensive character of insight—its emptiness. Little need be said about this, since we have long been familiar with the effects of its most momentous variety—intellecualization as defense (A. Freud, 1936). The vernacular it uses may be a varied one, that of the ego or that of the id, of depth or of surface, of the archaic or the cultural. The effect will tend to be equivalent: partial or pseudo-insight tends to become a façade behind which illness and charcter deformation can proliferate, sometimes successfully separated from the rest of the personality. The detailed features of such malformations tend to remain hidden unless the whole of the patient's behavior is viewed in the context of the analytic process. Hence the value of a careful attempt to extend interpretations even into areas where the gaining of insight is apparently very largely in the service of the cure. Even then—and in practice this means always—the function of integration of insight has to be scrutinized for its potential—however subsidiary—role as gratification or defense. The autonomy of this function is often established only through painful analytic work. This work, I believe, will in many instances not be complete without an analysis of infantile prototypes which give full meaning to the experience of insight during the analytic process, but are sometimes also responsible for its distortions.[8]

The closer study of the function of insight in analytic ther-

7. For the assumption that defensive ego functions work with less neutralized energy than autonomous ones, see Hartmann (1955).

8. There is a widespread notion in the literature on technique that "successful sublimation" should not and cannot be analyzed—a notion which, as far as I can see,

apy leads to one additional impression: we are faced with an extraordinarily wide range of individual differences. It is as if in every case the function of insight was differently determined, and its impact differently embedded in the balance of the personality. This is undoubtedly due to a multiplicity of factors, to both intersystemic and intrasystemic constellations. Little need be said about the first, since the unceasing labor of the ego to mediate between id and superego is well explored. The complexity of the intrasystemic constellations, however, has not been studied in comparable detail. To illustrate the problem, not to exhaust it, I refer to three functions of the ego, which are intimately involved in the gaining of analytic insight by integrative comprehension. I refer to the control of temporary and partial regression, to the ability of the ego to view the self and to observe its own functions with some measure of objectivity, and to the ego's control over the discharge of affects. In each instance the behavior of the patient during the good analytic hour supplies some basis for demonstration.

Early in the hour, I said, it was not clear what was to follow. Neither patient nor analyst knew it. The material came, and crystallized. At this stage the patient had relinquished conscious control of his thoughts and followed the analytic rule. This rule implies that the ego suspends part of its censorship, can let a partial regression of its functions carry on for a while, and is able later to regain its grip.

The ego's control over regression concerns a wide area of psychological problems. It was first noticed in the study of

---

goes back to one of Rado's comments in the Symposium on child analysis (1927). I believe the point has to be made that there may be cases, particularly in the analysis of latency and puberty children, in which the interpretation of sublimatory activity in terms of their instinctual roots may lead to resexualization or, in the terms here preferred, to deneutralization. There may be at times indications for avoidance of such interpretations in the analysis of adults: but no such principle of technique can be acknowledged. In principle no limitations of interpretative understanding can be justified by any of our theoretical assumptions on the mental apparatus; limitations are at best *ad hoc* adjustments. Many a time these adjustments seem unnecessary. The most familiar case in point concerns the alleged danger of analysis to the creative person, particularly in the arts. The apprehension that analysis must or may disturb creativity seems to me almost a disrespect to the forces that are at work in the creative, and of the contribution which ego autonomy makes to higher mental activity of all kinds. See also Kris (1952).

productive or creative activity, and in this connection described as the primary process in the service of the ego (Kris,
1934). Soon a wider set of implications became apparent. The
control of regression forms one of the nuclear parts of the integrative functions of the ego, which include the ego's capacity
to limit its own functions (Hartmann, 1939a). This offered
one of the points of distinction between the synthetic function
of the ego from a wider concept, for which Hartmann (1939a,
1947) suggested the term organizing function. In this paper I
have decided to speak of integrative function. This term, as
used here, includes the consideration of the economic point of
view. For rigorous use the term may be reserved for the
"organizing" functions, when they are also autonomous.

However, any closer investigation of the control of regression and the very use of the concept points to unsolved problems. Foremost among these stands the fact that we are hardly
informed about the genetic antecedents of the control over
regression—on the question how this function develops out of
the conflictual constellations of early childhood. According to
a plausible impression, individual differences are discernible
at a very early age; they possibly reach to the time when the
sharper differentiation between primary and secondary process normally occurs, during the first years of childhood. In
recent years interest has turned to the problem of controlled
regression in connection with indications for analytic therapy,
though the term itself has only rarely been used when the relevant phenomena are described.[9]

I have stressed that the analytic process places the patient in
a situation of purposefully chosen lack of structure. The very
fact that the transitions from one subject to the next are not
regulated gives the role of free association its central position.[10] It is a position characterized by the need to remain
comprehensible, to inform, to give accounts, to report or to as-
sociate to a dream. While the patient is referred to free associ-

9. See for instance Eissler (1953), who describes the phenomenon and does not use
the term, and Gill (1954), who uses the term when describing problems connected
with the transference neurosis.

10. In the supervision of a young analyst trained by one of the "revisionist" schools
of psychoanalysis, I was informed of the fact that patients were instructed first in
every hour to report on events of the preceding day, since without this precaution the

ation, he has to learn to establish in his contact with the analyst at which point that which he says or thinks can still be grasped by his silent listener. It is always of crucial significance when we observe that a particular patient tends to lose this contact, that when invited to follow the pressure of thoughts and images as they impose themselves upon his mind, he retires into soliloquy and mental isolation. Much more familiar is the opposite difficulty, the behavior of the patient who finds it impossible to relinquish control, to yield to the pressure of inner sources, or to acknowledge such pressure. In both extremes, and sometimes for the same reasons, analytic therapy seems unworkable. In the first case regression shows its power by destroying the contact with the analyst. We are faced with the approach of regression as uncontrollable force, loosened by the very requirement of the analytic situation. In the second case the same danger may exist, but countercathectic energy directed against the threat of dissolution produces absolute resistance to regression. Experience has taught us to respect the power and purpose of this defense. Sharply contrasted to these extremes are the minor fluctuations in the appearance of regression; these are part of the central core of behavior which analysts are wont to observe and to bring to the patient's attention. The interpretation of this behavior may either relate it to a specific context, or merely point to the relation to the free flow of associations, in the broad sense in which this term is used, when we view it in connection with the dynamics of resistance.[11] However, a pat distinction between

---

analyst might remain uninformed about the concrete reality in which the patient lived and patient and analyst left prey to a dilemma, inviting a regressive trend in the patient. It is hardly necessary to stress that the existence of this and similar "dilemmas" is part of the core experience of the analytic process.

11. It seems that the use of the term and the meaning of the "fundamental rule" of analysis are part of current controversies. "We no longer 'require' our patients to tell us everything that is in their minds. On the contrary, we give them permission to do so." This statement is supposed to describe "the analytic rule as it is usually worded nowadays" (Little, 1951, p. 39). This shift in emphasis seems to me to have far-reaching consequences for the structure of the analytic situation. It makes it more "personal," since the analyst who "permits" and does not "require" free association seems to me close to a parent who does not object to misbehavior. Perhaps this explains why in the paper quoted transference and countertransference are treated as fully equivalent phenomena.

the "normal" or "neurotic" and the severely psychotically endangered patient in their relation to the control of regression seems to obliterate the range of variations which we study in clinical practice. At least one of these variations deserves to be mentioned, since it directs our attention to a point of general importance: sometimes indivduals who seem severely impaired and whose regression in the analytic situation strikingly resembles severe pathology and often actually suggests the proximity of psychosis are more accessible to analytic therapy, can more easily acquire and more meaningfully use analytic insight, than others whose actual behavior in the analytic situation (and in life) does not point to the same danger. As far as the indication for psychoanalysis as therapy is concerned, this finding poses intriguing questions (Stone, 1954b). As far as our theoretical assumptions are concerned we are warned not to correlate the ability to control regression too closely to the depth that controlled regression may reach. One may well be reminded that Freud (1916/17) in a similar connection once pointed to the relevance of little explored individual differences; he did so when he spoke of the "flexibility of repression" in creative individuals. The possibility suggests itself that a considerable tension between the regression in the analytic situation and its more or less smooth control may characterize some of those rare individuals who show what one loosely calls a gift for analytic work, or at least a gift for it in an important respect.

But the control of regression itself, the ability of the ego to regain its full supremacy, is by itself clearly only one of the preconditions for the gaining of insight in analysis. A second step has to supplement the first. In the "good analytic hour" this second function emerges when the interpretation is offered. No pattern can of course be estabished. In my example I choose an extreme situation: sometimes, I said, the analyst can put what he has to offer into a question, and the patient himself can do the summing up; the patient's participation would thus be maximized. The principle involved is, I believe, fairly stated when we say that when interpretations are offered, the controlling function of the ego over the state of temporary and partial regression is expected to expand into an observing one. The object of this observation is the self. "The ego," Freud (1933) writes, "can take itself as an object, can treat itself like other objects, can observe itself, criticize itself, and do Heaven knows what with itself. In this, one part of the ego is setting itself over against the rest" (p. 58). Using a terminology here applied, it might be preferable to distinguish two cases, the one in which the ego observes the self and the other in which it observes its own functioning. In the latter case, one of the functions of the ego, that of observing, may be thought of as pitted against others. Once more the dangers of pathological distortions accompany the step in which insight is gained. Self-observation may in itself become compulsive and gain a symptomatic character. Best explored is the instance when its dependence on the superego exacerbates into the scrupulosity of the obsessional-neurotic, a case in which the aggressive investment of the function becomes discernible. Somewhat less familiar is the case in which the function is libidinized, when self-observation gains the character of narcissistic introspection. From some clinical impressions I believe that in this symptomatology we are sometimes faced with a fundamentally not much modified variation of narcissism in its literal meaning, the self-admiration of the mirror image. Self-observation, as autonomous function, tinged as it may be by both self-critical and self-loving components, is essentially characterized by its detachment, or, as one might say, by the individual's ability to achieve objectivity in his perceptions about himself. It is a goal never to be reached; the temptations of denial and self-deception can hardly be conquered (Hartmann, 1953). But degrees and shades and at least a tendency toward detachment may be all-important. The capacity to view oneself, an intricate subject for analytic observation and theoretical explanation, hangs closely together with the third function of the ego which contributes to analytic insight. I refer to the ego control over the discharge of affects. In my example this problem was represented by the incidents in which the affect was attached to the appearance of a memory. We are in the orbit of assured knowledge when we refer to the formula that remembering and repeating represent opposites, and that the control over acting out is one of the ideal requirements for the gaining of analytic insight. The interrelation can, I believe, not be discussed without leaving the cross-section, the "good analytic hour," and without turning to the analytic process in its time dimension: to the "good analysis."

The function of insight itself changes according to the phases and features of the analytic process. During early stages of analysis its place is much more limited than during later ones. The obvious difference concerns the area which insight covers or the stuff with which it is concerned. Only gradually is the patient—and every patient in a different way—enabled to view various parts of his unconscious self and the connections between them. But there is another, perhaps less obvious, but not less significant difference. It concerns the degree to which insight reaches awareness. Interpretation naturally need not lead to insight; much or most of analytic therapy is carried out in darkness, with here and there a flash of insight to lighten the path. A connection has been established, but before insight has reached awareness (or, if it does, only for flickering moments), new areas of anxiety and conflict emerge, new material comes, and the process drives on. Thus, far-reaching changes may and must be achieved, without the pathway by which they have come about becoming part of the patient's awareness.

If we view the analytic process as a whole, with the allowance for all its infinite variations according to the nature of illness and according to the style and even the principles applied by the analyst, it will, I believe, be found that, as analytic work proceeds, the short-circuit type of reaction to interpretation decreases, that more and more the flickering light stays on for a while; some continuity from one insightful experience to the other is maintained, though naturally what was comprehension and insight at one point may be obliterated at another. But by and large, even these phases seem to become shorter, and the areas of insight may expand. Some decisive changes in self representation, personal relations, and reality testing tend particularly to develop *pari passu* with a better understanding of the individual's past (see chap. 14).

Sometimes, not always concomitantly but rarely independently, a second long-term change seems to come about, as an analysis is set on its course, and particularly as the working through process shows genuine results. Although typical conflicts do not necessarily disappear, a change in their poignancy becomes noticeable if insight comes into its own. The amplitude between the phases in which the conflict and its manifestation in symptomatology dominate the patient's life is reduced. At the same time the tendency to acting out decreases. I should make it clear that I take the term here in a very broad, probably too broad, sense.[12] To serve my purpose, the tendency to act out should be distinguished from the acting out itself, and be contrasted with an internal constellation in which the incentive to "action" disappears. At this point the affect will not be fully experienced. It will be reduced to a signal. This does not mean that the affect is not genuine. The relation to its genuine counterpart is the same as that between anxiety and anxiety signal, and is due to a similar process of interiorization. Like the anxiety signal, any affect signal may mobilize adaptive responses of various kinds. Under conditions which would have to be specified further, this adaptive response may be no other than insight itself.

The ability to make this response would constitute one of the criteria of the "termination" of analytic work, a criterion that, though largely utopian if not qualified in many ways, might have some practical importance as one of the aims of training analysis. It might possibly help to assess the point at which the personal analysis can, as it were, pass over into self-analysis.

The hesitation with which I formulate this suggestion is due to the very great complexity of inter- and intrasystemic constellations that have to be considered in this connection. This complexity is, it seems, responsible for the wide range of effects that insight has as therapeutic agent. It has been said that insight is not a curative factor, but evidence of cure (Alexander and French, 1946). The statement is, I believe, fallacious, since it overlooks the circularity of the process (see

12. See Carroll (1954) and Silverberg (1955).

chaps. 11 and 15). Without other dynamic changes insight would not come about; but without insight and the ego's achievements which lead to insight, therapy itself remains limited and does not retain the character of psychoanalysis. However, the complexity of the ego functions which participate in the process of gaining and using insight may well account for the wide variations of the impact of insight on individual cases. In some individuals the result of analysis seems to be connected with a lasting awareness of their own problems, a higher degree of ability to view themselves; in others, this is not so—and yet the two groups of patients cannot be distinguished according to the range of therapeutic effects. This possibly finds a parallel in the study of what patients retain in memory of the course of analysis, a problem frequently accessible in repeated analyses. It is well known that the variations are extraordinarily wide. It seems that insight in some individuals remains only a transient experience, one to be obliterated again in the course of life by one of the defenses they are wont to use. And it is not my impression that these individuals are more predisposed to future illness than others (chaps. 14 and 15). This might well remind us how much remains unknown about the conditions under which the ego does its silent work.

We have learned to expand the range of our interpretations when pointing to its defensive functions. The area of interpretations here discussed was concerned with the vicissitudes of insight, the control of regression, the relation of remembering to acting out, and variations of self-perception, i.e., functions which contribute to the gaining of insight. But in spite of the extension of the range of analytic insight there is a core of the ego which tends to remain inaccessible. I refer to the capacity to integrate and to the range of integrative tendencies themselves. It seems that here we reach an area where some unknown factors (according to tentative impressions, directly related to inborn predispositions and earliest experiences) control the field.[13] We are reminded of a warning of Freud's,

13. Quite obviously this does not imply that there is no therapeutic access to gross deficiencies in integrative functions as they appear particularly in treatments of severely impaired individuals. For an example see M. Klein (1952, p. 204).

which may have gained a new meaning! We cannot guide patients in their "synthesis," we can, by analytic work, only prepare them for it.

I have spoken of the extraordinary individual differences which characterize the impact of insight as therapeutic agent. There is one group of analysands with whom we cannot, I believe, relinquish the postulate that the analytic process should achieve some degree of lasting insight. I mean the future analysts.

Many of the necessary steps which I have mentioned as connected with the emergence of insight in analysis are indispensable in the analyst's work. His mental attitude during his work, the freely hovering attention from which he starts off first into understanding and then into communication, has an unmistakable correlation to the ability to control regression. In his own affective reaction he is limited to the affect signal, and its use—sometimes confused with countertransference—becomes an important tool. The ability to detach himself from his own experience, the step from self-observation to self-analysis, remains his constant companion. The method of his work itself, the rationale of his therapeutic action, covers an area which is ambiguous in its structure: it extends from what is clearly regulated by scientific findings into areas in which new experiences are found to occur. At least at this stage of our knowledge every patient still has new things to teach and secrets of his own to reveal. The infinite number of steps left to new decisions requires in the work of the analytic therapist creative inventiveness. In the ambiguous position between the familiar and the unexplored the analyst can only trust the integrative capacities of his ego to guide his way.

14: The Personal Myth

A Problem in Psychoanalytic Technique

(1956)

The Autobiography As Screen

In the analysis of certain patients a particularly detailed and careful scrutiny of their life history seems essential in order to achieve meaningful results. In a number of cases in which this procedure proved to be indicated, I have gained the impression that these persons use their autobiographical memories—a term which I borrow from Freud's early (1899) writings—as a protective screen. In some cases this screen as a whole is carefully constructed, and built as some isolated screen memories tend to be (Fenichel, 1927, 1929; Glover, 1929; Greenacre, 1949, Reider, 1953a): the firm outline and the richness of detail are meant to cover significant omissions and distortions. Only after omissions have been filled in and distortions have been corrected, can access to the repressed material be gained. In other cases occurring more frequently, it is not the total life history but only a more or less well-defined period or isolated stretches of the personal history which have been worked up as screen; even then the well-knit structure suggests further and searching investigation. The question might well be raised which dynamic and developmental conditions favor the choice of this method of defense.

Presented on May 21, 1955 at a special meeting of the Boston Psychoanalytic Society in honor of Felix and Helene Deutsch. Some of the material had been part of various clinical, developmental, and theoretical studies of memory functions presented to the Psychoanalytic Societies in Baltimore, Chicago, Detroit, and (as the Siegfried Bernfeld Memorial Lecture) in San Francisco. First published in the *Journal of the American Psychoanalytic Association*, 4 : 653–681, 1956.

While I shall attempt at the end of this paper to suggest some answers to this question, my starting point is a more specific clinical experience: it refers to a small group of persons whose biographical self image is particularly firmly knit and embraces all periods of their lives from childhood on. Their personal history is not only, as one might expect, an essential part of their self representation, but has become a treasured possession to which the patient is attached with a peculiar devotion. This attachment reflects the fact that the autobiographical self image has become heir to important early fantasies, which it preserves. In this sense I propose to speak of it as of a "personal myth," which, as all living myth, extends from the past into the present. Some aspects of the patients' conduct of life could best be viewed as a reenactment of part of the repressed fantasies, which had found their abode in their autobiographical constructions.

The patients whom I have in mind were not inclined to propound their life histories or to proclaim the particular significance of any of the sequences of events they had or believed to have experienced. On the contrary, few of their friends or acquaintances knew about their lives, and they tended to be rather secretive about their past experiences—though without being aware of any special injunction. The very existence of a consistent autobiographical image was unknown to them, nor was the existence of a private personal myth revealed by any ideological substitutes.

The dynamic function of what I here call the personal myth has been studied in the extended analyses of three patients, who came into treatment during a period of about twenty years at approximately equal intervals. Their presenting symptoms did not suggest any analogies or structural similarities. They were different from each other not only in natural equipment, achievements in life, spread and degree of afflictions, but also in their behavior in analysis. Reactions to the transference situation ranged in intensity from regressive repetition of infantile experiences to a controlled reexperiencing in thought. The first common denominator which came to my attention was a special type of resistance to explorations of their personal history. The certainty that things could not have been different, that their recollection was both complete and reliable, was, though not explicitly verbalized, omnipresent whenever the past was first approached.

When several years after the first experience with this type of resistance I encountered it a second time, the feeling of familiarity imposed itself. Gradually other coinciding traits could be noticed, but only after the analysis of a third case had been well on its way was I able, in a review of the material, to arrive at an understanding of the congruent features. The patients whom I shall discuss showed superimposed upon essential features of an obsessional character structure, a large variety of symptoms, in two of the patients of considerable severity. In all three cases typical obsessional-compulsive formations played only a minor or transient role. In their reaction formations and along the pathways of their sublimations, derivatives of the anal-erotic triad were clearly discernible, as if one were faced with some raw material, molded by the complex experiences to which they had been exposed.

The nature of these experiences, their sequence in time, and their interaction with the predispositions of the patients—with their developmental state at the time of these experiences—seem to have stimulated the conditions in which the "personal myth" as defense and pattern of life could develop. In this sense I am inclined to claim specificity for a personality syndrome of which the personal myth is the secret core. Before I enter into a discussion of this claim I should like to present part of the case material. I shall present the analysis of the autobiographical image of one of the cases in some detail, since it offers an instructive illustration of the logic and extent of distortive biographical screening. This report, however, cannot aim at encompassing a study of even the essential psychopathology of the patient, nor can it give an impression of the course of treatment. From the analysis of two other cases I shall select some additional details to illustrate further points.

In the presentation of the first case I shall compare the biographical picture before and after analysis, in spite of the fact that the patient had been in analysis before he started treatment with me. At first one might have suspected that the life history as presented by the patient was in some considerable measure the result of his first analysis. Due to fortunate circumstances I was able to ascertain that this was not the case. It occurred to me time and again that the solidity and the cohesion of the autobiographical screen might reflect the fact that it had once proved its usefulness as a defensive structure during exposure to analysis. But there were no definite elements of the account which could be related to this presumably reinforcing experience. Instead of being a disadvantage, the fact that the material was gained in second analysis permits me to stress a point: the influence of the first analysis had been limited by the fact that the autobiographical screen had not been pierced and that the patient's life continued under the spell of the personal myth. It seemed reasonable to assume that certain essential and, according to follow-up impressions, lasting changes which the second analysis brought about were related to the fact that through the insistent analysis of a defensive structure the secret fantasy had been laid bare which the patient had reenacted in life.

CLINICAL DATA AND THEIR DISCUSSION

Case 1

The patient, a man in his late thirties, was extremely successful as a chemist both in an academic position, in a number of government committees, and in industrial enterprises in which he held important advisory or executive positions. The account of his working day had an almost dazzling quality. Though he seemed on the surace unruffled by the diversity and stringency of his commitments, those around him were left with the question how one man could get so much done in one day. While he took considerable pride in his achievements and their effect on others, anxiety had recently crept into his thinking.[1] He presented himself for a second analysis after

1. The immediate occasion which was responsible for the increase of anxiety will not be discussed.

some hesitation—though he was at that time not under the pressure of any extreme distress. His dominant complaint was the feeling of harassment and the fear that at this pace he would get "nowhere fast" and would die of a heart attack. One might say that his overt complaints and his awareness of his difficulties centered around the problem of time. The conflict showed many typical features. He was constantly struggling with time, and time was a commodity. His friends had urged him "not to go on this way" and he felt that his friends were right. Very soon in our contact a second reason appeared, which had made him decide to turn to analysis once more. He was married and his home life offered rich satisfactions. However, he was almost regularly involved in affairs with one or two women whom he neither respected nor loved and whom he saw at frequent though irregular intervals. He thus led a second life that subtly and sometimes not so subtly interfered with the family life, which he consciously cherished. It soon appeared that a somewhat similar duplicity dominated his professional activities. The urge to do many different things, to be involved in a variety of projects and enterprises, could easily be traced to a conflict between dominant sectors of interests. There was chemistry as a science, as a mathematical and physical science with the wealth of theoretical perspectives which it suggested to the patient, and there was chemistry as a technology, as part of acquisitive life with a particular stress on financial investments in patents and gadgets. Since he had terminated his first analysis with relief of certain symptoms six years earlier, the problems with which he had struggled had changed in one important respect: at the time when he had entered his first analysis he had felt disturbed by irritation and guilt feelings toward his parents. He could view them now in a more realistic light and was aware of his obligations and attachments to them.

At this point I turn to the life history which the patient presented during the early phases of our contact. The account I render emerged over several months. The patient was not aware of giving his life history as an account. And yet the way in which the various pieces fitted together seemed at times peculiar. There also was a striking insistence attached to the report of certain episodes, and to the impression they had made on him.

His parents, he reported, were simple people, who for years had been entirely dependent on his support. Both were immigrants to this country, but immigrants with very different backgrounds. The father was a Pole and a Catholic, whose unmistakably Polish name the patient had retained, though he used Americanized spelling and pronunciation. The mother was of German Protestant stock and better educated. The father, who had always been financially unsuccessful, as worker, small shopkeeper, and employee, was responsible for the sad childhood of the patient, from which, as he put it, he had escaped to success. He was one of several siblings of whom a three-and-a-half-year younger sister became particularly important in his development. There were no older brothers in the family.

During the patient's early childhood the family lived in a middle-sized Midwestern town. There life was happy. Later the father deserted the family, to live with another woman in a Midwestern metropolis. The mother and two children had to abandon their home and moved to the nearby farm of one of the mother's German cousins. Two years later, when the patient was between eight and nine, the family was reunited. The father had implored the mother to join him in the large city. But he had not been able to provide adequate facilities for the family. They lived under great financial restraint and not in the modest comfort of their former surroundings. The apartment was very small. The patient had to sleep in a windowless alcove, which was part of the parental bedroom. There was no door to separate it off. He was exposed to the noises of the parents' marital life, was auditory witness to intimacies of many kinds, some of which impressed him even at that time as obscene.

In these years he became conscious of hate and revulsion against his father, whom he resented as coarse and "dirty," and at the same time he became aware of the close attachment he had always felt to his mother. There was in the family some

German-Polish antagonism and the patient enacted this antagonism in his life.[2] He joined the *Turnverein,* an extremist German organization, veering very close to National Socialism,
which at the time was germinating in the *Vaterland.* And yet
the patient never learned the German language. (The parents
talked English to each other and the mother had had to learn
Polish early in her marriage in order to communicate with the
paternal grandmother.)

During these years the father opened a small hardware
store; after its failure he worked for other people. This suggested unfavorable comparisons with the mother's family.
They were better settled in life and considered themselves
skilled or professional people.

It was the German tradition, he said, which led the way to
his own career. The value scale was based on great respect for
"science" and "education" and the highest goal was to become
a "professor." To all such plans which the mother harbored
the father was sternly opposed. The son should work and earn
as soon as possible. The mother, on the other hand, insisted
he should "at least" go to college. During his years in school
the patient worked at odd jobs. He liked working, but he
hated the occasions when he had to help in his father's store
or later in the store in which his father was employed. He
preferred work in a small factory. The money he earned there
he delivered to his mother, who kept it for him in a secretly
guarded savings book. He was in constant contact with her
family—typical German Americans of early vintage—and was
liked and admired by them, since he had an unusual asset in
their eyes: an outstanding, one might say, unmatched school
record.

What now follows is of great relevance to my story and I
should like to draw special attention to it:

At fourteen he went to a local junior college, always working
at night, sometimes at the brink of exhaustion, since his father
remained opposed to his studies. At sixteen he left home and

2. This antagonism provided the form in which the psychological (largely instinctual) conflict could express itself. The dynamics of this conflict were at best somewhat
reinforced by the fact that the parents belonged to different subcultures.

the hometown. He went East, to one of the great universities, whose name had attracted the awe of the maternal family. There he was successful, could soon enter graduate school, and from then on his life, though full of hardship, consisted of a series of academic successes in various fields of science. He earned degrees and obtained teaching appointments. The very success of his career led, however, to a conflict which disturbed his life, and which, though it had been mitigated, had not been resolved by his first analysis. The detailed discussion of the current side of this conflict opened the door to the scrutiny of his life history and thus to the essential progress in analytic work. To put it briefly, it was a conflict between science and commerce.

Since his first analysis he had become a wealthy man and had faced the burden of supporting his parents. His family life also had taken shape. He had married a distinguished lady of Irish extraction whose energy and efficiency he admired, and with whose demands he was willing to cope. Their children were being brought up as Catholics. He had surrounded himself with a team of collaborators, most of whom had Slavic, some even Polish, names and were prominent in Polish nationalist affairs in this country. None of his present friends seemed to know about his Nazi connections, about the *Turnverein,* and yet from time to time he would see some of his old German friends from the Midwest, and to some of them he felt continued attachment—an attachment, I might say, which reverberated in the transference.

The first understanding of the true life history hidden behind the screen was offered when the question was raised how the conversion from German to Pole had come about. It was connected, he reported, with his experience at the Eastern university. There were two determinants of which he had become aware. A girl, to whom he had been devoted, German and fair-haired, had some time after his departure from home given her favors to another member of the *Verein* and he had never forgiven her. The second factor concerned ego interests of a peculiarly stringent nature. At the Eastern university to which he came during the first years of the rising influence of

Nazism in Germany, it was not opportune to have overt German or Nazi sympathies—at least, it was not opportune among the group of scientists with whom he associated. At this point, then, he suddenly turned to the allegiance with his paternal ancestry, an allegiance which he has preserved since. It is the conscious correlate to the unconscious identification with his father. The extramarital affairs which he conducted, to take only the most obvious instance, could easily be traced to the father's escapades in the patient's childhood. There had always been talk about "father's women," and long before the separation, marital discord used to reach its climax in violent fights between the parents. On one occasion the patient was present when his mother had a heated discussion with one of the strange women with whom his father associated. Thus the two sets of allegiances to paternal and maternal images and value preferences became gradually clear. They determined the patient's behavior in various avenues of his life. To put it in a schematic form: proclivities for science stemmed from the German side, the interest in gadgeteering, patents, in "hardware," was linked to business enterprise and to the father's hardware store. But these manifest connections were based on deeper and unconscious interrelations: the collecting of money and investments, the handling of time, was related to the anal side of his tradition. Not only were the Germans used to talking about "Polish dirt," but since early childhood the patient had been familiar with the father's flatulence, which in his early puberty became part of what he described as parental obscenities. In "chemistry" one was tempted to see a mixing of anal elements on a sublimated level, and at the same time part of the maternal world. Science was linked to its German admirers in his family. But "science" also proved part of an old fantasy; the fantasy of being a master of universal science, of being in command of things as a scientist, of being a superman of science, a prince of science. And when the small boy indulged in these daydreams, there was a princess to join him. By some simple displacement in the use of names the mother's German descent had in his fantasy been associated with some noble lineage and thus, out of varied ingredients, a family romance was built. But when did these fantasies take shape? Two phases could be distinguished. One led into early childhood, and the other into the end of latency or early prepuberty. In the later one the mother was unfaithful to father. At that time the patient had the thought that his mother had an affair with the owner of the small factory in which he worked, and where he earned the money which his mother saved for his college education. The factory owner and the mother, then, were the new and, in a sense, elevated parents of this version of the family romance. The father had been eliminated. The earlier version eliminated all men. There were superman and princess all by themselves. It was this fantasy which was deeply imbued with preoedipal elements, though its final formulation occurred only after the separation of the parents.

At this point I interrupt the account as given by the patient, which I have enriched by some additional understanding which the analysis offered. I should like to confront this account with the patient's life history as it emerged during the course of the analysis. I am using here some reconstructions from analysis, all supported or confirmed by recall or inquiry, and revisions which the patient himself added spontaneously from time to time, after the screen had been pierced.

Before the age of three and a half his closeness to his mother was absolute and his relation to her unbeclouded by any shadow. She was proud of the first sturdy male child and as devoted to him as she had been to his older sisters. A special aspect of this early relationship concerned the mother's joyful understanding and the child's happy compliance. He was, to give an instance, early trained, but in an almost playful manner, while oral gratifications were liberally granted. A screen memory illustrates the intermingling of the two areas. In this memory he saw himself eating coal in the cellar, and the mother happily laughing at the event. The scene must have been recounted to him in his later childhood years, since when he asked his mother about it, she confirmed the incident and put it at a time when the patient was eighteen months old. The early bowel training and the gratifying aspects of the mother's oral and anal preoccupations with him left their traces in his character. At three and a half the scene changed—a sister was born. While the mother was in the hospital for a week, the patient came down with measles. The mother returned as soon as possible to take care of him, but the day of her return or a few days later he developed diphtheria and had to be hospitalized. A separation of some duration ensued, leaving a residue of resentment against the mother. In his experience it seemed that the mother had deserted him for some long period of time. Here the ground was laid for his own pattern of desertion of people and allegiances. After the little boy's return from the hospital, he identified with the mother in her procreative function, and a phase of closeness to the father developed. In analytic reconstructions the two phases seemed sharply to be separated. Before three and a half, hostile feelings against the father were conscious. The father quarreled with his wife with great violence, and many detailed recollections could at least with great plausibility be related to the time before the birth of the younger sibling. After three and a half, the mother was occupied with another sibling, who was nursed like he had been. In joining the father, who was proud of the little boy, he was made to participate in the father's life; he went out with his father to a Polish worker's club, where the father played cards with his cronies, the little boy sitting on his lap. He became familiar with national Polish drinks and dishes. In analysis access to this material was gained when his preference for certain Polish dishes and drinks struck us as meaningful, since this spiced diet would regularly cause indigestion. There was a Polish restaurant in town in which he and his collaborators used to meet during the course of the analysis. Convivial experiences and elated moods during this feasting brought up the memories concerning the period of his early childhood when he had been close to his father.

At seven, when the father had left the family, the little boy suffered from a feeling of desertion. How would the family live, how would they survive? He could recall the fear of starvation which then invaded his life, the uneasiness which he felt when they had to accept support from the mother's cousin on the farm. It is in this context that he developed an interest in collecting, and was beset by the thought that only money and wealth would protect him from misery. This powerful and regressive trend, however, was in conflict with another set of feelings and interests. During these same years he also felt responsible for the mother, felt like the head of the family, but he suffered from the feeling of responsibility and could never quite eliminate the secret longing for the absent father. It is this secret longing which later in his life led him to look for powerful and eminent teachers whom he could admire and in turn protect. These aspects had appeared earliest in the analytic relationship. They had formed the basis of the transference in his first analysis, but had not at that time been related to the vicissitudes of his earlier experiences.

When the family was reunited, the close attachment to the father was resumed for a time. It is at this point that a memory gap in the patient's life became apparent. When the reunited family moved from their country home to the metropolitan town in the Midwest, events took place which had been eliminated from the first version of his biography. The family did not at first move into the narrow home in the German neighborhood. Prior to this they had lived for over a year in a deteriorated, but definitely Polish environment. During this time he had been very close to his father. The passive homosexual feelings of his earlier phase of life—after three and a half—were revived and, as it were, reexperienced once more. After a year the family moved in fact to the German neighborhood, close to the mother's relatives, and only then, when puberty approached, he turned away from his passive relation to the father. The danger, manifestly reinforced by the family's new sleeping arrangements, had become too great, and at the same time the father's failures, his whole demeanor, were experienced as disappointing. I am omitting many details of the analytic work concerning this renewed transition from one parent to the other during which certain minor but sharply defined and disturbing obsessional symptoms could be resolved. I am approaching the crucial point of his life story.

In the version first reported, a young genius went at fourteen to junior college and left at sixteen for the great Eastern university. This version had survived the first analysis. The data had been stated both before and after this first analysis in numerous life histories given out on several official occasions, but the facts were not correct. He had not gone to college at fourteen but at sixteen, and thus the superman fantasy was considerably curtailed. This fantasy had gained new vividness and great importance for him when he left home at eighteen, went far away into the "great" world, and when he lost the German girl to whom he had been attached. In the first version of his life history two years had been eliminated, but the two years between fourteen and sixteen replaced the years between nine and eleven. These were the years in which he had lived as a little Polish boy. These years, between nine and eleven, stood at the same time for the years in childhood following the age three and half when, in close association with the father, passive homosexual fantasies had been dominant.

It is at this point that we are enabled to understand the dynamic function of the autobiographical screen. The distortion of the life history had become necessary in order to maintain the repression of the negative oedipal attachment. At the same time the biographical self image was shaped into the pattern of a fantasy in which the intellectual superman wooed the German princess. The energy investment of the screen, I suggest, can be thought of as derived from two sources: anticathectic energies, derived, as Hartmann (1953) suggests, from aggression, maintain the repression, while energies, whose libidinal derivation is still traceable, endow the autobiographical screen with an investment originally attached to a set of old and cherished oedipal fantasies. It is this fantasy which the patient enacts in life. The superman, whose life he leads, is clearly recognizable as the idealized image of the father, whose role he has adopted in elevated stature. He combines success in science and commerce—in hardware, to use the bridge of words; he is a family man with colorful adventures, a German and a Pole; and yet the compromise formation remains unsatisfactory. The voice of conscience is alive and the enactment of the double role turns into a dangerous race of a self-destructive nature.

The problem in therapeutic technique as it relates to the topic of this paper can now be more clearly formulated. A first familiar step was concerned with the correction of distortions of the life history. Contradictions had to be discovered, the existence of memory gaps had to be established, and gradually their dynamic meaning had to be clarified. A second step was concerned with the analysis of the significance of the autobiographical screen itself, with its function as fantasy substitute and the meaning of the fantasies thus preserved. In speaking of two steps I naturally simplify the intricate texture of analytic work. No sharp separation between the two steps was attempted. In fact, the first glimpse of understanding which came to me concerned the patient's current occupational frenzy; I was impressed by its self-destructive character and its fantastic setting. The word "superman" presented itself and opened the way to the analysis of the patient's early fantasies.[3]

Another temporal division in the course of the analysis was more nearly maintained, though naturally it had not been intended. Only after the biographical screen had been pierced and its double function had, at least in part, become conscious, did the earlier material of the patient's history appear, or did what had been brought up gain cohesion and context. This material concerned the original attachment to his mother and its sudden interruption by the coincidence of the birth of the sibling and the patient's hospitalization on account of diphtheria. There was no doubt as to the nodal importance which this experience had gained. Thus early incorporative tendencies, surviving in the patient's hunger for identification with suitable ideals, had been dimly traced to feeding and weaning experiences. They could then be plausibly connected with the reaction to the feeding of the sibling, a situation which awakened dormant impulses in the little boy. The diphtheria seemed to have facilitated the tendency of turning aggressive impulses

3. A similar relation between a key word in an interpretation and the analysis of what I am inclined to consider a variant of the personal myth was described by W. Reich (1931).

toward the self and to select an organ which would carry their imprint. The patient had been a lifelong sufferer from respiratory distress which appeared at infrequent intervals but in most disturbing settings and, being allergic in nature, would yield only to ephedrine. The symptom disappeared after the reconstructive interpretation. A further ramification led to the understanding of a compulsive breathing ritual that had gained symptomatic character at the second transition from the negative to the positive oedipal attachment, at the age of ten, when he saw the dead body of his father's brother at a funeral home. Inbreathing meant the inspiratory incorporation of the dead, while expiration represented life; breath retention represented the death wish originally directed against the sibling, later against the father, and finally against the self.

The early history of my patient supplied at the same time an understanding of a developmental pattern which was found in similar form in the two other cases still to be mentioned. The essential parts of this pattern can be set out as follows: A happy and in every sense undisturbed relationship to the mother (and the father) dominates the period of infancy, the preoedipal years. For reasons to be discussed later, we may assume that it was a period in which rich and manifold stimulation led to a general precocity, but particularly to a premature development of important ego functions. The period of happy attachment to parental figures contributes to an early development of the phallic phase. During its first part a series of critical experiences occur. These experiences, apparently caused by external events, gain full traumatic significance through the fact that later life conditions continue or repeat and thus reinforce the original conflict situation.

I shall try to illustrate parts of this generalized formulation from the life history of this patient:

At a very early age he had become aware of the marital discord between his parents, had been witness to violent outbursts between them, and in his fantasy had assumed a role of substitute of the father and protector of the mother. This period, flourishing with experiences and fantasies full of conflict, was interrupted by the birth of the sibling and his temporary separation from the mother, which led him to a change in allegiance and direction of his oedipal strivings. While there is no doubt that an experience of this kind is in itself likely to leave important "traces," later experiences must have reinforced their effect. Not only did the fights between the parents continue, but a second separation ensued. This time the father was lost. When the family was reunited, the boy had reached prepuberty. Living arrangements forced him into a proximity with the parents' sexual life, presumably not experienced since earliest childhood. This proximity renewed the early infantile conflict and reawakened the fantasy of his earlier periods of life.[4]

The traumatic nature of the experiences during the early part of the phallic phase has a specific bearing on my subject. I am inclined to attribute to the nature and timing of these experiences some of the importance which fantasies have gained for the patient's life. At an unusually early age these fantasies were edited in various forms, all more or less loosely connected with the theme of the family romance. The material does not permit any definite statement of the age at which the integration of these fantasies into the pattern of the family romance occurred. Our clinical experience links the appearance of the integrated family romance fantasy to latency or prepuberty, and we are used to view it as a fantasy elaboration under the censorship of the superego. In this patient, at least one undistorted, frankly oedipal, and yet fairly cohesive and integrated version could be recognized, a fantasy in which the self and the object were both elevated, but no father figure was introduced and no displacement attempted. The role which the fantasy of the superman and the German princess played derives, it seems, from the fact that the conditions of its early origin, before three and a half, were duplicated at seven, when the family was separated and the little boy once more felt he was his mother's protector. This fantasy, which, as I said, was reenacted by the patient, was in itself not part of the biographical screen, but the construction of the screen oc-

4. [The role of separation experiences in this patient is also discussed in chapter 15.]

curred under the influence of the fantasy, which lent to the autobiographical self image the character of a personal myth.

The chronological conditions concerning the early formation of an integrated family romance fantasy are clearer in a second case from which I now present some illustrative material.

Case 2

A woman in her late twenties came for analysis because of deep dissatisfaction with her life. A painter of some distinction, she had remained emotionally untouched by a series of passing sexual involvements. She recently had felt powerfully attracted to a man of impeccable character and distinguished position who wanted to marry her. But she felt an almost irresistible urge to turn away from what she felt would be her happiness.

In describing her parental home and in speaking of her origins she showed a mixture of reluctance and distaste; not only had she come from low and insignificant parents, but from an environment so devoid of refinement that it was responsible for "the utter lack of breeding" on which she insisted. Everything in her past and in her present seemed unsatisfactory and dirty. The feeling of sloppiness and contamination had existed since earliest childhood and numerous but isolated recollections from her middle years of childhood were quoted in confirmatory evidence, from the years when the family had to flee from the invading Czarist armies during World War I. These reports seemed to some extent supported by her disorderly, slightly disorganized, and generally sloppy appearance, coexistent with immaculate bodily care and an almost faddish cleanliness.

The history which the patient offered was so contrived as to document that something had always been missing; more specifically, that there never had been a time when she had lived in a carefully guarded home, that there never had been somebody to take care of the house, that there never had been anything like an orderly atmosphere around her.

I shall not in this instance contrast the preanalytic life history with its second corrected edition. While there were few gross omissions, the distortions concerned mainly the very points on which she had initially insisted: the home was a distinguished one and the center of a rich social life. The father had achieved an eminent position early in life. He was professor of law and when the patient was born, he had just been elected dean of the law school, at one of the smaller Austrian universities, an office to which he subsequently was reelected. The mother, a beautiful, spontaneous, and high-spirited woman, ten years younger than her husband, was devoted to the child throughout her infancy and stimulated the child's early interests. She enjoyed the status which her husband's distinguished position offered, but frequented "the younger set" in the small university town in which officers of the garrison played a prominent role. The patient soon suspected her mother of an affair with one of these officers, and there was little doubt that what she had perceived or imagined either corresponded to reality or that reality was only completed by her imagination. The impact of these observations on the child was laid down in an early recollection, of which a part had been conscious and had served as a screen memory. During the course of the analysis a detail, which the mother confirmed, could be added. The patient saw herself sitting in the compartment of a railway train and was desperately trying to attract her mother's attention. But mother would shush the child, keep her away in order to continue her conversation with a young officer. The child, two and a half years old, was told to draw. The mother, herself interested in the arts, had early encouraged this activity. Thus equipped with pencil and paper, the little girl started to draw what represented the figure of a man. And whenever she had drawn it, she would energetically cross it out again. This was the detail which appeared only during the course of our reconstructive work, and which the mother could recall. The setting of the memory in the railway train was directly related to primal scene fantasies or possible early observations. When later in life one of her male friends threatened to leave her or when she felt that

she was impelled to terminate a relationship, she could cure
herself from secret longings or residual attachments by drawing his portrait.

When the first of many passing temporary alienations in the
marriage of the parents occurred, the patient was not yet
three years old. Apparently she turned to the father with violent affection, but met in him the hesitation which one might
have expected. Under the impact of the frustration caused by
the awareness of the mother's occasional distractions, the
sense of tension in the house and what she experienced as father's rejection, the girl turned to fantasy life. She did not
imagine herself the child of higher and elevated parents, but,
according to a variation of the family romance described many
years ago by Helene Deutsch (1930),[5] she was a child of lower
origin, the child of the family's cook, to whom she seemed to
have turned in her double distress. But the relationship to the
cook did not become a lasting one. Perhaps shortly thereafter,
at any rate before the patient reached her fourth year, the
cook left the family and had not been in touch with the house
since that time. The cook's name could best be translated by
saying that it sounded like slob. What the patient had projected into her life story and what she enacted in life were the
feeling of sloppiness, the idea of being the slob's daughter.
The coincidence of this fantasy with anal material and clear
masturbatory excitement suggests further determinants of this
fantasy,[6] but its early and nuclear version seemed to have occurred before the cook's departure or under the impact of the
separation from her. As one would expect, in a somewhat
later version of the fantasy the father did not remain out of
contact with the cook, and had an affair with her to compen-
sate for his wife's marital unfaithfulness. At this point, however, as far as I can judge, the fantasy was less well based on
reality. I shall not attempt to report about any other of the

5. At least one of the cases discussed by Deutsch reminds me in several traits of my
group of patients.

6. The relation of this fantasy to the patient's conduct of life reminds me of cases
referred to by Anna Freud (1949b) where masturbatory fantasy is translated into their
experience in life.

highly complex versions of this fantasy and about their incorporation into the "personal myth" of the patient. Suffice it to say that the relationship to her parents, though it underwent many fluctuations, appeared to the adolescent student of art in terms strikingly similar to those repressed ones which had set the scene for her development in early childhood. And it is in adolescence that the themes of the family romance and her early memories were finally condensed into the autobiographical screen of which I spoke. Experiences and impressions were scanned, sifted and combined, and the resulting picture was, as it were, painted over in the dark-shaded, distressing, and even repulsive colors in which she viewed herself and the course of her life—that of the illegitimate daughter of a slob.

The function of the biographical screen is in this second case even more complex than in the first one. With some simplification one might say that the patient has eliminated from her awareness the longing for her mother, but lived in her fantasy in union with the early substitute, the debased mother of her phallic conflicts.

Of the more complex set of dynamic interconnections only one still needs be mentioned. The autobiographical screen obtained its final version in puberty, when under the impact of germinating homosexual impulses the revision and reediting of the life history were required. I shall illustrate the function which adolescence plays in the final edition of the life history by a particularly dramatic episode from a third case.

Case 3

It is the fifth Christmas in a little girl's life. Both her parents, highly educated English people from the upper stratum of society, had devoted much attention to the child in spite of their manifold interests and obligations. They had taken the child along on many trips, one for over a year to the United States, when the little girl was three and four years of age. Though both had their own intellectual preoccupations, the father as a writer, the mother as an artist, they had not been able to separate from the child in spite of the fact that their economic situation would have made it easy for them. At this Christmas, then, the mother promises to the child a great surprise, and under the Christmas tree—an import from America—as a special present appeared a young friend of the family, Uncle Paul, who had arrived allegedly for the child's sake. The miscarriage of the surprise itself cannot have been more than slightly disconcerting to the child. It gained significance when a few months later the parents separated. The mother, in a nervous crisis, went to a rest home and while the little girl and a maid were living nearby, Uncle Paul appeared, to remain from then on the mother's inseparable companion. The parents were never reunited. The father departed for the United States and stayed there for the duration of World War I in the employment of his government. The mother stayed in England, close to the family of her friend, living in one of his houses, which she had allegedly rented, and went on trips with her little girl and Uncle Paul. During the years when World War I tore him apart from the new-found family, both mother and child waited for his return. The child had in these years developed into an energetic tomboy who could take over many duties of the head of the family. She protected her mother, looked after many affairs, and developed an identification with the two absent male figures. When the war ended, the separation agreement between the first husband and his wife was supplemented by divorce proceedings, and the mother married Uncle Paul. The life of my patient in the house of her mother and her second husband was made more difficult by the fact that soon children were born; but also by the fact that her own original fantasy relation to the new stepfather had never been discontinued, that some of the old teasing, some of the playful physical contact with which he had approached the child had survived. When the patient was between sixteen and seventeen, during a short absence of the mother, the stepfather attempted a sexual approach. This experience left a permanent trace in the character of the patient. It forced her to emancipate herself from stepfather and mother. She replaced these attachments by a definite attitude to life. She felt herself a stranger wherever she went—a stranger, I may add, a male stranger who comes and waits to be admired. In her life history the memory of the attempted seduction at the age of sixteen had never been eliminated, but the life history was edited in order to conceal the early traumatic events and their connection with later ones. Nothing was left which would indicate the course by which the early separation from paternal figures had driven her into male identification. All that survived was a story in which the feeling of strangeness and not belonging was attributed to the mother's lack of attention, to her shiftlessness. There was a sense of having been taken from place to place—without home or attachment. There were no dramatic memory gaps; no period of life was completely blanked out, but something essential was omitted from all periods, in spite of the apparent completeness and coherence of the patient's biographical sense.

Once more I shall point only to some of the dynamic functions of the biographical screen. The image of the neglected child, driven by the mother into "strangeness" and "homelessness," reversed the guilt feelings she felt after the stepfather's sexual approaches, which she had concealed from her mother. Her own repressed guilt feelings, however, were concerned not only with this episode but even more with her own death wishes against the mother early in life, in relation to both her own father and to Uncle Paul, whom the mother had given to her and taken from her. The "shiftlessness" of the mother, the lack of a home, which were contrary to the real conditions the autobiography had stressed, preserved the memory of the time when the three-year-old, alone with her young parents, traveled through the wide spaces of America, when she was close to both and in daily and nightly intimacy with them. Among the conscious feelings which survived this time, a longing for life in the United States had never been lost in this woman. She was herself slightly bewildered by this feeling. An admiration for America or a longing for it was in the circles in which she moved at the time still a minor offense and an admission of vulgarity. But in spite of her ingrained British upbringing the feeling persisted. It was a longing for the land

where she had been happy as a child and the land to which
the father had gone without her.

Conclusions, Additions, and Inferences

Part of the findings suggested by the material here discussed
can now be summarized. A coherent set of autobiographical
memories, a picture of one's course of life as part of the self
representation has attracted a particular investment. This investment serves a double function. It is defensive inasmuch as
it prevents certain experiences and groups of impulses from
reaching consciousness. At the same time the autobiographical
self image has taken the place of a repressed fantasy, from
which it derives part of its investment. The repressed fantasy
represents variations on the theme of the family romance,
which in the cases here discussed had been earlier integrated
than in other cases. This early integration of various fantasy
components into the family romance fantasy is due to the fact
that a relatively undisturbed preoedipal development was followed by traumatic experiences during the oedipal phase. The
continued persistence of similar conflict situations led, during
the revival of oedipal strivings in latency and particularly in
adolescence, to the need for a solid defensive structure against
the past, which at the same time retained essential features of
the original experience.

These findings do not exhaust the common feature in the
material of the analyses from which I have reported some
aspects and fragments. In fact, the most essential common denominator has been omitted: the structural properties which
these patients had in common. I mentioned in the beginning
of this presentation that they could roughly be classified as obsessional characters and that much in their behavior reminded
one of the so-called anal-erotic triad of traits. I am aware of
the fact that a fuller rendering and a different organization of
the material would have offered an opportunity to illustrate
these points and possibly even to clarify some of the questions
and problems which come to one's mind if one refers to "anal-
erotic traits" (Hartmann, Kris, and Loewenstein, 1951). How-

ever, some of the material invites some further comments in this direction. One might point to the fact that the first patient's frequent changes of allegiance which started in childhood and continued throughout his life—more often and more subtly than I could report here—had started as an active repetition of the desertion by the mother, as a desertion of the deserter, as one might say. But at the same time these changes in allegiance must be viewed as manifestations of unresolved ambivalence, as alternations of incorporation and expulsion, in line with the alternation which his breathing compulsion contained. Moreover, there is no doubt that the oral pathway enacts what genetically had been prepared by anal impulses. Ample material from the middle years illustrates the fact that his passivity in relation to his father was connected with an anal-regressive trend, presumably reinforced, at the time when he turned away from the mother. By inference I have pointed to the fact that the energies he used in his sublimation were tinged by anal derivation and that he treated his memories of the past as fixtures in a collection. He was a confirmed and passionate collector of things of all sorts, but also of thoughts and ideas. There was for the first kind of collection a visual prototype: the father's store with what appeared to the little boy as an endless array of treasures.

The second patient's drawing procedure, the drawing and crossing out, is magic and sorcery, doing and undoing in the essential meaning of the word. The mechanism survives on a higher level: later in life she first incorporates the model, then in setting it out on canvas she rids herself of it; she first submits to what she sees, then dominates it by creating; she destroys by intake and revives by output. Not only were these sequences, as they presented themselves in her analysis, clearly genetically connected with her anality; the sublimation of anal impulses remained a constant element in her creative activity and appeared as a precipitate in the leading fantasy of her life.[7]

The third patient, the little girl who became the parents'

7. At the same time some of these features represent essential characteristics of the creative process (Kris, 1952).

traveling companion, was the perfect lady of the dining car, admired and adored by her proud parents and a wide public. Her station in society imposed upon her a continued stress on manners and appearance—"shining like a Christmas tree"— and the tendency to rebellion remained suppressed. It found an outlet in a proclivity to criticism which had the character of a compulsive destruction of the object.

The obsessional elements in the structure of these patients' personalities deserve our attention since we have become used to look upon the early history of obsessional-compulsive patients and, though not with the same confidence, upon that of obsessional characters as distinguished by what the literature loosely designates as advanced, premature, or precocious ego development. It is generally assumed that this accelerated development of ego functions manifests itself initially and largely in the suppression of spontaneous discharges. The ego, it is thought—and by some authors, according to the use of the nomenclature they adopt, the superego—has "early" accepted the restrictions of the outer world and exercises pressure as its deputy. I do not wish to discuss at this point the number of important controversial views with which our literature is fraught whenever the topic of early manifestations of ego (or superego) development is discussed. I should rather, and, at this point, without support from further evidence, state my impression that, in general, early internalization is not limited to the internalization of inhibitory or restrictive adages, not restricted to identifications with the prohibitions coming from love objects (Hartmann, 1950a). This is especially true of the group of individuals to whom we refer as obsessional characters (in possible distinction to some obsessional-compulsive neurotics). The area of early internalization is at least initially much more impressive and much more universal. The observation of children who show this early tendency to internalization, in some cases during the earlier phase of the second year, and the early history of some obsessional characters (and even that of outright obsessional neurotics) supply not only well-known examples of early intellectual achievements, but also evidence of a flourishing fantasy life, or at least of richness of imagination, which makes some of these children self-contained without necessarily forcing them into actual withdrawal. They are in command of an inner world populated by creatures of their own, but at the same time they are prone to solve complex problems, until the onset of pathological development drives their activity into narrowed channels, into specialized pursuits. Then the richness dries up and the free play of thought is limited by the twin dangers of instinctualization and inhibition. This early internalization of a world of their own never arises without a close and satisfactory relation to primary objects, rarely without their special stimulation, and is not found in the form which I have in mind in children who in prelatency years show severe disturbances.

It is my impression that the first noticeable manifestation of prematurity of all ego functions related to internalization is originally linked to the early development of memory. This impression is derived from the longitudinal study of child development. Some of these observations on memory functions from the end of the first year on suggest a variety of assumptions, of which I shall mention one only: the earliest memory functions arise in the refinding of the needed and later of the beloved object. Out of this matrix all memory functions emerge; they might be distinguished according to their degree of autonomy. One set of memory functions, those with relatively high autonomy, comprehend what has occasionally been called "general memory ability," e.g., the ability to acquire, retain, and repeat learned material. Another extreme, one of low autonomy, are the memory functions concerning the self, i.e., autobiographical memories. The usefulness of this simplified distinction is illustrated by the selective character of what is traditionally called the period of infantile amnesia. It includes the experiences of the self, but does not include the impact of reality testing, skills, conceptualization or information acquired during the same period of time.[8] In all those areas where the self is concerned, where memory is autobio-

8. For the purpose of this paper I simplify some of Rapaport's (1951) suggestive propositions. I plan to return to the topic in greater detail and particularly to review the formulations on infantile amnesia by Schachtel (1949).

graphical, autonomy in the broadest sense is never fully
achieved, distorting influences never cease to play their part,
and recollections remain connected with needs and affects.[9]
The memory functions which have seemed to me most characteristic of prematurity are related to the special investment not
only of the remembered object but also of the process of remembering itself.[10] It is a pleasure which in different forms
persists throughout life, and which at times appears in pathological distortion. Its extreme is what I am inclined to call the
Proustian pleasure at reminiscing, an attitude in which more
and more of the investment has been shifted to the experience
of recall. I am here reminded of a patient in whom the dwelling on the past, in a somber and yet elated mood, proved to be
one of the most personal and yet serious resistances in analysis. When she was three and a half a number of adults in her
immediate environment had followed her own mother into
death: the investment of recall was substituted for the recall of
the deceased.

A certain investment of the process of remembering seems,
as I said, typical of early childhood, gaining in impact up to
approximately four years of age, and merging imperceptibly
with the pleasure in fantasy life, since in fantasy the lost is
always near and the wish always fulfilled. That this process
had a specific importance for the patients here discussed is a
plausible inference.[11] Another point is well documented. What
from the ego's point of view appears as advanced and specifi-

9. Hints for further elaboration of these problems can be found in Freud's first and
autobiographic treatment of memory problems in 1899.

10. This touches on a problem of some general importance for developmental psychology. I believe that in "childhood" the investments of the goal of an activity and
that of the activity itself are not sharply differentiated, and that no discussion of the
problem of "functional pleasure" can be complete without taking this genetic factor
into account. A wide area of problems opens before our eyes. At what age does the
differentiation of investment tend to occur; which goals favor and which discourage
this differentiation; which children are more and which are less likely to achieve this
differentiation; and under what conditions is this differentiation desirable or undesirable?

11. It seems best established in the second case. The extraordinary precocity of the
first patient was stressed by parental accounts. It has entered his biographical screen
as the way of the genius who leaves home at an early age.

cally invested functions—remembering and fantasy—is, from the point of view of the id, a valued and treasured holding. The analytic situation offered ample evidence. The extraordinary investment of the past, the difficulty in letting it be explored, the negative reactions to reconstructions deviating from the autobiographical screen—all had an unmistakable anal "retentive" tinge.

The special investment of memory and fantasy, merged in the autobiographical screen, naturally did not prevent the working of repression. In contradistinction to the traditional obsessional neurotic, repression and isolation worked in these patients in closest interaction, an interaction which I consider very largely typical of every repressive process.[12] The specific feature of these patients consisted in their ability to reunite what had been separated and thus to endow themselves with a continuous life history. Such attempts to establish one's past are familiar from the analysis of children in latency, and it is my impression that a continuous and relatively integrated memory identity as part of the self representation tends to develop only after the consolidation of the superego (Jacobson, 1954b). In the cases here discussed I believe that this integration of the past, under the impact of the question "how did it all come about?" originated earlier. The dynamics of memory function suggest that our autobiographical memory is in constant flux, is constantly being reorganized, and is constantly subject to changes which the tensions of the present tend to impose. The material concerning the autobiographical screen suggests that these changes reach a considerable intensity during latency. They tend to be accelerated from prepuberty on—with large individual variations—and tend to lead to a renewed "scanning" of memories in adolescence, when the need for a past becomes particularly pressing.[13] The best known manifestation of this need is the family romance itself, a fantasy of one's origin, born out of the pressure of the day. The

12. [For a more detailed discussion of the relation between repression and other mechanisms of defense, see chapter 15.]

13. The further discussion of this point would have to be related to Erikson's view on ego identity (1956), published after this paper went to print.

difference between my patients and other more or less similarly disposed individuals lies in the fact that the interaction of the sequence of early experiences with ego dispositions has made available to them nuclei of memories shaped into fantasy form which survived the various phases of scanning of memory material. These fantasy nuclei stem from a time when fantasy and reality were not sharply divided, when fantasy still was fully invested as a relatively integral and indistinguishable part of the self. Thus these patients made their life histories part of themselves, and they themselves remained actors in the history of their lives. This double relationship constitutes the specific character of the cases here discussed. The relation of the course of life to an infantile fantasy is a more general phenomenon which plays its part in almost every analytic treatment. A special case is represented by persons whose infantile fantasies later become attached to patterns of biography supplied by cultural sources, patterns frequently related to the tradition of a special vocation. Many years ago (1935) I presented examples of this kind in the attempt to show how the traditional "image of the artist" is enacted in the life of certain individuals. The patients discussed in this paper do not borrow their autobiography from cultural tradition or any general mythology. They are the creators, and their myth is a personal one.

15: The Recovery of Childhood Memories in Psychoanalysis

(1956)

This presentation might be compared to the visit to a familiar scene, repeated after a lapse of time. I propose to pass over a wide and well-mapped-out area and to stop at certain points in order to see in what way our reactions to the scenery may have changed. Though I do not set a definite date for our last visit, I have a period of a quarter of a century in mind. During these years we have been exposed to the impact of new observations and to more numerous, more varied, and (possibly through the advantages of cooperative teamwork) better recorded therapeutic experiences. Few, if any, parts of psychoanalysis as a body of knowledge have not profited by these developments. Though neither in theory nor in clinical or therapeutic practice can it be stated with general (or possibly even wide) agreement in which specific respects changes of assumptions or reformulation of hypotheses are required, it seems that the progress of which I speak permits in several instances fruitful perspectives where alternative hypotheses have been proposed, some as part of broader controversies.

The area of this survey is firmly established in psychoanalysis: the recovery of childhood memories by analytic patients. The advance in ego psychology and the more detailed understanding of childhood conflicts seem to have an immediate bearing on this study. I shall deal with these influences in the two major sections of this paper.

Presented to the Midwinter Meeting of the American Psychoanalytic Association, New York, on December 4, 1955. First published in *The Psychoanalytic Study of the Child*, 11 : 54–88. New York: International Universities Press, 1956.

Where any advance in our understanding, in our experience, or in our clinical practice can be reported, we tend to become aware of new uncertainties and limitations in our knowledge. We are forced to realize that some of our general assumptions need to be elaborated and some to be modified. Tentative suggestions of this order will be offered in a third, concluding section.

At no point can I attempt to pursue all of the ramifications of the problems on which I shall have to touch. My aim is to characterize these aspects as well as possible and to illustrate them by examples. If in the end even these aspects turn out to appear familiar, this would confirm the impression that at this time the progress in psychoanalysis tends to manifest itself by a gradual, sometimes imperceptible shading of our views and procedures, as a process of sifting, of constant adjustment of theory and practice—on the whole, as a process of learning adapted to the uniquely complex adventure in which psychoanalysis as a science is engaged.

As I mentioned, I shall be mainly concerned with the question how the recovery of childhood memories is brought about and with the dynamic context in which this occurs. This discussion implies certain impressions on the therapeutic effectiveness of the recovery of memories. It is well known that in this respect our views have undergone important modifications, since the model of hysteria has lost its paramount importance in psychoanalytic thinking. In a subtle way this model has overshadowed psychoanalytic discussions, even after it had lost its value as prototype, i.e., after the introduction of the structural approach in Freud's work. Since we no longer view repression as the only mechanism of defense, the tendency to measure results of psychoanalytic treatments in terms of "new" memories recovered is—as Glover (1927/28, 1940) suggested a number of years ago—outdated. And yet this tendency seems to linger on, as part of an unwarranted simplification in our thinking. But while it is comparatively easy to state what we no longer hold true, to say what we believe to be true is a much more difficult matter. At the end of the paper I shall briefly try to make explicit what I will have implied in its course.

EGO PSYCHOLOGY, RECONSTRUCTION AND RECALL

The bent to link present to past experience reflects the very structure of man's mental apparatus. It is part and parcel of many types of introspection and, in higher civilizations, part of the tradition of contemplative and speculative thinking. The study of the interaction between past and present stood at the beginning of psychoanalytic work and has remained alive throughout its development. An interaction it is. Not only does the present experience rest on the past, but the present supplies the incentive for the viewing of the past; the present selects, colors, and modifies. Memory, at least autobiographical or personal memory, i.e., the least autonomous area of memory function, is dynamic and telescopic.[1]

The central role of the interrelation of past and present in psychoanalytic work needs hardly to be justified. The psychoanalytic situation with its stress on partial and controlled regression—the request for free association being only the most obvious instance—is so designed that the borders between past and present tend to be blurred. The psychoanalytic situation encourages frequent and imperceptible transitions from reporting to remembering—even the yesterday is part of the past—and from repetition to recall. Certain extreme variations in these transitions and interactions pose well-known problems in therapeutic technique, of which the apparently simplest one is here taken as starting point. Both the patient's dwelling on the past and his persistent adherence to the present can function as resistance. In Freud's technical writings there is a notable rule of the thumb,[2] which advises the analyst to turn his attention to the past when the patient insists on the present and to look for present material when the patient dwells in his past. However, it seems that this aspect of resistance can be in-

1. I here summarize views best formulated in the study of screen memories, where Freud's (1899, 1901) own initial approach has been elaborated by Fenichel (1927), Glover (1929), and more recently by Katan (1939), Reider (1953a), and particularly by Greenacre (1949). For the relation of the present to the past in reconstruction, see particularly Loewenstein (1951a), Kanzer (1953), and Ekstein (1954). For a discussion of autonomy in memory function, see Rapaport (1951), and chapter 14.

2. See also Sharpe (1927).

finitely more complex, and that its understanding can in itself
provide important material for the course of analytic work.

I select an example from the beginning of my clinical experience, which illustrates a layering of resistance that suggests a
more general formulation. It occurred in the analysis of a
young female psychologist whose interest in psychoanalysis
had been stimulated by reading the analytic literature, which,
at that time and in her eastern European academic environment, was considered as somewhat extravagantly progressive
and not part of science in the proper sense. The young
woman, who under another name had gained distinction in
literary work, came to analysis with a detailed history of the
startling involvements through which a sense of adventure
had carried her during a period of a few years. The havoc
caused in her homeland by World War I, with its aftermath of
revolution and economic crisis, had affected the life of her
student years. A member of the aristocracy had been her
teacher and lover, and she was anxious to trace back the pattern of this relationship to her childhood, to the peaceful
years of the early century. Death had been a familiar specter
in her early years. Her mother died when she was three, and
in later years of childhood death had separated her from
some of those to whom she felt most closely attached. Peculiar
circumstances fortified the impression of an intimate linkage
of sexual love and separation by death. Attempts to focus on
these, at first dim, connections filled many months, in which
recollections played a dominant role. I was at the time much
less sensitized to the analysis of resistances than we all are
now, and followed the patient for some time on her way into
the past, until three features imposed themselves on my attention. They represented three aspects of resistance.

The talk of the past served to counterbalance the drab
present, in which the patient was forced to live. She spoke
about her current difficulties, but was constantly trying to
avoid the impact they exercised, both as humiliating reverses
of her fortunes and as challenging predicaments, which one
had to meet and conquer. The memories she produced were
in themselves likely to bring back pleasurable tensions with

varied and rapidly changing adventures, which had long become part of her fantasy life and crystallized in sadomasochistic masturbation fantasies of prepuberty. But while the tensions of the present were threatening, she was master of those she conjured up in recollection.

A second aspect of the wealth of "memories" was the repetition of a rivalrous relation to her brother in the transference. The productions of childhood memories became part of a competitive venture in analysis, part of a race for "reconstructing" early traumatic experiences. Self-analysis became the nucleus of the analytic experience and the analytic hour a mere supplement. The fraternal rival was raised to the position of a noble, but seducible teacher, whose interest might be gained by his pupil's stupendous progress.

The third aspect of resistance was more deeply rooted, and though its appearance had struck me first, its meaning became clear only gradually. I had at the time just become familiar with the work of Proust and was suddenly struck by the similarity between the patient's reminiscing mood and the delight and almost sensual pleasure which remembrance gains in Proust's writings. I was first inclined to connect the libidinization with the content of her recollections, but I soon learned to distinguish between this factor and the libidinization of the function of reminiscing itself. This investment seemed ultimately to be derived from the desire to be close to those she had lost early in life.

It was, of course, only in the context of the shifting aspects of the transference situation that the layers of multiple determination could be reorganized into a pattern of development; and only after this pattern of development had been established, could the dwelling on the past be replaced by insight into the life history and by changes in the patient's self representation. These steps, however, could be achieved only as the material which had been revealed in a Proustean mood gradually reappeared dynamically linked to current conflict situations, of which only the transference conflict has been mentioned in this digest. This then seems to throw light on the manifestation and function of resistance in this case. Nei-

ther the avoidance of reality conflicts nor the competitive
character of the transference, nor the libidinization of remembering—none of these elements (nor their combination) suffices
to characterize the dynamics of resistance involved. The resistance had broken the link between present and past and thus
the analytic process had been interrupted. I suggest that many
manifestations of resistance could well be described from this
angle.

It seems that during certain (presumably later) stages of analytic work this interruption is the hallmark of resistance,
whatever the defense mechanism utilized.[3] Best known is the
group of cases (sometimes seen in reanalysis) in which reconstructive work and the biographical connections established
remain either insufficiently invested and only intellectually
perceived, or isolated in other ways. Sometimes reconstructive
work may thus acquire the function of a screen behind which
relevant conflicts remain sheltered. However, the changes in
analytic technique which have come about during the last
twenty years reduce the danger that such separation of the
past from the present should establish itself. To repeat what
has been said on previous occasions (chap. 12): the change to
which I refer has not come about in a jolt or in the course of a
few years. It has crystallized gradually, starting from suggestions in Freud's technical papers, supported by his formulations on personality structure and on the nature of defense,
elaborated in the work of others—as far as defenses are concerned particularly by Anna Freud (1936)—and consolidated
in many years of clinical work, initially under the guidance of
textbooks and teaching manuals, of which Fenichel's (1941)
treatise on technique surely deserves separate mention.

The more systematic and more careful exploration of the
psychic surface, the greater consistency in a preparatory phase
in which attention is focused on the structure of defense,
seems to reduce the degree to which every one of the patient's
reactions is directly dependent on the analyst's interventions
(Loewenstein, 1951a). These interventions, it seems, have a

---

3. Among these mechanisms, "acting out" and "regression" play a particular part,
since both tend to lead to the substitution of repeating for remembering.

more limited purpose. With only slight exaggeration, one might say that the analyst watches a reorganization of forces in the patient's behavior and guides this reorganization by his interpretations. This interaction results in what we usually mean by "the analytic process." In the course of this process the past emerges into the present, and a readiness, a "need," for reconstructive interpretations may be noticed.

One of the oldest and most tenacious controversies in psychoanalysis rests on the fact that this readiness, this pressure exercised by the structure of the material, can be overlooked by the analyst. When more than forty years ago Jung found that Freud exaggerated the role of the past, when much later Horney found psychoanalysis "too genetic," they seem to have underrated the self-propelled elements in the patient's participation in the analytic process.[4]

But among writers on analytic technique there also were a few who felt that only the analysis of resistance and discharge in acting out were decisive (e.g., Kaiser, 1935). To others, such "purism" seems paradoxical. I take it that the guiding principle of analytic technique is firmly rooted in the idea that interpretation works on the border between unconscious and preconscious processes, and designates what with this help can become conscious. As far as the recall of the past is concerned, the interpretation may then be linked to the process of recognition. We suggest a connection of thoughts, feelings, or events which might have taken place in the past and, if this interpretation or this reconstruction has some validity and the material has entered the preconscious, the patient "recognizes" the picture drawn as familiar. At an earlier time, i.e., before the readiness had come about, he would have reacted differently (see also pp. 313–315). It is well known (but remains a matter of considerable clinical interest) that the reaction to recognition need not lead to positive verbalization and certainly not to (immediate) recall. The range of reactions may vary, from outright negation to gradual acceptance, from reinforcement of defense and reanimation of symptoms to relief

4. For the dynamics of these elements, particularly in relation to recollecting, see Nunberg (1932, pp. 348–352).

and the feeling of liberation—a series of reactions, on the whole still intriguing, to which Freud (1940) late in life devoted his attention. These reactions remind us once more of the fact that the communication with the patient is never exclusively regulated by the secondary process. Our interpretations may stimulate linkages between various strata of the mind which reawaken the flow of primary process connections.[5] Hence short-term predictions of specific reactions to an interpretation are in analytic work hazardous. The recovery of childhood memories is frequently one of the alternative or subsequent reactions to a specific interpretation or to preceding analytic work in general. The more restrained and gradual the interventions of the analyst are, the more they tend to fit into the flow of the analytic process (thus avoiding the danger that the search for memories becomes an intellectualized epiphenomenon), the more frequently memories seem to appear as if they had always been a part of the patient's recollections. While I shall later return to this point, I am here interested in the relation of various types of interpretations to the process of memory recovery. It is a process which interpretations set into motion but which in many instances seems to proceed on its own impetus.

An illustration, familiar in all essential features, is now offered as concrete basis for further discussion. It concerns an episode in the treatment of a forty-year-old member of a respected family of British merchants, who returned to analysis after two unsuccessful attempts with other analysts. The episode here reported occurred toward the end of the fourth year of his analysis. It seemed at first hardly connected with the patient's central complaint. This complaint had two major aspects. A widely diversified sexual life with many and attractive lady friends, facilitated by his social position, had followed a youthful failure in marriage; but the pleasure in these associations was limited by guilt toward his partners. None, he knew, would be able to retain his attention.

The patient's passing attachments had one feature in com-

---

5. See Hartmann (1951), who speaks of the multiple appeal of interpretations.

mon: the ladies, almost all of them somewhat lower in social status, would respond to him with feelings of devotion, and this devotion would stimulate a depressive reaction in him. He had to rescue them from the mortification which his future desertion would inflict upon them. This distilled presentation of a complex pattern which could be established only after several years of detailed scrutiny points to one of the unconscious determinants of the cycle. He himself is conqueror and victim, in part identified with the rejected partner, and he anticipates his own sadistic act by masochistic suffering. The whole sequence ultimately proved to be a reflection of the contrasting wishes of "eating" and "being eaten up."

I shall not enter into the further vicissitudes of this one group of symptoms, but limit myself to mentioning that the mechanism of identification had played a decisive part in his life. As if under fateful command, he had assumed shortcomings and pitfalls in the character and career of a successful father, who had achieved considerable recognition in a profession which he had pursued without having been trained for it. Because of his early failure, the father had been excluded from social and professional associations to which he would have been entitled by the position of his family and his own later achievements.

None of these limitations operated in the patient's life. His socioscholastic career—to coin a term adapted to the conditions under which he was brought up—was impeccable. He had gone to the right public school, and had been at one of the great universities. And yet he had joined none of the clubs to which he was expected to belong, but had sought association with one or two clubs in which members seemed to gather who, as a rule, had no access to the social set of which he was a part. He thus artificially created for himself the marginal position to which his father had been relegated. I might add that the choice of myself as analyst was determined by the same propensity: for an Englishman of his class it meant a conspicuous effort to turn to a foreigner of my kind.

The character of the precarious and marginal was apparent in other features. He suffered from a difficulty of recall, which affected his work less than his social contacts. He could frequently not recall the nature or topic of a recent conversation with one of his acquaintances. But even in his business activities, a sense of anxious tension maintained itself. He lived under the impression that a "bad memory" would prevent him from the full use of favorable opportunities.

At first it seemed that his memory problem mirrored his father's behavior. Immersed in the pressure of work, he appeared to the little boy preoccupied, distracted, and only half interested in the child's attempt to gain his attention. Gradually other determinants became apparent. We were able to establish a link between his bad memory and certain experiences concerning his genitals. Throughout the later years of his puberty he had been dissatisfied with his penis. In his early sexual exploits a feeling of "local inhibition" had prevailed. On slight provocation a physician whom he had met in the Navy arranged for a circumcision. After it, he felt as if liberated; the penis, he thought, had grown.

The episode of the analysis to which I refer and which covered a period of several months centered around two sets of experiences: the feeling of (memory) inferiority became heightened when the role which envy played in his life became meaningful to him. This envy centered at first on a sister, one year older, who since latency years had been the father's pet. She was recognizable as the prototype of many of his lady friends, but also supplied traits to his own personality. However, he had not identified himself with the radiant child, but with the suffering adolescent of later years. Envy also extended to his male competitors, mainly to members of the distinguished club which he had failed to join, and appeared in violent outbursts in which he would imagine how, in debates, he would destroy his adversaries by sarcastic remarks. If ever there was a doubt about the psychological meaning of sarcasm, this man's behavior and fantasies would eliminate it: the Greek root of the word means tearing apart with one's teeth.

Here we were on familiar ground. Memories of early rages, when he was kept waiting for food, fused with his mother's report on outbursts of the toddler, seemed not to fit the restrained gentleman of his later years, whose fastidiousness in eating was marked: meat had to be well done, sinews and gristles had to be carefully eliminated, so that eating was either a matter of indifference or an almost surgical procedure—once more a trait borrowed from his father and carefully integrated into the general restraint of the patient's manners. Material from dreams, unambiguous in their context and symbolic character, had long ago made clear that oral-aggressive tendencies had early predominated in his instinctual life. In his previous analyses this had been energetically stressed. In the period of analysis about which I report one of the leading themes had been the gradual realization that lethargy and paralysis appeared frequently when envy had been unsuccessfully suppressed. At this point the insight seemed to be near that various feelings of discomfort which pained the patient were equivalents of anxiety. The way which was to lead from the one point to the other seemed winding and extended. The emphasis shifted to the discovery of defects. His sarcasm was fed by a careful inspection of the opponent and what he feared was the opponent's retaliatory criticism, in the course of which his own defects—mainly his wanting memory—would be discovered.

It is at this point that in association to a dream the recollection of a childhood scene appeared in which his father inspected the patient's penis. The penis had been slightly inflamed and the foreskin had to be pushed away. It was on the mother's suggestion that this inspection had to be performed. Circumstances of a special kind permitted the dating of the episode. It must have occurred when the patient was four years of age, and all details seemed to fit into the picture we had gained. The slight adhesions of the foreskin (which twenty years later justified the circumcision) had been irritated by the masturbatory activity of the little boy—the masturbatory activity, I add, which had caused "intellectual impairment." In his association to the scene the patient who in his life and work had little contact with Jews reported suddenly and, as it were, abruptly that he had heard that certain "rabbis" who perform circumcisions on Jewish infants tend to bite off the foreskin. The interpretation was offered that as a child he had had the wish to bite off his father's penis and that he feared that his own genital would be bitten off by his father. The patient's reaction, however, was unexpected. He focused on one point: my remarks had implied that he had revealed a new piece of information, whereas he was convinced that he had not only always known about the scene of the inspection of the penis, but also that he had told me about it. Briefly, the *déjà raconté* experience (Freud, 1914a) appeared in the context of a memory rivalry.[6] Soon the connections became more meaningful. The feeling of memory insufficiency was suddenly experienced as pressure of the skull cap upon the brain, which was visualized as if it were compressed and hemmed in by this outer surrounding. The analogy with the glans penis and the quest for circumcision was unmistakable.

I cannot report on other interconnections in the material, but must limit myself to mentioning some which are directly related to the further piece of analytic material which I propose to report. The idea of circumcision was overdetermined: the foreskin represented at the same time a protection of the penis against attack, the protecting female and the patient's own femininity (Nunberg, 1947). As female he had been in vain competing with the sister for the father's love, after a period in which during a prolonged absence of the father he had felt extremely close to his mother and sexually attracted to her. The turning to the father, after the latter's return, culminated in a classical though transient obsessional-compulsive episode between seven and eight in which a ritual had to be adopted to protect the members of his family during the night. At the same time his intellectual interest had grown and found many outlets. While the prehistory of the patient's obsessional neurosis cannot be reported in detail, one episode which arose during this time of analysis must still be mentioned. In association to a dream in which a bird, whose name he could not recall, played a dominant part, he reported that during the years eight and nine he had been an eager student

6. For the dynamics of *déjà raconté*, see now Siegman (1956).

of the encyclopedia. While somewhat later the encyclopedia had attracted his sexual curiosity—particularly illustrations that showed exposed breasts—at this earlier age his interest had centered on an innocuous problem, on birds of prey. He studied their ecology, their behavior, and learned to distinguish ever rarer species. But even at that time he was already tortured by the difficulty in remembering their Latin names.

I interrupt this report. The choice of birds of prey as special objects of interest seemed overdetermined in several ways. It continued in sublimated form the older preoccupation with comparing the nature and sizes of male genitals. Moreover, beaks represented the fusion between phallic and oral-aggressive impulses whose derivations overshadowed his sexual life. These were also the years when he had first been forced to wear glasses, as his mother did, and the traditionally stressed sharpness of vision of birds of prey added a further incentive for exploration. In this attempt at sublimation the feeling of memory defect, i.e., the displacement of the feeling of defectiveness to the brain, made its appearance. This sign of intellectual inhibition entered his life at the time when his sister had found access to the father's interest by her intellectual exploits. The failure in sublimation was thus related to the envy of the sister, was self-punitive and a derivative of the conflict between the wish for and the fear of castration.

The sequence of material here reported suggests a number of generalizations on the relation of interpretation to the appearance of memories in the context of analytic work. In a schematic form we may distinguish various levels on which interpretations had been of influence. The atmosphere of prolonged analytic work had activated the patient's interest in his childhood in a general way. There had been times when this interest appeared as resistance, when he would repeat certain crucial screen memories on which he had worked in his previous analyses. This resistance, however, had not been operative at the time. Neither one of the memories, that of the inspection of the penis by the father and that of his interest in birds of prey, had ever been mentioned previously, at least not during his contact with me. The general activation of interest in his childhood may have facilitated the associative connection with the past, but this associative connection emerged in the context of the current conflict situation in which the role of envy had become an experience to him. Previous analytic interpretation may have facilitated the appearance of the association that rabbis perform circumcision by biting, with its obvious transference implications. But once more there had been no reference to oral material in the recent or even more distant course of the analysis. The material appeared because a previously repressed fantasy could at this time become conscious. The interpretations concerning the rivalry in his club life had established an understanding for the dynamics of aggressive rivalry in his mind. A situation was thus created in which impulses, long in abeyance, became more accessible and in which derivatives of repressed wishes could reach the preconscious. Interpretation, then, did not produce recall, but rather it established dynamic conditions under which recall became possible, conditions more similar to those which existed when the recalled scenes and events occurred.

The detailed analysis of current conflict situations and the recall of the past are therefore not accidentally but essentially interrelated, cannot exist without each other. Hence the impression that when the influence of instinctual forces and unconscious fantasies on current conflicts are analyzed, the reappearance of childhood material may follow spontaneously. We may thus schematically distinguish between the "dynamic interpretation" concerned mainly with conflicts in the current situation and "genetic interpretations" of various kinds (Hartmann and Kris, 1945). The continuum represented by these genetic interpretations may be characterized by an artificial, but possibly useful device: by characterizing extremes. One extreme would be represented by genetic interpretations pointing to archaic impulses, as they become accessible in current material. These impulses represent continuations of preverbal and nonverbal ideations, embedded in unconscious fantasies with later experiences.[7] The

7. The term "unconscious fantasy" is here not used in the sense defined by some authors who call the "original primary mental activity which usually remains unconscious . . . an unscious phantasy" (Riviere, 1952, p. 16).

other extreme would be represented by interpretations which try to establish a historical context between the various pieces of the patient's material. Next to numerous inferences drawn from all sources available in analysis, the inventory of always-remembered memory pictures (screen memories) and the recovered memories often foreshadowed in dreams are part of these interpretations, into which ultimately all interpretative work might be integrated. I believe that Freud (1937b) had this integration in mind when he said that ultimately interpretations are constructions (or reconstructions). The historical context into which these interpretations are fitted establishes a biographical picture. Even in the ideal case it is a biographical picture of a special kind, one which would not satisfy any requirements of ordinary biography. The nature and dynamic character of this biographical picture may become clearer if we approach our subject from another side.

PROBLEMS OF GENETIC INTERPRETATION

The discovery of the importance of ontogeny, first in the etiology of mental disorders and then in the development of personality, was one of Freud's most momentous steps and certainly the one least prepared by traditional views within the orbit of science. In no other area of psychoanalysis has the progress in knowledge been as continuous as in the understanding of the nature and vicissitudes of infancy and childhood. During the last thirty years the progress has gained in momentum, as if through the added interest in preoedipal development a barrier had suddenly been removed. The extraordinary richness of new insight, as it keeps accumulating, seems to defy any attempt at comprehensive classification. No such classification is intended when I here focus on a continuum characterized by its extremes, by the stress on *endopsychic* and the stress on *environmental* factors.

The dichtomy between these two approaches has its roots in Freud's early work. Shortly after he had become aware of the extreme importance of childhood experiences for the etiology of neuroses, he formulated a set of hypotheses which were "environmentalist" to the extreme: a seduction during childhood was viewed as cause of neurotic illness. Freud's assumptions went further. He thought that perversion in the seducer produced hysteria in the seduced. This hypothesis, which postulated a high incidence of adult (parental) perversion, enabled Freud to recognize first the improbability and shortly thereafter the incorrectness of his views. He himself described the crisis in his life and the emergence of new insight which evolved from the initial failure (Freud, 1950). Since his patients did not describe real events but reported fantasies, the study of fantasy life became essential. The study of these fantasies led to the discovery of the oedipus complex and to that of the various manifestations of infantile sexuality.

While the seduction hypothesis had maximized attention on concrete experiences to which the child was exposed, the later orientation was implicitly based on the supposition that relatively minimal external stimulation would produce the reactions observed; and these reactions, the working of the mental apparatus rather than concrete environmental conditions, were investigated in detail.

It is not my intention to trace the role of these alternative approaches in Freud's work. But it may be well to remind us of the changes his genetic constructions underwent in his clinical work. Detailed evidence seems available only for a period of fifteen years (1900–1915), and it seems appropriate to compare the cases of Dora and the Wolf-Man in this respect. The difference is not one which can be accounted for solely by the different duration of treatment. It is a difference in essence. In Dora's case (1905a), Freud's interest was focused on some general connections between her symptoms and her infantile experiences. In the case of the Wolf-Man (1918), a history of crucial conflicts is given, in which all then available knowledge on dynamic and genetic questions is combined. The Wolf-Man's development is not only seen as centered around phases of psychosexual development and their vicissitudes, but specific events are set in relation to each other. A dynamic biographical structure emerged which leads from event to event. But in the analysis of the Wolf-Man, Freud also made decisive advances in the understanding of repressed early fantasies of

a preverbal stage of development and laid the foundation for
the idea, which has since become one of the cornerstones
upon which much of our work rests: we take it for granted
that the impact of such preverbal imprints may determine the
modes of later reactions to environmental stimuli. The question whether at the age of one and a half years the patient had
witnessed parental intercourse or whether we are faced with a
primal scene fantasy was one which occupied Freud's thinking
for some time.[8] Out of this dichotomy arose Freud's formulations on psychic reality, which have proved their value, and
these formulations gave the search for unconscious fantasies
of a preverbal period their standing in analysis.

The advances in our understanding of such early unconscious fantasies through Melanie Klein's contribution are well
known. Much of her earlier work has become widely accepted
and many fantasy formations to which she first drew attention
have become familiar configurations in clinical studies. The
points of controversy have at the same time sharpened in other
respects. It is less the stress on endopsychic factors—somewhat
modified in her latest contributions—than the disregard of
maturational processes which constitutes the difference between her approach and that of others.[9]

Much less frequently is it stressed that in our notion of environmental conditions an increase in knowledge has occurred,
which has deeply affected our theoretical assumptions and
our clinical work. We are no longer satisfied to view the development of the child in terms of his psychosexual maturation only; we find that the development of ego functions and
object relations, to use convenient headings, are of equal and
intrinsic importance. Indeed, the history of the Wolf-Man's infantile neurosis would appear in a different light if it were observed today—by Freud.

The progress to which I refer has come from many sources.
Contributions from psychoanalytic work with adults, with children, combined therapies of mother and child in child guid-

8. It is a problem which twenty years earlier, in the "Project for a Scientific Psychology" (1895) had already captured his imagination (Freud, 1950).

9. See in this connection particularly Lewin's succinct comments (1950).

ance and treatment centers, and finally the impact of analytic views on the study of child development have all had their share.

It is at this point that I want to state an impression, or even advance a thesis. This increase in our knowledge, I believe, permits us to understand in greater detail the ways in which interpretations aimed at demonstrating in the patient's behavior the survival of deeply repressed, largely preverbal impulses can be enriched and supplemented by the recovery of memories.[10] Since our reconstructions tend to encompass more details and have become more specific, we are better equipped to learn how various levels of genetic interpretations "dovetail." It is one of the areas in analytic work in which the observation in the analytic situation once more discloses its stimulating potentialities as investigative procedure.

I first turn to findings to which child analysis has made the decisive contribution: to the importance of the early relationship of parent and child and more specifically the reaction of the child to peculiarities of the parent's personality. In our analytic work with adult patients we are only rarely able to include this factor. In my experience we succeed only in the course of long and on the whole successful analytic treatments, since interpretations which take the nature of the parents' personality into account obviously require particular caution and a wealth of affirmative impressions, such as in this instance only the prolonged analysis of reactions in the transference situation can provide. Only this caution can protect us against the distorting element of memory, which is hardly ever deeper ingrained than in the changing facets which characterize the report of adult patients on their parents.[11]

10. In terms of the controversy between the British school of psychoanalysis (Glover, 1927/28, 1945; Bibring, 1947; Zetzel, 1956; and others) this concerns not the question of the "existence" or "importance" of certain unconscious fantasies, but the criteria that decide at which point they become accessible in analytic material—a question which in turn is related to the "time" of their formation.

11. Global and stereotypical characterizations such as those given in anamnestic interviews prove almost regularly to dissolve under the analytic microscope. For a clinical illustration, see chapter 14; for one frequently neglected root of the changing images of the mother in the variations of her own reactions to the growing child, see chapter 8.

And yet, when we succeed in encompassing such details of a "traumatic situation" in our reconstructive work, we gain an essential and sometimes possibly crucial supplement. In the analysis of an, on the whole, successful but inhibited man of forty whose dominant symptoms were uneasiness in a number of specific situations, the attempt to reach an understanding of the origin of scoptophilic impulses played a significant part. These impulses had not invaded his adult sexual life, but were intertwined with attempts to master and control the human environment. The obvious relation to the displacement of oral impulses, the wish to incorporate with his eyes, was important in his relation both to currently significant objects and their infantile imagoes, particularly in his relevant but sharply circumscribed feminine identifications. But such elements of understanding were finally supplemented by one of a peculiar nature, dimly connected with memory images. One component of his scoptophilic propensities led to a specific phase in his childhood relationship to a mother who, as "beloved stranger," had later played a dominant part throughout his life. Behind this contradictory image in which closeness and distance were strangely intertwined, there emerged the reflection of a period when the mother, under the impact of a period of depression, found it difficult to relate to her child by means other than by her facial expression, which the boy learned to decipher.

Puzzled by the nature of these recovered circumstances, I discussed several years ago the type of reconstructive assumptions here involved with Anna Freud. To my astonishment, she mentioned that she had observed a "searching look" and an emphasis on visual contact with people in the treatment of children whose mothers suffered from various intensities of depression, and subsequent observations in the Hampstead Child-Therapy Clinic confirmed this finding.

One might at this point speculate as to antecedents of this reaction. We have recently been reminded of the fact that in the nursing situation the child's gaze is frequently centered on the mother's face, and that the ability to react to the human face as a configuration of forms is part of the child's early endowment (Spitz, 1955). May we not assume that oral and visual incorporations grow out of the same situational setup, and normally merge? The searching look, in the last analysis connected with the notion of the breast, would in the material of the adult patient appear colored and overshadowed by oral needs. I continue my speculation in assuming that if the nursing situation offers markedly less than the needed gratification, if there is—to speak in analytic shorthand—a breast but no maternal smile, then the two pathways of object relation, oral and visual incorporation, may become separated.

The child who feeds well may still be searching with his eyes as if the visual hunger remained forever pressing. The searching eye of toddlers in institutions is an unforgettable impression, even for the casual visitor.[12] Moreover, it seems that the historical setting in which extreme (i.e., perverse) voyeurism (or exhibitionism) originates might well confirm (or at least not contradict) the assumption of an early (and possibly specific) deficit in the nursing situation. In the case which I reported above, no such extreme disturbance had developed. As far as I could see from the analytic material, the mother's depression had not been severe, nor did it occur during the earliest infancy of the patient, but probably only after he was three years old (or alternatively it had gained importance only during the early phases of the patient's phallic development). The child's reaction had soon become part of an effort to sublimate the instinctual forces involved—an attempt which was only partially successful. The recovery of the memory concerned with the patient's relation to his mother contributed essentially to an understanding of this inhibition in sublimation, and thus to the analysis of the situation in which the symptom had established itself.

Another illustration refers to a traumatic situation, the impact of which was fully appreciated only during the last decade—the separation of mother and child. In the setting of Freud's theory the traumatic character of separation had been

12. I am indebted to R. Coleman and S. Provence for reports on their work on institutionalized children. For an observation of the searching look as distress signal in a two-year-old, see my own observations reported in chapter 7.

anticipated. When he developed in 1926 one of his most pivotal constructs, the sequence of crucial danger situations in the child's life, there was no awareness among analysts—and here I can bear witness as a contemporary—to what typical concrete situations this would apply. Nobody realized that the fears of losing the object and the object's love were formulae to be implemented by material which now seems to us self-evident beyond any discussion. We have become aware of the meaning which separation from the mother plays at various points in the child's development and will not hesitate to use it in our reconstructions, i.e., in establishing the frame into which we fit the material reaching us during the analytic process by the very extended set of avenues on which the patient communicates with us.

The early and fully repressed development of a negative oedipus complex in the life history of a patient could be traced back into his childhood years. But only when the need to relinquish one allegiance and to turn to the opposite one had been understood as a dominant pattern in his life, could the vicissitudes of his adult existence be traced back to a peculiar constellation of events, which threw light on its genesis. Before the recovery of the memories which I shall report, we knew that his mother had disappointed him. We assumed that he had reacted to the birth of a sister at the age of three and a half with a violent rageful revival of oral-aggressive impulses, presumably as to a repetition of "the weaning trauma." Slight but recurrent laryngeal spasms, allegedly on an allergic basis, and a compulsive symptom regulating inbreathing and outbreathing as part of retention and expulsion of objects during latency seemed to fit well to this assumption. But the way which led from these symptoms and discharge pathways to his characterological problems seemed obscure until a group of recovered memories appeared. The three-and-a-half-year-old had been suddenly separated from his mother. She, who had been wholly and warmly devoted to her first child, went to the hospital to give birth to a little girl. During the absence of the mother the boy developed a febrile illness which proved to be diphtheria. The mother accelerated her return from the hospital, but she either came the day when the patient had to be hospitalized, or even after he had been taken away. In the child's mind there survived the impression of a long-lasting separation. But it remained unclear who had gone and who was left. He turned to his father until further traumatic experiences drove him back to the mother's spell, but retained in life a need to change allegiances, to shift from one side of the controversy to the other, until, only in analysis, he found the way to compromise. The evaluation of the significance of the recollection had become possible only by our general knowledge of the impact of separation on children. Without that knowledge the memory might have suggested various causal relationships. One might have stressed the sibling rivalry as a central theme, or the idea that the absence of the mother had been experienced as retaliation for libidinal or aggressive desires, and a number of other possible interconnections. Although these and several other interpretations went through my mind and some were used, as subsidiary themes, as it were, the central avenue remained the active repetition of the passive experience of separation. Only gradually another line of interpretation was added, one which had suggested itself before the recollection appeared, but which at the time seemed not sufficiently connected with the pattern of joining and relinquishing allegiances. I had thought at the time that these interpretations would at best strengthen skepticism and resistance: I refer to interpretations which pointed to the connection of oral incorporation and expulsion of objects which covered both his somatic symptoms and his pattern of life. After the recollection the way seemed open to this expansion of our area of understanding (see Case 1 in chap. 14).

This example is not meant to illustrate that the "deep" interpretation of the archaic impulse group, i.e., the propensity to incorporate and expel, should necessarily follow the memory recovery. Any such suggestion would seem to me pedantic and unwarranted since it overlooks the nature of communication between analyst and patient. Interpretations of and inferences about opposing tendencies in object relations, specific manifestations of ambivalence, the importance of oral experiences in specific current situations had naturally been part of the preceding analytic work. How far such interpretations are carried at each given point obviously remains a matter of choice and is in the context of this presentation of secondary interest, provided that one outcome is avoided. The deep interpretation should not supply the patient with an empty "id vernacular" which can easily be used for resistance, and thus help to maintain repression. In the illustration offered this repression would presumably have been directed against the memory recovery. The recovery of memory, however, is only one of the reactions which might be barred by resistance. The much more general reactions concern the conviction that the patient must gain. The more archaic the material is that appears in the analytic process, the more will its derivatives be spread over wide areas of behavior. The broader the basis from which the specific reconstruction of early experiences and archaic impulses is reached, the greater is the chance of reawakening their full impact.[13]

The area where the most effective link between reconstruction and experience can be established is subject to great variations according to factors in the patient's personality and illness which I am at a loss to specify. To mention contrasting examples: I remember one instance in which the aggressive and teasing interplay between mother and child during early feeding was reconstructed mainly from the consistency and gradual sharpening of verbalizations in the transference situation—a reconstruction accidentally and spontaneously confirmed by an early observer, who had been in the house when the mother breast-fed the patient. In another instance, the discussion of the long-suppressed dissatisfaction in life was during later stages of analysis accompanied by burning sensations in the oral cavity and the palate. Interpretations of the traumatic experience in the suppression of rage, focused in earlier remembered events from the period of toilet training, could thus plausibly be extended into the nursing situation. In both these instances, however, the patient's conviction could arise

13. For a somewhat different emphasis, see Lampl-de Groot (1952).

only on the basis of experienced link between past and present. Through the lifting of anticathectic energies which makes the conviction possible (Lewin, 1950), the reconstructive effort gains new impetus. In the patient with the separation experience, the continued course of the analysis led to a more specific insight into what was incorporated and what expelled and the variations of patterns which can be studied when an unconscious fantasy is followed on its secret progression throughout a patient's life.

We assume that the fantasy whose reflections and reverberations we thus study retains reactions to and imprints of a traumatic situation. Hence the question now presents itself: what properties of this situation can reconstructive work in psychoanalysis hope to recapture? It is a question which, hardly posed, reminds us of intriguing limitations in our knowledge. Almost to our surprise we find outselves unable to answer questions which, we feel, are bound to be of considerable clinical relevance. Thus it seems that we are not always, and only rarely with the desirable sharpness, able to distinguish between the effects of two kinds of traumatic situations: between the effects of a single experience, when reality powerfully and often suddenly impinges on the child's life—the shock trauma, as I should like to call it—and the effect of long-lasting situations, which may cause traumatic effects by the accumulation of frustrating tensions—the strain trauma, as I would like to say. It is well known and has especially been emphasized by Anna Freud (1951, p. 157) that what the analytic patient reports as an event which occurred once appears in the life of the growing child as a more or less typical experience, which may have been repeated many times. Her suggestion, then, is that analysts tend to be misled by the telescopic character of memory. On the other hand, the single dramatic shock, e.g., seduction at an early age, usually does not appear in sharp outline; [14] the experience is overlaid with its aftermath, the guilt, terror, and thrill elaborated in fantasy, and the defense against these fantasies. We are misled if we believe that we are

14. For an example of this kind, see Rosen (1955).

able, except in rare instances, to find the "events" of the afternoon on the staircase when the seduction happened: we are
dealing with the whole period in which the seduction played a
role—and in some instances this period may be an extended
one. The problem is further complicated by the fact that the
further course of life seems to determine which experience
may gain significance as a traumatic one.

To illustrate the complexity of these processes I choose an
example which concerns not an actual but a prospective analytic patient. I should like to report on a brief sequence of experiences of a child and her dog, which were observed over a
period of several months. The data I offer stem from a longitudinal study at Yale University, Child Study Center, in which
a team of pediatricians, social workers, nursery school
teachers, and psychoanalysts attempt to follow the development of nonselected and hence presumably normal children
from birth on.

Dorothy satisfies in all respects the criteria of normal development. The well-developed and determined two-year-old
was, as the first-born, in the center of her parents' attention.
The marriage went through stormy episodes, and the child
learned early to find her way between the struggling parents,
to keep the mother closely attached to herself—she frequently
slept in her bed—and the father in the position of an interested suitor. There were definite areas in which she sided with
her father. He was an outdoor person, a lover of animals, and
Dorothy shared his interest. Except for a short period when
she was twelve to fourteen months old, she did not follow her
mother into her phobic tendencies. These tendencies included
an old dog phobia, reduced to a violent dislike of dogs.

When Dorothy was two years old, a brother was born.
Though the mother accorded to the newborn much attention,
the ties to her daughter were not loosened. Four months later,
shortly after the family had moved to a new home, the father
brought a small dog and cat home. Dorothy became very attached to the dog. She was constantly involved with him and
her body showed at the time innumerable scratches, which
were due to the dog's outbursts in response to her teasing love

play. The dog's attacks were not limited to Dorothy: he chewed the cat's tail, so that the father had to cut off the tail. During the same period—when Dorothy was twenty-six to twenty-nine months old—the relation of the parents to each other was a particularly stormy one, with frequent fights, in which Dorothy was using and sharpening her technique of both understandingly adapting to an environment in which she had a pivotal position and of manipulating the situation with some determination. Those who observed the child in the nursery school during these months were struck by two features, Dorothy showed extraordinary understanding for the emotional needs of the people around her. She was always aware of the needs of other children, and capable of poignant verbalizations. At the same time she showed an unusual determination (already manifest earlier) which seemed to spring from a substructure of stubbornness disguised by the engaging surface.

It was during this period (October) that her paternal grandfather died. Dorothy was then twenty-nine months old. Two months later the puppy was run over by a car and had to be buried. The family reacted strongly to the accident, the father with agitation, the mother with guilt, since she had not kept the dog leashed. In Dorothy's mind, the deaths of grandfather and dog were soon condensed. Immediately after the dog's death she had spoken about it in the nursery school (early December), but late in January the death and separation had gained for her a greater significance. For some time I had been particularly interested in Dorothy, and functioned in the nursery school as an assistant teacher. From September on, that is, from Dorothy's entry into the nursery school, I had been in regular touch with both her and her mother, so that the child seemed particularly attached to me. From mid-December to late in January I was kept away by one thing and another, and when Dorothy saw me again, her reaction clearly indicated that she had missed me; she greeted me with the words: "My dog has gone away, where Nonny is, very far." It is significant that she had substituted the pet name of the maternal grandmother, whom she saw daily, for that of the paternal grandfather, but equally indicative that she had equated separation from me with the thought that I might have died.

The attachment to the dog had not vanished in spite of the fact that shortly after its accident the father had introduced a new and different pet, a parakeet with whom Dorothy engaged in excited games, in this instance supported and aided by her mother. But the father must have realized that the child's mind was still occupied with the dead dog. Early in February a stray dog greeted by Dorothy with great pleasure joined the family for a few days. After its disappearance the father brought home a new dog, which had been given to him by a man whose wife had to be hospitalized (for hysterectomy). Dorothy welcomed the dog with great excitement. Four days after its arrival she was heard to communicate to one of the teachers part of the fantasy context which surrounded the new pet: *"My doggie died, my Mommy has a new baby—in the hospital."* She thus responded to the new dog with reinforced longing for the old one and with a fantasy taking her back to the time when her brother was born. A stimulus for the reminiscent thought may well be the fact that the former owner of the dog, whom Dorothy did not know personally, was in the hospital. The memory of separation, the fear of death, and the fear of her own death wishes were thus condensed—and the fact that the new dog was, to her, a child from father was denied by the double reference: she, Dorothy, had lost the dog, and mother had the baby.

This interpretation was firmly supported by a large number of data, and particularly by the mother's reaction. Her resentment turned against the new dog, which father and daughter shared, and she declared spontaneously that the fact that Dorothy did not share her own apprehension of dogs made her feel jealous, and made her realize that father and daughter were "ganging up" against her. It was a genuine outburst, uncontaminated by psychological indoctrination, which had not penetrated to the educational and economic stratum of the family.

Let me conclude by reporting that when the new dog's leg was hurt in an accident and he had to be left for a short period with the veterinarian, Dorothy developed her first acute fear of her otherwise beloved pediatrician, whom she had known since birth. But once more the sequence of events was confusing. A few weeks before the dog's accident, mother's menstrual pad had for the first time attracted Dorothy's attention. She was then thirty-two months of age.

May I engage your interest in an experiment in thought: let us imagine how after twenty years the recollection of the material here reported in considerable simplification may appear in Dorothy's analysis. The network of overdeterminations seems almost infinite: the wish for a child from father, the death wish against the mother, the fear about both sexual and destructive impulses, and finally the fear of castration, which seems age-adequately added and superimposed, are likely to baffle the future analyst's imagination.

In Dorothy's case we can follow the development of the transformation to which the memory of the experiences with the pet was exposed one step further. During her fourth and fifth year of life Dorothy was seen in play-therapy sessions, from four years and four months on regularly, three times a week by a young analyst under experienced supervision.[15] Early in this contact material concerning Dorothy's interest in dogs had appeared. It gained momentum when her dog, which had grown too big, had to be given away by the father and replaced by a smaller dog. Dorothy recalled on this occasion the death of her first dog. She could not verbalize and reexperience her affect fully. However, in describing her feeling, she said, "I feel like putting my head into a bucket with water." Whatever the source of the metaphor, it clearly expressed the painful affect in ascribing the tears to external influence. The thoughts originally associated with the death of the dog were not recalled, but the fear of Nonny's death, who had lately suffered from high blood pressure, reappeared. Even clearer and more significant was a second connection. The death of the dog was no longer closely connected to the loss of the fantasy child from father, but appeared as con-

15. The exploratory treatment was conducted by Dr. S. Perlswig under supervision by Dr. S. Ritvo.

nected to the loss of a penis, dimly linked to disappointment in the mother. In Dorothy's current conflict, the rivalry with her brother stood at that time in the foreground.

This simple example illustrates some steps in the elaboration of reactions to an early experience. The transformation, which occurred between the ages of two and a half and four and a half, might have had many intermediary stages, which we did not recapture. It seems likely that the transformation we observed is itself only preparatory to a further (gradual?) repression of the whole set of memories which, I suspect, might occur early in latency. But the complexity of the steps we observed makes us once more aware of the nature of reconstructive work in analysis. In one sense, one may say it is a hopeless task. Indeed it is, if it were our intention to reconstruct what had happened in Dorothy's life in the period of five months, during which the events with her pet occurred. But reconstructive work in analysis cannot aim at such a goal: its purpose is more limited and yet much vaster. The material of actual occurrences, of things as they happen, is constantly subjected to the selective scrutiny of memory under the guide of the inner constellation. What I here call selection is itself a complex process. Not only were the events loaded with meaning when they occurred; each later stage of the conflict pattern may endow part of these events or their elaboration with added meaning. But these processes are repeated throughout many years of childhood and adolescence and finally integrated into the structure of the personality. They are molded, as it were, into patterns, and it is with these patterns, rather than with the events, that the analyst deals.

Let me illustrate this point by some amplification of an example previously offered. It concerns the little boy who succumbed to diphtheria while his mother was away for her delivery and whom we met as a man with shifting allegiances. This pattern of behavior did not result from the infantile experience, but derived from the interaction of this infantile experience with later events. The years after the illness were years of extreme marital discord. The parents were involved in almost incessant nightly fighting in which, in more than one instance, the little boy felt the impulse to protect his mother against the violence of an attacker to whom he felt dedicated. This period was followed by years of separation, when the father had deserted the family with another woman, until, during the later years of latency, the family was reunited once more. This is the way in which even the single dramatic experience is built into the sequence of time, and merges into the course of the life history out of which, by reconstructive work, some episodes can be regained; it will be those episodes which have become dynamically operative, because they became— when they occurred, or later in life, at one of its crucial crossroads—invested with greatest "meaning." The memories of such events seem then to become nodal points. Hence the defense against the revival of certain memories becomes essential: anticathectic investment is directed against the reemergence of the derivatives of instinctual forces and the affects attached to the memory image.

Genetic interpretations aim at these investments rather than at the "original events": hence the well-known fact that the reconstruction of childhood events may well be, and I believe regularly is, concerned with some thought processes and feelings, which did not necessarily "exist" at the time the "event" took place. They may either never have reached consciousness or may have emerged at a later time, during "the chain of events" to which the original experience became attached.[16] Through reconstructive interpretations they tend to become part of the selected set of experiences constituting the biographical picture which in favorable cases emerges in the course of analytic therapy.

Conclusions

This seems to be the point at which we may finally, or at least explicitly, turn to some general aspects which this survey

16. See chapter 11, where this topic is discussed in some detail. When Freud formulated this principle for the first time (1916/17) he obviously was already under the impact of the analysis of the Wolf-Man [which lasted from 1910–1914, but was not published until 1918].

suggests. The recovery of childhood memories is part of the struggle between the ego and the id, and of another struggle, a rearguard struggle, as it were, which takes place "within" the ego itself.

In most instances the recovery of childhood memories is, as I said, an inconspicuous affair and at least initially not necessarily connected with any deeply moving experiences. The patient may have mentioned the particular recollection in an aside, as something he had always remembered. When the importance of the memory has gradually become acceptable to him, he may show some disappointment, which seems most marked in training analyses. The analysand had expected a startling revelation and seems to resent that what he considers a familiar reminiscence is now being advanced to key position in the biographical reconstruction of his childhood. Almost thirty years ago Glover (1927/28) seems to have expected that with the change in our views on the function of repression, this attitude would lose in poignancy, an expectation which my own experience does not confirm. While the hunger for dramatic revelations still persists, sometimes as an expression of passive desires, dramatic memory recoveries have probably become even rarer since interpretations tend to be better planned, more cohesive, and since surprise is considered a reaction, though germane to the inquisitive mind of the analyst, yet one which he does not intentionally elicit in his patients. We do not as a rule want to catch patients by surprise, we do not want to shock them into reactions or recall.

It seems therefore necessary to distinguish between memories which suddenly emerge from repression and memories which had been preconsciously available before they entered the patient's communication in analysis. They were, however, not sufficiently invested, stood outside of circumscribed mental contexts, and could not be mobilized without further instigation. In practice a sharp distinction between these two cases is only rarely possible. In theory the difference may lie in the reaction to recognition. The formula "what can be mobilized in recognition must have been preconscious" seems valid (see chap. 11).

The distinction between the two cases is made difficult by the fact that a constant flow of derivatives from repressed material enters the preconscious ego, especially during the analytic process; these drivatives, we say, move into the reach of interpretations. Of the variety of such transitions only one has been particularly studied by Freud (1914b), the phenomenon of *déjà raconté,* of which an instance was here reported. My patient's recollection of the inspection of the penis by his father had, I assume, gradually become available to the preconscious, was possibly for some time uninvested or cut off from other connections, and could then, on further instigation by analytic work, become part of a trend of thought, i.e., part of the integrative function of the ego, and thus appear in the patient's associations.

This description is based on the assumption of the regular or frequent interaction of repression and other mechanisms of defense.[17] Freud suggested that other defense mechanisms may have to operate where, for one reason or another, repression failed to eliminate the dangerous impulse, drive representation, or associated notion. Some of these mechanisms are more archaic than repression, of simpler construction, but not necessarily less effective or less powerful as sources of resistance. Their "strength," to continue in metaphorical terms, is difficult to assess, since in neurotic illness they tend to be sheltered by the main line of fortifications, behind the wall that we call repression. Freud's general assumption (1926) applied to the problem of memory recovery. "Forgetting impressions, scenes, or experiences," he wrote (1914a, p. 148), "nearly always reduces itself to shutting them off [*Absperrung*]." The words "shutting them off" [in earlier translations rendered as "dissociation"] here clearly stand for "isolation," a mechanism studied by Freud in his later work. Isolation excludes certain experiences from associative connections (which are said to be "suppressed" or "interrupted"), and can therefore not be "reproduced" in ordinary thought process (Freud, 1926, p. 120).

At this point a slight readjustment of current assumptions

17. For the following, see also Gero (1951, 1953) and Gero and Rubinfine (1955).

seems required, one already foreshadowed by Fenichel's treatment of the subject (1945) and by the use of the term "isolation" in current clinical understanding. Some degree of isolation is part of normal mental life and of all or almost all pathological configurations of defense. Isolation as resistance during the analytic process, then, can be studied not only in obsessional neuroses but in every analytic treatment at one time and in one form. The isolation of memories in the preconscious would be only one such instance.

The interaction between repression and isolation constitutes a parallel to the classical instance in which the appearance in consciousness of the formerly repressed (or isolated) thought is unsuccessfully warded off by a derivative of the former anticathexis; the thought appears in negative form. Repression has been substituted by negation as a reflection—in this instance, a feeble one. In other, less well-described instances, the memory, when it first appears, remains vague. A doubt may arise as to whether or not the event that is remembered actually occurred. I assume that in this instance repression is supplemented and followed by an attempt to use denial.[18] Much less often is it possible to study in the recovery of memories the interaction of repression and projection; the instances that I can recall seem to be particularly complex. In the simplest of these cases the memory is attributed to the analyst as one of his constructions.

The dynamics of memory recovery might be said to reflect, in some not too direct and not too regular sense, the functional distribution of various defenses in each personality, and particularly the interaction between repression and the more archaic methods, which in some individuals have remained part of their central equipment for the solution of conflicts. Although a wealth of clinical material is available on the interaction of various defenses in the great nosological pictures, only one group of afflictions has been studied in great detail from this angle: I refer to Lewin's (1950) classical study of elations. Through the homology between the interaction of re-

18. Alternatively one might think of "undoing"—but there are reasons, too complex to discuss here, which make me prefer the assumption of the working of denial.

pression with other mechanisms in memory recovery and in the structure of neuroses in general, the study of the former has strengthened two clinical impressions of possibly wider significance. The interaction of repression and isolation, which I here considered as part of the normal process of recovery of the repressed, is particularly significant in obsessional neuroses, where isolation seems omnipresent and specifically directed against the affect charge. (Hence the tempting danger of intellectualization in the treatment of obsessional characters.) However, it seems that not only the function of isolation but also that of repression can be particularly excessive. A certain proliferation of anticathectic energies, one may speculate, could well be related to the premature ego development, so frequently detected in the development of obsessional neurotics and obsessional characters, and to the interconnected need to invest large amounts of aggressive energy in anticathectic function. From the archaic equipment, of which, as Freud stresses, isolation is a part (in its derivation from the motor sphere of "do not touch"), particularly projection seems either to survive or, in the course of regression, to have acquired renewed power. One might assume that hysterias would offer an opposite picture—apart from the specific instance of phobias—but since hysteria as a clinical entity seems at this stage ever more amorphous, it is best to state that wherever clearly hysterical symptomatology plays a central part, repression is dominant, sometimes like an iron curtain, which, once one knows the mechanism, can be lifted easily, though previously it had seemed immovable. Although the subsidiary mechanisms are highly variable, it is my impression that at least in a group of cases in which typical conversion symptoms also tend to occur, particularly one mechanism of the archaic equipment often plays a subsidiary and perhaps in some instances an altogether important role: I refer to denial.

I cannot attempt to continue such a survey. Suffice it to say that the interaction of numerous archaic mechanisms can be studied in the transition from cases with clearer neurotic to those with clearer psychotic pictures, for instance, particularly where the combination of projection and denial in paranoid psychoses might be prototypical. The function of this interaction was indicated by Waelder (1951). However, in this connection it seems relevant to stress that the access to the understanding of some psychotic afflictions seems open only if one assumes that the hypertrophy of a large variety of archaic mechanisms of defense is at least sometimes concomitant with a dysfunction of repression. Memory phenomena studied in some psychotic children (Mahler and Elkisch, 1953), the memory hypertrophy in some schizophrenic process in adults, and the stream of reminiscences with which some borderline patients overwhelm the analytic process—all are well-known instances relevant to this point.[19]

I have briefly mentioned these phenomena, since a conclusion pertinent to the subject of this paper presents itself. The closer we approach the area where repression has lost its power as central defense, the less can the transition from past to present become one of the indicators of progress in analytic work and the less significant is the recovery of memories and the emergence of a biographical picture. The core of its therapeutic effectiveness rests in the dynamics of the lifting of anticathexes. The interpretation establishes the situation in which the lifting becomes possible. Then derivatives of repressed impulse groups enter the preconscious, the investment of the subsidiary defenses are lessened, and the released energies now at the disposal of the ego can be used for its integrative function. Thus memories enter the stream of thought, first in associative connections from which they had been excluded (Nunberg, 1931), then they take their place in the picture of the personal past, at which reconstructive work aims. The full investment of the causal connections established by the insight into the personal history in turn protects the preconsciously available memories against disappearing from the realm of the ego. Without that protection they can easily once more become part of the id, by repression and by other

19. For a clinical example, see Kramer (1955). For the vivid description of the "unnaturally strong" memory of a famous patient, see a letter of Charles Lamb (February 14, 1834, to Miss Freyer) in which he describes the "reminiscences" of his sister Mary, the matricidal psychotic with whom he had shared his life.

mechanisms, which will draw them back into the whirl of the primary process. Such vicissitudes of remembering and —to coin a term fashioned in *Through the Looking Glass*—of "unre-membering" are part and parcel of almost every analysis.

Memory recovery is thus part of a circular process. While it has been traditionally stressed that the lifting of repression (or, as I would say, of anticathexes) strengthens the ego, it is equally true that increasing the strength of the ego facilitates further reduction of anticathectic energies.[20] The emergence of insight, related as it is to the integrative functions of the ego, has its place in the center of these transactional events.

Reconstructive work offers insight into causal connections on various levels. To take the best documented area of ex-amples: the existence of traits or symptoms, which remain enigmatic when seen in the context of present behavior, may become meaningful once the veil that covers the past has been lifted (Hartmann and Kris, 1945). To refer to one of my illus-trations: the coexistence of the feeling of memory defect and the difficulties in object choice in my patient seemed isolated and unconnected. The recovered past established various in-terconnections and the memory concerning the preoccupation with birds of prey during latency brought an attitude and ex-periences into the analytic discussion, in which the investment of certain thoughts and ideas became particularly clear, as if a nodal point in a complex texture had been exposed. A similar insight into the genetic interconnection between two sets of symptoms, between upper respiratory complaints and the compulsion to change allegiances, appeared in another illus-tration where the recovered episode of the separation from the mother and the question of who was deserted and who the deserter played a decisive role.

In speaking of insight, the reaction of the analyst should be distinguished from that of the patient. The recovered memo-ries strengthen the analyst's conviction, fortify him against doubt, and may help him to gear his subsequent interpreta-tions more closely to such points in which the past seems to live on in the present.

20. Alexander (1948) and Alexander and French (1946) have stressed this point, and view recall only as a manifestation of increased ego strength.

In the patient himself the development of insight is once more a highly complex process and one subject to many vicissitudes [see chap. 13]. The intellectual and emotional acceptance should be sharply distinguished. To put it in the briefest formula: not only memories are screened and repressed; the same is true of the affective experience. I borrow the term of screen affects from Lewin's presentation of these issues (1950), to which I have nothing to add. To transform insight from an intellectual into a total experience is one of the essential parts of "working through"—hence the similarity between the patient's work in analysis and the process of grief and mourning. In fact, it seems that a repressed unconscious fantasy can be treated like a possession or a love object. One can sometimes actually observe how certain memories acquire such meanings. They may be treated as treasured possessions invested with energies derived from anal experience (see chap. 14) and may alternatively or concomitantly represent a part of the self, which is unwillingly relinquished to scrutiny.

Lewin (1939) has convincingly described how the sense of the real is added to that of insight when the sense of certitude is established by the reawakening of the past as a revival of infantile omniscience. When anticathexes are fully lifted, when autonomous ego functions are fully invested, the sense of conviction may be seen as essential progress in the individual's mental organization. While the dynamics of the process of assimilation of insight are thus clearly outlined, individual variations as to the course of this process and as to its final result are great, and there is at this time hardly any evidence available which would allow for generalizations.

In favorable or, one might as well say, optimal cases—they naturally need not be the cases in which analytic work produces the most dramatic therapeutic changes—some historical reconstructions, or even the total biographical picture, become part of the patient's changed self representation, and the patient remains aware of the relation of these changes to the analytic material. Part of this awareness concerns the preanalytic distortion of his past by defensive operations. After analysis the once recognized lines that connect past and present form a pattern which the patient is able to experience as familiar, and which in exceptional cases he may even be able to expand. These are, however, on the whole not too frequent results, and I see no reason why one should necessarily aim at such an outcome of analytic work, except possibly in training analyses. At least some analysts successfully pursue the arduous task of self-analysis, either as a concomitant part of their work or at times of personal crises. In this connection a wide area of awareness of their past has proved of value. But even here detailed information is at this time hardly available. The other extreme is represented by patients whose recollection of what occurred in their analyses is blurred; and yet some of these people seem to have no reason to complain about results. However, I would postulate that with many of these patients at one time during the course of treatment, particularly during the latter phase of the working through process, the effect of reconstructive work was operative. This period was apparently only a transient one, lasting for some time, until the acquired insight became warded off once more.[21]

At the present stage of our knowledge one may well find it difficult and futile to indicate clinical or structural conditions which favor one outcome or the other. But it is by no means a question which needs to remain outside the area of investigation. Material may be derived from several sources, from second analyses in general, particularly if analytic work with the same patient is resumed after several years of interruption. Moreover, empirical research in psychoanalysis could well expand its limits, and particularly if conducted by teams of investigators, it may in some instances help to replace opinion by decision. One might think of systematic analytic catamneses—utopian as such a suggestion may still seem at this time. In such investigations the question might be studied how after analysis the insight into his personal history has remained operative in each patient's experience or to what extent it has become blurred, and in what detailed way both outcomes are

---

21. This clearly does not take into account the interaction of various other therapeutically operative factors which constitute psychoanalytic treatment. Some of these other factors bring about the "corrective experience," the role of which has been stressed by Alexander.

related to therapeutic results in general and particularly to significant changes in the patient's self representation. It is in this area where I expected for some time a high positive correlation between the continued investment of the personal analytic biography and the effects of treatment. But when I examined the basis of this expectation, I found that I had stringent evidence at my disposal in only one instance, due to an unintentional experiment in psychoanalytic catamnesis, which had remained fixed in my mind.

Some years ago I prepared an extensive case history of a patient, of which I finally used a fragment for publication. At the time when I intended to publish it, I decided to let the patient, whose analysis had been concluded five years earlier read the whole report. The patient reported a feeling of full and intense familiarity and indicated which interpretations had seemed to him particularly crucial at the time. In one instance he definitely stressed that the awareness of a deep emotional reaction, of "a shattering experience," as he put it, had remained alive in his mind, though the intensity of his reactions had at the time not been fully noticeable in what he had told me. In this instance the lasting effect of analysis did, in fact, relate closely to the area of self representation. The patient was liberated from the pressure of guilt feelings and fantastic ambitions, which prior to his analysis he had reenacted in life.

Approaching our topic from several sides we have become aware of the central function of the ego in the recovery of memory, and in the assimilation of both the recovered memories and the analytic biography. The reconstructive approach in psychoanalysis is linked to the idea that changes in the structure of defense are indicated as part of therapy. They are not indicated in all types of illness, nor in all stages of one and the same process. Our theory can specify which of the functions of the ego has to be investigated, in order to make the decision as to the indication of psychoanalytic therapy reliable: it is the capacity to neutralize instinctual energy. The energy quanta, to continue in theoretical terms, set free by the analytic exploration of defense and repressed ideations, should ideally be discharged in a person's social functions—to repeat a well-known Freudian statement, in the capacity for work and love. In both these connections the discharge pre-supposes various degrees of neutralization (Hartmann, 1955; and chap. 9).

One of the relationships in which the importance of the ca-pacity to neutralize plays its part is the analytic situation itself. It is one in which the adjustment to changing levels of behav-ior, to regression and progression, to self-oblivion and re-emergent self-observation, plays its part. It is a situation in which, in the relationship to the analyst, the patient is required to learn and to experience the double discernment of the present liberated from the shadow of the past, and the past, liberated from defensive distortions.

Part III

HISTORY OF
PSYCHOANALYSIS

16: Review of *The Ego and the Mechanisms of Defense,* by Anna Freud

(1938)

In attempting in this final review to determine the significance of Anna Freud's book as a contribution to psychoanalytic psychology, to treat its bearing on questions of theory apart from its technical and clinical aspects, I cannot hope to do more than consider a few problems selected at random. For the close interdependence of technical and theoretical problems is a distinctive feature of this book; at the same time it determines in part the scope of its inquiry.

Historically speaking, problems of technique and their relation to psychoanalytic theory have obviously provided the author with her starting point. Indeed, the "prehistory" of this book seems to reach back as far as her book on the technique of child analysis (1927). There we are shown how in the analysis of children, where we are compelled to a large extent to forego the benefits of the free association method, analysis of the child's behavior is thrust into the foreground, with a view to helping the neurotic child to acquire insight into his illness and to observe the fundamental conditions of analytic treatment. Here, on the other hand, the general problems of ego psychology provide the setting for a discussion of the possibilities of an analogous procedure carried out in particular cases within the framework of the classical technique and of the extent to which such a procedure opens the way for analysis of

---

This review was written in German. It is not known who translated it for publication in the *International Journal of Psycho-Analysis,* 19 : 136–146. In the same issue, Anna Freud's book was also reviewed by Ernest Jones and Otto Fenichel.

the "unknown elements of the ego, its activities in the past." Discussing Melanie Klein's play technique in 1927, Anna Freud raised the question how far we may carry the symbolic interpretation of children's play; now she asks in general terms how we should prepare the ground for the interpretation of id content, which our knowledge of dream symbolism may have helped us to understand, and how we should steer the course which is to lead us via the patient's defensive positions and the unconscious parts of his ego to his instinctual life and early childhood fantasies.

Some of the other principal ideas in the book derive from papers read by the author at Oxford, Wiesbaden, and Lucerne, but never published.

In 1929 she described how the very elements which can ordinarily be shown to enter into the composition of an infantile animal phobia contributed to the formation of an animal fantasy, the mechanism of which can also be observed in dreams, fairy tales, and children's stories. What was then described with reference to a specific type of infantile fantasy as an achievement subserving the pleasure principle—the dreaded animal of the phobia elevated to the role of protector—reappears in chapter 6 of the present book as a stage in the developmental history of the ego. "Denial in fantasy" is described as one of the methods employed by the ego in its struggle with anxiety—a method which naturally loses its usefulness after the earliest period of childhood and comes into conflict with the need for synthesis required by a more mature ego adapted to reality. Cases in which this conflict is minimized or has never really arisen lie on the borderline of pathology. The neurotic mechanisms under the influence of education formed the subject of Anna Freud's paper in 1932, when she gave examples of the interaction between the internal and external world in the development of infantile neurosis. These are now discussed in chapters 6 and 7. Children who behave like adults are practicing denial in word and act. "Like a grownup," says the adult to the child; and this becomes for a time the guiding motive of the child's behavior and that of his environment. If the child in playing this game oversteps the line

which divides fantasy from action, he inevitably comes into
conflict with the outside world. But the fate of this fantasy activity does not depend solely on whether he meets with indulgence or disapproval. Encountering opposition from one
quarter, it will readily find a displaced outlet in harmless
forms of behavior; it would seem to lie at the root of much
that passes in life for eccentricity. Ego restriction, which the
author introduced into psychoanalysis in the same Congress
paper, illustrating her theme with examples of sudden
changes of interest and masked reactions of flight in children
during the latency period, offers as a contrast to these actions
of *denial* the case of *avoidance*. Just as denial may be distinguished from repression, so avoidance has a more serious
counterpart in inhibition. Denial and avoidance form a united
front against the dangers of the outside world. The chapters
of the book devoted to these forms of reaction are subsumed
under the general heading of "Examples fo the Avoidance of
Objective Unpleasure and Objective Danger." [1] They thus
take their proper place in the general scheme of the book, in
which the opening theoretical part ("Theory of the Mechanisms of Defense") is followed by three sections [2] corresponding to the threefold dependence of the ego on the
external world, the superego, and the instincts. This disposition alone suggests the point in the development of psychoanalysis from which the book departs, the "fresh direction taken
by Freud's writings," which, beginning with *Group Psychology
and the Analysis of the Ego*, "have freed the study of the ego
from the odium of analytic unorthodoxy." But Anna Freud
extends this new departure along quite definite lines. Whereas
other workers have sought to throw light on the early stages of

1. The contents of the third preliminary paper, in which the parallels between the
instinctual constellations of earliest childhood and puberty are further developed and
discussed, are elaborated in Chapters 11 and 12 of the present book, which are
devoted to the instinctual conflicts of adolescents. This 1934 Congress paper contained much of the substance of the corresponding sections of the book.

2. "Examples of the Avoidance of Objective Unpleasure and Objective Danger:
Preliminary Stages of Defense," "Examples of Two Types of Defense," and "Defense
Motivated by Fear of the Strength of the Instincts: Illustrated by the Phenomena of
Puberty."

ego development, on the origin and structure of the ego it-self—I refer to the line of investigation which has for some years been associated with the names of Melanie Klein, Ernest Jones, Edward Glover, and others—or to study specific types of primitive ego reaction, this book seems to take up the prob-lem of the way in which the mature ego functions at the point where *Inhibitions, Symptoms and Anxiety* left it in 1926. One of the basic problems of that book arose out of the freshly as-sumed obligation to show precisely how the forces of the ego interact with those of the id. This line of inquiry gave birth to the new theory of anxiety, but also to other doctrines of fun-damental importance, such as that dealing with the varieties of resistance.[3] It also forms the background of Anna Freud's book. Its derivation from *Inhibitions, Symptoms and Anxiety* also determines the point at which her exposition starts. Freud there reverts to the old concept of defense and describes re-pression as one form of defense. Anna Freud expands these arguments and reviews the state of our previous knowledge concerning the mechanisms of defense as revealed in psycho-analytic literature. She explores the various possibilities of classifying them, historically, according to the time of their ap-pearance, or systematically, according to the nature of their achievement, but maintains with evident justice that the time is not yet ripe for fulfilling this task. She discards it in favor of another which is approached in the book with penetrating in-sight; the nature and extent of the ego's achievements are ex-amined with a precision and lucidity which have seldom been attained in psychoanalysis before and which, compared with most of the earlier efforts in this direction, constitute some-thing entirely new, not only in point of form, but in the pene-tration of the material.

Here a word of explanation seems called for. We must be clear as to the position of new discoveries in psychoanalysis at the present day. By that I do not mean to ask whether it is possible to better Freud's achievement or to suggest that the greatness of that achievement excludes all possibility of fur-

3. See Waelder's review (1929) of Freud (1926).

ther discovery. It would be an absurd standpoint to adopt, bearing in mind what has been accomplished by the generation who have been Freud's followers since the first decade of this century; absurd, too, if we think of the developments undergone by psychoanalysis in the later works of Freud himself. The problem I have in mind is of a different kind. A now no longer insignificant number of scientists living in different parts of the world under different conditions are at work on material gained under the relatively constant conditions of observation determined by the technical requirements of analysis. New developments in psychoanalysis—leaving aside Freud's original great discoveries—are often due to changes in the material to be observed. I need hardly recall here the vital stimulus psychoanalysis derived and still derives from its preoccupation with the psychoses; or that a change in the actual forms of neurosis would seem to have cleared the way for the problem of character analysis; or again that interest in the child, both in his earliest years and in the latency period, has opened up fresh vistas: for even the present book seems to owe its first inspiration to a similar experience. But what this book has accomplished has been brought about not by any alteration in the material under observation, but by a silent change in the second constant factor, in the method of observation. In analytic circles such changes are generally received with a proper skepticism. For the history of psychoanalysis has shown that the great misunderstandings dictated by resistance often proceed from efforts to modify its technique. But no one will claim that that danger exists here. Decidedly not. I am much more inclined to think that in the case of this book the opposite danger exists: *the change in the mode of observation might pass unnoticed.* Up to a point the views sustained by Anna Freud are common to all analysts, her fundamantal position is theirs. But this is not equivalent to saying that the account she has given here really tallies completely with the position generally upheld until now. The points of divergence may appear trifling—and yet they are important enough.

Anna Freud's book advocates a method of observation which —putting it quite generally—is, above all, more detailed and exhaustive than has hitherto been usual; it sets to work more from the surface. Let me illustrate this. "Identification with the aggressor" and "altruistic surrender" are phenomena which we can easily verify from our clinical experience (once we have been made familiar with their features). They can be traced back to two of the great defense mechanisms, introjection and projection. But these two mechanisms and the relations between them do not cover the whole of the psychic event: this can be traced to them, but it remains a distinct condition with its own peculiar structure. Again, the dependence on instinctual life is transparent, the relation to aggression and masochism—but this, too, holds only for a part of the phenomenon. There is no need to insist what an advance it represents if we follow Anna Freud's lead in the technique of interpretation, first revealing the whole extent of a type of behavior, the activity of the ego, and only then penetrating into the deeper layers. This method promises to bring us decisively nearer our therapeutic goal, the modification and liberation of the patient's personality, but—and I say this simply to prevent misunderstanding—it is only *one* step in interpretation, which will remain unavailing unless it is reinforced by the others which have long been familiar to us. But it is desirable to emphasize what insight acquired in this way must mean for the *theory* of psychoanalysis, for *psychoanalysis as psychology:* the superficial layers of the mind, those functions of the psychic apparatus that are bound up with the ego, have for long remained beyond the reach of psychoanalytic psychology. Necessarily and inevitably so. Psychoanalysis is the natural science of the mind; it is not, and in its nature cannot be, a descriptive method. It cannot enter into competition either with those psychologists who have made it their object to describe mental phenomena with the help of empathy—I may mention Max Scheler as their most distinguished representative in recent times—or with the poets who perform the same task with a higher and more unimpeachable authority. Psychoanalysis has been repeatedly criticized for the schematic nature of its formulations and conceptions. It has been reminded of its undisputed claim to be considered *the* psychology of the innermost mental processes, of man in conflict—and some measure of satisfaction has been admitted from Freud's case histories alone. Sometimes it has been added that the intuitive genius of this one psychologist combined with his mastery of style have alone helped to overcome the inadequacies of the method of approach. We shall have no difficulty in recognizing the resistance, or perhaps had better say the misunderstanding, which has inspired this argument. For this criticism does but emphasize what was a necessary, almost unavoidable consequence of the historical development of our science. Psychoanalysis originated with the study of the unconscious, its interest was primarily in the id and its contents, on those strata of the mind which lay closest to man's biological nature and in which the individual comes nearest to being merged in the species. Moreover, in the interests of historical accuracy, we must repeatedly insist in the plainest possible terms that Freud's concept of psychoanalysis has from the very first, ever since the *Studies on Hysteria,* embraced the ego as well, the forces of defense as well as those they oppose, whether they appeared as the censorship or under some other name, without thereby sacrificing in any way its fundamantal position as a depth psychology. But the study of the ego, as Freud insisted, formed a second step after the first. Freud himself has specified the problems which this second step involves; the present book represents a decisive advance toward their solution. This advance leads back in the first instance to the phenomena themselves, it leads back to observation.

A gestalt psychologist, Koffka, once illustrated his point very simply by saying that if one wants to describe a machine, one must first *understand* its structure and function. *Mutatis mutandis* this holds good for psychoanalysis too. It is this which gives it its special position in psychology. The exposition of the mechanisms of defense contained in this book is based on an understanding of the way in which the mental apparatus works. One has only to read one of the passages describing some piece of behavior, for example, that of the little boy after visiting the dentist (p. 111f.), to see how the explanation, the insight into the process of "identification with the aggressor,"

embraces every aspect of the behavior in question. Let us see
how this conception differs from the ordinary psychoanalytic
version of the same process; the latter—for the sake of illustration I am presenting it in a crudely schematic form and am
even caricaturing it—would perhaps fasten on that element in
the boy's conduct which is mentioned at the end of Anna
Freud's account, his cutting string and breaking off the points
of pencils. Recognition of the symbolic meaning of these actions, of the effect which the assumption of activity typical of
play has in resolving castration anxiety, has never been wanting. But to have seen that here we have a specific defense gov-
erned by identification, forming one of the ego's *general*
mechanisms of defense and not confined to the individual
case,[4] to have grasped its range and nature, is an achievement
for the new standpoint. An explanation such as this presupposes the most careful observation in an attempt to see the
psychic situation as part of a connected whole, in a wider setting. Its advantage is that it draws closer to the concrete psychic events in its simultaneous grasp of the surface and the
depths of mental life. The author believes that it will surely
become possible to discover a number of other typical measures employed by the ego, beyond those mentioned in her
book. They will become accessible to us only through this new
method of observation; before they can be described or recognized, we shall require fresh insight into mental life as a whole
and, more especially, further information concerning the unconscious activities of the ego.

But let us approach the problem from another angle, and
ask in what respects this book differs from other attempts to
study the "ego's" mode of operation in the domain of the
psyche on the basis of certain assumptions concerning its essential nature. We find one such attempt in Adler's Individual

4. Perhaps I can also illustrate Anna Freud's standpoint by fastening on a terminological coincidence. In 1933 Ferenczi spoke of "identification of the menacing person
or aggressor." But Ferenczi was describing something entirely different, namely, the
child's reaction to a specific traumatic situation. The child's "weak and undeveloped
personality reacts to the sudden unpleasure induced by the provocative attitude of the
adult not by defence, but by anxiety-ridden identification and by introjection of" the
aggressor to whose will he submits (p. 163).

Psychology. (I have no doubt that many well-known critics of psychoanalysis and perhaps others who have failed to grasp the situation clearly will now discover that psychoanalysis is "becoming Adlerian.") In my view the gulf between psychoanalysis and Individual Psychology was never wider or more radical than at this point where there is a partial overlapping of the field in inquiry—partial, because we cannot speak of a strict correspondence when the two systems differ in what they include under the heading of ego function. Psychoanalysis runs counter to the theory of Individual Psychology in holding that the ego develops out of the id and bears the imprint of the process which gave birth to it.[5] Anna Freud constantly alludes to the processes by which the ego has been formed, revealing the *precise* instinctual situation from which a defensive attitude has been acquired, its essence and its ramifications. The little girl who practiced magic, so that she might take over the role of the ghost she was afraid to meet in the hall, was working over by means of this identification a definite experience, the effects of her penis envy. The patient who had the feeling that people were keeping some secret from her and in a certain phase of the transference became aggressive toward her analyst had herself kept her childhood masturbation a secret; the criticism with which she identified herself represented the criticism which her masturbation might call forth in her analyst. Thus the form of defense must be interpreted in the light of the patient's whole history. This idea is not sustained throughout the book, for it was not the author's intention that it should be given undue prominence; but, from hints scattered here and there, we may conjecture that she has been following a course of investigation initiated by her as long ago as 1922, perhaps without realizing where it would lead, in her first psychoanalytic publication. There she used the fantasies of a young girl patient to show how a certain infantile sexual fantasy (of the type represented by "A

5. A unified conception of the actual details of this process does not yet exist, although a number of valuable contributions to the problem have already appeared. It is one of the problems which psychoanalysis will in the near future have occasion to consider in its many aspects.

Child Is Being Beaten"), in spite of all the resistance and elaboration to which it was exposed, was endlessly repeated in the intricate network of fantasy fashioned by her daydreams. The reflections which in that early paper were prompted by the study of a patient's daydreams may also be applied to the genesis of certain methods adopted by the ego, and thus help us to understand the regularity or monotony of certain forms of defense.[6] I would accordingly define what I consider the crowning achievement of the book by saying that it inspires us to a further study of the ego and its activities, offers a method for approaching that study, and so opens up fresh prospects for psychoanalytic exploration.

How significant this achievement is we discover in the last two sections of the book, which in spite of their modest title give us the essentials of a psychology of puberty. This survey, to my mind the most finished part of the book, takes as its starting point the instinctual conflicts of adolescence and the ways in which they are worked over in asceticism, in the tendency to identification, and idealization.

The account of the instinctual conflicts of puberty gives Anna Freud the opportunity of urging a particular point of view, which she calls that of "the ego's primary antagonism to instinct." Under the peculiar condition of puberty, this primary attitude of the ego becomes an active defense mechanism, which according to the author expresses the ego's specific fear of the quantity of instinct. This idea, already foreshadowed in Freud's *Inhibitions, Symptoms and Anxiety,* represents a hypothesis of a kind that has so often in psychoanalysis proved its heuristic worth.[7] Accordingly, whether we accept or reject it, we cannot justify our decision by pointing to definite mental phenomena, any more than we can *perceive* a death instinct or a primary masochism when we study the processes of

6. In the discussions of the Vienna Psychoanalytic Society, Anna Freud amplified the views expressed in her book, and intimated that we find a uniformity in the methods to which the ego has recourse in dealing with the demands of instinct and affect, superego and outside world, and which it applies to them all indiscriminately.

7. "The ego's primary antagonism to instinct—its dread of the strength of the instincts, as we have called it—is not much more than a *theoretical concept*" (p. 157; italics added).

the mind itself—and yet many of us would not willingly dispense with these assumptions. For that a dread of the strength of the instincts does exist is not disputed even by those who reject a primary antagonism of the ego to instinct. Although familiar with the arguments to the contrary, I have not become convinced that there is anything in our clinical material or in the fundamental conceptions of psychoanalysis which militates against Anna Freud's hypothesis; rather I have a growing impression that the assumption of a primary antagonism to instinct on the part of the ego (specifically, on the part of the higher ego functions) resolves difficulties and contradictions. For the idea which lies at the root of Freud's views concerning the ego—its differentiation from the id—already presupposes a certain degree of repudiation of instinct. By way of defining the nature of the problem I would add: if the ego makes contact with the instincts and seeks to carry through its wishes, the instincts must be prepared to make concessions, must modify their aim under the ego's influence, must postpone satisfaction, perhaps in order to comply with the demands of reality.[8] To be sure, we are not entitled to rely on the processes heralding the onset of a schizophrenic illness or on the parallel or related processes occurring at puberty—which indeed are occasionally treated in the nonanalytic literature as a normal counterpart to the clinical picture in schizophrenia (Homburger 1926)—as *proof* of the ego's primary antagonism to instinct: and yet these phenomena are so convincing that the onus of finding an alternative explanation will fall on those who oppose the conception defended by Anna Freud. The author assumes that this anxiety is acquired very early in the development of the individual, in "the period during which an ego is gradually being isolated out of the undifferentiated id" (p. 165). Phylogenetically, it is to be regarded as "a kind of deposit accumulated from acts of repression practiced by many generations and merely continued, not initiated, by individuals" (p. 157). This is the point at which we come within range of Freud's idea of organic repression, the

8. Here we should have to discuss the (gradual) differentiation of genital from pregenital and aggressive impulses.

anthropological basis of the psychoanalytic psychology of the ego. It acquires an enhanced significance from the account given by Anna Freud.

I cannot attempt to enumerate here all or even the most important ideas contained in this book, or to develop the many suggestive remarks thrown out here and there almost in passing. Thus in a few words the author outlines the wole problem of psychoanalytic pedagogy. Or a chance sentence contains the solution of a remarkable and much debated problem: analysts are perhaps worse judges of human nature than one might expect, because the ego they see in the analyses of patients is an ego restricted by the analytic situation. Or in connection with the problems surrounding the ego's antagonism to instinct, she formulates afresh the problem of the indications for psychoanalytic treatment. I should just like to mention two other examples. One bears on the relation between affective and intellectual development in the child, a problem alluded to in several places.

Evidently we have hitherto been too one-sided in our readiness to concentrate exlusively on intellectual inhibitions and thought taboos and to attribute their presence to the operation of the castration complex. Anna Freud refers on the one hand to the factor of ego restriction which can seriously impair the child's intellectual development and aptitude for learning, and on the other to the intimate connection between the trend of intellectual development and the problems of instinctual defense. The simple statements, "instinctual danger makes human beings intelligent. In periods of calm in the instinctual life, when there is no danger, the individual can permit himself a certain degree of stupidity" (p. 163), that in the latency period children have no need to indulge in abstract thought (instead of the assumption that they *dare* not do so), suggest a complete program of research. It is inevitable, if we are to carry this out, that we should establish contact with academic psychology. In these relations it can really *only* be a matter of borrowing trustworthy information and results, not of electing to work along the same lines. I venture to predict that the result is more likely to be that the old gulf will reappear—

only elsewhere. But psychoanalysis is in a position to claim the
mental life of the child with its puzzles and problems as part
of its own territory. We should find ourselves in the same situation if we followed up the suggestions offered in several
places to explain a particular type of game which children
play, namely, games of impersonation. Here too we can draw
on material gathered in the field of academic psychology—Anna Freud has no hesitation in doing so—but, if I am
not mistaken, the task confronting psychoanalysis here once
again leads in a different direction. For psychoanalysis alone
may hope to inquire into the genesis of these games of impersonation and the conditions under which they can persist either to trouble normality or to enhance it in many fields of
artistic expression.

Thus we have glimpses again and again in the pages of this
book of the the problems and developments that await us. All
are characterized equally by breadth of vision, embracing systematically the whole range of mental life from the pathological to the normal and vigorously exploring the nature of
normality itself. The prospect of a psychoanalytic psychology
of the total personality takes shape, and I think that the stimulating effect of the book will be felt not only in clinical psychoanalysis but in all its applied branches as well.[9]

No one can foresee, looking at the developments inspired
by Freud's writings on the psychology of the ego, whether
more will be gained by pursuing the line of inquiry favored by
Anna Freud (as I prefer to think) or by following along the
path that others have chosen to tread. For the most widely
divergent efforts have a common purpose—to study the genesis and functions of the ego and so to advance the fulfillment
of a task which has confronted psychoanalysis for almost

9. I feel I must mention an attempt that I myself have made in this direction during one of the training courses in the Vienna Psychoanalytic Society under the immediate stimulus of reading Anna Freud's book. Starting from Jones's paper on Hamlet,
one of the most valuable—indeed, in my view, an altogether perfect example of an
essay in applied psychoanalysis—I endeavored to expand his study (first published in
1910) in the light of Anna Freud's ideas. The response which greeted my effort, schematic as it was, has left me with the impression that we have here a promising field of
research.

twenty years. But within the sphere of these efforts this book represents a position to which science has at all times adhered. It approaches mental phenomena in a spirit of fresh inquiry, travels the path which leads from observation to theory, and teaches us to strike an even balance between experience and reflection.

17: The Significance of Freud's Earliest Discoveries

(1950)

The subject of this paper is a number of Freud's early writings which have unexpectedly come to light (see Freud, 1950). The material consists of 168 letters addressed to a single correspondent and of nineteen manuscripts, clinical notes and various drafts of papers, a few comprehensive essays and of one monograph. None of it was intended by the author for publication. The editors, however, felt that publication was warranted, since the material represents a record unique in the history of science. While it seems at first that we can learn little from the new material that could not have been gleaned from a careful scrutiny of Freud's already published work, a more detailed study indicates some change of perspective. In thinking of the early history of psychoanalysis, we usually follow Freud's own account, mainly "On the History of the Psycho-Analytic Movement" (1914c) and "An Autobiographical Study" (1925). These were written at a distance of twenty and thirty years respectively from the experiences on which the new sources report, and were written by the man who had succeeded. The writings on which I am here reporting are by a man engaged in a desperate struggle with a new field of science, with a hostile environment, and with resistances within himself. In this lies the uniqueness of the record.

In what follows, no chronological report and no biograph-

Paper read at the 16th International Psycho-Analytical Congress, Zurich, August 1949. First published in the *International Journal of Psycho-Analysis,* 31 : 108–116, 1950; also in *The Yearbook of Psychoanalysis,* 7 : 31–46. New York: International Universities Press, 1951.

ical essay are intended. I shall omit much that is generally known, and focus on three interrelated problems in the early history of psychoanalysis: on the relation of psychology to physiology in Freud's thought, on the circumstances that led to the discoveries concerning infantile sexuality, and on the meaning of metapsychology in the development of Freud's ideas.

The relation of psychology to physiology stands in the center of the correspondence. Only Freud's side of it is extant. Its termination roughly coincides with Freud's reorientation toward physiology. Freud's correspondent, the closest friend he is known to have had, the Berlin physician Wilhelm Fliess, was by inclination a physiologist. Two years younger than Freud, whose neurological lectures he attended in 1886, Fliess combined the practice of otolaryngology with research in physiology and biology. While some of his clinical findings survive in footnotes in German textbooks of otolaryngology, his main work, the theory of periodicity in the life of both sexes, has long since been recognized as erroneous and as a kind of "numerical mysticism." However, for the history of Freud's thought this theory proved to be stimulating; it directed his attention toward the problem of bisexuality.

Freud and Fliess had both been trained in the doctrines of the school of Helmholtz and Du Bois-Reymond—a physiology based upon physics (see Bernfeld, 1944). Brücke, Freud's teacher in Vienna, considered himself their ambassador to the Far East. An eminently successful ambassador he was, who at the time had attracted many eminent scientists, among them Josef Breuer. We know from Freud's writings that, at the age of twenty-six, he reluctantly abandoned physiology and turned to the practice of medicine. It is not always equally well realized how far the immediate influence of his physiological training extended and what continued influence it exercised on his later work.

From physiology Freud turned to a field of its application, to brain physiology and clinical neurology. This interest predominated throughout his stay in Paris from the autumn of 1885 to February 1886; his first publication upon his return was his translation of a volume of Charcot's lectures (1886), published in German before they were published in French. In footnotes added to Charcot's text Freud records literature and catamnestic data on patients he had himself examined in Paris after their presentation by Charcot. Freud's return from Paris coincided with his marriage and with his appointment to the neurological outpatients department of a small children's hospital. On the basis of material collected during this work he published a considerable number of clinical communications on child neurology and several comprehensive monographs; the last of these was written in 1897. What by that time had become a cumbersome obligation compelled him to put other studies on one side: in particular his work on the interpretation of dreams. However, in the years after his return from Paris, Freud's interest in neurology and neurophysiology was by no means perfunctory. For years he planned a book on the anatomy of the central nervous system, negotiated with publishers, and finally composed several articles for a medical dictionary, in which he attempted to express his views. When without his permission the editor of the dictionary made radical cuts in his contributions, Freud felt so dissatisfied that he omitted the articles from the otherwise carefully compiled bibliography of his writings which he published in 1897. Only one of these articles was expanded by him into a monograph, published in 1891 and dedicated to Josef Breuer: *On Aphasia,* which has been described as "the first truly Freudian book," and in which the theory of localization was replaced by the first functional theory of aphasia.

Freud's interest in hysteria and psychopathology in general stood in the background during these years. Before his departure for Paris, this interest had first been elicited by Breuer's account of the cathartic treatment of "Anna O." (the case known from the *Studies on Hysteria*). To begin with, Freud's attitude seems to have been ambivalent. In his autobiography, (1925) he tells us how in his pride at his achievements in neurological localization he presented to his students "a neurotic suffering from a persistent headache as a case of chronic localized meningitis" (p. 12). His experience in Paris in-

troduced a change: the existence of hysterical phenomena attracted his interest and may have reawakened older impressions concerning the working of hypnosis to which he refers in
his autobiographical writings. However, Charcot's lack of en-
couragement when Freud told him of Breuer's case seems to
have fortified Freud's own hesitation. His first publications on
hysteria did not follow the path indicated by Breuer's findings: in his report on his experiences in Paris he defended
Charcot's views concerning the existence of male hysteria. For
several years he worked on a paper, the outline of which
Charcot had suggested, indicating diagnostic criteria for the
distinction of hysterical from organic paralyses (1893).

At this point of Freud's development one might have gained
the impression of a neurologist and neurophysiologist, whose
interest extended into the borderland of neuropsychiatry.

The change in his interest and outlook was brought about
by one great experience: his contact with patients in psychotherapy. Freud's interest was first centered on the differential
diagnosis of the cases of neurotic and psychotic disorders with
which he met in private practice. His interest in therapy grew
slowly. He turned from his initial tools, from electrotherapy
and hydropathy to hypnosis; he translated Bernheim's writings
"only to have a hand in something which is certainly going to
have a big influence on the practice of nerve specialists in the
next few years" (1950, p. 58). He visited Nancy in 1889 in
order to gain firsthand impressions of the working method of
Bernheim and Liébault—but he soon abandoned their technique. The practice of hypnotic suggestion seemed to run contrary to everything he discovered in the relationship existing
between physician and patient. "In the long run," he wrote in
1892, "neither the doctor nor the patient can tolerate the contradiction between the decided denial of the ailement in the
suggestion and the necessary recognition of it outside the
suggestion" (p. 141). From the use of hypnotic suggestion
Freud turned to the use of hypnosis for purposes of exploration, to the cathartic method which had been applied by
Breuer a decade earlier. Freud's growing interest in turn stimulated that of Breuer, who had withdrawn from the prob-

lem of hysteria, and joint publications were initiated: first the preliminary communication of 1893 and finally the *Studies on Hysteria* published in 1895. Freud's two independent contributions to the collaboration have become the cornerstones of psychoanalysis: first he established the connection between conflict, defense (repression), and symptom, which constituted the basis for all subsequent clinical approaches to the subject. His second contribution was of a theoretical nature: in 1892 Freud referred to it as "the law of constancy," postulating the existence of a tendency in the central nervous system to keep tensions constant. This formulation, foreshadowing the future pleasure and Nirvana principles of pschoanalysis, would account for the processs of "abreaction." It was soon to gain more general importance as the first of those general assumptions of psychoanalysis for which during the 1890s Freud coined a term which appeared in his published work only twenty years later, the term *metapsychology*. The importance of this approach for Freud's thought during the early 1890s can be shown by two considerations. In entering as a scientist into the study of human psychic conflict Freud was entering a field that had so far been accessible only to intuitive thinking, to philosophic insight, religious and secular, or to poetic imagination and empathy. Freud became painfully aware of this proximity, and only the rigor of scientific formulation promised to support his independence as an explorer. But science was not only a support against the temptations of intuition; it offered Freud the tools he needed for grouping clinical observations in a manner which would permit the formulation of further hypotheses. In 1894 he wrote:

> I should like, finally, to dwell for a moment on the working hypothesis which I have made use of in this exposition of the neuroses of defence. I refer to the concept that in mental functions something is to be distinguished—a quota of affect or sum of excitation—which possesses all the characteristics of a quantity (though we have no means of measuring it), which is capable of increase, diminution, displacement and discharge, and which is spread over the surface of a body.
>
> This hypothesis, which, incidentally, already underlies our

theory of 'abreaction' . . . (1893), can be applied in the same
sense as physicists apply the hypothesis of a flow of electric
fluid. It is provisionally justified by its utility in co-ordinating
and explaining a great variety of psychical states [p. 60f.].

In general we may say that the first principles of psychodynamics grew out of the fertile ground of the physiological
tradition. I shall enumerate only a few of the steps which followed immediately. The separation of anxiety neuroses from
neurasthenia was formulated after much hesitation and doubt.
For a while Freud took the view that anxiety neuroses could
not be cured but only prevented. Since incomplete gratification during sexual activity is responsible for their occurrence,
a new method of birth control or some indication concerning
fertility cycles might, he thought, constitute a great contribution to human happiness; this is a task that he assigned to his
correspondent. Soon, however, Freud's generalizations moved
in a different direction (1950, p. 93): "Where there is abun-
dant sexual tension but where it cannot be turned into affect
by being worked over psychically . . . the sexual tension is
transformed into anxiety." Thus the concept emerges that
covers both "the purely somatic excitation" of anxiety neurosis
and the "purely psychical" one of hysteria, which has been
evoked by conflict. The concept is that of the psychic energy
of the sexual impulses, the concept of libido, the most fruitful
conceptual tool in Freud's early equipment, which, within a
few years, was to make unexpected discoveries possible. Before we turn to them, we may here record that the formula
"anxiety is generated by repressed libido" was abandoned only
thirty years later, in *Inhibitions, Symptoms and Anxiety*, at a time
when that formula had become a limiting factor in the theoretical formulations of psychoanalysis.

Its earlier value for Freud's thought was at least twofold: it
made it possible to account for a large number of interconnections between apparently unconnected types of behavior,
which psychoanalytic observation had revealed. Toxicological
in nature, it also faced physiologists with the question as to the
"chemical" or the "real" explanation of this spectacular trans-

formation. Much in the correspondence with Fliess was explicitly or implicitly devoted to this problem.

Freud's attempt at integrating his new and his former spheres of interest during the mid-90s were still not restricted to any one field of his observation. He felt compelled to consider all his new discoveries in the light of brain physiology and to organize them into a system. By 1895 these new discoveries embraced some nuclear hypotheses concerning the mechanisms operating in various neuroses and in paranoia and extended into a field which at that time still seemed apart from psychopathology, the psychology of dreams. When in July 1895, apparently all of a sudden, the wish-fulfilling tendencies of the latent content of dreams became apparent to Freud, the idea of integrating his various findings presented itself for the first time. It occupied his thoughts for more than two years. The plan of writing a treatise obsessed and haunted him, a treatise that he first called *Psychology for the Neurologist.* Later both title and purpose were repeatedly changed. Draft after draft is mentioned in the correspondence, hypotheses were modified and revised, but the whole of the planned monograph was never completed. We are familiar with its main ideas. They form the backbone of psychoanalytic theory as it was formulated in 1900 in Chapter VII of the *Interpretation of Dreams,* in which Freud presented his first sketch of the psychic apparatus, his first inferences on the distinction between primary and secondary processes as modes of discharge, his first hypotheses of mobile and bound energy as motive forces in these processes, of hallucination and perception as stages in the development of a single function— thoughts and ideas which had gradually gained shape but were already clearly outlined in Freud's mind in the autumn of 1895.

In September of that year, returning from a short visit to Berlin, Freud composed a draft of his treatise which has come down to us. It was started in his railway carriage and continued at his desk. Material that fills some eighty typewritten pages was written down in three days; the rest of the manuscript, seventy more typewritten pages, was produced during evening hours and intervals between patients in the course of the next few weeks. Some weeks later, Freud's enthusiasm gave way to skepticism; he spoke of his condition while he was writing it as "a state of mind which I can no longer understand." There is, however, nothing of rapture or enthusiasm noticeable in the manuscript itself, the most condensed and most closely argued work of Freud's which we possess. The first words set the tone:

> The intention of this project is to furnish us with a psychology which shall be a natural science: its aim, that is, is to represent psychical processes as quantitatively determined states of specifiable material particles and so to make them plain and void of contradictions. The project involves two principal ideas:—
> 1. That what distinguishes activity from rest is to be regarded as a quantity (Q) subject to the general laws of motion.
> 2. That it is to be assumed that the material particles in question are the neurones [p. 355].

This is the pupil of Helmholtz and Brücke trying once more, for the last time, to combine his past and present fields of investigation.

The contents of the essay resist any attempt at condensation or abridgement; the work is condensed to the utmost and written not for readers but as a summary to be expanded later; that expansion, as we know, filled the whole span of Freud's life, and throughout forty-four years, up to the time of the last notes found on his desk at his death, the ideas first expressed in this essay did not lose their hold over his thoughts. In 1895, however, these thoughts were expressed in terms of neurophysiological hypotheses. Four types of specifically differentiated neurons are distinguished, and two types of psychic energy; and a host of very detailed assumptions are made on sense perception, and the paths in the central nervous system. A special group of neurons is charged with control and direction. They constitute a special organization, the ego. These neurons are distinguished by the fact of their being permanently invested with psychic energy; it is their function to inhibit or to delay certain processes of discharge within the system of neurons, and in particular to control the secondary process, in opposition to the primary process, which follows the wish, i.e., the impulse to immediate discharge.

These brief examples will strike us as a condensation of many parts of psychoanalytic theory, of passages familiar to us in the *Interpretation of Dreams,* or *The Ego and the Id.* But what strikes us as condensation is in fact their common root: the anticipation of future hypotheses in Freud's earliest formulations. This anticipation accounts for what one might call the hidden texture of Freud's writings. I am referring here to the well-known fact that what first appeared as an enigmatic footnote or sentence in one of his publications was later expanded, and that every new contribution of Freud's used to throw light on some feature or aspect of a previous one. We can now understand these interconnections as the gradual unfolding of ideas that had matured over decades, and we realize that the whole of Freud's writings must be seen as a continued attempt to revise and check theory against experience. The draft of 1895 is in itself evidence of the working of Freud's mind. It uses examples that hint at a field which, to judge from Freud's publications and the content of the letters, had not yet played an important part in his conscious thinking. I refer to the field of genetic hypotheses.

Freud's hypotheses on dynamic relations could draw on familiar thoughts in neurophysiology and even in psychology itself; it has been shown, for instance, that Herbart's influence shaped some of Freud's formulations (Dorer, 1932). No such model existed for Freud's ontogenetic hypotheses. While in his phylogenetic speculations he followed the pattern of contemporary evolutionism and Darwinian tradition, the idea of studying the individual's past as a source of etiology had grown entirely out of clinical data, at first focused on the repression of sexual traumata.

But at what time of sexual life were sexual experiences traumatic? During the years from 1895 to 1897 this question was in the foreground of Freud's attention. In comparing his clinical impressions he gradually came to look for ever earlier limits; at the same time he tried in an apparently endless series of observations to relate the age at which the trauma occurred to the type of neurotic disorder observed. He was in search of the "fixation point." At the time when he wrote the Project (1895) the danger zone was considered to be limited by puberty; sexual impressions before that age were likely to be experienced as traumatic. And yet in this same essay the uniqueness of the mother in the life of a child, the dependence of a newborn human being on his environment, the crucial importance of the relief of tension in the situation at the breast are quoted in order to illustrate the stresses that account for the formation of the psychic apparatus, an instance of the anticipation of insight to which I referred earlier.

Clinical impressions soon suggested the second dentition as a crucial age; a year later Freud was induced to look upon the third year of life as crucial and to take even earlier experiences into account.

During this search the need to make the nature of the trauma concrete became ever more intense, until in 1896 the hypothesis of seduction was advanced. This hypothesis stated that all neuroses are due to seduction by an adult. The seducer is more likely to be a pervert or an obsessional, the child seduced likely to become a hysteric.

We recall from Freud's writings how deeply he was impressed by the discovery that these hypotheses were erroneous. In his autobiographical writings (1914c) he has described his reaction to the insight into his mistake:

> Influenced by Charcot's view of the traumatic origin of hysteria, one was readily inclined to accept as true and aetiologically significant the statements made by patients in which they ascribe their symptoms to passive sexual experiences in the first years of childhood—to put it bluntly, to seduction. When this aetiology broke down under the weight of its own improbability and contradiction in definitely ascertainable circumstances, the result at first was helpless bewilderment. Analysis had led back to these infantile sexual traumas by the right path, and yet they were not true. The firm ground of reality was gone. At that time I would gladly have given up the whole work [p. 17].

And yet Freud's mood, as we see it in the present correspondence, was at least initially very different. For example, in a letter dated September 21, 1897, he wrote:

Here I am again—we returned yesterday morning—refreshed, cheerful, impoverished and without work for the time being, and I am writing to you as soon as we have settled in again. Let me tell you straight away the great secret which has been slowly dawning on me in recent months. I no longer believe in my *neurotica*. That is hardly intelligible without an explanation; you yourself found what I told you credible. So I shall start at the beginning and tell you the whole story of how the reasons for rejecting it arose. The first group of factors were the continual disappointment of my attempts to bring my analyses to a real conclusion, the running away of people who for a time had seemed my most favourably inclined patients, the lack of the complete success on which I had counted, and the possibility of explaining my partial successes in other, familiar, ways. Then there was the astonishing thing that in every case . . . blame was laid on perverse acts by the father, and realization of the unexpected frequency of hysteria, in every case of which the same thing applied, though it was hardly credible that perverted acts against children were so general. (Perversion would have to be immeasurably more frequent than hysteria, as the illness can only arise where the events have accumulated and one of the factors which weaken defence is present.) Thirdly, there was the definite realization that there is no "indication of reality" in the unconscious, so that it is impossible to distinguish between truth and emotionally-charged fiction. (This leaves open the possible explanation that sexual phantasy regularly makes use of the theme of the parents.) Fourthly, there was the consideration that even in the most deep-reaching psychoses the unconscious memory does not break through, so that the secret of infantile experiences is not revealed even in the most confused states of delirium. When one thus sees that the unconscious never overcomes the resistance of the conscious, one must abandon the expectation that in treatment the reverse process will take place to the extent that the conscious will fully dominate the unconscious.

So far was I influenced by these considerations that I was

ready to abandon two things—the complete solution of a neurosis and sure reliance on its aetiology in infancy. Now I do not know where I am, as I have failed to reach theoretical understanding of repression and its play of forces. It again seems arguable that it is later experiences which give rise to phantasies which throw back to childhood; and with that the factor of hereditary predisposition regains a sphere of influence from which I had made it my business to oust it—in the interests of fully explaining neurosis.

Were I depressed, jaded, unclear in my mind, such doubts might be taken for signs of weakness. But as I am in just the opposite state, I must acknowledge them to be the result of honest and effective intellectual labour; and I am proud that after penetrating so far I am still capable of such criticism. Can these doubts be only an episode on the way to further knowledge?

It is curious that I feel not in the least disgraced, though the occasion might seem to require it. Certainly I shall not tell it in Gath, or publish it in the streets of Askalon, in the land of the Philistines—but between ourselves I have a feeling more of triumph than of defeat (which cannot be right) [p. 215ff.].

At this point the writing of the letter was interrupted: a communication from Fliess arrived, suggesting that Freud should come for a weekend to Berlin. In a parenthesis in his letter Freud expressed some hesitation about going:

To go on with my letter. I vary Hamlet's remark about ripeness—cheerfulness is all. I might be feeling very unhappy. The hope of eternal fame was so beautiful, and so was that of certain wealth, complete independence, travel, and removing the children from the sphere of worries which spoiled my own youth. All that depended on whether hysteria succeeded or not. Now I can be quiet and modest again and go on worrying. . . .

There is something else I must add. In the general collapse only the psychology has retained its value. The dreams still stand secure, and my beginnings in metapsychology have gone up in my estimation. It is a pity one cannot live on dream-interpretation, for instance [p. 217f.].

Freud undertook the trip to Berlin. From the subsequent letters we gather that in Berlin he discussed with Fliess the second of his secrets, the secret of his self-analysis. It is more than probable that it was the self-analysis that had led to the recognition of the errors in his theory or had at least helped him in rejecting them. For almost a year the study of the fantasy life of his patients had occupied Freud's mind. In letters and clinical notes he reported on his findings, described the regressive character of these fantasies and asked himself the question how childhood experiences and their elaboration in fantasy were related to each other. But however close he came to a solution, at one point or another he returned to the quest for a prototype, the scene of seduction. At this point Freud's own infantile fantasies seem to have limited his capacity as an observer. When in his autobiography (1925) he referred to the seduction hypothesis he put it clearly: "I had in fact stumbled for the first time upon the *Oedipus Complex*" (p. 34). That his self-analysis dealt very largely with his relation to his father he has stated himself in the preface to the second edition of *The Interpretation of Dreams*. Freud's father had died in the autumn of 1896, at the age of eighty-one, and Freud's self-analysis started in July 1897, a few months before the letter I have just quoted was written. It has been tacitly assumed that Freud's self-analysis was a more or less intellectual experience, concomitant with his study of dreams and undertaken to fortify his theory. The new material reveals a different state of affairs. While the interest in dream psychology played its part, the incentive came from pressing unconscious conflicts.

It was not the first time during the years of great discoveries that Freud suffered from neurotic difficulties. In 1894, when his relation to Breuer went through a crisis, he described cardiac symptoms, which he himself evaluated as psychogenic. While we do not know how far this evaluation was justified, *The Interpretation of Dreams* and the letters familiarize us with other symptoms, with a fear of premature death and with a railway phobia, symptoms that disappeared after his self-analysis. When in the summer of 1897 he became aware of his renewed difficulties he decided to take up the battle. In June 1897 he writes:

Incidentally, I have been through some kind of a neurotic experience, with odd states of mind not intelligible to consciousness—cloudy thoughts and veiled doubts, with barely here and there a ray of light [p. 210f.].

[Three weeks later:] I know that I am a useless correspondent just now, with no right to any claims to consideration, but it was not always so and it will not remain so. I still do not know what has been happening to me. Something from the deepest depths of my own neurosis has ranged itself against my taking a further step in understanding of the neuroses, and you have somehow been involved [p. 211f.].

[And again a few weeks later:] My little hysteria, which was much intensified by work, has yielded one stage further. The rest still sticks. That is the first reason for my mood. This analysis is harder than any other. . . . But I believe it has got to be done and is a necessary stage of my work [p. 213f.].

[For months the letters contain hints or statements:] I can only crawl, and wait until a next dream will bring clarity. . . . I can only analyse myself with objectively acquired knowledge (as if I were a stranger); self-analysis is really impossible [p. 234].

The self-analysis did not remain isolated; what he discovered in his patients he applied to himself and insight gained concerning himself facilitated further progress in therapy. A dream allowed him to reconstruct one of his childhood experiences; he turned to his mother for a confirmation of the reconstructed experiences and reported triumphantly that at least a great part of his reconstruction was correct in detail; and he thus gained confidence in the reliability of the procedure. The validity of the reconstruction opened the way to a further discovery, one that had repeatedly announced itself but had always been rejected or forgotten: the discovery that his interests in dreams and neuroses were not separate fields of interest, but that the two problems were in fact one and the same. Hence the note of triumph in the midst of depression. That note grows through the months to come. After the autumn of 1897 the great discoveries followed each other in rapid sequence: the oedipus complex, infantile sexuality, and particularly the anal phase of libidinal development, became visible in the clinical data. The draft of *The Interpretation of*

Dreams, started in 1898, was written and finished in 1899, the first inklings on parapraxes announced themselves and—perhaps the greatest step of all—the therapeutic technique of concentration was transformed into the method of free association. The concept of resistance appeared. Within two years the understanding of the phenomena of transference was to follow.

The speed with which insight accumulated and ideas matured seems at least in part related to the progress of Freud's self-analysis. Through his publications, mainly the sequence of editions of *The Psychopathology of Everyday Life* and *The Interpretation of Dreams,* we know that it extended over many years. I am inclined to think that it initiated a lasting process of analytically orientated self-scrutiny, an attitude which may well have formed the background of some of the views expressed in one of Freud's latest papers, "Analysis Terminable and Interminable" (1937a).

One of the consequences of the internal liberation initiated in the autumn of 1897 deserves our special attention. Freud's attitude to the physiological tradition was being modified. Not that he ever wished to establish psychological thinking as something independent of physiology; the closest relation, even identity of terms as an ultimate goal, was never in doubt. But the question that now arose was one concerning the appropriate relation between psychological and physiological concepts. Freud had for some time tried to free himself from the rigorous views of German neurophysiology. In his studies *On Aphasia* (1891) he had followed the ideas of Hughlings Jackson, who viewed psychological processes as "dependent concomitants" of physiological processes; a year later, in the introduction to his translation of Charcot's *Leçons du mardi,* he expressed his admiration for French neuropathologists who did not insist on the immediate link with physiology which was postulated by German neurophysiologists. Freud's search for the appropriate degree of separation between physiology and psychology had started during those years. The Project of 1895 represents the greatest approximation to the physiological tradition—possibly emphasized in opposition to Breuer, who took a different attitude in his theoretical chapter in *Studies on Hysteria*. But Freud's own position changed, when his insight into the rudimentary facts of psychodynamics was supplemented by his first findings in the field of ontogenetic hypothesis. The extension of psychoanalytic propositions to embrace the whole of the individual's life history, the introduction of social considerations into the study of conflict, enriched his views and gave him a feeling of independence. When Fliess attempted to link the unconscious to the problem of bisexuality by stating that the impulses of the opposite sex are regularly repressed, Freud revolted against this attempt to "biologize psychodynamics," and the relation between the two came to an end.

A few years later (1905c), Freud described his new position in these terms:

> My experiences of the displaceability of psychical energy along certain paths of association, and of the almost indestructible persistence of the traces of psychical processes, have in fact suggested to me an attempt at picturing the unknown [the psychical apparatus] in some such way. To avoid misunderstanding, I must add that I am making no attempt to proclaim that the cells and nerve fibres, or the systems of neurones which are taking their place to-day, are these psychical paths, even though it would have to be possible in some manner which cannot yet be indicated to represent such paths by organic elements of the nervous system [p. 148].

Later in his life he reformulated the same idea in somewhat different terms (1915c):

> Research has given irrefutable proof that mental activity is bound up with the function of the brain as it is with no other organ. We are taken a step further—we do not know how much—by the discovery of the unequal importance of the different parts of the brain and their special relations to particular parts of the body and to particular mental activities. *But every attempt to go on from there to discover a localization of mental processes, every endeavour to think of ideas as stored up in nerve-cells and of excitations as travelling along nerve-fibres, has miscarried completely* [p. 174; italics added].

In these last remarks one might well detect a recollection of the failure of his own attempts, of which the newly accessible material gives us evidence.

The problem of "the suitable degree of separation" is still with us. Recently, a distinguished neurophysiologist, E. D. Adrian (1946), has formulated the problem in terms similar to those I have just quoted. We have recognized that the appropriate degree of separation between physiological and psychological concepts has to be determined by the specific character of the data on which psychoanalysis is based. Contemporary discussions concerning the concept of instinctual drive offer the best illustration of this problem. The Freudian concept, sharply distinct as it is from that of instinct in the sense used in animal psychology, is one that allows for the fruitful integration of the various aspects of maturation and social learning on which psychoanalysis is based (Hartmann, 1948). It was formulated not to fit into a system but in order to allow for a comprehensive explanation of the data which psychoanalytic observation had provided.

Examples of this kind are not isolated. They should be stressed in order to meet a frequent objection to psychoanalysis. This objection maintains that since the terminology used by Freud derives in part from the neurophysiology of the 19th century, the concepts of psychoanalysis are antiquated. We readily grant that historical overtones may make psychoanalytic terminology confusing to some students in the field, but the problem is one that concerns the terms only and not the concepts. With the verbal tools of the age in which he was educated, Freud constructed concepts that were novel, closely linked to the data of observation and yet broad enough to allow for far-reaching generalization.[1]

Freud's search for the appropriate degree of separation between psychological and physiological thinking has enabled psychoanalysis to occupy a position in the center of modern

1. [For a more detailed discussion of the implications of Freud's early discoveries, see Ernst Kris's Introduction and footnotes to *The Origins of Psychoanalysis*. For further statements concerning the relation of brain physiology and psychoanalysis, see Kris (1953a).]

science: firmly rooted in clinical thought, in biological and physiological hypotheses, it extends into the social sciences and constitutes a link between the two. Recent extensions of psychoanalytic research into the area of psychosomatic medicine on the one side of this continuum and into the area of psychoanalytically orientated sociology on the other are evidence of the fruitfulness of the position that Freud established in his early years. In those years and in his own experiences another fundamental discovery was made: the discovery that the calibration of the observer by psychoanalysis is an essential prerequisite for fruitful observation—a discovery which is equally valid and equally important in every department of the study of man.

18: The Development of Ego Psychology

(1951)

In speaking of psychoanalytic ego psychology I refer not only to a part or sector of psychoanalytic theory but also to a decisive reorientation of this theory as a whole. The fundamental assumptions on which psychoanalytic ego psychology rests were formulated by Freud during the early 1920s—more than a quarter of a century after he had first approached the field out of which the theory and practice of psychoanalysis grew. The new formulation compelled Freud to revise more or less radically many of his earlier views. He never attempted a complete and systematic revision or synchronization. Although many authors have since supplemented his attempts, a systematic revision has not yet been spelled out in all essential details, a circumstance that may well be responsible for some of the cross-currents in psychoanalytic writings during the last twenty years.

Freud's reformulations have had decisive consequences. Let me here briefly state that psychoanalytic ego psychology has encouraged and facilitated the integration of the psychoanalytic approach with other approaches in the biological and social sciences, particularly in psychiatry and, to a lesser degree, in psychology; its influence has spread rapidly to all fields in which psychoanalytic propositions are being applied, particularly to psychoanalytic therapy itself, the area from which the major incentive for the reformulation of older views had come. Psychoanalytic ego psychology not only influenced the very matrix from which it had grown, but its influence ex-

First published in *Samiksa*, 5 : 153–168, 1951.

tended to all psychoanalytically oriented psychotherapies and to many techniques in mental health and education which implicitly or explicitly are geared toward prevention.

This influence led to, and at the same time was supported by, an extensive, if not always systematic, research activity that opened up new vistas. The very foundation of the psychoanalytic approach to psychosomatic medicine has its roots here. The extension of psychiatric techniques to the practices of social work and the penetration of social psychology may be designated as the psychiatric revolution of our day.

In order to understand how this expansion can at least in part be related to the development of psychoanalytic thinking, it seems necessary briefly to turn to its history. Since this history is to a large extent the work of *one* individual—to a larger extent than in any other branch of science—it is justified to follow traces leading to the stages of Freud's thought after more than fifty years of its development (see Kris, 1950).

When at the age of thirty-five Freud turned part of his interest in a gradually increasing degree to psychotherapy, his starting point was the assumption of a connection between mental conflict and mental illnesses. At the time he was painfully aware of the fact that the study of mental conflict had never been attempted by means of science, that knowledge about it was derived from nonscientific exploration, from poetic intuition, philosophic introspection, or the speculative interpretation sanctioned by theological tradition. This proximity to extrascientific approaches was bound to constitute a challenge to a man who, though deeply imbued with admiration for the humanities, had grown up as a scientist in the strictest sense of the word, one who looked upon physics as the basic science and on all other endeavors as derivations or applications. This was the approach of the particular physiological environment in which Freud had passed the formative years of his youth (Bernfeld, 1944, 1947). Only reluctantly had he abandoned histological investigation and physiological experimentation in order to devote himself to the practice of neuropathology. When apparently accidentally and allegedly for merely external reasons his attention was directed toward psychiatry, he had already achieved a compromise between his earliest physiological and his later neurological interests. He planned a comprehensive treatise on the anatomy of the central nervous system, which was intended as a revision of the then current views in neuroanatomy and neurophysiology. At that time, Freud was one of the first who, following Hughlings Jackson, attempted to stress the importance of dynamic thinking in neurology in contrast to rigid localization. The newly discovered Fliess correspondence and the notes and drafts dating back to the 1890s (Freud, 1950) permit us to establish the link between his early training, his later interest in neurophysiology, and his first steps in theoretical thinking in the area that was to become psychoanalysis as a coherent body of hypotheses [see also chap. 17].

The first attempt to understand the nature of mental conflict and to establish a rationale for therapeutic action was based on neurophysiological assumptions, which Freud at the time designated as "the law of constancy"; it referred to the tendency of the central nervous system to keep energy tensions constant. The law of constancy permitted Freud to formulate his assumptions on the interaction of conflict, mounting tension, defense (repression), and abreaction in the therapy of hysteria.

During the mid–1890s Freud was engaged in writing a treatise on general psychology and psychopathology for neurologists. In this Project (1895) a very large number of detailed assumptions are made in order to explain in terms of neurons and their functions such concepts and processes as the symptom formation in hysteria and the transformation of the dream wish into the manifest content of the dream. To make these processes understandable, Freud assumed the existence of four qualities of psychic energy in the central nervous system and of several anatomically differentiated types of neurons. One such type is distinguished by its permanent investment with psychic energy; neurons of this type form a coherent organization in charge of inhibitory and control functions. Freud designates them the ego neurons and speaks of an ego organization.

Freud's writings during the first and second decade of the new century abound with passages in which he asserts that the attempt to replace psychological by specific neurophysiological assumptions had not succeeded. In view of the intricate character of the psychological assumptions themselves, we should not lose sight of the notion that ultimately whatever was expressed in psychological terms refers to physiological processes.

This is the methodological orientation of Freud's continued attempts to represent the processes he studied as interrelated manifestations of the function of the "psychic apparatus" as a whole. His interest in the anatomy of the central nervous system has found its continuation and its fruitful expansion when in the course of these attempts the structural concepts of psychoanalysis were introduced, and after a time lag of thirty years, next to the id and the superego, the ego as an organization reappeared in Freud's writings. The way in which these constructs were defined leaves no doubt as to the scientific tradition which Freud follows. The id, the ego, and the superego are defined as physiological organ systems are defined—they are defined by their functions (Hartmann, Kris and Loewenstein, 1946).

Let me pause here for a moment. There are passages in Freud's writings in which the word ego is used not to describe an organization, but the total personality, the self; there are also passages in which the attribution of functions to the one or the other of the organizations is not consistent—and nothing is easier than to quote Freud in order to contradict Freud. Apart from a fair degree of semantic inconsistency which may be the particular prerogative of the great explorer, contradictions in Freud's writings are the expression of the function of these writings; they represent not the codification of a system, but a constant attempt to unify explanatory concepts and at the same time to adapt theoretical assumptions to the findings of the clinician. The tension between the theoretical assumption and the clinical observation accounts for the particular texture of Freud's thinking and for the fact that many assumptions that had been kept in readiness for years emerge in his writings at a time when new observations seem suddenly to have called for them.

After the grandiose but forced attempt of the psychology for the neurologists, the concept of an ego in the sense of an organization disappeared for two decades from Freud's writings. With the disappearance of this one concept, another that had originally led to the concept of an ego organization—the concept of defense—lost its dominant position. Of the variety of defense mechanisms which Freud had early described, the mechanism of repression attracted his attention. The great discoveries that led Freud into this direction need only be enumerated: the insight into the formative importance of earliest experiences for the etiology of neuroses and the discovery of infantile sexuality, the understanding of the mechanism of dreams, and detailed insight into mechanisms operating in various types of psychoneuroses and perversions. These included an understanding of typical ontogenetic patterns, i.e., of the occurrence of fixation and regression in each of the major clinical pictures studied. Freud's interest, one may be tempted to say, was turned toward the id, a statement which can be supported by his own later views on the significance of this period (Freud, 1925), a statement, however, that can be viewed only as extreme simplification. Freud's attention remained centered on the nature of mental conflict, on the interplay of opposing forces. The repressing agent was required by the study of the repressed, the censor by the study of the dream. They remained isolated until the incentive came to revise the earlier assumptions, and to revive the older concepts in the light of new findings. To put it briefly, the ego as an organization played a part in the study of some of its function.[1]

Some of these incentives can be clearly traced to psychoanalytic therapy. The ever-growing insight into the dynamic function of resistance was bound to direct the attention to the ego. One might say that in Freud's papers on psychoanalytic technique, his advice to start therapeutic work from "the surface,"

---

1. See Hartmann, Kris, and Loewenstein (1953) in which the relation of the history of psychoanalysis to its systematic presentation is examined.

to interpret defense before content, already implied some principles of psychoanalytic ego psychology. Other stimuli came undoubtedly from the clinical pictures Freud studied.

During the early years and decades of his work, limited by the conditions of private practice, Freud had hardly any access to the study of psychoses. Through the suggestions of some of his early disciples, particularly of Jung and later of Abraham, the question of what psychoanalysis could contribute to the study of psychoses was brought to his attention. This then focused his observations on pathological reactions of a new type, which forced upon him a new approach. In introducing the concept of narcissism (1914d), a first attempt was made to turn from isolated functions of the ego to one of a coherent organization with an independent energy cathexis. The nature of this organization was to be more closely scrutinized when new types of cases appeared in psychoanalytic observation.

It is doubtful whether the appearance of what I here briefly call new types of cases can be explained by the effect of cultural change or social factors on the manifestation of neurotic illness, or to changes in the type of cases which came for treatment. These alternative explanations, or the assumption that both these factors operate, seem to exist whenever we are faced with reports on changes in hitherto familiar clinical pictures or on changes in their frequency distribution under psychiatric observation. It is probable that as far as psychoanalysis is concerned, at least one additional factor has to be considered, a factor to which I am inclined to attribute decisive importance: the potentialities of psychoanalytic therapy had gradually increased and this increase had influenced the concept of what was to be considered illness in a psychiatric sense. The new types of cases to which I refer were character neuroses of various types, foremost among them being individuals in whose life not symptoms but distress and misfortune were dominant. It is in the treatment of these cases that new types of resistance, the uncanny negative therapeutic reaction, and other manifestations of unconscious guilt feelings and self-punitive impulses could be studied. In the study and the treatment of these manifestations of conflict and resistance, psychoanalysis gained a new dimension.

These, then, are some of the clinical and therapeutic experiences that suggested a revision of older theoretical assumptions. It was no longer possible to account for mental conflict by assuming the opposition of various strata of consciousness to each other. Defense and resistance, the power of which had only at this point been fully understood, were not processes mobilized by consciousness, and neither the regulation of moral behavior nor the onslaught of self-punishment on the individual's life proceeds within awareness. Moreover, there was the clinical aspect of psychotic regression, which could not be accounted for by the older conceptual tools. A new concept of the psychic apparatus was needed in order to establish once more the link between clinical work and theoretical assumption.

Partly the same clinical experiences that had created this necessity, partly similar ones, directed Freud's attention into another direction. Not only the organization of the psychic apparatus but also assumptions on the nature of energies operating in this apparatus had to be revised. Freud's great clinical discoveries up to the second decade of the current century had been based on a concept of sexuality that had grown out of the data of clinical observation (Hartmann, 1948). These data had pointed to the ontogenetic connection between early infantile needs and bodily functions and the later development of genital gratification, a connection that at the same time threw light on never suspected vicissitudes and transformation of the impulses studied. Based on these data of observation, Freud formulated in gradual steps the concept of "instinctual drive" that has proved so eminently fruitful. At this period of development the need for structural concepts was felt by Freud. He temporarily envisaged the necessity to assume that the ego as viewed at that time, the inhibitory and self-preserving part of the personality, was endowed with drives of its own, with ego drives, in contradistinction to sexual drives (Bibring, 1941; Hartmann, 1948; Hartmann, Kris, and Loewenstein, 1953). This assumption, in turn, could not withstand the pressure of clinical experience.

When later in his life Freud discussed the reasons which had led him for years to overlook the importance of aggres-

sive impulses in man, he was inclined to make his own unconscious tendencies responsible for this time lag. Be this as it
may, if we envisage for a moment what part in contemporary
psychiatric thinking the reference to aggression plays, how
our views on large sectors of clinical phenomena are determined by our insight into the economy of aggressive impulses,
we will realize the importance of the next stage in the development in Freud's ideas (see Menninger, 1938, 1942). It may
seem unfortunate that at this point of his development Freud
combined two steps: the introduction of a new assumption on
the role of aggression in mental conflict with a speculative extension of his theory of instinctual drives in general, i.e., the
speculation concerning life and death instincts.

   This is not the place to account for the development of
Freud's instinct theory, but without the introduction of aggression as an instinctual drive none of the great advances that
psychoanalysis made are understandable. Insight into the
functions of the superego, especially into the importance of
internalized aggression, which largely motivates these functions and their unconscious nature, was the first decisive contribution to appear. Somewhat later attention was focused on
the ego. Its energy cathexis was no longer attributed to drives
of its own but rather was accounted for by the assumption that
the energy of instinctual drives could be sublimated or neutralized; desexualized and de-aggressivized energy contributes
the motor power for the complex functions of the ego (Hartmann, Kris, and Loewenstein, 1949).

   At this point I shall not attempt to enumerate these functions. Any such enumeration leads into intricacies of definition, which I am not prepared to approach, and suggests the
need for further clarification. In order to demonstrate some
of the problems involved, I mention that in speaking of the
ego's control of motility, perception, and thought, we imply
that the testing of reality and the anticipation of further
events are part of the ego's function. In assigning to the ego
the function of mediating between the requirements of reality,
the pressures of the id impulses, the postulates of the superego and its own interest, we have not only assumed the ex-

istence of an integrating, organizing, or synthetic function of the ego, which accounts for the multiple determination of human behavior in general, but have implied that the ego is more than a mediator,[2] that there are independent—or better, relatively independent—ego interests and autonomous ego functions, which may be, but are not necessarily, a part of mental conflict (Hartmann, 1939a, 1947).

Freud's assumption that ego functions are being exercised on various stages of awareness has opened the way for a new understanding of the importance of these functions for a psychoanalytic theory of the total personality and has gradually gained very great significance indeed for all areas of psychoanalytic thinking. I should like to illustrate this significance in two ways: first, in discussing briefly at least one example of reformulation of previous views that had become necessary; and second, in discussing some of the new problems that have become accessible.

During the 1890s when, as we saw, Freud, was anxious to maintain or to establish the link between his psychological findings and the tradition of physiology in which he had grown up, at a time when he was not yet able to determine a fruitful distance between the two, he proudly formulated the hypothesis that nondischarged libidinal energy tended to be transformed into anxiety. This hypothesis seemed at first to account for the data of observation provided by clinical cases in which the symptomatology seemed related to direct sexual frustration. The frequency of such cases at that time may have been determined by the Victorian standards of sexual morality prevailing in the society in which Freud practiced. The proposition suggested can be characterized as toxicological (Hartmann and Kris, 1945; Orlemans, 1949). Freud maintained it for almost thirty years (1926). The revision was a radical one. Before I point to the theoretical consequences of this reformulation, let me remind you briefly of some of his new statements. The physiological mechanism of anxiety acts as a signal by which the ego warns the organism of dangers to come. In

2. See, for example, Nunberg (1931), Waelder (1930), Hartmann (1939a), and French (1941).

the case of successful warning, defenses are being mobilized. When warning tends to be unsuccessful, i.e., when a specific anticipated danger situation, or in extreme cases, when the anticipation of danger situations in general is experienced as traumatic, anxiety as signal tends to grow into anxiety as a symptom beyond control. Traumatic danger situations are those in which the individual experiences helplessness and is unable to discharge tension. Situations of this kind are regularly experienced during infancy and childhood. During each phase of early development, other typical dangers tend to be experienced as traumatic because the fear of the mounting tension of certain physiological needs leads in early infancy to the fear of the absence of the need-satisfying human object— the mother. At a somewhat later stage, during the second year of life, the need for the presence of the object is partly replaced and largely supplemented by the need of retaining the lasting love of the object. During the fourth year of life, in connection with the stage of maturation which Freud designated as the phallic stage of development, and during, the involvement in oedipal conflicts, the fear of castration gains a paramount position, to be largely replaced at the end of this phase by the fear of conscience, the fear of the superego—in normal cases, more or less sharply distinguished from the fear of sanctions of the community, i.e., from social anxiety.

The four specific danger situations obviously cover a vast array of phenomena and refer to a considerable number of developmental phases including the reaction to the environment. Before continuing this discussion, I shall briefly indicate in what way the newer theory of Freud deviates from the older one. The difference points at least in two directions. When Freud speaks of reaction to danger situations, his model is the reaction of the organism in a given environment, hence the problem of adaptation. A physiological, or more specifically, a toxicological way of thinking has been replaced by one oriented toward a general biological approach. Second, the clinical manifestations studied, even those in which anxiety is apparently instigated by mere frustration, are being viewed in relation to the individual's past history, if in no other sense than in one which assumes that the ego's way of reacting has been patterned by the past. Such an extension of the importance of ontogenetic factors in the formulation of psychoanalytic theory was bound once more to stress the viewpoint of adaptation, and at the same time to place emphasis on what is designated in current psychological theory as learned behavior.

The new theoretical formulations had several consequences. The understanding that the individual mobilizes defenses in danger situations in order to avoid danger or the rise of undue and no longer protective anxiety stimulated a reorientation. Shortly after the formulation of the new theory in 1926, the attention of many workers turned to the systematic study of the mechanism of defense. These investigators started from the assumption that the types of behavior which in psychoanalytic observation appear as defense correspond in part, but only in part, to the mechanisms which, during early phases of development, are normally being used in the adaptation to new situations. The technical starting point—though in itself part of the new theory—was Freud's insight into the relationship of resistance during psychoanalytic therapy to defense against danger. If I here refer to Anna Freud's contribution, *The Ego and the Mechanisms of Defense* (1936),[3] I have also pointed to the influence of ego psychology on psychoanalytic technique, an influence which I believe can hardly be overestimated, and refers to an area in flux. There is no doubt that even the goals of therapy have become better accessible to formulation, and this is true for psychoanalytic therapy proper. I have little doubt that a closer analysis of the theories used by those experimenting in the therapy of borderline cases, psychoses, or in general psychoanalytically oriented psychotherapy, would indicate a high degree of success during the last quarter of a century, and would reveal that the *improvement of integrative* capacities of the ego has become the goal of, and with it the guide for, therapeutic improvements.[4]

3. For a summary see Fenichel (1945). See also French (1938), [and chap. 16].
4. See the numerous contributions of Alexander; see also Greenacre (1941), Federn (1943).

In turning to the second area to which I pointed previously, to the relation of ego psychology to personality development, we are faced with many and divergent trends of investigation. Only some of them can be mentioned here.

The psychoanalytic method of observation achieved one of its most significant results in the area of child development. Through data provided by the study of regressive behavior of adult neurotics, under the rules of psychoanalysis, Freud was able to describe a normal sequence of maturation. The stages of psychosexual development, the sequence of oral, anal, and phallic erotogenicity, were related by Abraham (1924) and others to the discharge of both libidinal and aggressive impulses (though the link to aggression is by far the looser one).

Under the impact of Freud's formulation of the functions of the ego, these theories were elaborated in various directions. One group of workers turned its attention to the earliest stages of preverbal behavior and attempted to explain a large number of clinical phenomena by the defense against one particular group of impulses, those of an oral-aggressive nature. In some of the formulation of this group, particularly in those of Melanie Klein, the assumption is implied that defense is as old as impulse, the ego as old as the id, largely an innate organization whose functions are essentially dependent on developmental and maturational processes. Others take exception to this idea and visualize the process in a different light (Waelder, 1936; Glover, 1945; Bibring, 1947). They study the formation of the ego, the contribution of each of the stages of psychosexual maturation and each of the critical phases in the child's ego development to this formation. Investigations of this type have attempted, at least in part, to supplement material gathered in psychoanalytic observation by direct observation of the growing child.

The most general question that these investigators pose is concerned with desirable or optimal conditions for the distribution of indulgence and deprivation or discipline in child rearing and education in general (see chap. 4). The formula that seems to tally best with clinical experience and experimental findings suggests that indulgence should be maximized as long as deprivation of a specific need is likely to create traumatizing tension, that indulgence should be regulated by discipline at the point when the child's ego organization is ready to accept the requirements of his environment, and hence not only learns to bear tension, but gradually acquires the pleasure in its mastery, and in mastery in a more general sense (Hendrick, 1942, 1943a, 1943b).

This distribution of indulgence and discipline, related as it is to the formation of the ego, implies, at the same time, the establishment of the child's identification with his love objects.

The closer study of this relation was once more initiated by clinical psychoanalytic observations. Under the guide of the newly formulated ego psychology, it became possible to distinguish more sharply between oedipal and preoedipal conflicts in the child's development. These findings suggested to Freud some of the formulations on typical early anxiety situations which I quoted above—mainly, the distinction between the early need for the presence of the love object and the somewhat later need for the object's love, a formulation which, in monumental brevity, refers to the development of a unique relationship, that between mother and child.

I need not here report in detail how much and how decisively our understanding of this relationship has increased, how clinical study and systematic child observation have taught us to evaluate the effects of separation on the child.

Some of these studies have a direct bearing on ego psychology. Clinical impression in the analysis of schizoid personalities pointed to the influence of insufficiently intense or generally unsatisfactory object relations on the ego development of the patient (H. Deutsch, 1934). Studies of institutionalized or severely disturbed children have reaffirmed and enlarged this impression. There seems little doubt that the intactness of ego functions in the adult is to a higher degree than was previously anticipated, determined by the nature of the child's earliest object relations.[5]

The time has not yet come to evaluate fully the significance

5. See, e.g., Ribble (1941), Fries (1935), Malcove (1945), Spitz (1945, 1946), Spitz and Wolf (1949), Rank (1949b), Putnam et al. (1948).

of these findings. To everyone familiar with the data presented, the fascination of the topic and the uncertainties that still prevail, must be obvious. In concluding, therefore, I shall try to indicate how these findings could be fitted into the structure of theoretical thinking in psychoanalysis.

If we assume, as Freud does, that the investment of the human object with psychic energy, both libidinal and aggressive, prepares the child's way to life, then we may expect that a satisfactory relation to the object regulates the economy of psychic energy in a particular way. In identifying with the object, part of the energy vested in it becomes available to the ego. We may assume that this energy, fused in object cathexis, can be neutralized, i.e., lose the hallmark of either libido or aggression, be at the free disposal of the ego, and constitute one of the sources of that evasive and yet unavoidable concept, ego strength, which expresses itself in autonomous functions. In the opposite case, the cathexis of the ego will not be neutralized. This, then, may lead to narcissistic and self-destructive tendencies and the defenses against these.

These or similar hypotheses do not contradict other more general assumptions on the formation of the ego, which have been discussed by many authors since Freud formulated his original hypothesis. He visualized this process as one of gradual differentiation of the ego from the id. Hartmann (1939a) has, I believe with better grounds, suggested that the assumption of an undifferentiated phase out of which ego and id develop, may be preferable (see also Lampl-de Groot, 1947). Common to both assumptions is the idea that early stages of development can be described in terms of growing distance between ego and id—an assumption that, I believe, throws light on many aspects of child development. This vast area of research, the subject of so many investigations during the last half century, is still rigidly departmentalized, particularly the processes of physiological maturation which have been studied in considerable detail. If we turn from the study of this one sector to that of the child's personality, if we learn to include the psychoanalytic and psychiatric knowledge, new problems and also new possibilities of integration of existing knowledge are offered. We may say, as Hartmann does, that maturation concerns the apparatus which the ego organization controls; that among ego functions some are likely to be more involved in mental conflict than others; that certain functions which, early in childhood, at the proximity of the id, are still part and parcel of conflict, may later become autonomous, so that their original involvement in conflict has acted as an incentive to future development.

At this point a new outlook on the future seems possible. The study of the development of the ego in childhood is likely to give renewed emphasis to the study of normal child development by observers with psychiatric and psychoanalytic training. The study of normalcy, however, is bound to include consideration of the influence which changing cultural conditions exercise.

The development of psychoanalytic ego psychology, which I have tried to survey in an admittedly abbreviated and sketchy form, constitutes, to my mind, not a completed chapter in the history of psychoanalytic theory, but a series of attempts to arrive at useful formulations. Their further development is difficult to predict. There seems to exist a tendency to select parts of this theory for elaboration and to neglect others. Thus recently the theory of the mechanisms of of defense has been recommended as closer to the possibility of verification by experimental procedures to be carried out in the laboratory. In view of similar tendencies, it is appropriate to state that however complex the assumptions of psychoanalytic theory seem to some, to others they still seem comparatively primitive. The latter are impressed by the magnitude of the unknown areas in a field that extends from psychiatry to normal psychology; they are also impressed by the distance from other areas in science in which we still operate. It is this distance which, at the beginning of his venture, bewildered Freud and formed one of the incentives for the development of his theoretical thinking, some examples of which I have tried to quote. It seems likely that the impact of similar uncertainties will form one of the incentives for the further development of psychoanalytic ego psychology.

19: New Contributions to the Study of Freud's
The Interpretation of Dreams

A Critical Essay

(1954)

The preface to the first volume of Wilhelm Wundt's *Völker-psychologie* is dated March 1900. In it the author sets out to explain and justify the bold plan that had led him, the master of experimental psychology, late in life, in his sixty-eighth year, to enter into a new venture. Psychology, Wundt felt, was ready for greater tasks and should no longer be confined to the rigorous limitations of a "psychophysical" approach. The study of man in a new and broader sense should not be left to anthropologists and historians; it was the psychologist's business. Wundt devoted the major part of the subsequent twenty years of his life to the twelve volumes of his work. Half a century after he started on his venture, the *Völkerpsychologie* is rarely quoted; it has never been translated into English. And yet no other man's work left an imprint on academic psychology in Great Britain and the United States comparable to that of Wilhelm Wundt, the experimentalist. However, as far as the *Völkerpsychologie* is concerned, the intention more than its execution is memorable. No access to the study of man was possible from Wundt's point of departure. *The Interpretation of Dreams* (1900) offered this access. The aim of conceiving a new approach to psychology had been on Freud's mind during the

This review of James Strachey's new translation of *The Interpretation of Dreams* and *On Dreams* (published 1953) and Robert Fliess's *The Revival of Interest in the Dream* (1953) was first published in the *Journal of the American Psychoanalytic Association*, 2 : 180–191.

long years he had prepared for his task. When Wundt wrote his preface, Freud's book had been for sale for four months, and it was already clear that the high hopes of its struggling author would be disappointed and that the book would arouse but little immediate attention.

Historians of science, experts in the history of ideas, are left to ponder the question why the access to the psychology of the 20th century led through psychopathology and psychotherapy rather than through insights gained by laboratory procedures, why Freud succeeded where Wundt failed. Part of this question, however, concerns the unique position of *The Interpretation of Dreams* not only in the history of science, but more specifically in the development of Freud's thought and in that of psychoanalysis. The question has gained new scope by information which has become accessible during the last few years. We have learned to understand some of the circumstances and developments which led Freud to select the dream as the initial field of intense study.

There are two roots to Freud's devotion to his subject: one leads to the structure of the problems he was investigating, the other to the structure of the personal conflict which the inquiry into unconscious processes had stimulated in the investigator. Before they could finally be separated, the two roots were intertwined in many ways. Our information stems from two sources: Freud's letters to his bride (1882 to 1886) indicate that dreams had early played a part in Freud's interest; the letters to W. Fliess and previously unpublished manuscripts sent to the latter permit us to trace in some detail the various steps which led, during the years 1895 to 1899, first to the direction of Freud's interest and then to this intense concentration on the subject. Ernest Jones (1953a) has wielded the information which these sources offer with other material into a masterful account of Freud's development as man and investigator. The picture he offers not only immeasurably enriches our understanding of Freud's life and work, but it may well influence our image of the personality of great explorers. We may well be led to understand that the measure of proximity and distance between personal and objective incentives to his work

constitutes one of the characteristics of the great. One encounters not a mere compromise of conflicting forces, as any
sublimation may offer, but rather a specific condition: namely,
during the process of work the functions of the ego emerge
from involvement in intense conflict to full and supreme autonomy. In Freud's study of dreams these requirements are
fulfilled in a unique fashion. His self-analysis became part of
an investigative process which was constantly enriched by personal experience, and the investigative process served in turn
the function of liberation from suffering as well as from fateful error.

Freud's interest in dreams must have been of long standing.
During the 1880s it became part of a more than accidental
preoccupation. He compiled a collection of his own dreams
and applied self-observation to their study: self-observation
and self-experimentation were to him legitimate tools of investigative procedure used in his work on cocaine and in neurological studies. Applied to the dream, they yielded at the time
astounding insight. In a letter to his bride (June 30, 1882) he
mentions that in his dreams only such themes occur "as were
touched on once in the course of the day and then broken off"
(Jones, 1953a, p. 351). Fourteen years later this discovery of
one of the principles for the selection of day residues is utilized in Freud's writings, in a footnote to one of the case histories in the *Studies on Hysteria.* (p. 69).

It may be worth mentioning that this first discovered and,
topographically speaking, "most superficial" hypothesis of psychoanalysis is among those which in the experimental psychology of the 20th century have found most attention. The host
of investigations, stimulated by Kurt Lewin, on the completion
of incomplete tasks—investigations which are supposed to
make the study of psychological dynamics accessible to the laboratory—are based on the self-observation of a young man,
who had not yet decided in which of the medical specialties he
would find satisfactory opportunities. When Freud wrote the
above-quoted letter, he still held the position of "demon-
strator" in the Physiological Institute.

More than a decade later Freud, the neuropathologist,

could link this accidental discovery to the experiences suggested by his therapeutic work with the method of free association; but the key was still missing. In March 1895, Freud mentions in one of his letters, accidentally, as it were, and with half-humorous intention, the dream of the tardy medical student who dreams of himself as being in the hospital—thus recognizing a relationship to hallucinatory wish fulfillment. In July 1895—we do not know under what immediate stimulation—he turns to self-experimentation. A dream which must obviously have impressed him, the dream of Irma's injection, is the first to which he collects his own associations. He discovers the wish-fulfilling function of the dream. He was at the time engaged in thoughts which deeply preoccupied him, had gradually emerged, and were to direct his thinking for the rest of his life. He was abandoning his intense interest in neuro-anatomy and neurophysiology, the field to which he had devoted himself when he had entered practice, and was dominated by the idea of combining his experience as psychotherapist with his neurophysiological thinking. An external circumstance supplied the motivation of which he may not have been fully aware. Breuer had just completed the theoretical chapter of the *Studies on Hysteria,* in which he wisely had declined to establish too close a correlation between psychological and physiological theory. Spurred by the urge to improve on Breuer's approach, Freud attempted the opposite, a treatise on "Psychology for the Neurologist." It is preserved on loose, sometimes scarcely legible sheets which he sent to Fliess (see Freud, 1950). The psychology of dreams based on the idea of their wish-fulfilling function is part of the "Project," the most closely argued piece of Freud's writing, which he put to paper under tremendous inner pressure during a few weeks in the fall of 1895. The idea of the Project centered on the problems of energy discharge, which led Freud to the distinction of primary and secondary processes. This distinction seems to have suggested the renewed interest in dreams. The discovery of the wish-fulfilling function of the dream viewed as a problem in energy discharge proved in turn the value of this distinction. It is this insight which the analysis of the dream of Irma's injection supplied: self-experimentation seems to have been called upon to solve a crucial problem.

Many of the essential insights in the structure of dreams were at Freud's disposal when he wrote the Project. In the four years which elapsed until the manuscript of *The Interpretation of Dreams* was completed, two further essential steps were made, which are closely interrelated. The idea to translate psychoanalytic findings into the language of contemporary neurophysiology was abandoned; instead psychoanalytic theory was formulated in such a way that its ultimate dependence on neurophysiology could never be questioned, but that within this broad area its conceptual framework was kept independent. Psychoanalytic theory was established at a distance from neurophysiology, which proved fruitful and not paralyzing—to neurologist and analyst. This first step had become possible to Freud mainly through the set of discoveries concerning the importance of the individual's childhood for his later development. The dramatic unfolding of the great problem areas which we designate with the key words of "infantile sexuality" and "oedipus conflict" fills the years in which *The Interpretation of Dreams* gained shape.

But these developments were threatened by a fateful distortion: the idea that not the child's instinctual development but seduction by adults was responsible for neuroses. This assumption, a projection of Freud's own oedipal fantasies concerning the relation of his father to his sister and his younger brother, had first been stimulated and supported by many reports of patients. Later, doubts appeared in Freud's mind—and yet he was unable to discard the seduction theory. The conflict with Breuer, the involvement with Fliess, in which hostile impulses were painfully kept in abeyance by almost adoring devotion, and finally the death of his father in 1896 had brought Freud's own neurotic conflicts to the fore. Self-analysis imposed itself on the struggling man. The first steps in this direction already led Freud to recognize the extent and the nature of his error. The seduction theory could finally be abandoned, and man's struggle with his own instinctual impulses was recognized in its continuity, reaching back into infancy: the theory of wish fulfillment had gained its historical and social dimension.

In the interpretation of his own dreams, Freud had made a fateful step; from self-observation and self-experimentation he had proceeded into a new and definite direction, to systematic self-analysis. The self-analysis, the second root out of which *The Interpretation of Dreams* grew, seems to have taught Freud much more than we can estimate today. It almost certainly sharpened his eye for much in the dynamics of resistance and regression, but also for much in the understanding of dreamwork, on which the interpretation of any dream rests.

A brief survey of the prefaces Freud wrote to the various editions of *The Interpretation of Dreams* makes us realize that this, his first *opus magnum,* retained a special meaning throughout his life. The preface to the first edition (1899) justifies the venture in the eyes of neuropathologists. The preface to the second edition (1908) is no longer directed to a professional group but to the "wider circle of educated and curious-minded readers, whose interest has led me to take up once more after nine years this difficult, but in many respects fundamental, work." It is in this preface that Freud mentions that the book had revealed itself to him as part of his self-analysis. But he also stresses another aspect: "During the long years, in which I have been working at the problems of neuroses I have often been in doubt and sometimes been shaken in my convictions. At such times it has always been *The Interpretation of Dreams* that has given me back my certainty." We know from other of Freud's utterances that this refers to the theoretical considerations first developed in the Project of 1895, and finally revised, expanded, and elaborated in Chapter VII of *The Interpretation of Dreams.* During the 1890s this interest in the psychological blueprint stood side by side with his clinical work, and it seemed difficult to establish a link. From his letters to Fliess we know that Freud discovered three times a fact that seems to us elementary: that dreamwork and symptom formation follow analogous principles.

Three times the discovery was obliterated for reasons which, I believe, can be inferred. Only after the new insight had been integrated, after all contradictions within his thinking had been resolved, could the relation of dreamwork to symptom formation not only be "discovered" but also retained. When, finally, *The Interpretation of Dreams* was published, it offered both a theory and its application, a unity of view which in his clinical work Freud was far from achieving. These are some of the factors which explain Freud's attachment to *The Interpretation of Dreams*. It is most clearly and openly expressed in the Preface to the third English Edition, dated March 15, 1931. "*The Interpretation of Dreams*," Freud says, "contains even according to my present-day judgement, the most valuable of all the discoveries it has been my good fortune to make. Insight such as this falls to one's lot but once in a lifetime" (p. xxxii).[1]

Freud's attachment to the first of his great books has manifested itself by his constant amendments of and additions to earlier editions. These revisions made *The Interpretations of Dreams* difficult to read and presented to the editor of *The Interpretation of Dreams* an extremely difficult task. It is one which has now been solved with supreme skill and foresight.

The first two volumes of the new English edition of Freud's works to be published are devoted to *The Interpretation of Dreams*. It was obvious that this contribution of Freud's should thus be selected, in order to convey the magnitude and importance of the overall venture. Strachey has long been associated with the translation of Freud's writings, and has long been recognized as Freud's most careful, conscientious, and skillful translator. I believe he never before has reached the level on which he now has solved the infinitely complex task of rendering Freud's German. *The Interpretation of Dreams* was written under difficult circumstances. Freud sent parts of the manuscript to the printer when others had not yet gained final shape. There are chapters which he rewrote or at least

---

1. Strachey's footnote to this Preface indicates that no German text of this exists. I have learned from Bertram D. Lewin, and am authorized by him to report, that Freud had sent the German text to A. A. Brill, who had asked Lewin to translate it. Strachey's edition gives Lewin's translation.

reorganized several times, and others whose manuscript went to the printer in a first, scarcely corrected draft. Freud was dissatisfied with his own German style and remarked on the inequalities not only of construction but also of expression that existed from one chapter to the other. The reader who approaches the original of *The Interpretation of Dreams* with these, Freud's own reservations in mind, may well find them justified if he ever can detach himself from the grandeur of the exposition of thought.

There is no such unevenness in Strachey's translation. His style is in perfect balance. It is not that this cohesion and fluidity of style are superimposed upon Freud's text; it brings, I believe, the clarity of Freud's thought fully to the fore. It combines the most painstaking accuracy with a supreme sense for phraseology and structure.

Strachey not only keeps abreast of the stream of Freud's exposition; but by rearranging sentence sequences and paragraphs, he has clarified Freud's meaning in many instances. It is indeed a fortunate coincidence that the erudition and psychoanalytic training of a translator are here combined with literary craftsmanship of high order and rigorous standards; a craftsmanship which, as we have recently learned, was, if not acquired, still trained and strengthened through Strachey's early work for the *Spectator* of London.[2]

In addition to the problems of style and meaning in every translation of Freud's contributions, numerous questions of terminology arise which have to be solved. Strachey has never avoided the translator's responsibility. He has not been intimidated by the conventions of either language, German or English.

To quote only one example, I feel that psychoanalysts will always be grateful to Strachey for having the courage to translate the German *Unlust* by a neologism "unpleasure," thereby adding precision to current English psychoanalytic usage. In the present translation of *The Interpretation of Dreams* there are some noteworthy instances of terminological choice with

2. For a bibliography of James Strachey's contributions to the *Spectator,* see Charles R. Sanders (1953).

which Strachey found himself faced. At least one of them needs to be mentioned here. He replaced the term "secondary elaboration" by "secondary revision"—a simpler and more pleasant word, and one significantly borrowed from the area of editorial work.[3] Whether analysts will readily accept Strachey's suggestion or be prone to long for the customary "elaboration," because it had become customary, remains to be seen.

Instances where Strachey has not adequately conveyed Freud's meaning seem extremely rare. This is undoubtedly in part due to Anna Freud's collaboration, who has undertaken a sentence-by-sentence comparison of text and translation.[4] But it is not only the mastery of the translator and writer which will give to Strachey's work its place in the history of psychoanalysis. As Ernest Jones (1953b) recently intimated, the new edition should not be looked upon merely as a new translation. It is not only the Standard Translation of Freud into English; it is, as the title proudly proclaims, the Standard Edition of Freud's Psychological Work in any language.

Strachey undertook the task to improve in several ways on the work of previous editors and of Freud himself insofar as he assumed the role of editor. There are many instances in *The Interpretation of Dreams* where Freud refers to preceding or following passages of the text; in many of these instances no specific page reference is indicated. The new edition not only remedies this, but adds references even where Freud has omitted them altogether. Those who have tried to use the bibliography attached to *The Interpretation of Dreams* have frequently been baffled by inaccuracies; Strachey has revised

3. To indicate changes in a work from one edition to the other, we speak of a "revised" edition; this renders the German *"durchgesehene" Auflage*. More radical editorial changes may in German be designated by *"bearbeitete" Auflage*. There seems to be no special translation in English of this distinction.

4. A similar, partial comparison was recently made by one of our colleagues. In discussing Chapter VII with his students at the New York Psychoanalytic Institute, Dr. Frederic Weil made a number of observations, one of which he authorized me to use: in his comments on the difference between primary and secondary process Freud speaks of thoughts which are *korrekt* or *inkorrekt;* Strachey's translation has "rational" and "irrational" (p. 597 and later).

the vast majority of references. These represent only the minor editorial improvements. There are two ways in which Strachey's editorial work has rendered a service to psychoanalysis which will be fully appreciated only in years to come. First, he has indicated in every instance when a passage was added; the reader can now read, as it were, the first edition and at the same time be aware how original statements were enriched, qualified, and elaborated upon. Briefly, this is not the translation of any given edition of *The Interpretation of Dreams;* it is, in Strachey's words, an "editio variorum" in which discarded passages and altered formulations are recorded in footnotes. Strachey has made a second decisive editorial step: he has added annotations, in which he traces the treatment of any specific subject matter and of many hypotheses to Freud's earlier and later writings. There will be in the course of this essay an opportunity to illustrate how useful these annotations are to anyone who pursues a concrete problem and wishes to consult Freud's views.

In surveying Freud's additions to the various editions of *The Interpretation of Dreams,* we not only learn to assess how gradually the study of symbolism gained shape in his mind and how great the influence of Stekel was in this matter; we also become aware of the fact that every detail of the vast topic of dream interpretation retained Freud's interest over the years and decades. I have little doubt that few of us realized that this interest extended to the last German edition of 1931 which was revised by Freud in some telling details.

Freud's revision, however, did not extend to Chapter VII—a contradiction which deserves special comments. I have spoken of the unique position of *The Interpretation of Dreams* in Freud's work and in the history of psychoanalysis, but have not, on this occasion, taken one particular aspect into consideration. There is no other area in Freud's work where the relationship between general theoretical assumptions and their concrete applications, between hypotheses of various degrees of generality, have been elaborated in such detail. The attempt is made to cover the totality of an area of problems— not, indeed, all that one wishes to know about dreams, but all about their interpretations.[5] In none of his work has Freud demonstrated with such great insistence how the fascination with the details of observation can be coordinated with various and even the most general levels of theoretical formulation.

There were obviously various reasons why no additions were made to Chapter VII. It is unique in its composition, one of the greatest pieces of writing in psychological theory, but one which might easily be disrupted by any addition or even by any change. And many additions and changes would have been necessary.

At the time when the second edition of *The Interpretation of Dreams* appeared (1909), the thoughts which a few years later found their way into Freud's metapsychological papers were already germinating. Freud may have found that they could not be mixed with his previous formulations. Indeed, we now feel that such an attempt would have been confusing. However great the shortcomings of some of the formulations in Chapter VII are, compared with Freud's later conceptualization, the whole of the theory is satisfying in one respect: it is suited to the purpose of the study of dreams and represents a level of thinking on which many alternatives can be clearly stated and many concrete clinical problems can be decided. Comparing older to newer formulations of Freud's metapsychology, Bertram D. Lewin (1952), for instance, speaks of two terminologies which one might use alternatively: "the older when discussing dreams, the newer one when writing about the neuroses."

While this represents a convenient practical solution, there are certainly a number of questions in which the synchronization of theory would be of great advantage. An attempt to express the whole texture of general hypotheses contained in Chapter VII of *The Interpretation of Dreams* in structural terms has never been made.[6] This task will fall to a generation of analysts who have not grown up with at least part of the ear-

---

5. "There was a reason for my choosing as the title of my book not *The Dream* but *The Interpretation of Dreams,*" Freud wrote, in a footnote added in 1935 to his *Autobiographical Study* (1925, p. 46).

6. For a valuable beginning, see Rapaport (1950).

lier history of psychoanalysis, but have been educated to view psychoanalytic theory as a whole, synchronizing the various phases of its development and extending its confines from psychopathology to the psychology of normal behavior. They will thus resume the original intention of Freud's Project of 1895. It is the source of much of what in different formulation is still the common basis of our thinking.

> Students of Freud's theoretical writings [Strachey says in his thoughtful introduction to the volume] have been aware that even in his profoundest psychological speculations little or no discussion is to be found upon some of the *most* fundamental of the concepts of which he makes use: such concepts, for instance, as 'mental energy,' 'sums of excitation,' 'cathexis,' 'quantity,' 'quality,' 'intensity,' and so on; . . . The paucity of explanation of such basic notions in Freud's later writings suggests that he was taking it for granted that they were as much a matter of course to his readers as they were to himself . . . the posthumously published correspondence with Fliess . . . throws so much light precisely upon these obscurities [p. xvi].

In Strachey's annotations to *The Interpretation of Dreams* a special emphasis is laid upon references to this material, particularly to the Project. This helps us to understand and reevaluate Freud's concepts in the light of implications which he himself has never spelled out. I believe that through Strachey's insistent and detailed commentary our understanding of psychoanalytic theory has gained a new, historical dimension.

The publication of the two volumes of the new *Standard Edition* coincides happily with *The Revival of Interest in the Dream*. This is the title of a small volume by Robert Fliess, in which a selection of "post-Freudian" contributions are skillfully reviewed. Fliess's point of departure is a change which has occurred during the last twenty years. "Freud's complaint, expressed almost two decades ago, of a lack of interest in the dream among analysts is well known: he accused us in the first of his *New Introductory Lectures* of behaving as though we 'had nothing more to say about the dream' and 'as though the

whole subject of dream theory were finished and done with.' "
Fliess's volume gives evidence that the interest in dream psychology not only has been revived, but that significant contributions and new hypotheses have been offered. The
immediate and, as far as I can see, very general reaction of
readers seems to be that this is indeed a fruitful and stimulating way of presenting material; it permits distinguishing between the new and the old in any one contribution, eliminates
misunderstandings which personal idiosyncracies of an author
or minor shortcomings of his paper may have created; most of
all, however, it draws attention to controversial points,
suggests alternative formulations, and points to questions
which deserve more detailed study. One feels certain that this
type of survey will be extended to other areas of psychoanalytic writing, and one can but hope that Fliess's successors will
try to reach the level of critical frankness and the standards of
learning which make the present volume eminently useful. I
found Fliess's comments on the contributions by Alexander
and Wilson, Federn, French, Grotjahn, and Wisdom, among
others, particularly enlightening.

There are naturally instances where I feel that I cannot
share the reviewer's approach. Thus, I cannot find it useful to
assume that Bertram D. Lewin's "dream screen" is meant or
should be viewed as a "tracer concept." Since Fliess's review
and discussion of Lewin's contribution was written, Lewin
(1953a) himself has stated that he does not share Fliess's interpretation and has clarified in some detail the relation of the
dream screen to the wish to sleep, a problem discussed with
particular care in Fliess's commentary. "The dream screen,"
Lewin (1953b) writes, "is the hallucinatory fulfilment of a wish
to sleep, not a real fulfilment. It represents the idea *sleep* during the state of sleep" (p. 196).

However deeply Fliess enters into the discussion of one
given problem, in most of his comments he stays close to the
questions which the author's contribution has suggested. He
has, in his own words, limited himself sometimes "to supply
opinion" when controversial questions were at stake, in other
instances he "need only supply or explain references from
Freud."

There is, however, one exception to these self-imposed limitations. A recently advanced hypothesis stimulated Fliess to elaborate his comments in particular detail in a special chapter "On the 'Spoken Word' in Dreams," which he distinguishes from other sections of the volume. In a 1948 panel meeting of the American Psychoanalytic Association, Otto Isakower advanced the hypothesis that spoken words in dreams are a contribution of the superego. Fliess's comments are based on a brief report on the Panel Meeting by Robert Waelder (1949). In his unpublished manuscript, which I was privileged to see, Isakower points to the fact that Freud's original thesis, according to which spoken words in dreams are derived from remembered speeches, is not integrated into Freud's dream psychology or psychoanalysis as a whole. This integration becomes possible through Isakower's previous studies (1939) on the role of "auditory incorporation" in the formation of the superego. In the course of these studies, Isakower described the process of going to sleep as one in which "the frontiers of speech" are gradually crossed and pointed to the reverse phenomena in the process of waking up. Based on these previous observations, Isakower developed his new thesis, according to which "speech elements in dreams are a direct contribution from the superego to the manifest dream content." Isakower illustrates his observations by a particularly striking dream, and concludes with reference to the fact that his view was not altogether unexpected, but that Freud had anticipated something similar. He refers to a footnote, added in 1909 to *The Interpretation of Dreams*, in which Freud mentions an exception to his rule. In the dreams of an obsessional patient, speeches did not reproduce words he had heard or spoken, but contained the undistorted verbal expression of his obsessive thoughts. If we use Strachey's edition, we are told that the dreamer to whom Freud refers is well known to us; it is the Rat Man. In the case history itself the fact is duly noted. Freud (1909b) mentions that the obsessional may not be aware of the text of the obsessional command, and continues: "Such texts appear in dreams in the shape of speeches, and are thus an exception to the rule that speeches in dreams are derived from speeches in real life" (p. 223).

In Volume X of the new *Standard Edition,* the last of Freud's unpublished manuscripts will appear in Strachey's translation: the notes which Freud took after sessions with the Rat-Man. In this "Original Record of the Case," we find the report of a dream of the patient which ends—true to Isakower's findings—with the sentence: "I said to myself, 'you mayn't.' " While the patient assumes that these words were suggested to him by his pride, Freud is able to trace them back to a similar sounding remark of the patient's father. And in the epigrammatic fashion of his clinical diary, Freud adds: "The speeches in his dreams need not be related to real speeches. His *Ucs.* ideas—as being *internal voices*—have the value of real speeches which he hears only in his dreams" (p. 274).

That Freud did not draw the conclusions from his observation, which Isakower drew, and did not reconsider the implication of a similar hypothesis in the light of other of his hypotheses, as Fliess did, is not without deep significance.

In leaving the old theoretical framework untouched, in not integrating the various new approaches with the initial approach, some of the problems which occurred to Freud are, as it were, left marginal and remain unintegrated. At a time when interest in the dream is revived, such uncompleted problems turn up again and can now be solved with greater ease.

The revival of interest in the dream, well documented in Fliess's monograph, is powerfully stimulated by observations in areas which only during the last decades have been given their full attention in psychoanalysis. Hypnagogic phenomena during the process of falling asleep, which Isakower (1938) first described in a contribution which has since become a classic, were familiar to Freud. He actually mentions in one of his writings (1917, p. 155, n. 2) an "Isakower phenomenon," but the access to its understanding was not open to him, no more than that of the understanding of Lewin's blank dreams and the dream screen. Only years of detailed exploration of the reflection in clinical material of the pregenital organization, in general, and of the experiences of the oral phase, in particular, have made these addenda to Freud's dream theory possible.

The revival of the interest in the dream can be fruitful only if one follows the general principle which Fliess has suggested: "What Freud has observed must be learned in order to be augmented, and what he has abstracted must be understood in order to be revised." His own contribution to the subject, Fliess has modestly circumscribed: "If the student, closing this small volume, feels that besides having been acquainted with some new ideas and stimulated to clarify old ones, he has had a practical lesson in the reading of *The Interpretation of Dreams,* my purpose is virtually achieved."

I feel that Fliess has achieved considerably more than he has set out to achieve. But his "lesson" in the reading of *The Interpretation of Dreams* will in the future lead the student to a text which Strachey has established with admirable scholarship and skill.

Part IV

APPLIED
PSYCHOANALYSIS

20: The "Danger" of Propaganda

(1941)

THE PROBLEM

If a statement is shaped into a slogan, the power of its appeal may overwhelm that of reason; the slogan calls for emotional response. The slogan of the "danger of propaganda" has, in fact, called into being responses of this kind, the most typical being "beware of propaganda." I shall later discuss one such response. At the moment I should like to retransform the slogan into the statement and ask what people have in mind when they say that propaganda is dangerous.

For the sake of simplicity I shall have to overlook one obvious difficulty. Not all who make this statement refer to the same danger; they mostly imply that only their opponents' propaganda is dangerous.

If we attempt, however, to understand the satement in a more general sense and to investigate what it *may* mean—irrespective of the connotation attached to any particular kind of danger—it seems safe to assume that it regularly refers to one or more of three things: to the fact that man is suggestible; to the technique devised in order to take advantage of this fact; and to the pressure groups using this technique.

The statement also implies that this danger of propaganda is a comparatively "new" one, which either has arisen only recently or of which we have become aware only at this stage of our civilization. The recent experience is World War I—the first "mass war" in centuries, fought by nations, not merely by technicians, mercenaries, or volunteers. In this war, pro-

Read to the Boston Psychoanalytic Society, January 17, 1941. First published in the *American Imago*, 2 : 3–42, 1941. Only the first three sections of this paper are reprinted.

paganda as a means of social control and of actual warfare played a noticeable part. "There is little exaggeration in saying that the world war led to the discovery of propaganda by both the man in the street and the man in the study" (Lasswell, 1938; see also Doob, 1935).

In the years which followed that war, liberal and progressive minds all over the world explored the working of the propaganda machinery during the war. Under the impact of the slogan "it can't happen again," the consciousness of a danger connected with propaganda was widely promoted.

The statement that propaganda is dangerous referred, I said, to three spheres. We shall now have to ask to what extent each of them has been subject to changes in recent history: our mind, the technique of appeal, or the nature of the pressure groups.

In other words, man was always suggestible. Is he more suggestible now than he was before? Those who wanted to influence their fellow beings have always used certain techniques. Do the ones used now evoke a reaction different from those of former days? The few in power were always concerned with gaining the support of the many. Is it the particular brand of pressure groups or ideologies which constitute the danger?

These questions concern some of the fundamental problems of social science, of which psychology is a part. Any answer to these questions can be of two kinds: either it will be based on research carried out with the intention of answering these very questions, or it will be based on the anticipation of results, which may or may not be confirmed by subsequent research. For various reasons, I decided on the second method. Scientific "anticipation," however, and research are not, as a rule, inseparably divided. Their interrelation is obvious: research starts with assumptions. My intention in this paper is no other than to report on some such assumptions. A certain vagueness seems to be their most advantageous characteristic.

My reason for dealing with this subject is not the challenge which its highly flavored topicality may exercise. It is rather a sense of duty. Since the outbreak of this war I have been in touch with problems of propaganda, most of the time as senior research officer of the monitoring service of the British Broadcasting Corporation in London.[1] My experience is limited. It is based mainly on a fairly detailed knowledge of broadcast propaganda from totalitarian countries. While it is not my intention to report here in detail about the experience gained in this connection, some of the deductions achieved under the impact of this material may be of value for those who want to determine in which way research and action can be interrelated.

SUGGESTIBILITY AND SOCIAL CHANGES

Notes on Suggestibility

Psychoanalytic experience and theory have contributed largely to a better understanding of some of the phenomena of human suggestibility. The magnitude of these phenomena, however, evades to some extent our attempts at explanation. I shall limit myself here to summarizing briefly such evidence and such theoretical conceptions as seem to be well established, without attempting in any way to exhaust the subject; the selection is determined by the aim: ultimately to gain insight into the working of propaganda.

Suggestibility designates originally the fact that man is "open to hypnotic suggestion" (Oxford Dictionary). In technical usage this meaning has been considerably enlarged. The word "suggestion" itself is used without qualification as a term in the sense coined by French psychiatrists, that of a—mostly verbal—command given when the subject is awake. The borderline between suggestion and persuasion is difficult to establish.[2] The first definition which therefore may be accepted,

1. I wish to take this opportunity to express my gratitude to those with whom I had the privilege to collaborate: John Salt, Director of the European Department of the British Broadcasting Corporation, conceived the idea of the potential value of psychological analysis of totalitarian propaganda and of research in this field; Dr. Mark Abrams, formerly Director of Research at London Press Exchange; and Allison Outhwaite, who gave me the inspiration of their assistance. Much of what is said in this paper is derived from our teamwork.

2. For a differentiation, see Lameere (1938), Birnbaum (1927), Floyd Allport (1924).

states that suggestibility designates "open to hypnotic suggestion, suggestion and persuasion."

The usage of the term suggestibility is, however, not limited to any connection with these techniques. It is made to designate quite generally the fact that man can be influenced by determined actions of his fellow beings. This wider sense, however, has always a certain connotation: the influence is exercised without the full cooperation of the subject. Something within ourselves makes us accessible to influences from others, without our agreement or, at least, our awareness. In psychoanalytic terminology: suggestibility refers to conditions not fully under the control of the adult ego.

The classical explanation, first formulated by Ferenczi (1909),[3] states that the phenomenon of suggestibility is related to the child in man. Under certain conditions, most clearly represented by hypnosis, infantile reactions recur; they find their expression in states of more or less complete dependence of one adult upon another, the patient's on the hypnotist. This dependence is constituted by libidinal and anaclitic attitudes; they correspond to two main wishes in the child's life: the wish for love and the wish for protection, both once attached to the parental figures. These wishes never die and under specific conditions they may again awake in full strength; they are the motor powers of transference. This term designates the phenomenon that relationships between adults reflect to some extent relationships between the child and his first objects. Man's attitude in hypnosis is a special case within this general framework. We speak of "hypnotic transference." Its main distinction is its intensity.

While these conceptions seem, as I said, hardly satisfactory, if compared with the manifold problems with which observation confronts us, their heuristic value is such that they explain a greater number of features than any other theory yet brought forward. It is with this reservation that I continue: neither the anaclitic nor the libidinal attitude of the subject toward the hypnotist can always, or can clearly, be distin-

3. See also the various publications by Schilder, especially (1926).

guished by observation. They coexist, as it were, in the subject's passivity. He is under the influence of a *spell*. In this spell, reactions seem to survive which reach beyond the ancestry of man. These reactions represent what Freud (1921a) calls the "unexplained and mysterious" features of hypnosis; he speaks of "an additional element of paralysis derived from the relation between someone with superior power and someone who is without power and helpless—which . . . may afford a transition to the hypnosis of fright which occurs in animals" (p. 115). This latter hypothesis seems best to fall in with the data of observation, if we add that the archaic reaction of fascination appears in hypnosis in a new shape: that of sexualization. It is hardly necessary to add that its power is increased since sexual satisfaction remains excluded and the level of experience is one in which, as a rule, no instinctual gratification approaches consciousness. We recall that Freud describes the relationship existing between the subject and the hypnotist as an exuberant variety of the normal phenomenon of being in love. The hypnotist's command has taken over some of the main functions of the subject's psychic apparatus, those generally attributed to the superego. Closer analysis, however, seems to show that the range of its influence is somewhat wider.

The nature of this influence, great and impressive as it is, and extraordinary as are both motoric and psychic activities which the subject may perform under the "spell" of hypnosis, is restricted in many ways. None, or few, and only minor, criminal actions are executed under hypnosis. The ego activities are asleep, but not totally excluded. An even more decisive limitation may be recalled. The hypnotist does not, as a rule, gain permanent influence. His influence does not outlast his command. No permanent transformation of the subject's ego is achieved.

We cannot hope to gain any new insight by comparing the conditions prevailing in hypnosis with those existing in suggestion. The phenomena are either too similar, though somewhat diluted, or the technique of suggestion may approach that of persuasion. The difference between persuasion and hypnosis,

however, will for a moment attract our attention. It can best
be understood if we recall that with the techniques here discussed, the power of "spell" and the activity of the ego, something in the nature of compulsion and actions based on the
free interplay of psychic forces, form a complemental series.
In hypnosis, the "spell" is paramount, the ego activity is reduced to the consent of being hypnotized. The situation in
persuasion is more complex. In studying it, I shall restrict
myself to a brief outline and to only some of its aspects: for
the time being I shall limit my discussion to persuasion in the
psychotherapeutic sphere. Using this as a model, I hope to
study conditions which to some extent exist in various spheres
of life where people are influenced by determined actions of
others; some of these actions are referred to as propaganda,
which Lasswell (1927) defines as "the management of collective attitudes by the manipulation of significant symbols."

   In describing the process of persuasion, we are faced with a
difficulty of a special kind. In spite of the existing variations of
the patterns of procedure, hypnosis is a homogeneous technique. There is no one technique of persuasion, and those authors who describe their individual technique rarely mention
all that takes place in the relationship between themselves and
their patients. The existence of an interhuman relationship
distinguishes persuasion from suggestion or hypnotism. In
this human relationship the therapist takes sides. The patient
is in a conflict and the therapist strengthens one part of his
personality against the other.[4] He will be most successful if he
can limit himself to an appeal to reason. He may do so either
by what he expresses or infers, or he may do so by his example, as if he were to say: "Look at me." He thus offers himself as an object for identification. His influence is in many
ways limited; he cannot do more than appeal to what there is
in the patient. Within this range, however, his influence may
be effective. His main instrument, even in this human contact,
is once more the element of "spell"—the transference. I need
not go into detail and describe what amplitude there exists in

---

   4. If he takes the side of the instinctual wishes, his influence may be in the nature
of seduction.

the handling of transference and what limitations there are, though a detailed investigation might actually throw some unexpected light on some of the devices of propaganda. I shall mention only two of the limitations of the technique of persuasion. The one concerns the reliability of the process; it may at any time lose its effect, for instance, when the positive transference turns into a negative one. In order to ascertain the duration of the therapeutic contact, the therapist may have to take measures of various kinds. He may, for instance, instruct one of his colleagues, who attends the physical ailments of his patient, how to behave; he will, as it were, use him as a kind of lightning rod in order to deflect aggression from himself. I do not contend that this is a regular technique. I mention it only for the sake of some parallels in propaganda.[5] But even if no such arrangements are made, the psychotherapist will watch the emotional equilibrium of his patient in order to assess how far his influence is endangered by the vicissitudes of transference.

The second limitation I wish to mention is of a more general character. It concerns the range of influences based on persuasion or similar techniques in psychotherapy. Their value will be the greater the more strictly they are confined to facilitating solutions of definite problems in the patient's life, and the less they aim at a permanent transformation of his personality.

There are, of course, no sharp boundaries between "the solution of a problem"—especially if we keep the neurotic symptom in mind—and the "permanent transformation of the personality." The difference, however, becomes more obvious

5. [In a section of this paper that has not been included in this volume, Ernst Kris states: "The part of the second doctor whom the psychotherapist uses as a lightning rod in order to safeguard his own position is assigned by propaganda to a 'common enemy.' His first function is that of attracting and thus relieving the relation of the audience to the propagandist of the danger threatening from a latent aggressive undercurrent. . . . By manipulating the aggression of his audience the propagandist strengthens his own position and safeguards what in a parallel might be called the 'transference situation.' Man is, however, not likely to indulge in aggression without moral justification. Aggression for the sake of an ideology will be more widely accepted. And thus man is made whenever possible to fight a concrete foe who embodies evil, but to fight him in the name of ideals."]

when we turn to two applications of the technique of persuasion within the framework of other psychological techniques.

Only one needs to be mentioned here: it is psychoanalysis. Persuasion is an ingredient of our technique. The human understanding which we use in order to establish contact with our patients, the process which precedes the "establishing of transference," is of that kind. It depends largely on the analyst's personality how much more of it enters into the process itself. This process is, in principle, different from that of persuasion. It aims at making conscious what was unconscious and thus at freeing the ego from some of its entanglements. The result in successful cases will be better control of ego functions, especially of the function of integration. The ultimate aim, therefore, is to strengthen independence (Nunberg, 1926, 1932, 1937).

The second technique is education of the child and the adolescent. Education, too, is to some extent based on persuasion, which in this instance, however, has a different function than in psychotherapy. It excludes gratification less strictly, it uses more extensive contacts, and most of all aims at "transformation" of the personality largely through *permanent* identification.[6]

The problems of education are in various ways directly related to suggestibility. While at a later stage I shall refer to some of these interrelations, I must here point to a terminological difficulty. All education is ultimately based upon the "plasticity" of the personality of the young, upon the fact that children and adolescents are influenced with comparative ease. It remains, however, doubtful whether we should use the term suggestibility in this connection. It refers, I said, to conditions which are not fully under the control of the adult ego; the process in childhood and adolescence seems to be of a different order: suggestibility is here the basis of ego formation.

6. In this paper I do not discuss the relation of the technique of education to social ideologies. No other subject of applied psychology, however, seems more urgently to require a discussion of methodological principles.

The Function of Suggestibility

Psychoanalysis has taught us how fruitful it is to study the phenomena of normal psychic life in their enlargement in pathology. The attempt, however, to apply this method to the study of suggestibility does not meet with success. No clear-cut answer has yet been given to the question under which pathological conditions suggestibility is regularly increased.

The most obvious cases concern certain lesions of the brain, especially of the cortical parts. We may learn from this that a disturbance of the central nervous system, the apparatus of the ego, may make man less independent up to the point where he automatically reacts to all influence from another person as if it were a determined command. No such clarity exists in those cases where the "organic" reason of the ailment has not yet been discovered.

There is a full agreement, however, on certain questions, on the fact, for instance, that hysterics are more suggestible than obsessional types; in other neurotic syndromes, the factor of suggestibility seems not to be specific.

We may at first be tempted to assume that a correlation between ego weakness and suggestibility may help us clarify the clinical problem; we shall soon discover, however, that this is of little avail. The concept of ego weakness is not well enough defined, and its bearing on clinical matters is by no means established (Nunberg, 1939).

There are a number of cases in which severe disturbances of ego functions are apparent, but no increase of suggestibility can be observed. In some of these cases we find an avidity for influence from others, a desire to establish contacts and to strengthen the ego from outside. Some of these cases have been described as people who act "as if" (H. Deutsch, 1934). Others show clearly that their desire for object relations is of a schizoid type and serves the purpose of "clinging to the world"; neither the one nor the other group is suggestible in our sense. It is hardly necessary to say that the deeper we enter into the purely psychotic symptomatology, the less we will meet with suggestibility. Where we are faced with the problem, it has a different character. The "suggestibility" of the catatonic is unreliable and sometimes no more evident than his negativism. In disintegration, both types of behavior seem open, and the almost automatic succession of reaction and resistance to command makes any reference to suggestibility as a phenomenon "not fully under the control of the ego" inappropriate.

No less a difficulty exists if we confine our attention to normal personality types.[7] We do not know what type of person is likely to show an "increased suggestibility" in life. It seems, therefore, more promising to study, without any relation either to clinical pictures or to personality types, the *conditions* which seem regularly to coincide with the change of a person's level of suggestibility. The most important of these conditions are, generally speaking, a certain insecurity or anxiety and certain libidinal conflicts. If a person is in danger, he will ask for protection or advice; while the external danger persists, he will be ready to accept the influence which he sought. If the danger is of a more permanent nature, if it is not merely an external danger but one which is reinforced from internal sources, the need for support may take the shape of a desire for guidance. People in such conditions may want to be influenced. Analysis shows that in all such cases we are faced with a conflict in which support is sought from outside. The behavior is similar to that of the child who turns to the parental figures.

I may be reproached here with having shifted ground. I set out to discuss suggestibility as a quality of the mind and I discuss it here as fulfilling a function which I correlate to a desire. I do so not without intention. Only if approached from this angle, as fulfilling a function within the dynamic framework of our mind, can the problem of suggestibility be successfully studied. In order fully to appreciate this point, we shall have to turn our attention once more to certain problems of childhood. I have said that in childhood the influences

---

7. See the bibliography in Bird (1939) and Hull (1933).

from others are used for the formation of the ego. One part of this process needs to be described in greater detail. The child's wish for love and protection stigmatizes his relation to his adult environment. It reflects the biological conditions of his helplessness. Part of this protection is concerned with his adaptation to reality. The child is taught what dangers there are, that fire burns, that water wets. That lesson, however, is not limited to the physical environment. Adaptation is concerned with the child's behavior in a wider sense, with actions to do and not to do in order not to offend those on whom he depends, with desires to satisfy or to suppress in order not to endanger himself. The desires and strivings of the small child cannot remain unrestricted; while in the world of animals the instincts seem rarely to produce a conflict between what the little animal wants and what is reasonably good for it, the life of man is based on the antithesis of this, and the very differentiation of our psychic system has been explained with reference to these conditions (Hartmann, 1939a).

In terms of current psychoanalytic theory we speak of a conflict between the id and the ego, between organized and unorganized parts of the personality. We know the role that is played in the child's life by the revolt against restrictions; only comparatively late have we come to realize that under certain conditions an opposite reaction may occur: a "desire" for restriction from outside. The child has learned to control some of his wishes, but that control is neither complete nor firmly established. It may at any moment be overrun. "In the educational influences brought to bear upon him," the child's "feeble ego has a powerful ally against his instinctual life," against the nondomesticated part of the personality.

The observations which should illustrate these problems in detail have been published only in part. Much further clarification may be expected. Anna Freud who in various publications (1930, 1936) has developed the theme to which I refer was also the first to draw general attention to one of the practical consequences of overlooking the need for restrictive guidance in the child; to the erroneous interpretation of psychoanalytic theory in progressive education. It had for a certain time become a fashion to assume that education should aim at avoiding restrictions; this theory had even entered the field of didactics. This situation can find no better illustration than the child who upon entering class in a new school is supposed to have said: "May I work or must I do what I like?" The child's need for guidance and his desire for restrictions are ultimately connected with his "suggestibility."

Better known are the corresponding problems in the life of the adolescent. The biological and psychological revolution of that age has endangered the established equilibrium of the prepubertal personality. Threatened by the new onslaught of demands, the ego has the difficult task of achieving compromises. This conflict may be solved in various ways, by rebellion or by submission, by gratification or by self-restrictions. In each case, however, influences from outside, new ideals or concrete personalities representing those ideals are sought. The adolescent is suggestible and his suggestibility fulfills an important function.[8]

Later in life similar situations may recur when the equilibrium is disturbed, and the ego is in danger of losing control. But the demand for influence from outside does not remain restricted to the realm of the ego; it may correspond to an instinctual desire and aim at gratification. The patient who looks for guidance may reveal another aspect of his desire when in an analytic treatment he expresses the wish to be hypnotized. He wants to be released from his own responsibility; he desires to be dominated. So regular is this demand in certain cases that I have no doubt that it regularly requires the same interpretation. It is related to the sexualization of the desire for guidance and is, in the male, the expression of a passive homosexual attitude. This is the most widespread and at the same time the most dangerous condition of increased suggestibility.

8. See Anna Freud (1936) and my discussion of one of the most important conceptions of her presentation, "the ego's primary antagonism to instinct," in chapter 16.

Suggestibility and Skepticism

It is now appropriate to relate the fragmentary and certainly not fully satisfactory evidence gained from the psychology of the individual to conditions in the social sphere. No comparison is intended, nor a mere application of one kind of insight to another field. We have learned from Freud that individual psychology is in fact part of social psychology. The object of our study is the individual in society. The world he lives in is part of man. We never can hope to understand man unless we see him in relation to his environment.

This is not only a statement of principle; methodology encroaches here upon practice. Our conception of health in a psychological sense does not fully coincide with the conceptions in the field of physical functions. We describe psychological health and illness either in terms of adaptation or in terms of equilibrium (Freud, 1937a; Hartmann, 1939b). Both descriptions, however, refer to and imply a social structure to which to adapt oneself and in which to maintain balance. Though this social structure may be of considerable latitude, we should like to know more about its specific influence upon the mind. No definite answer, however, seems as yet to have been crystallized and we have to rely upon conjectures.[9] The general impression prevails that social changes are not without relations to certain types of neurotic diseases, and though this problem has to my knowledge never been treated in great enough detail and with tangible results, I should like to refer to one example, that of the change in hysterical symptoms. I remember Paul Schilder discussing it almost twenty years ago with reference to existing attitudes of society to the problems of sex life: "I cannot," he said in one of his lectures in the Psychiatric Clinic in Vienna, "demonstrate a hysteric arch; such cases have become extremely rare of late and if I see a case of this kind, it is one from the east, say from Bucharest where

9. See, for example, Williams (1934) and Eder (1935).

social conditions are different and more traditional types of mores still prevail." We stand here at the fringe of a vast field. The problems of comparative psychology and psychiatry open up in front of our eyes, a subject to which Seligman (1924) devoted his attention, without, however, finding adequate response.[10] We cannot dare to enter it. All we can attempt is to continue for a moment to walk along its contiguous borders.

The traditional psychoanalytic approach to the relation of man and society was for a time one-sided. One was used to describing man and society in terms of antithesis; society inhibits his desires. I believe this conception to be only half of the truth—to give not more than one aspect. It is the aspect which may be compared to that of external influences gradually domesticating the child. I have mentioned the opposite problem when I described that phase in the child's life in which the formation of the ego is endangered by instinctual desires and wishes; then educational restrictions may gain a protective function. In his attitude to society the individual is to a certain extent inclined to repeat attitudes of the child to his environment, and many of the irrational trends in our social life are determined by this fact. How does man react, we may ask ourselves, if the protective and restricting powers of society are shaken, if the framework of society itself lacks stability? Sociologists have asked this question. Lasswell (1935a) has devoted a book to the problem and Karl Mannheim (1939) has reformulated it in these terms: "Recent experiences have shown us the starting point for our investigation by teaching us that there must definitely be a deeper correlation between the disorganization of society and the disorganization of individual behavior, and even of certain levels of the human mind, and vice versa, that the more strongly a society is organized, the more strongly forms of behavior and the corresponding attitudes of the mind seem to be integrated. . . . But it is not enough to make the general statement that collective insecurity may suddenly change human nature; one must

10. See also Róheim (1939). The problems involved are of considerable heuristic importance in order to check on some of the "recent" theories in psychoanalysis. This has been stressed by Dooley (1939) in a review of the work of K. Horney.

define the specific forms of insecurity and the ways in which they react upon the individual" (pp. 117, 125).

In spite of variability of conditions and reactions, we can attempt to follow Lasswell's example and discuss for a moment certain typical reactions. One of them seems to deserve our particular attention. If in a rapid survey we try to comprehend some of the features of instability in our times, our attention may first be directed toward economic problems. Not the real maladjustments in a given state of social development are, however, important for our purposes; not the real reasons for an existing crisis. We should like to know how all this may appear to man. "Here they are," he may think, "the wise and well-learned experts and yet they are not able to control the machinery. The crises follow each other and take away from us all we have." In this doubt another of the main foundations of modern civilization is involved; the belief in progress, of which economic security may well be said to be a part. "What is the good of this progress which seems to aim at greater safety for all if it does not lead to safeguarding some of the essentials of life?" I shall not continue to enumerate in detail the various aspects of these reactions. The authors who have devoted their attention to them have described some of these reactions in great detail. The need for increased protection and a certain inclination toward aggression as a reaction to fear and frustration seem to be paramount (Lasswell, 1935a).

I should like, however, to mention one more feature which is most closely connected with the present war. It was accepted fatalistically by the belligerent nations. Nowhere was any enthusiasm shown and nowhere was any "will to war" alive among the people. A dense layer of depression was spread over the world; a desperate regret that man had failed to arrange things in a more intelligent way. This attitude cannot be understood without reference to World War I. "We were promised that it would never happen again and now once more war is swaying the world." This one-sided and impressionistic description [11] should focus our attention on one reac-

11. It simplifies the situation if we do not discuss certain pressure groups.

tion which I believe to be widespread; not that it is the outstanding or the most important reaction, it is only one closely related to the problem of suggestibility. This reaction is disappointment.

If we wish to study reactions to an experience, individual psychology can give us answers which may be of value for sociological research. The relation of individual to social psychology in this respect is that of a model to reality; the decisive question concerns the accuracy of our model. In human development we regularly meet with disappointment. In early latency the child discovers that the parents are not as powerful and mighty as he had believed them to be. Reality may accelerate this insight. It is astonishing, however, how slight its influence is. The reaction to the discovery is a typical one. The child attempts displacements and is in search of new authorities. The cook or the janitor become important in the child's life. These are intermediary solutions. They teach us how easily accessible the child is to influences from outside at that time. He is, we may say, in search of authoritatives figures. This process as a rule comes to a temporary standstill, until teachers or figures endowed with similar prestige become the objects of the child's adoration and emulation. At the time, however, when these displacements are still unsettled, we may speak of an increase of "suggestibility" in the child. While his environment offers the objects for displacement, man in the society of our days chooses them under the impact of propaganda. "Disappointment" as a normal phenomenon becomes a motor for social changes. Its most rational aspect exists in the electorate of a democracy, when people consider the question of a redistribution of power in relation to success or failure of an administration. In the ideal case the reaction is not influenced by emotional elements. We may not even be justified to speak of disappointment; the reaction is that of dissatisfaction.

Disappointment, however, is rarely of such a rational nature. It is likely to appear in conjunction with and to form the basis of a great number of emotional attitudes. It is no more than one motor of social changes, in the same way as it is only

one impulse in the child's quest for new authority, which is intimately linked up with the conflicts of his age, the oedipal
conflict.

The approach which I have advocated implies a distinction.
While traffic lights fulfill the function of regulation, there
seems to exist an inclination in man to invest traffic lights with
the halo of the irrational. One aspect of authority leads back
to religion. However briefly, I shall therefore have to mention
in this connection that gravest problem of our time—the part
religion has played throughout the last centuries. Its position
has frequently been endangered, and it has frequently been
reinstated into its rights. Not only must the question be asked
how few and how many people have registered at any given
moment and register today as religious believers, the questions one would like to ask are: how firmly is religious belief
rooted in those who are believers; how deeply has the wave of
relativism shaken the foundations not only of ethical practice
but of the groundwork of ethical beliefs? In the framework of
religion, ethical values are imposed upon and inspired into
mankind by the external powers of the divine; to maintain
these ideals without that external influence presupposes a
high degree of internalization. Has this degree been reached;
has it been proven that, independent of such obligation and
inspiration from the projected authorities of the divine, man
can at this stage of his development stand free without support?

Thus we understand that the insecurity of our time, activated by recent experiences, may in fact be related to a cen-
tury-old process of a wider range which may strengthen the
desire for new authorities, which in its turn is one of the
sources of suggestibility. "Propaganda increases with depar-
tures from equilibrium" (Lasswell, 1935b, p. 26).

In describing some of the factors which the sociologists
mention in discussing the present social situation, we have, as
it were, referred to artificial conditions. We have talked about
the man in the street in our time and seem to have overlooked
that in reality everything depends on who is the man and
what is his street. While we cannot avoid describing such phe-

nomena, on this level of abstraction one more objection must be raised. Our description of the various factors which may be responsible for an increase of suggestibility, culminating in and related to the quest for new authorities to make the world safe, does not fit the picture with which we are faced daily in this country and to a lesser extent in other countries. We are not, this objection says, faced with a general increase of suggestibility. On the contrary, people *believe* less than they ever did before. They believe neither their newspapers nor their leaders. They see propaganda everywhere and have in some countries—in Great Britain and in the United States in a higher degree than elsewhere—been taught to do so. They are not more suggestible; on the contrary, evidence proves that they are more skeptical.

This is, indeed, a grave objection, one which may seem to endanger our thesis. In fact, however, it strengthens it. That skepticism is a defense. It was acquired mainly in these last twenty years; it grew out of the process of debunking the propaganda of World War I; it has been applied to the analysis of advertisements in the work of the consumer organizations; and it is, in these days, maintained against odds. It does not, I claim, make suggestibility as a whole less dangerous. The desire which calls the reinforced suggestibility into being exists in spite of the defense which has been mobilized.

The artificial skepticism which leads people no longer to distinguish between the truth and the fallacy of a statement but to apply the one criterion of "Why does he say so?" instead of "What does he say?" is witness not only to their distrust but also to their apprehension. They are suggestible and are striving against it. From clinical experience we know the patient who suffers from anxiety of anxiety, from fear of his own fear. This is most common if his anxiety refers to passive wishes. He knows about his own passivity and lives through a second level of anxiety. His knowledge of his own passivity increases his anxiety. We know how difficult it is to control these states without the help of the psychoanalytic method. They may in the end lead to a breakdown, or they may make the patient more inclined to some unexpected gratification of his passive desires. If the attack comes from a side against which he was not guarding, it may well succeed. To some extent a comparable phenomenon seems to exist in the social sphere. The propaganda phobia of the early months of this war in the United States has not protected people from propaganda. It has made them more accessible to one kind of it. The antipropaganda movement has become propaganda itself, and Dorothy Thompson, who, to my knowledge, was the first to describe this phenomenon, has drawn attention to the propaganda tendency in the activity of those whom she calls the antipropaganda propagandists. As always, however, the desire of the public to accept the propaganda of these antipropagandists was well founded in something of the nature of an ego interest. People wanted to stay out of the war and they wanted to be propagandized. And thus the propaganda phobia grew into a propaganda movement.[12] While this movement maybe considered an episode, it directs our attention to a more general question. There seems no reason to believe that at any time—with the exception of the consumer movement and in relation to advertising—has the fear of suggestibility and of propaganda worked as an inoculation. I am, on the contrary, inclined to believe that this fear paralyzes active response to the pressure of propaganda. This active response is no other than the preparedness at any time to set one's own opinion against that of the propagandist. It rests on the self-assured power of conviction. In the state of double anxiety, however, if no gratification of the passive wishes is granted, one is likely to give way to the voice of doubt. "Perhaps he is right," an inner voice may say. The critical sense may gradually exhaust itself. The power of the propagandist and that of the dictator for whom he speaks is made to grow steadily until it appears to be irresistible. If it is irresistible, we are released from the duty of defense. Surrender is less shameful. We have found what we wanted.

12. An analysis of this phenomenon will be undertaken separately [see Kris (1942a, 1942b), Kris and White (1942/43), Kris et al. (1944), Kris and Leites (1947), and chap. 21]. In this description I have once more isolated the facts and not taken into account that movements of this kind are sponsored by powerful promotors.

And thus one of the dangers of propaganda in our time seems to appear in a clearer light. Man's own unconscious desire acts as disposition. The appeal of propaganda meets with an unconscious wish. This, I believe, is the aspect of the danger of propaganda as it relates to our suggestibility.

NEW TECHNICAL DEVELOPMENTS AND RECENT PROBLEMS OF PROPAGANDA

Whenever men form a community, some media of social control exist. The tribal drum is their ancestor. The historian who takes the broad view of a distant spectator may be inclined to believe that this relation is static; each society, he may say, finds the media it requires. Should he, however, study the phenomena at closer range, he will be faced with a more complex problem. He will have to take the interrelation between the technical development of the media and the nature of social control at a given time into account, and he may well find that at some crucial moments of history the technical development becomes a driving power. The invention of the printing press and the nature of social control in the 16th century were related in that way.

Any attempt to study the interrelation of the "new" media, the motion picture and the radio, which have been fully developed in the last twenty-years, with the social conditions of our time remains outside of our immediate consideration. A further delimitation, however, is forced upon us. Each medium offers different kinds of stimuli; it addresses another part of our suggestibility, or if we do not admit such differentiations, it appeals to us from another side.[13]

I feel, however, that in spite of valuable results recently achieved,[14] our knowledge is not yet detailed enough to recommend any such approach. It seems advisable to consider

13. This approach to the problems of suggestibility will be found in G. and L. B. Murphy (1931). I do not, for the purpose of this paper, discuss the otherwise all-important distinction between ideomotoric and prestige factors in suggestibility.

14. So far as radio communication is concerned, see G. W. Allport and Cantril (1935) and Lazarsfeld (1940).

only one problem. The new technical development results in an increase of stimuli. How does this increase in quantity, how does the fact that we are exposed to symbols of social control wherever we turn, affect our suggestibility? This is not an aspect that is often discussed in the psychoanalytic literature. It is a problem of experimental psychology. Suggestibility in this sense is limited to conditioning. The problem which attracts our interest is this: "How far can adult men be conditioned by the repetition of stimuli of a symbolic nature?" An answer to this question is hardly possible, but in order to clarify some of its implications, we shall have to discuss some aspects of advertising.

All advertising is based upon two elements—the symbol which is offered and the reaction of the public to it. This reaction is initiated by an ego activity, that of attention.[15] Attention need not manifest itself on the level of consciousness; preconscious attention "will do." Only if our attention is concentrated on another subject, in the case of anticathexis, shall we fail to react. The reaction itself, of course, may be limited to the formation of a temporary memory trace.

The symbol in advertising is, however, not as a rule offered in isolation. A variety of appeals may be attached to it. The paramount appeal is directed to reason. We are told that certain purchases are advantageous. This advice, however, is supported by additional elements of appeal, which in principle seem to be of equal, if not of greater, importance. If we are made to buy toothpaste, an association may be created between the toothpaste and a smiling face of a girl with her mouth open. The beauty of her teeth has undoubtedly a very special kind of "appeal." If we are to buy a patent medicine, another additional appeal will be presented, that of apprehension, of fear, which in turn will be allayed by the promised therapeutic effect of the drug. In Britain a certain product of the nutrition industry was sold in order to prevent "night-star-

15. The latest contribution of Freud to this problem has been quoted by Marie Bonaparte (1940). According to Freud's ideas, the attention which we bestow on objects is due to rapid but successive cathexes, which might be regarded in a sense as quanta issuing from the ego.

vation"; a danger is created, a bogey is shown, and at the same time means of protection are offered. These are only a few examples. A great number of additional appeals may be mobilized—patriotic, ethical, or aesthetic appeals in different variations. In this manifold and colorful activity, the play upon our emotions is carefully blended. Never should the response be too violent; it is on the whole intended only to assure increased attention. If this goal is reached, the ultimate aim will be achieved almost automatically. We will buy the merchandise (see Zilboorg, 1938).

I cannot help feeling that we as psychologists have not sufficiently appreciated that this is so, and that "advertising pays." It is a factor of some considerable importance when the same technique is made to serve other purposes and to appear in a different framework. In our society advertising follows the laws of supply and demand, even if as a first step it may create the demand. We ourselves regulate the intensity of advertising by our response to it. Advertising directs our purchasing power. It does not aim, or not primarily aim, at any central part of our personality. Let us remove two restricting conditions: the intensity will no longer be related to any economic consideration, nor will it be subject to the laws of supply and demand; the object will not be our purchasing power; the intention will be not to sell goods, but opinions. If such alterations are admitted, we may be faced with the use of the principles of advertising in political propaganda. At first sight there is nothing new about this. Symbols have always been used in social control; the coat of arms, the flag, the cross and the crescent. They have always inspired mankind and proven to be useful to those at the helm; they were related to group situations, with a clear division of the many and the few, the led ·and the leaders. The flag always flies in front of the marching troop. The appeal of symbols in this sense has remained unchanged, and wherever man has become part of a unit, he may be influenced by such methods. Today, however, the stimuli come to the individual through what he reads in his paper, what he sees in the cinema, what he hears at his fireside, if he tunes in to a local radio station. All the symbols he receives are meant to solidify his allegiance to some larger unit. Not only has the potential quantity of stimuli been increased, they have become more manifold and they may follow us wherever we turn.

What is man's response in this new situation? We do not know. At no point have facts been established—facts that are reliable and detailed enough to be trusted and to throw light on the manifold implications. All we may attempt at present is to collect some haphazard and fragmentary impressions, two of which seem intimately related to our main problem: the first concerns the attitude of certain individuals to radio advertising. They actually experience the repetition of the slogan as a pressure. "I will buy that drink in order to get rid of it," is what they say; the "it" being that friendly voice which at given intervals repeats a vivid description of the advantages and delightful qualities of the liquid referred to. The second concerns a more general problem. There seems to exist, even with advertising, a phenomenon which might be called "resistance." While on the whole the reaction of consumers corresponds to the quantity of reasonably varied stimuli, there arises something in the nature of a negative response, even if such variation is attempted, and no economic or practical reasons prevent its effect. One may, of course, always pretend that the "variation" was unsuccessful, either too small in order to give enough new accessories, or too great, thus interrupting the cumulative effect. But there apparently is an optimum, a kind of saturation point, related not only to one stimulus, but to a group of stimuli.

Both of these reactions are greatly reinforced in political propaganda; out of microscopic fluctuations they may become visible attitudes. The appeal of political propaganda is in the nature of a command; it is, in the last analysis, a hypnotic command, in which the person of the hypnotist may remain invisible. By many it is experienced as pressure. One widespread reaction is docility.[16] The other reaction is that of indifference. The nature of this indifference, its extent and

16. We recall that we are dealing with that aspect of suggestibility which is related to conditioning, and we may add now that the conditioning through command, however camouflaged this command may be, is a most powerful weapon in the arsenal of education of the small child.

character, will depend on a great number of factors. With those who for a long time have attempted to resist the pressure and who are finally paralyzed, it is of the nature of apathy. The best observers have described in these terms the present attitude of those Germans who were initially opposed to the National Socialist regime.

The relationship of the new media of communication to the totalitarian practice of control goes, however, much further. In relating advertising to political propaganda, I must emphasize one of the differences between them that concerns the economic side. Advertising expenditure, I said is related to the market, to the laws of supply and demand. Such limitations do exist even for political propaganda in a democracy. They never exist in a totalitarian state, and only under the conditions of an unrestricted propaganda expenditure does the whole impact of the problem unfold itself before our eyes. Only one voice is heard. The arsenal of new stimuli is monopolized. It is not only directed as propaganda against the adults; it is incorporated into the personalities of growing men: whatever stimuli the young totalitarians receive, they are of one kind in thought, in vision, and in sound.

In conclusion, we may say that while we have not answered the question how far man can be conditioned by the increase of symbolic stimuli to which he is exposed, we have understood that the control of these media is of decisive importance. All will depend upon those who exercise this control and upon its limitations. The conditions of total control existing in totalitarian countries are an essential factor of the "danger" of propaganda in our time.[17]

17. [The sections on "German Broadcast Propaganda in the Present War" and "National Socialist Propaganda and Propaganda in a Democracy" have been omitted here because these topics are again taken up in chapters 21 and 22. See also Kris (1941a).]

21: Some Problems of War Propaganda

A Note on Propaganda New and Old

(1943)

The Distrusts of Propaganda

Discussions of propaganda in this world crisis tend to be highly practical; they usually culminate in recommendations on how to propagandize. Without adopting the pretense of detachment, to which I have no claim, I shall attempt in this paper to widen the scope of the discussion by reporting on two concepts of propaganda upon which, explicitly or implicitly, I believe propaganda practices are based. These two concepts are to some extent opposed to each other; they coincide largely with two systems of government, if those systems are taken as "ideal types" (Max Weber), and with two doctrines of men. Antitheses like democratic and totalitarian propaganda, good and bad propaganda, have been used to describe them. Another antithesis may be even more telling: the psychological hypotheses underlying the concepts here discussed are different in their relation to modern psychological insight, the one being based on an overage psychology, the other on what more recent findings suggest. We may therefore speak of propaganda, old and new.[1]

Read before the American Psychoanalytic Association at Boston, May 19, 1942. First published in the *Psychoanalytic Quarterly*, 12 : 381–399, 1943.

1. See The University of Chicago Round Table (March 1, 1942) on *Propaganda Good and Bad*, in which Archibald MacLeish, Harold Lasswell, and Richard McKeon participated. (The University of Chicago Round Table, No. 207, with bibliography.) The views expressed in the following pages partly supplement a trend of thought first developed in 1941 (chap. 20).

Without discussing the definition of propaganda, I here use the term in the widest sense of communication from authority and start with the assumption that in every society some means of social control of this nature exist, which establish contact between the responsible leaders and the community. The scope of such communication is largely determined by the situation in which the group lives, by the reality it has to face. The situation of "being at war" is one which tends to stigmatize all such communication. Men of all ages, Thucydides, Dr. Johnson, John Dewey, have stressed the high degree of uniformity of all war propaganda, of the theme "Our cause is right, we will win" echoed throughout time. Thus modern war propaganda was compared to the battle cry of yore, which was meant to encourage one's own group, frighten the foe, and impress those who did not participate in the fight. A similar division of the functions of modern war propaganda is in fact widely accepted. We distinguish propaganda in wartime directed to the home front, to the enemy, and to neutrals. In the following pages reference is made only to the first—home propaganda. In the war of 1914–1918 it was successful. Waves of enthusiasm and hatred were aroused, and swayed even those who before the outbreak of war had championed other and higher ideals. The phenomenon was not limited to one nation; it happened in all belligerent countries.

In this war all seems different: propaganda has not been able to "do the job." The crisis of propaganda is one common to Western civilization, which in this case includes our European enemies. (No statements on conditions in Russia, China, or Japan are possible at present.) All forecasts made before the war were proved false—men went to war in sadness and in silence, not only in the democracies but even in the totalitarian states.

The course of the war has not decidedly affected the picture. The belligerent governments continue to be faced by the distrust of propaganda existing among their people. It is to some extent independent of the form of government. It is not limited to countries where mass communication is monopolized, planned, and linked to coercion. It exists in the democracies, where free enterprise in mass communication prevails, where only the outgoing military news is controlled, where there is no relationship between communication and coercion (see Kris, 1942b). This leads to the quest for the origin of this distrust. It may tentatively be related to two phenomena, here isolated for the purpose of analysis: the *disappointment in government* and the *inflation of persuasion*. Both developed fully after the last war, at different times in each of the countries of our civilization. The first, the disappointment in government, is related to the feeling that the world has grown out of control. It is a phenomenon apparently typical of industrialized mass society under the impact of war and postwar conflicts. It is connected with the weakening of religious and other traditional values and with a diffidence to the ideals of progress. The economic crisis in all countries, though it occurred at different times and with different intensity, has heightened the disappointment in government into a feeling of general insecurity (Lasswell, 1935a; Mannheim, 1939).

The reaction to this disappointment has taken various forms. One reaction—known in the development of the child after the discovery that "parents are human"—is the search for new ideals and new "imagoes." The manipulation of this disposition by reactionaries who financed and by militarists who supported demagogues has contributed to the rise of dictatorships in Europe. No such successful manipulation occurred in the democracies, protected by greater wealth and by a greater adaptability of government rooted in tradition. In the democracies, too, demagogues—those who did not make demands for sacrifice—had their chance; hence the success of irresponsible government, of Tory appeasers in Britain, and of isolationists in the United States.

The distinction between the general disappointment in government and the reaction to the inflation of persuasion is, as said, artificial.[2] The term inflation of persuasion indicates the increase in publicity which during and after the last war

2. Persuasion in this sense describes psychological techniques without reference to the social context. For a psychoanalytic discussion of general problems of persuasion in relation to propaganda see Zilboorg (1938).

swayed the world. Two of the three media of mass communication were introduced in these decades—radio and film—and the impact of publicity on life has grown from year to year. In the United States, where research has provided reliable data, distrust, so far as we know, is not essentially a distrust of commercial advertising. It applies to the relation of the average American to persuasion in politics; even when more than three fourths of the media of communication supported one candidate, this did not change the results of the election (Waples and Berelson, 1941).

The Western world is propaganda conscious. In the democracies this was initiated after the last war, when members of the propaganda committees wrote their memoirs, described "how it all was done" and how they swayed their people. This was followed by the consumer movement and the antipropaganda drive. The latest of the attempts at debunking is still fresh in memory: the propaganda phobia which pretended to inoculate the public by teaching them to analyze not the content of statements but the "intention" of those who made them.

The sequence of reactions was different in Germany. The distrust of propaganda was canalized soon after the war by the slogan of the broken promises of Versailles. It was turned against democratic propaganda and finally democratic government. Under the National Socialist regime the distribution of trust and distrust was at first related to political allegiance; later, especially after the outbreak of war, distrust and apathy became very general phenomena. Many independent observers agree that few people read the papers, listen to the radio, or go to the movies before the news reel is over.[3]

In both totalitarian and democratic countries measures were adopted or recommended to deal with this situation. Here our problem crystallizes: what were these methods and on what general psychological assumptions were they based? While I cannot here discuss whether or to what extent the views of our enemies have changed since the outbreak of the war, a brief

3. See Kris (1941b), in which some of the more recent lines of German propaganda were predicted.

case study will show how they attempted to adapt their techniques to the existence of distrust.

The views expounded in the democracies are not homogeneous. Everybody agrees that truth should prevail. Beyond this, difference of opinion exists. There are two extremist groups: those who stand for intensification of propaganda, for the use of all devices of publicity and advertising in order to create enthusiasm—the radicals among them state that the methods adopted by the Nazis are the best possible. This group of experts professes not only an absolute trust in the various promotional activities; they also advocate in propaganda directed to the enemy a most aggressive and violent attitude.[4] And then there are those who refuse to give any credit to propaganda. The community, they say, will be united if existing grievances are eliminated. Then, they seem to assume, there will be no need for propaganda (Shulman, 1942).

Apart from these extremists, a vast body of opinion advocates a new type of propaganda. Its principles are not yet well established, the consequences of the new approach are not yet clearly visible, but the attempt exists; a propaganda based on the "strategy of truth," to quote Mr. MacLeish on "Facts and Figures," and integrated into the process of democracy at work. Thus a new and an old concept of propaganda oppose each other. While in reality the differences frequently are blurred by the demands of a given situation, the problem is clarified if the comparison is extended to that of psychological concepts.

HYPNOTISM AND GUSTAVE LE BON'S THEORY OF PROPAGANDA

The competence of psychoanalysts to comment on this problem of social technique is well founded in the history of the

---

4. The unconscious meaning of this point of view was revealed to me in the analysis of a professional propagandist, broadcasting to one of the enemy countries: words have become magic weapons, speech is supposed to kill. Phylogenetically this leads back to the origin of the battle cry; ontogenetically this "aggressivization" of speech was related to oral fantasies.

subject. The concepts upon which the old type of propaganda is based, and which found expression in the propaganda of World War I and more generally in the inflation of persuasion, are closely linked to pre-Freudian psychopathology. Social psychology at the end of the past century stood under the shadow of the great newcomer to the science of man, hypnotism. The effect of the admittance of this neophyte on the development of psychopathology has been described by Zilboorg (1941). Its influence on social psychology has not yet been fully realized. The later works of Hippolyte Taine are linked with those of the Italian pupil of Lombroso, Sighele, with the great and frequently misinterpreted concepts of Tarde, and finally with the work of Gustave Le Bon, whose Psychology of the Crowd was first published in 1895. The central problem in the work of these men was the transformation of the individual into a member of the crowd, i.e., what we today know to be one aspect of regression. The model of this behavior is found in the dynamics of the hypnotic situation.

The doctrine gained popularity in Le Bon's presentation. It is one in which the emphasis is shifted from science to politics: the fact that the crowd is easily influenced by the hypnotist and leader may be used for purposes of control—the leader may manage the crowd. Le Bon's Psychology of the Crowd was, in his own words, written as a reedited Machiavelli. Born in 1841, the author was one of those French reactionaries who had seen revolutions in plenty. He was terrified by the specter of socialism. His life—a peculiar sequence of endeavors on the fringe between journalism and science—was intrinsically devoted to warding off this peril. A physician by training, he started as a physical anthropologist. He returned from India imbued with the idea of the danger to the white race. What he wrote in the 1880s against extending European education to the colored was repeated fifty years later by Oswald Spengler.

In Eastern Europe, this pupil of Gobineau learned to hate the Jews. In his own country he opposed the forty-eight-hour week, the abolition of child labor, the expansion of education to lower-income groups. In the '80s Le Bon won fame by a detailed study of the training of horses, written for the use of the French cavalry. The subject, he said, taught him much which was applicable to human affairs.[5]

This is the atmosphere out of which grew *The Crowd,* the first treatise on psychological management in the modern sense. It is written with considerable psychological acumen and with complete cynicism. The mental life of crowds is, according to Le Bon, on the level of hallucination, dominated by images; all ideas presented to the crowd merge into such images, and there is a craving in the crowd for a steady supply of ideas: the illusions. Leaders have to create the illusions as means of domination. (It may be worth recalling that the Bible is to Le Bon a textbook of managerial control, full of obscene absurdities—and much of what he says in this connection might well be quoted as from Alfred Rosenberg.)

The student of the history of ideas will note in Le Bon the parallel with Nietzsche and the reaction to Marx, but he will also be able to quote chapter and verse in order to prove how closely statement after statement by Le Bon reappears in the concepts of propaganda developed by Hitler and Goebbels.[6]

The success of Le Bon's writings, especially of *The Crowd,* was largely dependent on a specific public: translations, except into English and German, were sponsored by Grand Dukes, Ministers of Justice and General Staffs. His biography was written by a Japanese Foreign Minister. When Mussolini came

5. Here is the bridge to the doctrine of conditioning. The impact of this theory on that of propaganda and advertising, though considerable, will not be discussed. Dr. Ley, the leader of the National Socialist Labor Front, in describing the training and selection of the party elite, says: "We want to know whether these men have the will to lead, to be masters, in one word, to rule . . . we want to rule and enjoy it . . . we shall teach these men to ride horseback . . . in order to give them the feeling of absolute domination over a living being" (Ley: *Der Weg zur Ordensburg.* Sonderdruck des Reichsorganisationsleiter der NSDAP; quoted by Heiden (1937) and Fromm (1941).

6. This influence, direct or indirect—i.e., conveyed by some of Le Bon's vulgarizations—gains in significance if we hear that years after the publication of *The Crowd,* in one of the many books which reiterate the basic thesis of the managerial control of the masses, Le Bon developed in his *Psychologie de la politique* (1910) a blueprint of fascism; shopkeepers and militias were entrusted with social defense since the upper classes of France had refused to see the danger.

to power, he professed the influence of Le Bon's doctrine. Le Bon, almost ninety years of age, became the admirer of the · "new order" in Italy. His closest contacts in France were members of the military elite.

The contamination of science with politics does not negate the truth of a doctrine. The content of truth in Le Bon's analysis of social events is considerable if limited to its object of investigation. He has described, in terms of his generation, the psychology of mob formation, of man under the spell of a temporary regression. He has erred in extending the concept to human group behavior at large; the crowd to him has become mankind.

The function of propaganda in Le Bon's scheme is clearly outlined. Its model is the address of the orator; its function is to drive the crowd into submission and to promote its regression. If one rereads how Hitler, with the experience of the agitator of genius, has elaborated these thoughts—age-old thoughts of the demagogue—one will find that the attack upon reason under various disguises is paramount: let the audience be tired, the lesson be repetitive, then all depends on the propagandist's conviction. The essence of National Socialist propaganda before and throughout this war has been to reconstitute on a nation-wide scale the conditions of the assembly place, and on a worldwide scale conditions approximating it. The strategy adopted, the tactics used, and the devices so ingeniously varied have one common goal: ultimately to establish between the propagandist and his audience a relationship akin to that between the hypnotist and his medium.

SOME COMMENTS ON PRESTIGE, PROPHECY, AND INITIATIVE IN GERMAN WAR PROPAGANDA

German home propaganda consists to some extent of repetitions and variations of Hitler's own views. Each of his speeches is a blueprint of propaganda. Before each speech some of the themes come up, then he summarizes them, and then the radio waves carry the message daily and with due variation. The main lines of propaganda are under his authority.[7]

The image of this authority, however, has undergone changes. As long as he was not independent of his industrialist and militarist promoters, he was a brother figure—a savior. After that time the buildup of omnipotence started. The pathway was that of success: every success was hinted at so that when achieved it could be represented as a fulfilled prediction. Thus each of the fateful steps—the German rearmament, the march into the Rhineland, etc.—was described in terms of an achieved goal. In wartime the manipulation of predictions naturally is handled with the greatest care; planning and preparation, omniscience and foresight, are daily enacted. Studies conducted at the Research Project on Totalitarian Communication illustrate this point. The analysis of words indicating foresight and planning, the essential qualities of magic leadership, in German High Command communiques, show that reports on and reference to military success gradually take the place of such words. A technique of "Let the facts speak for themselves" becomes the substitute for other means of prestige building. It is this publicity technique which helped to create the impression of irresistible and supreme, omnipotent organization.[8]

Another study deals with the use made of predictions of German actions in their radio home news bulletins. A first finding shows that predictions are generally frequent before action. Without specifying what concrete events are to hap-

7. This section is based mainly on material provided by the Research Project on Totalitarian Communication, directed by Hans Speier and myself. The material analyzed is contained in the Daily Digest of Foreign Broadcasts, published as a confidential document on behalf of the British Ministry of Information by the British Broadcasting Corporation and released by courtesy of the B.B.C. for research purposes to the Research Project on Totalitarian Communication, at the New School for Social Research. [For publications deriving from this research project, see Kris and White (1942/43), Kris, Speier, Axelrad, Herma, and Loeb (1944), Kris (1945), Kris and Leites (1947).]

8. As an illustration of this technique, the following well-documented device may here be recorded. In a German town eggs have arrived. They are *not* distributed; rather it is announced that in three weeks at four o'clock, two eggs per head will be available.

pen, they create a situation in which success of action will reflect upon the wisdom of the predictor. Such, for instance, was the situation in the spring of 1940, before the campaign in Norway, the Low Countries, and France. After victory less manipulation was thought to be required. At that time distrust was allayed by conquest.

Predictions increased, however, later in the year and early in 1941, when the Battle of Britain was lost. Not all predictions at that time were fulfilled. A crisis of the technique became apparent in the Russian campaign. A host of predictions accompanied initial successes and when late in the autumn of 1942 the failure became evident, a new device was adopted—that of "negative predictions." Not action, but the failure to act was forecast. In this sense, Hitler's announcement of November 29, 1941, in which he proclaimed that from now on the German Army would renounce the offensive in Russia, is unique in military history. It is, however, in line with the psychological technique here described. Prediction is the implement of omnipotence and thus of initiative. Passivity is identical with or even more dangerous than temporary failure. Thus while the German Army was harassed by the cold and by an undaunted enemy, and while the people at home went through hardships of unexpected severity, in this war's third winter, the grim news was advertised. Plight and sacrifice were as repetitiously discussed as planning and success in more fortunate times. While here, as in all similar cases, various psychological appeals were carefully blended, one device was outstanding. In discussing the bad news the appearance of frankness was given, and a "we can take you into our confidence" technique was adopted whenever possible. In this sense, activity remained with the leader.[9]

9. Finally in January 1942, the traditional history of Hitler's career was rewritten. Instead of an irresistible rise to power, it became the history of success painfully interrupted by setbacks. For the first time Hitler's own personality was measured against one of German history. A new film of Frederick of Prussia's life was hastily arranged, and all official comments stressed the historical parallelism. Here, too, there was victory in spite of setbacks—and the conquest of destiny by endurance was added to the paternalistic equipment. [For a detailed analysis of German war films, see "The Imagery of War" (Kris, 1942c), in which the author also discusses the relation between art

This survey naturally is misleading by its very brevity, since it does not discuss how the manipulation of trust in the deified leader is supplemented by the manipulation of distrust against information coming from enemy countries. While I cannot in detail scrutinize what evidence there is of failure or success of the National Socialist propaganda management of the German people, there are indications that it fails when its roots are shaken; i.e., when success, even though temporarily, recedes. In the winter of 1941/42 the broadcast day of the German radio had to be reorganized; light music was given preference over all other programs. In order to attract the attention of a propaganda-weary audience, propaganda was sandwiched between entertainment programs. In those days of intense cold, spring was described by propagandists as the time when special announcements of victories would be broadcast once more. When later in the spring of 1942 the German offensive in Russia started and the Russians retreated, German propagandists were busily attempting to reestablish the older pattern. Every suitable quotation from Hitler's speeches was produced in order to show that he had predicted that the Russian winter offensive would fail and the German spring offensive succeed. Thus German propaganda was directed toward recuperating the prestige lost throughout the winter. Not the present, not the future—the past was of paramount importance.

Only when seen as part of the National Socialist concept of propaganda, based as it is on the model of the hypnotic situation, can this policy be fully appreciated. The propagandist who wishes to address a spellbound audience cannot afford any gap in his record. Complete success and complete submission are closely linked to each other.[10]

If we now turn for a moment to democratic propaganda

and propaganda and the extent to which documentary films capture and distort reality.]

10. In a survey of German propaganda throughout the war, Dr. Goebbels stated of late that only once was a prediction wrong: in the autumn of 1941, when the Russians were underestimated. It is significant also that in the campaigns of 1942, German propagandists were explicitly instructed to refrain from any prediction. A second failure might be fatal and seriously endanger the concept of paternalistic omnipotence.

under similar conditions, the differences are obvious. The democracies, unfortunately, had in this war more occasion to justify failure to their people than totalitarian states. There are
certain patterns of justification which are ubiquitous. Victorious enemy forces generally are described as superior in
numbers, the gallantry of defeated troops generally is
stressed, the tendency to distract attention from the theater of
war where defeat was suffered to other theaters where one's
own forces were successful is equally general. At first sight one
might well be inclined to say that differences between totalitarian and democratic communications are in this respect differences of degree only. This, however, is only a first
impression, on the whole misleading, which is corrected by experience provided by every further month of war.

At no time in the democracies did criticism vanish. But
while in the first year of the war mainly the French and also to
some extent the British government covered their news and
propaganda policy with the mantle of secrecy, in Britain the
sequence of defeats gave more and more importance to the
criticism of government by parliamentary institutions and
public opinion; later the compensatory patterns such as "the
numerical   superiority   of   the   victorious   enemy"   were
dropped—I refer to the discussion of the British defeat in
North Africa in spring 1942—and concerns for home morale
no longer reduced the bluntness and vehemence of criticism.
In ever-increasing measures detailed information is given, limited only by the requirements of military secrecy, and nonmili-
tary experts participate increasingly in what the people are
being told.

Thus, while defeat in the totalitarian system leads to a crisis,
in the democracies it led to a process of gradual adjustment of
paternalism and participation.[11]

11. This process of adjustment accounts to my mind for organizational failures
such as those much discussed by the British Ministry of Information and the Information Services in Washington. Out of trial and error the new patterns develop. The importance of free controversy for morale was discussed by French (1938/39).

THE NEW PROPAGANDA

The methods used in order to influence public opinion are closely linked to the system of government. The concept which totalitarians have in mind is that of the people as the crowd which follows the leader; that prevailing in the democracies refers to integrated groups (MacIver, 1937; Waelder, 1939b). For more than thirty years the discussion of similar problems has played a decisive part in social psychology. It started out from the criticism of Le Bon's work and the confusion created by his extension of the crowd concept to any kind of community. Freud's contribution in this connection was rarely, if ever, fully taken into account although it facilitates greatly a clearer formulation of certain psychological aspects of that difference.[12] His *Group Psychology and the Analysis of the Ego* (1921a) was not written as a treatise in social psychology. Problems are only discussed so far as they contribute to his main objective, to clarify further the structural model of the personality which he was developing at the time. The main conceptual tool used is that of identification. To the best of my knowledge, no satisfactory attempt has as yet been made to exhaust fully the catalogue of problems to which Freud refers in discussing "Further Problems and Lines of Work." They include the study of motivation and origins of group formation, the differences between types of groups according to types of leadership, the unifying function which common interests, wishes, and ideals may have.

In applying Freud's basic concept to my specific problem, I should like to elaborate on a model frequently used by him. I refer to the construct on the origin of ritual and social communication. In a schematic form it permits us to describe changes of function of both leadership and communication as a change of mechanism used in participation.

On a first level, that of tribal dance, the reaction of the group to the communication of the leader is total: they act

---

12. In Freud's presentation this formulation is implied and only part of it is explicitly stated.

together. Individual differences on this level are of little importance. Action, however, is not always essential. In rituals of communication, such as the holy mass, where the leader functions not as the supreme authority but rather as a representative of the supreme ideal, actions are reduced to symbols—but instead, a rigid code prescribes the emotional reaction members of the group are expected or required to have.

A different level is reached where the ritual is gradually secularized and the leader develops from priest to bard or poet. The conformity of reaction then vanishes. The message may mean something different to each member of the group—according to his individual experience. While on the level previously discussed the unity of response was institutionalized, here response is free, only the stimulus is common to all.

Differences in reaction develop gradually into differences in evaluation and in agreement. On this level criticism comes into play. Criticism, however, presupposes a new type of identification: one in which the critic identifies himself with the criticized, to however small an extent, in adopting an attitude of "I in his place. . . . " Such criticism may bear on the content of the message or on the way it is presented; it may be rough and unreasonable, or it may be that of the expert. It does not necessarily destroy the fascination which the message may inspire. It introduces, however, a process of testing and of scrutiny as a new element. Some psychological aspects of this process are apparently most accessible to analysis if we turn to the appreciation of art. The response of the audience is an aesthetic one if to a slight degree the audience identifies itself with the artist as creator of the work of art. Only if such an even distant approach to connoisseurship is realized, the aesthetic illusion is maintained and is achieved in what Coleridge calls "the willing suspense of disbelief" (see Kris, 1952, chap. 1).

In reformulating these types of participation in terms of processes of identification, two main cases may here be distinguished: one in which the leader and communicator is "accepted as ego ideal"—we may here speak of "identification in the superego—the case of the ritual dance; and one in which identification in the superego is supplemented by ego identification; this case is linked to what I described as the birth of criticism.[13]

The two concepts of propaganda, the totalitarian and the democratic, easily can be related to this differentiation: totalitarian propaganda clearly is based on the assumption that the message of the leader should be fully "accepted as ego ideal." Identification should take place in the superego. Democratic propaganda, on the contrary, is based on a concept in which two types of identification, identification in the superego and in the ego, are more evenly distributed.

So general a formulation clearly describes ideal types of attitudes. In the social reality we may expect to find more complex pictures which require more refined concepts. In the present context devoted rather to preliminary clarification than to a detailed analysis, we may well stress the outstanding contrasts. Totalitarian propaganda, I said, aims at establishing conditions approximating the market place. This was more than a metaphor. If one of the totalitarian leaders addresses his people, he regularly speaks from a mass meeting—and the nation as a radio audience is made to participate in it. They hear how the meeting assembles, they hear the music, they wait in tension, and when the leader appears and while he speaks, they are made to watch the carefully staged reaction of the multitude of which they are made to be a part. Thus the organized spell of the crowd extends to the radio homes. This, then, is the situation which creates the conditions under which the submissive type of identification grows. It grows where individuals have renounced their intellectual and moral independence, where regression rules.

Democratic leaders speak from their study. They address the individuals in their nation, their speeches are "fireside chats," from one home to another. Not a difference of prestige or power, but one of responsibility exists between the

---

13. The case represented by rituals of communication might be described as one in which a "partial" superego identification with the communicator takes place, while the "total" identification concerns the ideal shared by both communicator and audience.

speaker and the listener who is left to weigh, to test, and to consider. Attempts to sway his judgment are rare.

This clearly does not mean that there are no Germans who, in listening to Hitler, can resist his spell. There are many, we know; nor does it mean that we are not touched, although we may guard it as a secret, when we listen to those legitimately speaking for our cause. Rationality does not determine the life of the free; they, too, are subject to enthusiasm of various kinds, and normally so. We all know that we are suggestible and, while we are aware of it, many of us let ourselves for a time be carried away.

The antithesis of regression and ego control, of irrational and rational behavior, is a dangerous simplification. No such exclusion exists. To put it in the negative: he who cannot *pro tempore* relax, let loose the reins and indulge in regression, is according to generally accepted clinical standards ill. Regression is not always opposed to ego control; it can take place, as it were, in the service of the ego.[14]

I return to my initial remarks on distrust and disappointment. Many observers have complained about the fact that enthusiasm in this war seems to be suspect in the democracies. Spy fever or hate campaigns are rejected by the people—even by those who, like the British, have gone through the ordeal of total war. They want victory; they do not want orgies of hate.

Thus, based on the experience of the last war, they strive for more and more reasonable apprehension, for more and better information; and have, by their very attitude, created an atmosphere in which the new propaganda may grow. It will, I believe, by later historians be classified as the third revolution in psychological techniques to occur within half a century. And seen together the three revolutions are one. First came the new psychotherapy; the new education followed; the new propaganda is about to emerge.

---

14. In a paper read at the International Psychoanalytic Congress in Lucerne, 1934, I tried to establish this as one of the assumptions necessary to explain human reaction to the manipulation of symbols—in art or social control (see Kris, 1952, chap. 6). See also Hartmann (1939a, 1939b). The clinical aspects of the problems discussed here have recently also been mentioned in various papers by Otto Fenichel.

The essence of the revolution in psychotherapy is well known to us. The command of the hypnotist was replaced by the guidance of the psychoanalyst. We do not in psychoanalysis renounce all elements of suggestion, but they are reduced to a minimum. Some trust and confidence of the analysand is a precondition. The ultimate therapeutic aim is, however, increased self-awareness and increased ego control. It is achieved in the ideal case by lifting the veil of infantile amnesia and thus replacing the compelling forces of fixations by newly and freely made decisions; it is in this sense that Freud termed psychoanalytic therapy reeducation.

The new education was born out of many impulses. The one which came from Freud undoubtedly was decisive. Authoritarian was replaced by cooperative education; automatic obedience, the repercussions of which had become known, by agreement based on understanding. Again authority was not discarded—where it was, it had soon to be reintroduced—but it was modified in its function.

It was and is a painful revolution. It was easier and quicker to cure by hypnosis; but what cures there were, were no longer satisfactory. The scope of therapy had grown. It was easier to educate by stern command, but the results did not meet any longer with general approval; the necessity for more and better guidance had become obvious in the ever-expanding complexity of our lives.

It is now similar to what here is termed the new propaganda. It does not require less; it requires more labor. Again guidance cannot be discarded; it has to be reoriented. Talking down or inciting will no longer do. The task is to explain. Lasswell (1941), one of its advocates, has stressed what he calls balanced presentation—a presentation which states alternatives and thus enables independent evaluation of facts (see also Bruce Smith, 1942). Were this principle fully adopted, an agreement would have been reached on the essentially educational function of the new propaganda: to make his social and physical universe understood by man. This is a task so great, so necessarily integrated with the dynamic process of expanding democracy, that an increase of graded communication beyond all precedent seems warranted. The traditional channels hardly will suffice, and a new personnel will be required. Training may gradually fill the gap, but at least initially the job to be done is more general. It is clearly one for the opinion leaders, for the educational elite.

If I return for a moment to the model of participation I studied, I may now say that what I described as the place of expertness and connoisseurship in the growth of criticism illustrates the function of a democratic elite. Their function as intermediaries between the communication emanating from a representative leadership and the people may be said to represent the equivalent of their educational status. Their function is essential and irreplaceable—and may well be clarified by reference to its opposite. "Opinion leaders" in totalitarian countries are the elite of the party, the supervisors of the people, the specialists in violence. They organize totalitarian life with its sham participation, its parades and marches. In their hands, propaganda becomes a supplement of violence, and violence a prerequisite of propaganda. And thus psychological management supplants guidance of public opinion.

In the democracies, on the other hand, the new propaganda, in agreement and sooner or later in cooperation with the other newly developed psychological techniques, aims at individuals having higher freedom and greater responsibility. It is that aim which, for the psychoanalytic therapy, Freud formulates in saying: "Where id was, there ego shall be."

The oldest meaning of the word propaganda encourages so utopian a view. A moral philosopher of the 3rd century A.D., who wrote under the name of Cato, said:

> *Disce, sed a doctis, indoctos ipse docto*
> *Propaganda etenim est rerum bonarum doctrina.*

> Learn from the learned and teach the unlearned
> For the teaching of things that are good must ever be planted
> anew.

22: Danger and Morale

(1944)

In a world at war, man—normal or abnormal, alone or in association—lives under temporarily changed conditions. This offers the psychologist a special opportunity, the greater since the nature of the changes can be described in reasonably concrete terms. The opportunity is twofold, for enlarging data, and for evaluating hypotheses. I limit myself to the latter. I should like, in the experimental situation of men at war, to test the validity of some of Freud's views which seem of considerable importance for a better understanding of the relation of danger and morale.[1] For the sake of simplification I shall contrast hypotheses which can be derived from Freud's views with popular opinion and select two examples where forecasts based on such opinion have proven to be erroneous.[2]

The first of these examples refers to the expected reaction of urban populations to aerial bombardment. At the outbreak of the war "the organization of civilian mental services" in England "was based on the assumption of a tremendous blitz which . . . would give rise to huge waves of war neuroses, both acute and chronic." These "alarmist anticipations" have since been termed "the mass-neurosis myth" (Glover, 1942, pp. 17f., 36).

Presented at the 1943 meeting of the American Orthopsychiatric Association in New York. First published in the *American Journal of Orthopsychiatry*, 14 : 147–155. Copyright 1944, the American Orthopsychiatric Association, Inc. Reproduced by permission.

1. I refer to hypotheses "of Freud's" and not of "psychoanalysis," since at the present stage what remains as a noncontroversial body of views among groups of workers in the field of psychoanalysis to my mind hardly presents a unified set of assumptions.

2. The selection of these forecasts aims at giving representative examples and not at scornful exposure. It should be said that prognostications in wartime are particularly risky since, as a rule, they have to be based on incomplete data.

The second forecast concerns the reaction of a specific military group to dangers of a particular intensity. I refer to the embarkation of the British Expeditionary Force at Dunkirk in May 1940. The army, it was said, would be demoralized and, in turn, demoralize Britain. History proudly records what in fact took place.

Freud's views which I should like to contrast with these forecasts were formulated in 1926, partly revising his earlier assumptions; they concern the relation of anxiety and danger. Freud distinguishes between real and imaginary danger. Anxiety acts in both cases as a signal. In the case of real danger the signal leads to protective action; this signal need not reach the level of awareness. In the case of imaginary danger the signal does not lead to protective action or the protective action is not the only reaction to the signal: anxiety, as it were, gets hold of the person.

Let me illustrate this by a typical example which, however, has one merit: the objective danger situation the subject had to face and the danger situation he imagined have much in common.

A young man in his early twenties, Jewish, intellectual, whose interest in modern psychology was the conscious reason for his wish to be analyzed, suffered from a severe anxiety neurosis. The anxiety attacks reached considerable intensity. They were related to situations in which unconscious passive-homosexual tendencies predominated. The center of the apprehension was the situation of being overpowered: former Gentile playmates and friends in the neighborhood were the preferred objects of the fearful fantasies. The case was analyzed in Vienna. When Hitler came to power in March 1938 the fantasies of the patient suddenly met with supporting conditions in the environment. The objects of his fantasies had gained the power which in his imagination he previously had attributed to them. One day he was confronted with a gang of young Nazis. A street fight ensued. He was a young man of athletic appearance, who had repeatedly been encouraged to train as an amateur boxer. His neurosis, however, had prevented him from availing himself of these opportunities. In the brawl mentioned he did well indeed. Impressed by his courageous initiative, his violent and skillful defense, the gang did not try to prevent his retreat. Since their code of behavior had not yet been corrupted by National Socialist education, they also refrained from subsequent retribution.

I saw the young man shortly after the encounter. He described how he felt anxiety rising when he met the gang on a narrow street. In his own words: "I switched to action."

In the days after the encounter his anxiety grew. The encounter was gradually brought into relation to the fantasies which usually disturbed his falling asleep. However, no great attack crystallized. A number of reasons may have been responsible for this omission. First, there *was* the danger that the gang might retaliate and hand the patient over to those specialists in violence who controlled life after the National Socialist occupation; second, his activity did not stop. He prepared for escape from Vienna with such untiring energy that, despite many adverse factors, he succeeded in an astonishingly short time.[3]

This example shows, I believe, with considerable clarity that the set of functions of the psychic apparatus which Freud calls the ego [4] includes the control of danger situations in which highly coordinated actions may be required.

Wartime experience, as described by the participants or reported in the daily press from all battlefields, gives ample and astounding examples of how far this control of danger situations can go when the individual is not only threatened, but when the threat comes from the enemy and when active response to danger is self-protection and duty at the same time. Such reactions are not limited to those trained in endurance,

3. The anxious fantasies of this patient followed a pattern which has been described as "libidinization of fear" (Anna Freud, 1936); it is, if we follow Anna Freud's classical exemplification, a play with the object of fear from which satisfaction, frequently masochistic satisfaction, is derived. The fantasy is used as a stimulant, but the stimulation may fail and then the anxiety attack comes into its own. Similar processes occur in a more normal setting. Anxious tension acts as a stimulation of the ego. Among intellectual workers or students, one not infrequently finds individuals who require anxious tension or anxiety in order to achieve success. Some cases of stage fright have a similar structure; the stimulation of activity by the "anxiety signal" (Freud, 1926) becomes a device for the improvement of action. Generally, similar psychological mechanisms were described as appeasement of the superego. Anticipation of failure, it was said, was the price of success. In my experience, this is sometimes only a subsidiary explanation.

4. This is one of the meanings in which he uses the word "ego."

to the men in the fighting services. The resistance of the people of Britain to the German aerial attacks in 1940 and 1941 seems to indicate that those forecasters who expected mass neurosis had formed an erroneous conception of human nature. They had overestimated man's craving for safety. As a reaction, a new myth seems about to arise, which Edward Glover (1942) calls the "no neurosis myth." While it is infinitely nearer to truth, it does not promote our understanding. The purpose of this paper seems best served if we inquire into the exceptions. Who were the few who, when their lives were threatened by aerial bombardment, reacted in a way approximating mental illness?

Surveys published in Britain such as Glover's case studies or Aubrey Lewis's statistical presentation (1942) have assembled data which, while they do not yet allow for a systematic symptomatology of nervous reactions to air raids, seem highly significant. The vast majority of specialists reporting on observational data stress the importance of the pretraumatic personality for the study of the reaction to traumatic experiences. It is not pretended that all nervous casualties must have a neurotic history, though many have. Our knowledge of psychodynamics rather invites the idea that the pretraumatic personality might have been characterized by impaired stability; instability of balance being a precondition favoring pathological reaction to exposure to danger. Such pathological reactions were discussed in Freud's schematic exposition in the following terms. Freud distinguishes between realistic and neurotic anxiety, corresponding to objective and imaginary danger. Realistic and neurotic anxiety may be related to each other in various ways: they may be "mingled"; the danger, in Freud's words, may be real, but the anxiety in regard to it may be "over-great, greater than seems proper to us. It is this surplus of anxiety which betrays the presence of a neurotic element" (1926, p. 166).[5]

---

5. I would add that the relation may also be one in time; past real danger may later be experienced as imaginary danger, and I have little doubt that this transformation may be of some considerable importance for further research on traumatic neuroses, where this time relation has always been considered but has lately not been sufficiently stressed.

Freud comments further on the nature of this neurotic element. Neurotic anxiety, he asserts, reacts to "instinctual danger." I shall not comment on this expression but assume that what he meant is understood: an element in the actual situation may mobilize needs or drives which regularly refer to the past of the individual, as a rule to his childhood. This process remains unconscious.

The impressions concerning the pretraumatic personalities of psychological air raid casualties in Britain were interpreted by many observers in line with these assumptions. Data recently published in Britain seem to bring confirmation of Freud's views independent of the impressions of observers. The data were collected by trained observers "who had experience of the effects of raids upon unevacuated children in bombed areas" and were published by Cyril Burt (1941), one of the pioneers in British child psychology.

The data refer to children "whose own houses or immediate neighbourhood was so severely damaged that they had to move at once, usually at night." The figures are concerned with children not physically injured who showed "nervous symptoms during the following week." The commonest symptoms to be noted by casual observers were "abnormal restlessness and distractability of attention" rather than conscious fear; "but many different kinds of minor neurotic symptoms are traceable beneath the surface." By the end of one month most symptoms had disappeared.[6]

Of children under two years, 5 percent showed a nervous reaction. In commenting on this extremely low figure, one is reminded of the qualitative data reported by Anna Freud and Dorothy Burlingham (1942), who have elaborated on the fact that anxiety reactions in the small child are frequently what one might call reactions of "induced anxiety"; the child's fear is that of his mother.

In the next group, age two to five, 37 percent showed nervous aftereffects. From the psychoanalytic point of view we might have wished for a different age breakdown, one to in-

6. The curve gives, in Burt's words, an approximation only. Owing to wartime conditions, no more exact procedure was apparently possible. No absolute figures are quoted.

clude the sixth year. This would have been especially important in view of the subsequent figures.

In 26 percent of children from five to eleven nervous aftereffects to the exposure were found. We wonder what the drop in the curve might have been had the figures been limited to the latency period. The trend clearly continues in an accentuated form. Children age eleven to fourteen showed the reaction mentioned in 13 percent. There is little to comment upon here. It is the next set of data which deserves our attention. The trend is suddenly reversed. In 21 percent of adolescents, age fourteen to sixteen, nervous aftereffects appeared. Not only is the trend reversed, but the rise is considerable.

The curve has two peaks, at age two to five, and at age fourteen to sixteen. *The two peaks coincide roughly with two periods in which "instinctual demands" gain ascendance in human life.* The first peak period includes that part of prelatency in which the larger portion of the oedipal conflict is enacted. The second includes puberty proper, which is somewhat late in certain areas of Britain.

The increase in tension which coincides with an increased frequency of nervous reaction indicates that in the age groups at the two peaks reaction to real danger was more frequently "mingled" with one to imaginary danger than in other age groups. The methodological relation of Freud's hypothesis and the data here discussed deserve some attention. Hunches provided by the microscope of psychoanalysis direct our interpretation of quantifiable data from macroscopic observation.[7]

In another field of observation supporting data seem to be available, though their interpretation may be said to be less suggestive. Our starting point is an impression formulated at the end of the last war by some observers who studied war neuroses of soldiers. The term "war neurosis" itself was suggested by David Eder, who, like many others, was impressed by the fact that in spite of the specific symptoms of some of these cases—those originally termed shell shock and usually

7. The first peak has clearly to do also with the increased awareness of danger; but this supplements our explanation without contradicting it.

considered as typical traumatic neuroses—a variety of other cases showed similar traits, structurally at least, if not symptomatically.[8] It is to the general relationship between these structural traits of nervous casualties in soldiers and neurotic predispositions to which I refer. In a paper read in April 1918 before the Royal Society of Medicine in London, Ernest Jones took the view that the only men who suffered from war neurosis were those whose "libido organized on a homosexual-narcissistic basis was so attached to the Ego as to become stimulated when the latter was threatened, i.e., in situations of danger." Jones arrived at this formulation (which he would now probably be inclined to reformulate in terms more in line with recent psychoanalytic concepts) from clinical studies of war neuroses of soldiers.[9] His findings were corroborated by psychoanalysts in other countries (Abraham et al., 1919).

Some incomplete data available from this war may be interpreted in the light of Jones's assumptions. In Britain soldiers in camps or barracks and civilians in their habitual dwelling places were subject to the same amount and kind of danger. While figures of nervous casualties for the armed forces were not released, Aubrey Lewis, the Director of Maudsley Hospital in London, who was given access to these data, reports the following. *The incidence of mental illness in the fighting services is not high, but is "higher than in the corresponding civilian population, [though insofar] as enemy attacks are concerned, they are in Britain in the same position as civilians."* The difference in reaction may be interpreted in various ways. Civilians and fighting men live under vastly different conditions. The latter lack the relative freedom of the former; their initiative, if faced with an emergency, is more limited. While civilians have mostly been able to adapt themselves to extreme hardships without being fully deprived of their peacetime existence, the soldiers are separated from their family and their peacetime

8. It seems that not all relevant problems of the traumatic neuroses of wartime have yet been solved. Neither the question of their relation to the "flight into illness" seems to be definitely explained, nor has the decisive importance of the quantitative element of the duration of strain, of psychological wear and tear, as one might say, as yet been fully elucidated. See Kardiner (1941), and Rado (1942).

9. For his later views, see Jones (1929).

environment.[10] The civilians, says Lewis, have been able to make for themselves an environment in which they fit; the soldiers have not. While it is clearly impossible to isolate any one causal element in so complex a picture, we may well feel inclined to stress that the life in the services, in a male society subject to command and all the concomitant features of this life, may adversely affect those soldiers whose pretraumatic or, more accurately, prewar, personality might clinically be classified by the somewhat amorphous term of latent homosexuality. We may venture this interpretation since many who have been in touch with cases of mental illness in the fighting forces in Britain, including the psychological casualties after air raids, are inclined to form an opinion which might best be rendered in these terms. Those who react pathologically to war situations and, more specifically, to aerial bombardment as part of it, are men with an unstable libidinal organization, men "not sure of themselves." [11]

We may thus hope to have gained some corroboration of Freud's views on the relationship of realistic and neurotic anxiety. Our examples tend to show that those individuals who react to real danger with "a surplus of anxiety" are individuals in whom conflicts and tensions predominate. In the examples here discussed the tension is of a sexual nature—sexual of course in Freud's sense of this term; clinical experience shows that similar tensions may also be created by pressures of a different nature.

I have dealt in some detail with one part of Freud's views, that concerning the difference between realistic and neurotic anxiety and the reaction to both. I did not refer to other parts of his theory concerning the nature of danger and its relation to helplessness.

10. For the phenomenological differences of civilian and army life, see Glover (1942).

11. Glover (1942) mentions the following three conditions for what he terms neurotic anxiety in the face of danger: "1) The anxiety character group; 2) The so-called narcissistic type; 3) Groups having strong unconscious homo-sexual leanings" (p. 37). Glover's impressions thus corroborate the findings suggested by the material quoted above.

Real danger, Freud says, is danger that is known. Unknown danger tends to be magnified. Freud equates, therefore, imaginary and unknown danger.

Man facing danger tends to measure his forces. The greatest threat is that of being helpless. Freud calls a situation where helplessness is actually experienced, traumatic. These situations are frequent in the child's life, when the threat of losing the love object looms large. The anticipation of a traumatic situation and the preparation for its occurrence enable the ego, "which has undergone the trauma passively," now to react actively. This active response is set into motion by (initial) anxiety acting as a signal.

Group psychology supplies impressive examples. I shall first refer briefly to an illustration which the America of prewar days has provided: the panic reaction to Mr. Orson Welles's broadcast on *The Invasion from Mars*.[12] It will be remembered that the news broadcasts with which the play was interspersed announced the invasion of a part of New Jersey by terrifying monsters of unknown nature and that these broadcasts were taken as real by a considerable part of the listening audience. Though the conditions for investigation were severely restricted, the response data collected by Cantril and his collaborators show that among those who fell subject to panic and whose critical ability did not suffice to face the confusing situation, there were many who impressed the investigators as unstable personalities—personalities predisposed, as it were, to pathological reaction. However, I am here mainly concerned with the reaction of the audience as a whole. In order to appreciate this reaction we must realize that the play was broadcast on October 30, 1938, at a time when the American radio audience lived under the impression of the Munich agreement. In those days, when news broadcasts raced with each other for the ultimate and fatal scoop, an atmosphere of tension took hold of the Western world. Briefly, the reaction described by Cantril was not to Mr. Welles's broadcast alone; not

12. Mr. Welles's broadcast might be considered as another case of erroneous forecast. Nobody anticipated the reaction it created. For the following material, see Cantril (1940).

only the alleged sudden, unanticipated appearance of unknown nightmarish monsters created the panic—the panic was
also a reaction to the total situation of October 1938 in our civilization; it was a reaction to Hitler's war of nerves.

It is the secret of the war of nerves that the initiative is retained by one side; that while tension mounts, the world is
kept guessing. In each phase of the war of nerves Hitler's next
step was an unknown danger. A situation of this kind, where
activity cannot be directed toward any one goal, creates a feeling of mental paralysis and helplessness, one directly related
to what Freud calls traumatic. How National Socialism has
elaborated this principle of the war of nerves in its political
warfare has repeatedly been described in great detail. The
strategy of terror and intimidation carried out by German
propaganda against Poland and France, and unsuccessfully attempted against Britain, has made this principle generally
known (see chap. 20). And with familiarity it lost part of its effect. Its final collapse, however, took place when the saga of
German irresistibility was shattered on the battlefield.

Reference to the war of nerves has carried us into the midst
of the problem of morale, which for the purpose of this study
may be defined as the endurance of a group in a common enterprise under hardship and strain (Lasswell, 1933). While the
complexity of these problems is impressive, the present context calls only for a few remarks.

Two of the important functions of the leader of an
endangered group seem to be implied in Freud's hypothesis.
To be acceptable to the group, leadership has to prove its anticipation of the danger. The leader, acting for the group,
thus fulfills a function similar to that of the ego in the individual. In the social context, the information of the group on
what the future may bring becomes a necessary means of psychological prophylaxis. By making adequate information accessible, the leader transforms "unknown" into "known"
danger; he gives, as it were, the danger signal. By actually
turning himself against the danger and by thus inviting identification in action, but naturally also by providing outlets for
the group's desire to participate in "protective activity," the

leader prevents the transformation of real into imaginary danger. Under his guidance the extent of the danger is estimated in reasonable terms.[13]

Instead of presenting a theoretical discussion, I shall comment briefly on a case history in social psychology which illustrates with great clarity the problems of morale under danger. It is a complex history, and its implications lead beyond the area of the problems discussed in this paper. I refer to the British retreat from Dunkirk. The prognostication was, as I said, that on its return the army would be demoralized, and the possibility was anticipated that it might in turn demoralize the British Isles. This prognostication was made not only and not mainly by the enemy, but more often by British observers. It was repeated up to the second day of the evacuation, when the arrival of the first troops gave the lie to the panic of the forecasters. They—the forecasters—were in a panic. They saw the specter of an army which was defeated, which had lost its equipment, and had to return home—if the return ever succeeded. But the forecasters had not shared the life of the troops. Much has been said about how the Battle of Flanders and the retreat took place. Better than any of the accounts by nonparticipants, the dispatches of the British Commander, Lord Gort, enable us to follow step by step those ventures.[14] He reports in parsimonious but admirable style the sequence of decisions which had led him to realize that first retreat and then reembarkation were unavoidable. We learn how sub commanders and troops were made to understand a situation which, while painful and confusing, was not shameful for the British forces. The French army, their admired ally, had been

13. These are naturally not the only functions of the leader in a danger situation; others may be deduced from Freud's *Group Psychology and the Analysis of the Ego* (1921a). All functions of leadership are related to the nature of the group. In this connection see chapter 22, where types of identification with the leader are discussed in relation to social structure. The structure of the group, its cohesion, the satisfaction of the people with conditions under which they live, the unifying factors of danger, and other problems cannot be discussed here. See Watson (1942) and Hocking (1941).

14. Supplement to the London Gazette, October 10, 1941, *Despatches received by the Secretary of State for War from General the Viscount Gort, Commander-in-Chief, B.E.F., France & Belgium, 1939–1940*, pp. 5899–5934.

beaten, the French defenses had been broken, their own equipment was insufficient, and finally the Belgians had surrendered. From day to day Gort adapted his decisions to the deteriorating situation. There is no trace of exasperation in the measures he chose; they follow each other logically. He determined at which point each group must make its last stand in order to delay the enemy; he announced at which crossroads each army corps, division, and brigade had to drop its equipment in order not to encumber the road leading to the port; and continuously the greatest care was taken to keep the army informed of the course of events.

So far goes foresight and leadership. The anticipation of danger by the home authorities went further. When the British troops came to the beaches of Dunkirk, there appeared not only a navy to save them—a strange navy of little boats, manned by their kin—but also, for the first time in their experience, the Royal Air Force. The latter had failed to protect them during the Battle of Flanders; now at the beaches of Dunkirk the fighter planes of the Home Command could intervene. Dunkirk was just within their reach, and flying from the outer ring of British aerodromes they could stay in the air over the beaches for just fifteen minutes. And in those fifteen minutes, 200 to 300 of the German bombers which were trying to disrupt the waiting units, were shot down in a day. The dogfights were fought in the clouds and, from above, the Dorniers and Heinkels fell into the sea. There can be little doubt that to the waiting men this meant "protection from above." The ordeal and the danger did not end with the embarkation. On some days men had to change boats three or four times if the small vessels which had given them shelter were bombed out of action. But since on at least two days a protective haze supported the heroic skill of the skippers and, by and large, the embarkation succeeded beyond any expectation, the troops, when they arrived on the home soil, had not the feeling of flight or disintegration. From the moment when they turned from advance to retreat they had fought danger. From Belgium to the Channel they had delivered their fight. Danger had not ended when they were waiting on the beaches and danger had accompanied the crossing of the Channel. It was danger courageously met each time by action of their own and their leaders.

The example does not end here. The psychological aftermath of the conquest of danger may be varied. In some the traumatic effect sets in after the danger is past, others show manic reaction. Neither type was infrequent among the men from Dunkirk. But in the vast majority the conquest of danger acted as an invigorant. If we turn from the men of Dunkirk to the people of Britain as a whole, we find a similar reaction repeating itself on a nation-wide scale. They conquered their danger in the lonesome year after the fall of France. At no time, either with the men of Dunkirk or with the people of Britain, has there ever been an absence of apprehension. Apprehension, one might say, is anxiety under the command of the ego. Anxiety never did take hold of the situation; not for a moment did the people lose the consciousness of the danger in which they were living, nor were they allowed by their government to lose it; and what in the first part of this paper was said about the rarity of incidents of mental illness under aerial bombardment should be related to this social context, to this climate of British morale.

Before the war and before the danger became real, current opinion expected that man, under the threat to his safety, would be likely to develop psychological illness. Panicky forecasts were made, and some ill-advised scholars went so far as to draw conclusions from the reaction to the Orson Welles broadcast as to the behavior of man with his life at stake.[15]

Wartime experience has corrected these assumptions. We have learned that the threat to safety was more easily overcome than the threat to the social side of human life. Evacuation and not bombing, the disruption of families and not the casualty lists, have become the concern of those studying the morale problem in Britain. This is once more in line with Freud's assumptions. In childhood, where the reaction to the traumatic situation is rooted, helplessness is a part of all

15. In this connection, see *New York Times,* Dec. 6, 1942, *Panic is to be avoided,* letter to the *Times* by the Committee on National Morale.

human beings; helplessness which later in life may be re-created by external conditions and the internal response to them. In childhood, however, the first and greatest threat is that of loss of love. Out of the matrix of love grow the values which enable man to face the threat to his safety in order to retain his self-respect and to serve his ideals.

23: Notes on the Psychology
of Prejudice

(1946)

Only in a society such as ours, whose values include the belief
in the equality of all men and in the dignity of the individual,
can the fight against prejudice be meaningfully carried on.
Hence, the effort to secure general recognition of those values
is basic to any effort to combat prejudice. Only when the im-
morality of prejudice has been established can the educator
point to the contradiction between moral standards and the
existence of prejudice as a latent proclivity or as a manifest attitude; only then can he create in his audience a state of mind
truly receptive to what he has to say.

As an educator he can never hope to change the behavior of
those who are satisfied with their prejudices, or whose prejudices are of great intensity. Extremists cannot be convinced;
they can only be converted; and conversion is rarely, if ever,
achieved by insight. The educator must focus his efforts on
those in his audience who, while they hold prejudices against
groups within or outside of the community, wish that they had
no "reason for prejudice." That wish may never become conscious; it may manifest itself only as a feeble echo of some self-
reproach. How many in the community reach this stage of maturity it is hard to estimate; they surely are only a fraction of
those who practice prejudice, and yet they are the only ones to
whom argumentation, at least of the type I shall try to develop
here, can be successfully presented.

First published in *The English Journal*, 35 : 304–308. [The author dealt with the
same topic, as well as the roots of hostility, in 1949.]

Any discussion of prejudice leads, by necessity, back to the quest for the part that nature and social nurture play in the growth of the individual. Evidence accumulated throughout the last decades suggests that the influence of hereditary factors on human behavior has previously been greatly overestimated. Those who tend to exaggerate the importance of racial characteristics frequently do so out of ignorance or for the purpose of deceit. Anthropologists have taught us that many types of behavior previously attributed to racial factors can be explained as resulting from cultural learning. Controlled observational procedures—for instance, studies on identical twins—suggest that the same hereditary predispositions can manifest themselves in vastly different types of behavior, according to the nature and to the sequence of the child's experiences. Findings in both those areas and in many allied fields do not eliminate the factor of heredity and the potential importance of racial characteristics—though the nature of these characteristics has to be defined with greatest care—but they limit their importance considerably. They give impressive and incontrovertible evidence of the plasticity of human nature.

That plasticity decreases sharply after adolescence, and recent studies of the emotional development of children tend to indicate that many fundmental traits of the human character are formed in the nursery years. Thus the adopted infant who stems from a foreign land but has been brought up from the earliest months of his life in an American home will only in special cases later in life be distinguishable from his fellow Americans; the immigrant child, on the contrary, who comes to America with his parents, though educated in an American school, acquires in his home modes of expression and behavior that are part of a different cultural pattern. Such learning takes place in the earliest interplay between parents and child; its vehicle is the process of identification. How the influence of the home and that of the new environment will merge into one another is hard to predict. Needless to say, the result may prove to be of high social value, and its cultural potentialities may be manifold.

The flow of change in society is slowest where basic ideals rooted in tradition, customs, and institutions are concerned. Some of these ideals are transmitted at an early age. Throughout the Western world we frequently find the phenomenon of a time lag in human affairs due to these transmissions. Traditional ideals that one might expect to have been long discarded live on in the human mind; they may offer tenacious resistance to the acceptance of social change. In the process of the assimilation of the immigrant, that cultural time lag gains considerable importance; the immigrant child may still transmit to his own descendants some of the behavior patterns that were active in his own upbringing. Assimilation is a slow process. Under the disguise of full compliance with the new environment, cultural heritages of the past, though attenuated by time and intermarriage live on among men.

In touching upon the survival of cultural differences, I have deviated from the proper sequence of this presentation; I have not yet dealt with the question of what relation to prejudice differences between groups may have. At first one might be inclined to assume that the correlation will be positive and that the greater the differences between the groups, the more intense will be the prejudice. However, the data of observation contradict this assumption. Even the smallest difference can be stressed and overstressed and may become a focal point around which prejudice may crystallize. One can go even further: propinquity seems to invite such overemphasis; thus a slight deviation in accent or pronunciation in one and the same language can be experienced as indicating a wider gulf between groups than the use of a different language; "brethren in blood," like the Spanish and the Portuguese, can hold against each other no less embittered prejudices than people of differently colored skins.

Such overemphasis of the smallest differences can draw our attention to the true relation between difference and prejudice in group life. That relation is determined by the danger to the integrity of the group. The emphasis on difference or on social distance, be it small or great, serves mainly the purpose of maintaining that integrity. If one difference tends to disappear or to lose its importance, i.e., to appear less crucial to group members, another one is called upon to take its place. Hence, when in western and central Europe during the 19th century Jewish assimilation proceeded rapidly, so that ever more persons of Jewish descent became indistinguishable from the dominant groups, and, simultaneously, the religious distinction was felt by many to be less decisive, it was suddenly claimed that the difference between Jews and non-Jews rested upon racial inheritance; racial reasons were called upon to supplement religious reasons for segregation and discrimination.

The desire to keep groups apart is not inborn in human nature; there is no gregarious instinct that would hold ingroups together and erect barriers against diffusion. But there are many psychological ties that connect members of the ingroup and make it easier for men to understand each other if they have common symbols of identification. And yet, observation indicates that, at least under conditions of Western civilization, one of the strongest motive powers, if not the strongest, for maintaining the integrity of a group and its social distance from other groups is the fear of competition. Under modern conditions the fear of sexual competition has lost some of its power. And yet it survives. The stranger to the tribe—and even modern man is in some sense still tribal—may be, at the same time, peculiarly attractive and repulsive as a sexual object. He owes both these qualities to the fact that he is further removed from the barrier of incest; there is adventure and danger in his approach. More important in the modern world is the economic aspect of competition. The dangers of competition grow when the newcomers or the intruding group are socially mobile and their social status is potentially rising.

At this point I have to return to the beginning of my discussion. When, in a social order, the belief in the equality of all men has been established, social mobility has become possible, and the danger of economic competition necessarily grows. Everywhere in Western civilization there exists some sort of link between equalitarian beliefs and the growth of prejudicial attitudes. Prejudice replaces social barriers of another kind. Moreover, the intensity of prejudice is related to the level of indulgence and deprivation under which the group lives. Prejudice invariably grows where deprivation increases. If there are fewer jobs, the tendency toward increased discrimination against underprivileged groups is bound to grow. There can be little doubt that economic hardship is the most important and tangible reason for the increase of prejudice; but it is not the only reason. Prejudice is likely to grow wherever a group is exposed to hardship of any kind.

Social processes are not anonymous; there are those in the group who influence group activities more than do others. In any community there are opinion leaders: the doctor, the vicar, the teacher, the barber, the union organizer; they and many others may lead opinion both inside and outside the framework of a political group or of an institution, stimulating decisions on problems of common interest among fellow citizens. Some opinion leaders not only guide the formation of decisions, but agitate in favor of one or the other pressure group. They become manipulators of group activities either in the service of others or for aims of their own. In both cases they aim at creating an organization of their followers.

Group cohesion can be strengthened by a common ideal or tradition or by admiration for a common leader—in brief, by unity in devotion. But group cohesion can also be strengthened by a common enemy, against whom all hostility is directed; the enemy fulfills an important function in the dynamics of most group formations, since he becomes the target for hostilities which otherwise might endanger relations within the group. The age-old strategy of political propaganda takes this fact into account; the agitator frequently chooses as his target of abuse a group against which prejudice exists, and that group, most frequently a minority, becomes a scapegoat. Whenever hardship of any kind arises—not economic hardship only—and aggressive tendencies within the group increase, that aggression will be conveniently directed against the scapegoat; he functions as a catalyst in social living.

The scapegoat acquires definite characteristics. Some of these characteristics may correspond to the behavior exhibited by some, or even by a majority, of the members of the abused group; but in every case other characteristics are added. These additions usually follow a definite pattern; the clearest case of such a pattern is that in which the scapegoat is satanized. Thus we find in anti-Semitic propaganda statements which refer to the "pushing," highly competitive character of the Jews, merged with statements about their dirtiness and trickery and their scheming character, their bad odor, their destructive and hateful impulses, their lust, and their depraved mores. The image of the Jew is thus made in the shape of Satan.

This merging of true and alleged characteristics of a group is a process of considerable importance in group relations, both intranational and international. All human relations are based on a generalized picture that man carries of both the self and the other. Every people has an image of every other people with whom it has had contact. Beef-eating John Bull of the Napoleonic era, solid and stout as he was, changed in the 19th century into the haggard, scheming hypocrite who "with Bible and checkbook corrupts the people," the stereotype created during the Boer War, with which German propaganda has successfully operated during both German attacks on the Western world. Such changes do not occur rapidly; the ancient imagery tends to persist. Even at a time when beef eating has become a fading memory in a hungry island, at a time when a Labor government struggles for survival, and the checking account of an empire has been overdrawn, the ancient images that cluster about it still are propagated. Even while Jews were being tormented and exterminated as no religious or national group ever was before, rabblerousers and agitators spoke of their dangerous satanic power. Imagery of this kind, based upon the merging of stereotypes from various areas, constitutes an element of retardation; it tends to disrupt the spontaneity of our judgment and to endanger understanding between groups. The work of the agitator who purposely manipulates such imagery aims at perpetuating prejudices and at canalizing hate in a chosen direction.

The work of the educator can be no other than to undo the evil the agitator has created. The teacher has powerful arguments at his disposal. He can demonstrate how prejudice is rooted in social conditions, how it is manipulated for the purpose of agitation; and he can do better, by demonstrating that those in a democracy who follow the agitator are prey to the wickedness or the weakness of a small group of individuals, frequently unfit for leadership in any other field than that of demagogy.

There is little to be said about individuals whom one might call "wicked" agitators, men who coolly calculate what type of incitement would best serve their purpose in a given situation. They are cynical technicians, frequently responsible for the planning of agitation. Sometimes the calculating agitator is, at the same time, a man who has the capacity for making himself believe what it is useful for him to say. "Sincerity," therefore, is not a concept with which we can successfully operate. Rather is it essential to understand what personal needs are satisfied by agitation as a profession. Research in the personality of agitators during the last decades has produced some useful hunches as to their unconscious motivations.

Agitators tend to be individuals of various degrees of psychological unbalance. Maladjustments in their personal lives and failures in their careers in society are so frequent as to be almost regularly recurrent factors. They are persons whose early experiences have created a predisposition for intense ambivalence, i.e., contradictory feelings toward one person or object. In order to escape that ambivalence, they tend to polarize positive and negative attitudes. The world to them is divided into the best and the worst, and thus the contradiction between love and hate seems "rationalized." In other words, the mechanism of projection provides for them the solution of personal conflict. We resort to projection when we attribute to another person attitudes or emotions whose existence in ourselves we refuse to admit. By projecting negative values on the scapegoat, by satanizing his enemy, the agitator tries to escape from the battle within himself. But the mechanism of projection alone does not constitute the agitator. He is also a man who strives for applause that he cannot obtain otherwise, who dramatizes his beliefs, and who has the uncanny ability to convince others of his views. One should add here that not all agitators correspond to this somewhat simplified picture; but many do, particularly the small fry of demagogy—those who rouse the passions of the people at street corners and who, in the community, act as obedient servants of pressure groups interested in the persistence of discord and in the growth of distrust.

The educator can point to these examples and he can tell his audience that, if they accept what the agitators profess, they follow a doubtful attraction. If they harbor prejudice, he might imply, his listeners are trying to project their own unsolved conflicts into the world of thought and opinion, as the agitator does.

But the teacher's work is not completed at that point. He cannot stop at the negative phase; he must try to make not only their own motivation understandable to those who hold prejudices, but must also explain to them the reaction of those against whom the prejudice is directed. There is no better means of dissipating prejudices than familiarity between one group and another. The educator's work will therefore not be completed unless he includes in his scope the group against which prejudice is directed. There is no such thing as unilaterality in human affairs; where there are two, there is mutuality. The response to prejudice is frequently counterprejudice; the response to distrust, counterdistrust. Thus, groups linked to each other by prejudice are unified by hate and counterhate that in turn tends, many a time, to justify prejudice.

Briefly, education has to act in the social situation of conflicting groups. In making both groups face and understand each other, in bringing into the open the dynamics of the interplay between prejudices, education against prejudice becomes group therapy in the truest sense.

24: Psychoanalysis and the Study of Creative Imagination

(1953)

"Creative Imagination" indicates a mental property which we usually connect with achievements in the arts, in the broadest sense of the word. But scientists and "thinkers" also rely upon creative imagination during certain probably crucial phases of their work; and in one way or another this same mental property may manifest itself in the personal or professional lives of us all.

Common to all manifestations of creative imagination, in the first place, is subjective experience. This tends to be infinitely differentiated in intensity and duration and to appear as an ingredient or accessory in many moods. Three characteristics of this experience seem outstanding.

1. Subjects are aware of the limitation of conscious effort.

2. They are aware of a specific feeling. It is never a neutral one. There is always some, and frequently a very high, emotional charge involved.

3. Even if excitement rises, the mind tends to work with high precision and problems are easily solved. If we adopt a broad meaning of the term "problem solving," we can say that some "problem solving" is always going on, even in art.

A further common element concerns not the subject's experience but the reaction of others to him. Wherever creative imagination is at work, for better or worse it tends to establish some distinction between the one and the many.

Delivered as Freud Lecture under the auspices of the New York Psychoanalytic Institute, May 6, 1952 at The New York Academy of Medicine. First published in the *Bulletin of the New York Academy of Medicine*, 29 : 334–351, 1953; also in *The Creative Imagination*, ed. H. M. Ruitenbeck. New York: Quadrangle Books, 1965, pp. 23–45.

This is not, I know, a satisfactory and certainly not an exhaustive description. However, a certain vagueness may not be out of order since we are dealing with a difficult topic. And in the end, the impression must and should prevail that, significant as the contribution of psychoanalysis is, it is limited in various ways. We have started on a voyage with our course largely uncharted.

I shall attempt to characterize the contribution of psychoanalysis to the study of creative imagination with particular reference to art—art in a very broad sense—and loosely follow the guide of the history of psychoanalysis, since its contributions to the study of creative imagination constitute an important part of this history.

The present position of psychoanalysis, its status in science and society, offers a starting point. I shall characterize this status by stressing two aspects. There is one which will hardly preoccupy us on this occasion. Largely based on psychoanalytic insight for some twenty years, a movement has been under way which later historians may well decide to describe as the "psychiatric revolution." There is, for one, the rise of psychiatry within medicine, the obsolescence of a rigid distinction between the "physical" and the "mental" in approaches to illness, in the emergence of psychosomatic medicine; there is, moreover, the ever-broadening concept of mental health itself, modifying procedures in education and transforming our views on welfare to the point where charity as an institution has come to include considerations of the individual's psychological balance. During the last decade these and other related trends seem to have converged into one direction. It is this, that therapy is gradually being supplemented by prevention; and a program which has existed in a somewhat utopian sense since the earliest days of Freud's work is thus being carried further.

The second aspect of the current status of psychoanalysis is externally characterized by the growing contact of psychoanalysis with other disciplines. It is not a contact in which psychoanalysis and sociology, anthropology or political science—to mention only some currently much emphasized examples—establish an interdisciplinary cooperation, but rather one in which psychoanalysis provides the focal point for a new science of man of which the outlines are here and there visible. Psychoanalytic therapy and psychoanalytic psychiatry in general provide the most essential set of data in the building of this new science.

How did this come about, how could two so far-reaching developments grow out of one root, originally out of the experience of one investigator?

I here turn to a quotation from Freud's earliest writings which describes his own reflections on the first extensive psychiatric case histories which he presented to the public after considerable delay, in the fall of 1895:

> I have not always been a psychotherapist. Like other neuropathologists, I was trained to employ local diagnoses and electroprognosis, and it still strikes me myself as strange that the case histories I write should read like short stories and that, as one might say, they lack the serious stamp of science. I must console myself with the reflection that the nature of the subject is evidently responsible for this, rather than any preference of my own. The fact is that local diagnosis and electrical reactions lead nowhere in the study of hysteria, whereas a detailed description of mental processes such as we are accustomed to find in the works of imaginative writers enables me, with the use of a few psychological formulas, to obtain at least some kind of insight into the course of that affection [see Breuer and Freud, 1893/95, p. 160f.].

These words describe the scientist's struggle with a new and particularly challenging subject matter. It was not, as Freud thought at the time, one syndrome or one illness; it was the study of man's psychological conflict, an age-old topic and part of the tradition of Western civilization. Freud's predecessors were not scientists; they were the masters of intuitive insight, poets, writers, and thinkers. Closest to Freud's formulations are those of some of the great men of the century of his own youth, the formulations and approaches of Schopenhauer,

Nietzsche, Dostoyevsky, and those of some minor, and yet very great men, like Samuel Butler; the coincidences which we observe are largely rooted in the similarity of cultural predispositions. This in turn makes us aware of the fact that the demand of the age and the creative effort of the individual must be in some harmony with each other; creative imagination can in some measure anticipate the future, but in empty space, out of tune with at least hidden trends, genius will not emerge; his work must fit into the structure of the problems which he solves, with which he struggles and which he modifies.

In Freud's work the confines of sciences were widened; an area of phenomena never before approached scientifically was investigated through the formulation and testing of hypotheses. The practical consequences of this step were to be seen in the enlarged orbit of therapeutic intervention, the slow, steady, and uninterrupted progress of the therapeutic technique of psychoanalysis during almost six decades, and the more recent development of psychotherapy in psychoanalytic psychiatry. In one point, at least, these developments were different from those in most other fields of medicine. When unhappiness and self-made destiny proved in some instances to be amenable to therapeutic intervention, not only a cure of illness was offered, but also a cure where previously the existence of illness had not been recognized. The widening of the perimeter of science has thus led to a widening of the confines of medicine itself.

Let me briefly characterize some of the consequences of Freud's first steps for the development of psychoanalysis as a theory. The few "psychological formulas" to which he referred in the passage quoted above expanded rapidly into a cohesive set of propositions. At first, Freud could borrow his main conceptual tools from the area of his previous interests, neurophysiology. The general approach, the idea of seeing human conflicts in terms of an interplay of forces, the distinction of various types of discharge processes and of principles regulating the economy of psychic energy, were derived from this field. But the therapeutic experience with psychiatric cases forced upon Freud not only modifications of his early concepts, but also a radical extension of his approach. Two interconnected observations became of decisive importance: the realization that earliest experiences tend to leave lasting imprints on personality development; and the recognition of the role of instinctual drives, particularly in connection with the earliest phases of development. The realization of the importance of man's early total dependence on maternal care, unique among mammals, led Freud to supplement his physiological by a biological approach. But this biological approach received in Freud's context a new dimension. It is not limited to the consideration of genetic, biochemical, or physiological forces within man; it also includes the continuous social influences upon the growing human organism. In this approach the dichotomy between the biological proper and the social is eliminated as spurious, a dichotomy which in the past had obscured many psychological formulations. There are still those who tend to reemphasize its existence and thus to support the distinction of two kinds of sciences, natural and social sciences. The position of psychoanalysis as scientific theory and that of psychoanalytic psychiatry as therapy, and hence as source of data, illustrate the value of an approach which has made it possible to integrate various fields of investigation around a core of central assumptions. The fact that the committee of the New York Psychoanalytic Institute responsible for the Freud Lectures has selected as its topic for this year one which demonstrates the range of psychoanalytic thinking may well be taken as evidence that the integrative potential of psychoanalysis seems to us to be one of the most valuable parts of Freud's heritage.

The psychoanalytic contribution to the study of creative imagination should be seen with this in mind, as a contribution to an inquiry basic to any science of man. This view has determined the selection of the topics which are to be discussed as examples; they deal with phenomena of the nature of art, and art in turn is viewed as a particular, and as the most complex, type of communication in society.

I shall deal with three problems for which I have chosen the

following headings: (1) the problem of thematic generalization; (2) the emotive or aesthetic potential; and (3) creative
communication.

The problem of *thematic generalization* is concerned with narration, whatever the mode of presentation; it is story-centered
and hence deals largely with content. The starting point is the
relative uniformity of all narration, of myth, folklore, fairy
tale, novel, and even drama, or, to put it more cautiously, the
very high frequency of recurrent themes.

Previous explanations accounted for this recurrence mainly
by two interdependent types of inquiry: thematic similarity
was explained by pointing to historical reasons, to the migra-
tion of accounts, and thus to the influence of one narration
upon others. Influence, however, posits a predisposing factor,
a universal experience which explains the readiness to accept
influence. As such experience, the reactions to cosmological
and physiological cycles in nature and man have been most
thoroughly investigated. Both the historical and the cyclical
explanations are not superseded by the approach of psychoanalysis, which relates the uniformity of themes to the uniformity of conflict patterns in man's life. This uniformity is
rooted in what I mentioned as the biological approach in psychoanalysis. Hence the uniformity of conflict patterns refers
not so much to the conscious experience of the adult but
largely to the experiences and hence also to the thought processes of the child. Universal human experiences, modified by
specific conditions of the cultural environment, account for
the extent to which the themes of narration tend to resemble
each other.

The typical content of many of these themes was first discovered in the reconstruction of childhood fantasies during
the psychoanalytic investigation of adults and later elaborated
in the observation of the growing child. We are familiar with
the emergence of many such typical fantasies as the response
of the child to the riddles of his own existence and to those of
the adult world surrounding him—riddles not only in an intellectual sense, although this is part of it. For there is also the inherent conflict of many of the child's most basic strivings with

each other and with his environment; there is, moreover, the task of adjusting to a social world in which one is still a child with wishes and desires no less intense and even more unbending than those of the adult.

The best-known coincidence between myth or great narration and individual fantasy concerns accounts which have the hero of miraculous descent, separated from his original parents, adopted by foster parents up to the day when he splendidly emerges. These accounts, widely spread in Western and particularly Mediterranean tradition, but frequent also in other cultures, have lost nothing of their emotional relevance [see Kris, 1935].

Some 30 percent of the Americans of this generation are consciously aware of having thought of themselves at some time between the ages of five and fifteen as adopted or foster-children, and of having invented "true" parents of higher or— much more rarely—of lower status. There is hardly a psychoanalytic treatment where some such fantasy fails to play its role; some of its parts tend to have remained conscious; other, dynamically more significant, parts tend to be repressed. The very fact that I can here quote percentiles of the occurrence of the conscious version is due to a special circumstance: Freud's assertion of the frequent occurrence even within consciousness of a similar fantasy is, to my knowledge, one of the first psychoanalytic hypotheses to have been experimentally tested (by what are called objective scientific methods) more than thirty years ago in this country and repeatedly retested since.

The relation between the individual's fantasy life and the thematic repertory of narrative art opened our eyes to two problems which interact independently. The first concerns the transition from individual fantasy to narrative account. The finding says that the fantasy of the individual, particularly the daydreams of those normal and abnormal individuals who habitually weave their reveries in continued stories, are closely related to the wish for immediate gratification, frequently derived from older, repressed, masturbatory fantasies, and have retained some of the characteristics of their origin (A. Freud, 1922).

Let me report to you how this problem presented itself to me in my days of apprenticeship. A twenty-year-old youth, interested in many aspects of his medical work, showed by his behavior the wish to impress his teachers as the most gifted and most effective student of a large class, in order to become the one who would, in each of the specialties in which he happened to be interested, make decisive contributions, and thus acquire in the professor a new and more powerful paternal protector. Apart from more obvious and typical dynamics, this behavior repeated the course of a "continued story" which since the age of five or six had dominated the young man's life in many variations. In this fantasy he was the son of the crown prince of Austria, Rudolph, and had been placed as foster-child in a middle-class family. For years the stories which he told himself dealt with the topic of how he would gloriously come forward and rescue his country; how he would meet his grandfather, the emperor, and gain admiration from his own, real parents. This moment when he would meet *them* was the focal point. Whenever this scene approached, a new setting had to be invented, since the fantasy would start to roll off fast and faster; then the details became unimportant, the "need" to get there dominated his thought, until the whole setting had become unusable and a new version had to be elaborated, soon to become subject to the same fate. The climax had swallowed the plot.

The storyteller, professional or amateur, has liberated himself from similar urgency, can dispose and distribute where the daydreamer is subject to pressures since he cannot delay gratification. Here we have a first and basic precondition to the socialization of what previously was a private experience.

The second problem which impressed psychoanalysts early in their work concerns a finding first established by analytic observation and since corroborated in the study of child behavior. What narrative art offers to the child tends to be treated unconsciously as if it were a fantasy and appears in dreams as its substitute. But a borrowed fantasy can be less guiltily used since it comes from outside. The quest for such external stimulation, the need to "borrow" fantasies instead of elaborating one's own, tends to grow under the pressure of certain typical conflicts, particularly those of the phallic phase of psychosexual development.

Among the accounts which stimulate the child's fantasy life a special place is reserved for those which early in their development the parents or significant substitutes tell or read to their children; these are the stories which tend to remain imbued with the memory of a specific shared experience and to be assimilated with particular ease.

Taking this as an example, we may generalize on the function of the narrator in society. He is the one who under given circumstances, in any specific cultural environment, fulfills a need of his audience. In primitive society it is the bard's prerogative to speak of the unspeakable, of incest, parricide and matricide, of the gods and the demons. However much has changed, some such prerogatives still remain peculiar to the professional narrator. We ascribe to him the faculty of adapting what he knows from personal experience, from his own fantasy, to the needs of a community. We do not necessarily assume that what he tells is a tale all his own or all about himself. His faculty includes the capacity to assimilate many patterns of conflict, to react to minimal experiences with empathic understanding. In speaking of thematic generalization, I have this set of faculties in mind.

Among the narrator's public there are those who have remained on the level which I have discussed: they follow the quest for fantasies which they can borrow. And yet, this is quite obviously only one of the possible attitudes to narrative art.

To meet the demands of a public may mean a variety of things and neglects differences as fundamental as those between the Broadway hit or the pulp magazine and the great work of literature, differences which can, in some instances, be established by common sense, but which in other instances become subject to the verdict of the literary critic whose function I am not prone to underrate. It is to him that we as psy-

choanalysts hope to supply some tools. The two contributions
of psychoanalysis to the study of creative imagination, to
which I now turn may be said to serve this purpose.

The consideration of the *emotive* or *aesthetic potential* is
derived from the study of dreams. The texture of dreams,
woven out of the day's unfinished thought and repressed and
reawakened impulses, presents us with an imagery that is only
in rare instances of "meaning" to the dreamer. Only the psychoanalytic method enables us to understand it.

The overdetermination of single elements in the dream or
of whole parts, the condensation of many thoughts into one
element or the representation of one thought in various
disguises, these and similar mechanisms are an intimate part
of the dreamwork, which produces the manifest dream content. The study of the mechanisms of the dream has suggested
that similar mechanisms play a part in the working of creative
imagination, in the production of the work of art. But it is a
similarity particularly important for its clear differences.

The language of the dream, which is in force when we are
asleep, becomes a tool of the creator. The trance or reverie in
which it emerges has the capability of most efficient communication. What in the dream impresses us as *overdetermination* becomes the *potential* of the artwork. This principle has
been applied to the study of various media. It is by no means
limited to the understanding of narrative creations, and it contributes decisively to our understanding of especially the great
masterpieces. The oedipal conflict in Hamlet or in the
Brothers Karamazov is represented not in one but in several
versions. There is no one theme that does not have its variations; in the relation of several sons to their fathers the central
conflict is treated in various interconnected aspects in both
these works. Without an understanding of the interaction of
those thematic variations, or of the decomposition of one central figure into various characters, of one conflict into its
various components, even the most elementary approach to
the great thematic compositions cannot be attempted. Such
variation of one theme may coexist with the condensation of
various different themes into one incident and finally with the

condensation of various meanings into one account. When Shakespeare scholars point to the meaning of *Hamlet* in terms of the contemporary Elizabethan scene, this does not contradict other interpretations: contemporary and mythological themes are interwoven. The public is faced with a multiplicity of meanings, integrated into one work and supporting each other.[1]

The similarity of artwork and dreamwork has been best explored and demonstrated in the study of poetry, particularly by William Empson (1931, 1935, 1951), whose critical writings have been fertilized by psychoanalysis. Poetry is "filled with meaning" more than any other type of verbal communication; words are stimuli to associations which lead in various directions, and when Eliot, as critic, wishes to appraise the work of one of his contemporaries, of, let us say, Marianne Moore, we find him saying that her poems have "a very good spread of associations." Eliot should know, since the extraordinary richness of his own "spread of associations" seems to have given to his work his unique position in the poetry of this age.

Let me resume: The multiple meaning constitutes richness; the dichotomy between appropriate ambiguity and hidden precision, the latter more stringent as the lines flow into the stanza, becomes an important criterion in the study of poetic language [see Kris and Kaplan, 1948]. There are poets who are masters of multidimensional vagueness, without leading finally into the growing precision; there are others, whose lines differ from ordinary verbal communication only by meter, rhythm, and setting, by the "music of poetry"—but who hardly use the very complexity of meaning. All this seems to have become more understandable to us through our experience with contemporary poetry: here complexity of words tends to be maximized, multiple meanings abound, and uncertainty of interpretation tends to prevail. There can be little doubt that in this the modern poet is more than accidentally akin to the dreamer; nor is the phenomenon limited to any

---

1. It is not implied that this approach "exhausts" the meaning of the artwork, whose structure, naturally, may be, and frequently is, infinitely richer.

one artistic medium. It is one of the distinguishing features of
much that appears in modern painting. It reveals, I believe, in
part the influence of psychoanalysis on modern thought—not
of psychoanalysis as a science, but of some of its findings acting as a social force. There is a trend in modern art to consider the work of art as a documentation of the creative
process itself, a tendency which expresses itself in a shift in the
traditional or previously existing relation between the artist
and his public.

This then brings us to a third area of problems upon which
psychoanalysis has thrown light. I propose to refer to it as *creative communication*. Psychoanalytic insight has helped to clarify
some of the experiences which creators in many fields have
described as long as a tradition of introspective writing has existed in Western civilization. These reports can be briefly summarized in the following terms. Creation tends to be
experienced as a dichronous process; it has two phases which
may interact with each other in various ways. They may vary
in duration, frequency of occurrence, and intensity. In the
first the creator is driven; he is in an exceptional state.
Thoughts or images tend to flow, things appear in his mind of
which he never seemed to have known.

> A thought suddenly flashes up like lightning: it comes with ne-
> cessity. I have never had any choice in the matter. . . . There is
> the feeling that one is utterly out of hand, with the very distinct
> consciousness of an endless number of fine thrills and titillations
> descending to one's very toes. There is a depth of happiness in
> which the most painful and gloomy parts do not act as an-
> titheses to the rest, but are produced and required as necessary
> shades of color in such an overflow of light.

The sudden character of the experience described in this
quotation from Nietzsche's *Ecce Homo* stands in contrast to the
second phase of productivity, when all is labor, when the creator looks upon his work, as it were, from the outside, and
concentration and endeavor predominate. No one in recent
decades has more sharply contrasted these two phases than
A. E. Housman, to whom we owe not only one of the most

vivid descriptions of creative inspiration, but also of the "hell that is to pay" when the flow has tarried. Since the manuscripts of his poems have become accessible for study—some in the Library of Buffalo University, where documents on the process of creation are being collected—we can watch the differences which he describes, the instances when lines or a stanza flew to the mind, and the others, when ease was absent and purposeful concentration had to substitute.

Psychoanalytic observation of creative individuals leads to a somewhat better understanding of such descriptions. In the state of inspiration the psychic apparatus is in an exceptional condition. The barrier between the id and the ego has temporarily become permeable. Impulses reach preconsciousness more easily than under other conditions, and their translation into formed expression can proceed painlessly. Forces previously used for repression are being used by the ego for another purpose. All energy seems to be vested in the process of coming to consciousness; hence the similarity between inspirational experiences and those of a hallucinatory kind, a similarity once more clearest in its difference [Kris, 1939].

The coming to consciousness in the case of creative effort presupposes a long unnoticed process of shaping: it is this process which, entrusted to preconsciousness, is geared to integration and communication. But the process of creation is not completed during its sudden and inspirational phase [chap. 11].

When the first phase gives way to a second, when the artist steps back to view his work, one might say he identifies with his public; he views what "the spirit" has done. He views it, temporarily, from the outside.

The reaction of the public repeats in reversed order and in infinite variations some of the processes which the artist experienced. These variations are determined by cultural and social factors as well as by individual predispositions. Though these reactions may vary in depth, the core of the process, a gradual moving from the fringe to the center, seems to occur with great frequency. It is impeded when we read the narration as if it were a daydream to be borrowed, or when the artwork becomes the pinup girl, i.e., when we miss the distance from immediate gratification; then we are taken back to more primitive modes of reactions. Clinical observations of such incomplete reactions to the creative effort constitute a promising field of investigation in their own right. It is not of these failures that I intend to speak, but of the successful reaction: then the process from the fringe to the center means that gradually a change in the attitude of the audience is taking place.

This change may have various dimensions. It may lead from the borrowed-fantasy stage to the appreciation of the complexity of thematic composition, from *what* is being said to *how* it is being said, and here again from the pleasure in rhythm to a gradual understanding of first one, then many interacting and integrated meanings. These changes have one factor in common. They are all changes involving the movement of the audience from passivity to activity. In the end the audience may experience some of the excitement and some of the release of tension which arises when the barriers separating unconscious from preconscious or conscious processes have been loosened: "Next to the seizures and shapings of creative thought—the thing itself—no comparable experience is more thrilling than being witched, illumined and transfigured by the magic of another's art" (H. A. Murray).

In speaking here of re-creation I stress that the shift in psychic levels which operated in the creative process is repeated, and that in this sense the public identifies itself with the artist. The process of identification to which I refer does not concern the artist as an empirical individual [Kris, 1952].

How could we assume that biographical familiarity should be essential when the greatest artist's personal life is shed in anonymity? And yet, no other compares to Shakespeare as master of creative communication. The identification with the artist's biographical person may be the conscious business of the critic, and re-creation at this point may become reconstruction, the reaction of the connoisseur. What I, here, mean by identification with the artist is an unconscious process in which the audience becomes in its own right creative by being re-creative. It follows the spell of the emotive potential. The understanding then leads to the unconscious mechanisms which the artist had used, to the impulses he had mastered; the audience is with him both in reaching downward and in mastery. I do not assume that the audience's experience need be or can be identical with that of the poet. "A poem," says Eliot, "may appear to mean very different things to different readers and all these may be different from what the author thought." The readers' reaction may be richer in implication than the creator ever supposed. There is that old word, the core of all psychology of the great, which says: "The genius builds better than he knows."

At this point the psychoanalytic approach may turn out to be useful to the critic in a new sense. It is conceivable that some of the attributes which lend artistic value could be measured by the study of response, and, more particularly, by the survival of great artworks as effective stimuli. The study of their emotive or aesthetic potential may account for the lasting appreciation of such unique formulations as that of Sophocles in his Oedipus Trilogy, or for many comparable achievements in the arts which seem to triumph over changes in social affairs. Many generations of men repeat what seems to be the fundamental reaction to creative imagination in art: they accept the invitation to an experience of the mind in which a specific and particularly intensive kind of intrapsychic communication is temporarily established, in which controlled regression becomes pleasurable since the experience stands under the firm and unabated control of the ego, which has reasserted its functions: it has become creative, or re-creative.

This outline of some of the problems which occur in creative communication cannot be terminated without a brief mention of two of the sources of insight which have proved particularly valuable. One large field of study which has attracted the attention of many investigators concerns the specific function of creative processes in the therapeutic situation: the creative communication is then limited to the creator and the therapist. Story, poem, or picture facilitate the "coming to consciousness"; the creative experience becomes part of the therapeutic procedure. Whatever the limitations of this technique, even its disadvantages, it has proved, with certain individuals, to be of considerable value. If we try to generalize the conditions under which this is the case, we may say that when free association itself is too threatening, when it might lead to a regressive rush which can no longer be controlled, canalized into production and shaped by the ego, the onslaught of the repressed can still be organized.

This experience has sharpened our eyes to similar processes outside of treatment situations, in which psychological balance is being reestablished by creative activity. When in the course of a particularly intensive conflict, narcissistic regression threatens the creative act, an attempt to communicate with others and to establish contact may act as a catalyst. The very intensity of conflict may lend particular impact to the work thus created. This is true of some of the productions of later psychotics produced during the prepsychotic phase of their illness. A normal counterpart to the extraordinary richness and sometimes deceptive fascination of their productions may be found in the expressive ventures of some adolescents who solve the age-specific intensification of their conflicts by sudden and frequently transitory spurts of creative activity.

The second area of clinical experience in which the study of creative communication has become particularly fruitful concerns the artistic productions of the insane; here the variety of meanings which the process of creation gains for the individual becomes apparent; words are not signs but acts, pictures tend to become verdicts, and creation may mean "making" in a literal and magical sense. In extreme cases the artist identifies himself with God, the creator; he destroys and restores, rules and organizes in creating. The delusion of the psychotic artist has its counterpart in the unconscious fantasy of many creative individuals and determines some of the complex attitudes of the artist toward his work; foremost among these, the striving for perfection and the feeling of responsibility in exercising his power as creator. What appears as diffusion of instinctual drives, as magic destruction and reparation in the work of the psychotic, plays its part in many creative processes, but the regression to magical procedure is only partial and temporary. This difference becomes clearest when we realize that the product of the psychotic is created as an act to influence the course of events, while the work of the nonpsychotic plays upon an audience from which it aims to elicit responses [Kris, 1952, 1953b].

The value of the study of psychotic art for a deepening of our understanding of creative processes in general should not lead us to underestimate differences, a tendency particularly significant in the contemporary scene. The interest of certain artists and of sections of the public in productions of the psychotic has suggested to some a comparison between modern and "psychotic" art, a comparison which points to similarities as evidence of disintegration in our civilization, or of "cultural psychosis." I feel unable to share in, or even to discuss in detail, speculations leading in this direction and find it more useful to refer to what has been briefly suggested before. The fact that productions by psychotic creators have gained aesthetic significance for part of the contemporary public is, I believe, due to the fact that their extreme and often badly integrated ambiguity is experienced as a challenge. "Psychotic art" serves as a screen for a generation to which the exercise of projective power has become, to some extent, pleasurable in itself. I have spoken of the influence of psychoanalysis on the artists. I have now to add that such influence naturally includes the reaction of the public. The preference for forms which stimulate projection, which enhance the creative activity of the public, is not unique in history. Although it seems that it has never been as consistently pursued as during the last decades, it has occurred with varying intensity during various historical periods. Psychoanalysis can only point to the existence of a psychic mechanism, which manifests itself as a partial shift of roles in creative communication. The importance of this shift during various historical periods may be established in studies by experts in cultural change to whom psychoanalysis may have here suggested a new perspective.

The three problem areas which have been reviewed represent only a selection of what psychoanalysis has contributed to the study of creative imagination. Let me now for a moment speak not of what was achieved but of that which we would most like to know; not of results but of questions. All that concerns the typical predispositions of the masters of creative imagination, if such a "typical predisposition" exists, all that concerns the ontogenetic approach to the creator, remains in darkness.

Who are those best equipped for creative work, those whose creative imagination functions with greatest ease and most appropriately? Needless to say that no answer can be offered; we have not been able to solve a problem which during the ages has puzzled all and has evaded even speculative approaches; and we remember Freud's modesty when dealing with it (1910b).

When as psychoanalysts we study the artist's personality we are subject to the limitations imposed by the therapeutic situation. Hence most of the statements of psychoanalysts seem to focus on relevant but not on specific factors. There is the impression that in the early history of creative individuals traumatization may play an unusually great part; there is some evidence that there are definite peculiarities in the function of certain defense mechanisms—a problem to which Freud referred when he spoke of "the flexibility of repression" in the artist, which he shares with many severely impaired individuals. With some of them the creative individual is said to share the proclivity to a passive attitude manifest in the high incidence of homosexuality. But again it is the difference which seems most suggestive; the passive abandonment is the matrix of the artist's inspirational experience. Let me at this point turn to speculation: the biological nature of man, one might say, accounts for the fact that on the verge of his greatest and supremely active effort, in creation, his experience tends to be mixed with passive elements; he receives from outside what he is to elicit; he incorporates before he produces, and experiences even his own thought as reaching him as benevolently tendered from an outside agent [Kris, 1939].

The quest for the specific confronts us with insight into the limitations of our knowledge. All that I can attempt is to point to certain trends in current research which seem to lead in a definite direction.

When we speak of talent and gift we assume the interaction of inborn endowment and environmental influences. For some decades the first area had been neglected; during the last few years it has resumed some of its importance and gradually more and more investigators in various fields turn in this direction. The psychoanalyst expects most of the attempts to study the endowment of the human infant in his earliest stages, to watch how it is molded by the mother, and how the mother responds to what appears to be the specific individuality of the newborn. Only in long and painful study will such observations lead into the area where the development of properties in any sense akin to gift and talent may become observable.

Observation here as elsewhere may well follow the path outlined by the clinical impressions gained in psychoanalysis. Let me illustrate this by some examples. The influence of early traumatic experiences on creative activity, their reflection in the artist's work, has been mentioned. In approaching the study of the child's first forming activities in the development of his fantasy life, we realize that the reaction to and impact of threatening experiences become equally apparent. Imagination tries to cope with threats; fantasy arises in part as a defense against danger. Clinical observation in psychoanalysis has pointed to the role which the interplay of libidinal and destructive impulses plays in the artist's work. Observation of children in their creative activities confirms these impressions. Two-to-four-year-olds studied in their behavior at the easel, playing with paint, building blocks, give us a picture of the dynamics of the creative process, more dramatic and richer in detail than expected. There is the child who tentatively approaches the easel, who gingerly puts down line after line, color neatly next to color; then colors are mixed, movements become more rapid, excitement grows, immediate discharge rules. The child has followed the seduction which brush and colors have exercised. Over the months that temptation is gradually mastered. With order, even meaning may accrue to the painting; the impulses to smear may return at times of pressure, and yet the distinction emerges between a completed work and one which is not completed—whatever completion may mean to the child. The child learns to resist the temptation to destroy what he has just produced, and the functions of expression and communication come to the fore. Such observations are far from the realm of art; they describe what, with a term which has grown somewhat loose, we mean by sublimation. But observations of this kind are part of the empirical study of the development of creative behavior as part and parcel of the development of personality [see chap. 9].

In one fundamental respect these directions of research and the first tentative impressions seem to prove that recent progress in psychoanalytic theory may help to clarify even complex problems. At the outset I stated that the influence of psychoanalysis upon science and social organization as well as its unique place in medicine was initiated by the scientific study of conflict. But human faculties emerge from conflict. The peeping Tom becomes painter or scientist; children who wildly and excitedly brush colors on paper may develop highly differentiated skills; their painting activity may successfully emerge from conflict and may develop into a special aptitude. Such detachment of activity from conflict, its fundamental autonomy, is facilitated by certain types of endowment, facilitated further by an infinite range of possible life experience and their interaction.

If we look from the battle for creation in the child, back to the clinical data which psychoanalytic investigation reveals, i.e., to the battle of creation observable in some analytic patients, a certain affinity becomes apparent. *It seems that in every process of creation the gradual emergence from conflict plays its part.*[2] It may start out in serving a fantasy of the individual, in meeting an individual's needs, but to the extent that it emerges from conflict, certain properties may be acquired which are akin to, and some of them identical with, gift or skill. I men-

2. [To test this and similar hypotheses, Ernst Kris initiated The Gifted Adolescents Project at the Treatment Center of the New York Psychoanalytic Institute in 1954. For a description of this Project, see Loomie, Rosen, and Stein (1958).]

tioned that themes may be generalized, the emotive potential may grow, and the process of creative communication may be initiated. All that is not only the result of conflict; it is at least in part due to the integrative, and in this instance autonomous, powers of the ego. And thus creative imagination may lead to concrete achievements; some of them art, others devoted mainly and solely to problem solving, to inventiveness in science, or simply to the enrichment of the individual's existence. At this point the problem leads back to the broad stream of our work; for next to therapy stands not only, as was said, the problem of prevention but also that of turning from the infinite variety of the mentally ill to the equally infinite and less explored variety of the healthy. The study of conflict embraces both the well and the sick, it is part of human life, and no basic science of psychopathology can avoid being at the same time basic in the psychology of normal behavior.

In what preceded I have reviewed the thoughts and contributions of many analysts. I have not mentioned names, since this is the occasion when we all join in grateful remembrance. If I have given you the impression that our curiosity is far greater than our knowledge, that we are moving under the guide of clinical experiences to tentative generalizations, I will have been able to convey to you the spirit under which psychoanalysis has developed in the work of Freud.

Bibliography

ABRAHAM, K. (1919), A Particular Form of Neurotic Resistance Against the Psycho-Analytic Method. In: *Selected Papers on Psycho-Analysis.* London: Hogarth Press, 1927, pp. 303–311.

—— (1924), A Short Study of the Development of the Libido. *Ibid.,* pp. 418–501.

—— et al. (1919), *Psycho-Analysis and the War Neuroses.* London: Hogarth Press.

ADRIAN, E. D. (1946), The Mental and Physical Origins of Behaviour. *Int. J. Psycho-Anal.,* 27 : 1–6.

AICHHORN, A. (1925), *Wayward Youth.* New York: Viking Press, 1935.

ALEXANDER, F. (1933), The Relation of Structural and Instinctual Conflicts. *Psychoanal. Quart.,* 2 : 181–207.

—— (1935), The Problem of Psychoanalytic Technique. *Psychoanal. Quart.,* 4 : 588–611.

—— (1948), *Fundamentals of Psychoanalysis.* New York: Norton.

—— & FRENCH, T. M. (1946), *Psychoanalytic Therapy.* New York: Ronald Press.

ALLPORT, F. H. (1924), *Social Psychology.* Boston, New York: Houghton Mifflin.

ALLPORT, G. W. (1937), *Personality: A Psychological Interpretation.* New York: Holt.

—— & CANTRIL, H. (1935), *The Psychology of Radio.* New York: Harpers.

ALSCHULER, R. & HATTWICK, B. W. (1947), *Painting and Personality: A Study of Young Children.* Chicago: University of Chicago Press.

BALINT, M. (1942), Ego Strength and the Education of the Ego. *Psychoanal. Quart.,* 11 : 87–95.

BARKER, R., DEMBO, T., & LEWIN, K. (1941), Frustration and Regression: An Experiment with Young Children. *University of Iowa Studies Child Welfare,* Vol. 18, No. 1.

BATESON, G. (1944), Cultural Determinants of Personality. In: *Personality and Behavior Disorders,* 2 : 714–735, ed. J. McV. Hunt. New York: Ronald Press.

—— & MEAD, M. (1942), *Balinese Character.* New York Academy of Sciences, Special Publications, Vol. II.

BEACH, F. A. (1949), A Cross-Species Survey of Mammalian Sexual Behavior. In: *Psychosexual Development in Health and Disease,* ed. P. H. Hoch & J. Zubin. New York: Grune & Stratton, pp. 52–78.

—— (1950a), The Snark Was a Boojum. *Amer. Psychologist,* 5 : 115–124.

———— (1950b), Sexual Behavior in Animals and Man. *The Harvey Lectures* 1947/48. New York: Science Printing Press.

BENEDEK, T. (1938), Adaptation to Reality in Early Infancy. *Psychoanal. Quart.,* 7 : 200–215.

———— (1949), The Psychosomatic Implications of the Primary Unit: Mother-Child. In: *Psychosexual Functions in Women.* New York: Ronald Press, 1952, pp. 339–372.

BENJAMIN, J. D. (1950), Methodological Considerations in the Validation and Elaboration of Psychoanalytic Personality Theory. Round Table on Approaches to a Dynamic Theory of Development. *Amer. J. Orthopsychiat.,* 20 : 139–156.

BERGMAN, P. & ESCALONA, S. K. (1949), Unusual Sensitivities in Very Young Children. *The Psychoanalytic Study of the Child,* 3/4 : 333–352.

BERGMANN, G. (1943), Psychoanalysis and Experimental Psychology: A Review from the Standpoint of Scientific Empiricism. *Mind,* 52 : 122–140.

BERNFELD, S. (1925), *The Psychology of the Infant.* New York: Brentano, 1929.

———— (1934), Die Gestalttheorie. *Imago,* 20 : 32–77.

———— (1944), Freud's Earliest Theories and the School of Helmholtz. *Psychoanal. Quart.,* 13 : 341–362.

———— (1947), Freud's Scientific Beginnings. *Amer. Imago,* 6 : 163–196.

BIBRING, E. (1941), The Development and Problems of the Theory of the Instincts. *Int. J. Psycho-Anal.,* 22 : 102–131.

———— (1947), The So-Called English School of Psychoanalysis. *Psychoanal. Quart.,* 6 : 69–93.

———— (1954), Psychoanalysis and the Dynamic Psychotherapies. *J. Amer. Psychoanal. Assn.,* 2 : 745–770.

BION, W. R. (1946), The Leaderless Group Project. *Bull. Menninger Clin.,* 10 : 77–81.

BIRD, C. (1939), Suggestion and Suggestibility: A Bibliography. *Psychol. Bull.,* 36 : 264–283.

BIRNBAUM, K. (1927), *Die psychischen Heilmethoden für ärtzliches Studium und Praxis.* Leipzig: Thieme.

BLITZSTEN, N. L., EISSLER, R. S., & EISSLER, K. R. (1950), Emergence of Hidden Ego Tendencies during Dream Analysis. *Int. J. Psycho-Anal.,* 31 : 12–17.

BONAPARTE, M. (1940), Time and the Unconscious. *Int. J. Psycho-Anal.,* 21 : 427–468.

———— (1945), Notes on the Analytic Discovery of a Primal Scene. *The Psychoanalytic Study of the Child,* 1 : 119–125.

———— (1953), *Female Sexuality.* New York: International Universities Press.

BORNSTEIN, S. (1937), Missverständnisse in der psychoanalytischen Pädagogik. *Z. psychoanal. Päd.,* 11 : 81–90.

BREUER, J. & FREUD, S. (1893/95), Studies on Hysteria. *Standard Edition,* 2.*

* See footnote to Freud (1892).

BRUNSWICK, R. M. (1940), The Preoedipal Phase of the Libido Development. *Psychoanal. Quart.,* 9 : 293–319.

BURT, C. (1941), *Under Fives in Total War.* London: British Psychological Association.

CANNON, W. B. (1945), *The Way of an Investigator.* New York: Norton.

CANTRIL, H. (1940), *The Invasion from Mars.* Princeton, N.J.: Princeton University Press.

CARMICHAEL, L. (1951), Ontogenetic Development. In: *Handbook of Experimental Psychology,* ed. S. S. Stevens. New York: Wiley, pp. 281–303.

CARROLL, E. Y. (1954), Acting Out and Ego Development. *Psychoanal. Quart.,* 23 : 521–528.

CHARCOT, J. M. (1886), *Neue Vorlesungen über die Krankheiten des Nervensystems insbesondere über Hysterie,* tr. S. Freud. Leipzig & Vienna: Toeplitz & Deuticke.

COLEMAN [LIPTON], R. W. & PROVENCE, S. (1957), Environmental Retardation (Hospitalism) in Infants Living in Families. *Pediatrics,* 19 : 285–292.

DAVIS, H. V., SEARS, R. R., MILLER, H. C., & BRODBECK, A. J. (1948), Effects of Cup, Bottle and Breast Feeding on Oral Activities of Newborn Infants. *Pediatrics,* 2 : 549–558.

DELACROIX, H. (1939), L'invention et le genie. In: *Nouveau traité de psychologie,* ed. G. Dumas, Vol. 6, Pt. 4. Paris: Alcan.

DEUTSCH, H. (1930), Zur Genese des Familienromans. *Int. Z. Psychoanal.,* 14 : 249–253.

―――― (1934), Some Forms of Emotional Disturbance and Their Relationship to Schizophrenia. *Psychoanal. Quart.,* 11 : 301–321, 1942.

―――― (1939), A Discussion of Certain Forms of Resistance. In: *Neuroses and Character Types: Clinical Psychoanalytic Studies.* New York: International Universities Press, 1965, pp. 248–261.

―――― (1944/45), *The Psychology of Women,* 2 Vols. New York: Grune & Stratton.

DOLLARD, J. (1949), Do We Have a Science of Childrearing? In: *The Family in a Democratic Society: Anniversary Papers of the Community Service Society of New York.* New York: Columbia University Press, pp. 44–51.

―――― DOOB, L. W., MILLER, N. E., & SEARS, R. R. (1939), *Frustration and Aggression.* New Haven: Yale University Press.

DOOB, L. W. (1935), *Propaganda: Its Psychology and Technique.* New York: Holt.

DOOLEY, L. (1939), Review of K. Horney's *New Ways in Psychoanalysis. Psychiatry,* 2 : 420–424.

DORER, M. (1932), *Die historischen Grundlagen der Psychoanalyse.* Heidelberg: Winter.

EDER, M. D. (1935), Review of F. Williams: *Soviet Russia Fights Neurosis. Int. J. Psycho-Anal.,* 16 : 108–111.

EIDELBERG, L. (1945), A Contribution to the Study of the Masturbation Fantasy. In: *Studies in Psychoanalysis.* New York: International Universities Press, 1948, pp. 203–223.

EISSLER, K. R. (1953), The Effect of the Structure of the Ego on Psychoanalytic Technique. *J. Amer. Psychoanal. Assn.*, 1 : 104–143.

EKSTEIN, R. (1954), The Space Child's Time Machine: On "Reconstruction" in the Psychotherapeutic Treatment of a Schizophrenic Child. *Amer. J. Orthopsychiat.*, 24 : 492–506.

ELKISCH, P. (1945), Children's Drawings in a Projective Technique. *Psychol. Monogr.*, Vol. 58, No. 266.

—— (1947), The Emotional Significance of Children's Art Works. *Childh. Educ.*, 23 : 236–240.

EMPSON, W. (1931), *The Seven Types of Ambiguity*. New York: Harcourt Brace.

—— (1935), *Some Versions of the Pastoral*. London: Chatto & Windus.

—— (1951), *The Structure of Complex Words*. London: Chatto & Windus.

ERIKSON, E. H. (1945), Childhood and Tradition in Two American Indian Tribes. *The Psychoanalytic Study of the Child*, 1 : 319–350.

—— (1950), *Childhood and Society*. New York: Norton.

—— (1956), The Problem of Ego Identity. *J. Amer. Psychoanal. Assn.*, 6 : 56–121.

ESCALONA, S. K. (1949), The Psychological Situation of Mother and Child upon Return from the Hospital. In: *Problems of Infancy and Childhood*, ed. M. J. E. Senn. New York: Josiah Macy, Jr. Foundation.

FEDERN, P. (1943), Psychoanalysis of Psychoses. *Psychiat. Quart.*, 17 : 3–19.

FENICHEL, O. (1927), The Economic Function of Screen Memories. In: *Collected Papers of Otto Fenichel*, 1 : 113–116. New York: Norton, 1952.

—— (1929), The Inner Injunction to "Make a Mental Note." *Int. J. Psycho-Anal.*, 10 : 447–448.

—— (1941), *Problems of Psychoanalytic Technique*. Albany: Psychoanalytic Quarterly, Inc.

—— (1945), *The Psychoanalytic Theory of Neurosis*. New York: Norton.

FERENCZI, S. (1909), Introjection and Transference. *Sex in Psychoanalysis*. New York: Basic Books, 1950, pp. 35–93.

—— (1928), The Elasticity of Psycho-Analytic Technique. *Final Contributions to the Problems and Methods of Psycho-Analysis*. London: Hogarth Press, 1955, pp. 87–101.

—— (1933), Confusion of Tongues between Adults and Children. *Ibid.*, pp. 156–167.

—— & RANK, O. (1924), *The Development of Psychoanalysis*. New York: Nervous & Mental Disease Publishing Co., 1925.

FISHER, C. (1953), Studies on the Nature of Suggestion: 1. Experimental Induction of Dreams by Direct Suggestion. *J. Amer. Psychoanal. Assn.*, 1 : 222–255.

FLIESS, R., ed. (1948), *The Psychoanalytic Reader*, Vol. 1. New York: International Universities Press.

—— (1953), *The Revival of Interest in the Dream: A Critical Study of Post-Freudian Psychoanalytic Contributions*. New York: International Universities Press.

FRENCH, T. M. (1936), A Clinical Study of Learning in the Course of a Psychoanalytic Treatment. *Psychoanal. Quart.,* 5 : 148–194.

——— (1938), Defense and Synthesis in the Function of the Ego. *Psychoanal. Quart.,* 7 : 537–553.

——— (1938/39), Social Conflict and Psychic Conflict. *Amer. J. Sociol.,* 44 : 922–931.

——— (1941), Goal, Mechanism and Integrative Field. *Psychosom. Med.,* 3 : 226–298.

——— (1945), The Integration of Social Behavior. *Psychoanal. Quart.,* 14 : 149–168.

FRENKEL-BRUNSWIK, E. (1940), Psychoanalysis and Personality Research. *Selected Papers* [*Psychological Issues,* Monogr. 31]. New York: International Universities Press, 1974, pp. 36–57.

FREUD, A. (1922), Beating Fantasies and Daydreams. *The Writings of Anna Freud,** 1 : 137–157.

——— (1927), Four Lectures on Child Analysis. *Ibid.,* 1 : 3–69.

——— (1930), Four Lectures on Psychoanalysis for Teachers and Parents. *Ibid.,* 1 : 73–133.

——— (1936), *The Ego and the Mechanisms of Defense. Ibid.,* 2.

——— (1945), Indications for Child Analysis. *Ibid.,* 4 : 3–38.

——— (1949a), Aggression in Relation to Emotional Development: Normal and Pathological. *Ibid.,* 4 : 489–497.

——— (1949b), Certain Types and Stages of Social Maladjustment. *Ibid.,* 4 : 75–94.

——— (1951), Observations on Child Development. *Ibid.,* 4 : 143–162.

——— & BURLINGHAM, D. T. (1942), *Young Children in War-time.* London: Allen & Unwin; also as Report 12 in *The Writings of Anna Freud,* 3 : 142–211.

——————— (1944), *Infants Without Families.* New York: International Universities Press; also as Part II in *The Writings of Anna Freud,* 3 : 543–564.

——— & DANN, S. (1951), An Experiment in Group Upbringing. *The Psychoanalytic Study of the Child,* 6 : 127–168.

FREUD, S. (1891), *On Aphasia.* New York: International Universities Press, 1953.

——— (1892), Preface and Footnotes to the Translation of Charcot's *Tuesday Lectures. Standard Edition,*† 1 : 133–137.

——— (1893), Some Points for a Comparative Study of Organic and Hysterical Motor Paralyses. *Ibid.,* 1 : 157–172.

——— (1894), The Neuro-Psychoses of Defence. *Ibid.,* 3 : 43–68.

——— (1895), Project for a Scientific Psychology. *Ibid.,* 1 : 283–397. Also in

* *The Writings of Anna Freud,* 7 Volumes. New York: International Universities Press, 1966–1974.

† *The Standard Edition of the Complete Psychological Works of Sigmund Freud,* 24 Volumes. London: Hogarth Press, 1953–1974.

The Origins of Psychoanalysis. New York: Basic Books, 1954, pp. 347–445.

—— (1897), Abstracts of the Scientific Writings of Dr. Sigmund Freud. *Standard Edition,* 3 : 225–257.

—— (1899), Screen Memories. *Ibid.,* 3 : 301–322.

—— (1900), The Interpretation of Dreams. *Ibid.,* 4 & 5.

—— (1901), The Psychopathology of Everyday Life. *Ibid.,* 6.

—— (1905a), Fragment of an Analysis of a Case of Hysteria. *Ibid.,* 7 : 3–122.

—— (1905b), Three Essays on the Theory of Sexuality. *Ibid.,* 7 : 125–243.

—— (1905c), Jokes and Their Relation to the Unconscious. *Ibid.,* 8 : 3–236.

—— (1908), Character and Anal Erotism. *Ibid.,* 9 : 167–175.

—— (1909a), Analysis of a Phobia in a Five-Year-Old Boy. *Ibid.,* 10 : 3–149.

—— (1909b), Notes upon a Case of Obsessional Neurosis. *Ibid.,* 10 : 153–320.

—— (1910a), The Future Prospects of Psycho-Analytic Therapy. *Ibid.,* 11 : 139–151.

—— (1910b), Leonardo da Vinci and a Memory of His Childhood. *Ibid.,* 11 : 63–137.

—— (1912a), The Dynamics of Transference. *Ibid.,* 12 : 97–108.

—— (1912b), Recommendations for Physicians on the Psycho-Analytic Method. *Ibid.,* 12 : 109–120.

—— (1913), On Beginning the Treatment. *Ibid.,* 12 : 121–144.

—— (1914a), Remembering, Repeating, and Working-Through. *Ibid.,* 12 : 145–156.

—— (1914b), Fausse Reconaissance (Déjà Raconté) in Psycho-Analytic Treatment. *Ibid.,* 13 : 201–210.

—— (1914c), On the History of the Psycho-Analytic Movement. *Ibid.,* 14 : 7–66.

—— (1914d), On Narcissism: An Introduction. *Ibid.,* 14 : 67–102.

—— (1915a), Instincts and Their Vicissitudes. *Ibid.,* 14 : 111–140.

—— (1915b), Repression. *Ibid.,* 14 : 141–158.

—— (1915c), The Unconscious. *Ibid.,* 14 : 159–215.

—— (1916/17), Introductory Lectures on Psycho-Analysis. *Ibid.,* 15 & 16.

—— (1917), A Childhood Recollection from *Dichtung und Wahrheit. Ibid.,* 17 : 145–156.

—— (1918), From the History of an Infantile Neurosis. *Ibid.,* 17 : 3–123.

—— (1919), Lines of Advance in Psycho-Analytic Therapy. *Ibid.,* 17 : 157–168.

—— (1920), Beyond the Pleasure Principle. *Ibid.,* 18 : 7–64.

—— (1921a) Group Psychology and the Analysis of the Ego. *Ibid.,* 20 : 67–143.

—— (1921b), Introduction to J. Varendonck's *The Psychology of Day-Dreams. Ibid.,* 18 : 271–272.

FREUD, S. (1923a), The Ego and the Id. *Ibid.*, 19 : 3–66.

—— (1923b), Remarks on the Theory and Practice of Dream-Interpretation. *Ibid.*, 19 : 109–121.

—— (1925), An Autobiographical Study. *Ibid.*, 20 : 3–74.

—— (1926), Inhibitions, Symptoms, and Anxiety. *Ibid.*, 20 : 77–175.

—— (1931), Female Sexuality. *Ibid.*, 21 : 225–243.

—— (1933), New Introductory Lectures on Psycho-Analysis. *Ibid.*, 22 : 3–182.

—— (1937a), Analysis Terminable and Interminable. *Ibid.*, 23 : 209–253.

—— (1937b), Constructions in Analysis. *Ibid.*, 23 : 255–269.

—— (1940), An Outline of Psycho-Analysis. *Ibid.*, 23 : 141–207.

—— (1950), *The Origins of Psychoanalysis: Letters to Wilhelm Fliess, Drafts and Notes, 1887–1902*. New York: Basic Books, 1954.

FRIES, M. E. (1946), The Child's Ego Development and the Training of Adults in His Environment. *The Psychoanalytic Study of the Child*, 2 : 85–112.

—— & WOOLF, P. J. (1953), Some Hypotheses on the Role of the Congenital Activity Type in Personality Development. *The Psychoanalytic Study of the Child*, 8 : 48–62.

FRIESS, A. (1952), The Study of a Child: Her Paintings and Personality. *Sarah Lawrence Studies*, VI.

FROMM, E. (1941), *Escape from Freedom*. New York: Farrar & Rinehart.

GERO, G. (1951), The Concept of Defense. *Psychoanal. Quart.*, 20 : 565–578.

—— (1953), Defenses in Symptom Formation. *J. Amer. Psychoanal. Assn.*, 1 : 87–103.

—— & RUBINFINE, D. L. (1955), On Obsessive Thoughts. *J. Amer. Psychoanal. Assn.*, 3 : 222–243.

GESELL, A. & AMATRUDA, C. S. (1947), *Developmental Diagnosis*. New York: Hoeber.

—— & ILG, F. L. (1937), *Feeding Behavior of Infants*. Philadelphia: Lippincott.

—— —— (1943), *Infant and Child in the Culture of Today*. New York: Harper.

GILL, M. M. (1954), Psychoanalysis and Exploratory Psychotherapy. *J. Amer. Psychoanal. Assn.*, 2 : 771–797.

GLAUBER, I. P. (1951), The Mother in the Etiology of Stuttering (abs.). *Psychoanal. Quart.*, 20 : 160–161.

GLOVER, E. (1927/28), Lectures on Technique in Psycho-Analysis. *Int. J. Psycho-Anal.*, 8 : 311–338, 486–520; 9 : 7–46, 181–218.

—— (1929), The Screening Function of Traumatic Memories. *Int. J. Psycho-Anal.*, 10 : 90–93.

—— (1940), *An Investigation of the Technique of Psycho-Analysis*. London: Baillière, Tindall & Cox.

—— (1942), Notes on the Psychological Effects of War Conditions on the Civilian Population. *Int. J. Psycho-Anal.*, 23 : 17–37.

—— (1945), Examination of the Klein System of Child Psychology. *The Psychoanalytic Study of the Child*, 1 : 75–118.

GOLDMAN-EISLER, F. (1951), The Problem of "Orality" and of Its Origin in Early Childhood. *J. Ment. Sci.*, 97 : 765–789.

GORER, G. (1942), Japanese Character Structure. Mimeographed memorandum. New York: Committee on Intercultural Relations.

—— (1943), Themes in Japanese Culture. *Trans. N.Y. Acad. Sci.*, Ser. 2, Vol. V, No. 5.

—— (1949), Internal Monsters: Review of Melanie Klein's *Contributions to Psychoanalysis. New Statesman and Nation*, Feb. 5, 1949.

GREENACRE, P. (1941), The Predisposition to Anxiety. *Psychoanal. Quart.*, 10 : 66–95, 610–637.

—— (1944), Infants' Reaction to Restraint. *Amer. J. Orthopsychiat.*, 14 : 204–218.

—— (1949), A Contribution to the Study of Screen Memories. *The Psychoanalytic Study of the Child*, 3/4 : 7–17.

—— (1952), *Trauma, Growth, and Personality*. Preface by Ernst Kris. New York: International Universities Press, 1969.

GROTJAHN, M. (1950), About the "Third Ear" in Psychoanalysis. *Psychoanal. Rev.*, 37 : 56–65.

HADAMARD, J. (1949), *The Psychology of Invention in the Mathematical Field*. Princeton: Princeton University Press.

HALLIDAY, J. L. (1948), *Psychosocial Medicine*. New York: Norton.

HALVERSON, H. M. (1940), Genital and Sphincter Behavior of the Male Infant. *J. Genet. Psychol.*, 56 : 95–136.

HARROWER, M. & GRINKER, R. R. (1946), The Stress Tolerance Test: Preliminary Experiments with a New Projective Technique Utilizing Both Meaningful and Meaningless Stimuli. *Psychosom. Med.*, 8 : 3–15.

HARTMANN, H. (1927), *Grundlagen der Psychoanalyse*. Leipzig: Thieme.

—— (1933), An Experimental Contribution to the Psychology of Obsessive-Compulsive Neurosis: On Remembering Completed and Uncompleted Tasks. In: Hartmann (1964), pp. 404–418.

—— (1934/35), Psychiatric Studies of Twins. In: Hartmann (1964), pp. 419–445.

—— (1939a), *Ego Psychology and the Problem of Adaptation*. New York: International Universities Press, 1958.

—— (1939b), Psychoanalysis and the Concept of Health. In: Hartmann (1964), pp. 1–18.

—— (1947), On Rational and Irrational Action. In: Hartmann (1964), pp. 37–68.

—— (1948), Comments on the Psychoanalytic Theory of Instinctual Drives. In: Hartmann (1964), pp. 69–89.

—— (1950a), Psychoanalysis and Developmental Psychology. In: Hartmann (1964), pp. 99–112.

—— (1950b), Comments on the Psychoanalytic Theory of the Ego. In Hartmann (1964), pp. 113–141.

HARTMANN, H. (1951), Technical Implications of Ego Psychology. In: Hartmann (1964), pp. 142–154.

—— (1953), Contribution to the Metapsychology of Schizophrenia. In: Hartmann (1964), pp. 182–206.

—— (1955), Notes on the Theory of Sublimation. In: Hartmann (1964), pp. 215–240.

—— (1964), *Essays on Ego Psychology: Selected Problems in Psychoanalytic Theory.* New York: International Universities Press.

—— & KRIS, E. (1945), The Genetic Approach in Psychoanalysis. *The Psychoanalytic Study of the Child,* 1 : 11–30.

—— ——& LOEWENSTEIN, R. M. (1946), Comments on the Formation of Psychic Structure. *The Psychoanalytic Study of the Child,* 2 : 11–38.

—— —— —— (1949), Notes on the Theory of Aggression. *The Psychoanalytic Study of the Child,* 3/4 : 9–36.

—— —— —— (1951), Some Psychoanalytic Comments on "Culture and Personality." In: Hartmann, Kris, & Loewenstein, (1964), pp. 86–116.

—— —— —— (1953), The Function of Theory in Psychoanalysis. In: Hartmann, Kris, & Loewenstein (1964), pp. 117–143.

—— —— —— (1964), *Papers on Psychoanalytic Psychology* [*Psychological Issues,* Monogr. 14]. New York: International Universities Press.

HEBB, D. O. (1949), *Organization of Behavior.* New York: Wiley.

HEIDEN, K. (1937), *One Man Against Europe.* New York: Penguin Books.

HENDRICK, I. (1942) Instinct and the Ego During Infancy. *Psychoanal. Quart.,* 11 : 33–58.

—— (1943a), Work and the Pleasure Principle. *Psychoanal. Quart.,* 12 : 311–329.

—— (1943b), The Discussion of the "Instinct to Master." *Psychoanal. Quart.,* 12 : 561–565.

—— (1951), Early Development of the Ego. *Psychoanal. Quart.,* 20 : 44–61.

HENLE, M. (1942), An Experimental Investigation of the Dynamic and Structural Determinants of Substitution. *Contributions to Psychological Theory,* Ser. 7, Vol. II, No. 3.

HERMANN, I. (1934), *Die Psychoanalyse als Methode.* Wien: Internationaler psychoanalytischer Verlag.

HEROLD, C. M. (1939), A Controversy about Technique. *Psychoanal. Quart.,* 8 : 219–243.

HOCKING, W. E. (1941), The Nature of Morale. *Amer. J. Sociol.,* 47 : 302–320.

HOFFER, W. (1945), Psychoanalytic Education. *The Psychoanalytic Study of the Child,* 1 : 293–307.

—— (1949), Mouth, Hand and Ego-Integration. *The Psychoanalytic Study of the Child,* 3/4 : 49–56.

—— (1950), Development of the Body Ego. *The Psychoanalytic Study of the Child,* 5 : 18–24.

HOFFMAN, F. J. (1945), *Freudianism and the Literary Mind.* Baton Rouge: Louisiana State University Press.

HOFFMANN, E. P. (1935), Projektion und Ichentwicklung. *Int. Z. Psychoanal.*, 21 : 324–373.

HOMBURGER, A. (1926), *Vorlesungen über Psychopathologie des Kindesalters.* Berlin: Springer.

HULL, C. L. (1933), *Hypnosis and Suggestibility: An Experimental Approach.* New York: Appleton Century.

HUNT, J. McV. (1941), The Effects of Infant Feeding Frustration upon Adult Hoarding in the Albino Rat. *J. Abnorm. Soc. Psychol.*, 36 : 338–360.

ISAACS, S. (1933), *Social Development in Young Children.* New York: Harcourt Brace.

—— (1935), *The Psychological Aspects of Child Development.* London: Evans.

ISAKOWER, O. (1938), A Contribution to the Patho-Psychology of Phenomena Associated with Falling Asleep. *Int. J. Psycho-Anal.*, 19 : 331–345.

—— (1939), On the Exceptional Position of the Auditory Sphere. *Int. J. Psycho-Anal.*, 20 : 340–348.

JACKSON, E. B. & KLATSKIN, E. H. (1950), Rooming-in Research Project. *The Psychoanalytic Study of the Child*, 5 : 236–274.

JACOBSON, E. (1954a), Contributions to the Metapsychology of Psychotic Identifications. *J. Amer. Psychoanal. Assn.*, 2 : 239–262.

—— (1954b), The Self and the Object World. *The Psychoanalytic Study of the Child*, 9 : 75–127.

JONES, E. (1910), The Oedipus Complex As an Explanation of Hamlet's Mystery. *Amer. J. Psychol.*, 21 : 72–113.

—— (1918), War Shock and Freud's Theory of the Neuroses. *Papers on Psycho-Analysis.* London: Baillière, Tindall, & Cox, 3rd ed., 1923, pp. 577–594.

—— (1929), The Psychopathology of Anxiety. *Brit. J. Med. Psychol.*, 9 : 17–25.

—— (1933), The Phallic Phase. *Papers on Psycho-Analysis.* London: Baillière, Tindall, & Cox, 5th ed., 1948, pp. 452–484.

—— (1946), A Valedictorian Address. *Int. J. Psycho-Anal.*, 27 : 285–286.

—— (1953a), *The Life and Work of Sigmund Freud*, Vol. 1. New York: Basic Books.

—— (1953b), Review of Freud's *The Interpretation of Dreams*. *Times Lit. Suppl.*, September 25, 1953.

KAISER, H. (1935), Probleme der Technik. *Int. Z. Psychoanal.*, 21 : 490–522.

KANZER, M. (1953), Past and Present in the Transference. *J. Amer. Psychoanal. Assn.*, 1 : 144–154.

—— (1955), The Communicative Function of the Dream. *Int. J. Psycho-Anal.*, 36 : 260–265.

KARDINER, A. (1939), *The Individual and His Society.* New York: Columbia University Press.

—— (1941), *The Traumatic Neuroses of War.* New York: Hoeber.

KATAN, M. (1939), Der psychotherapeutische Wert der Konstruktionen in der Analyse. *Int. Z. Psychoanal.*, 24 : 172–176.

KAUFMAN, F. (1944), *Methodology of the Social Sciences.* New York: Oxford University Press.

KLEIN, H. R., POTTER. W., & DYK, R. B. (1950), *Anxiety in Pregnancy and Childbirth.* New York: Hoeber.

KLEIN, M. (1932), *The Psycho-Analysis of Children.* London: Hogarth Press.

—— (1948), *Contributions to Psycho-Analysis 1921–1945.* London: Hogarth Press.

—— (1952), Some Theoretical Conclusions Regarding the Emotional Life of the Infant. In: *Developments in Psycho-Analysis,* M. Klein, P. Heimann, S. Isaacs, & J. Riviere. London: Hogarth Press, pp. 198–236.

—— RIVIERE, J., SEARL, M. N., SHARPE, E. F., GLOVER, E., & JONES, E. (1927), Symposium on Child Analysis. *Int. J. Psycho-Anal.,* 8 : 339–391.

KRAMER, P. (1955), On Discovering One's Identity: A Case Report. *The Psychoanalytic Study of the Child,* 10 : 47–74.

KRIS, E. (1934), The Psychology of Caricature. In: Kris (1952), pp. 173–188.

—— (1935), The Image of the Artist. In: Kris (1952), pp. 64–84.

—— (1936), Comments on Spontaneous Artistic Creations by Psychotics. In: Kris (1952), pp. 87–117.

—— (1938), Ego Development and the Comic. In: Kris (1952), pp. 204–216.

—— (1939), Laughter as an Expressive Process: Contributions to the Psychoanalysis of Expressive Behavior. In: Kris (1952), pp. 217–239.

—— (1941a), Approaches to Art. In: Kris (1952), pp. 13–63.

—— (1941b), Morale in Germany. *Amer. J. Sociol.,* 47 : 452–461.

—— (1942a), German Propaganda Instructions of 1933. *Social Research,* 9 : 46–81.

—— (1942b), Mass Communications Under Totalitarian Governments. In: *Print, Film, and Radio in a Democracy,* ed. D. Waples. Chicago: University of Chicago Press.

—— (1942c), The Imagery of War. *Dayton Art Institute Bulletin,* 15.

—— (1944), Art and Regression. *Trans. N.Y. Acad. Sci.,* Series II, Vol. VI, No. 7.

—— (1946), Review of Hoffman, *Freudianism and the Literary Mind.* In: Kris (1952), pp. 265–272.

—— (1949), The Roots of Hostility and Prejudice. In: *The Family in a Democratic Society: Anniversary Papers of the Community Service Society of New York.* New York: Columbia University Press, pp. 141–155.

—— (1950), Introduction to Sigmund Freud: *The Origins of Psychoanalysis: Letters to Wilhelm Fliess, Drafts and Notes, 1887–1902.* New York: Basic Books, 1954.

—— (1952), *Psychoanalytic Explorations in Art.* New York: International Universities Press.

—— (1953a), Discussion of Kubie's "Some Implications for Psychoanalysis of Modern Concepts of the Organization of the Brain." *Psychoanal. Quart.,* 22 : 64–67.

—— (1953b), Review of M. Naumburg's *Schizophrenic Art: Its Meaning in Psychotherapy*. *Psychoanal. Quart.*, 22 : 98–101.

—— (1954), Problems of Infantile Neurosis: A Discussion (Chairman). *The Psychoanalytic Study of the Child*, 9 : 16–71.

—— & Kaplan, A. (1948), Aesthetic Ambiguity. In: Kris (1952), pp. 243–264.

—— & Leites, N. (1947), Trends in Twentieth Century Propaganda. In: *Psychoanalysis and the Social Sciences*, 1 : 393–409. New York: International Universities Press.

—— Speier, H., Axelrad, S., Herma, H., & Loeb, J. (1944), *German Radio Propaganda*. London: Oxford University Press.

—— & White, H. (1942/43), *The German Radio Home News in Wartime*. New York: Duell Sloan, Pearce.

Kris, M. (1957), The Use of Prediction in a Longitudinal Study. *The Psychoanalytic Study of the Child*, 12 : 175–189.

Krötzsch, W. (1917), *Rhythmus und Form in der freien Kinderzeichnung*. Leipzig: A. Haase.

Kubie, L. S. (1941), The Repetitive Core of Neurosis. *Psychoanal. Quart.*, 10 : 23–43.

—— (1953), Some Implications for Psychoanalysis of Modern Concepts of the Organization of the Brain. *Psychoanal. Quart.*, 22 : 21–52.

Kunst, M. S. (1948), A Study of Thumb- and Finger-sucking in Infants. *Psychol. Monogr.*, 62 : 290.

Lamb, C. (1903), *Life, Lectures and Writings*. London: Templeton Edition.

Lameere, N. J. (1938), L'art de persueder. *Rev. l'Instit. Sociol.* (Brussels), 18 : 749–830.

Lampl-de Groot, J. (1946), The Preoedipal Phase in the Development of the Male Child. *The Psychoanalytic Study of the Child*, 2 : 75–83.

—— (1947), On the Development of Ego and Superego. *Int. J. Psycho-Anal.*, 28 : 7–11.

—— (1950), On Masturbation and Its Influence on General Development. *The Psychoanalytic Study of the Child*, 5 : 153–174.

—— (1952), Re-evaluation of the Role of the Oedipus Complex. *Int. J. Psycho-Anal.*, 33 : 335–342.

Lasswell, H. (1927), The Theory of Political Propaganda. *Amer. Pol. Sci. Rev.*, 21 : 627–631.

—— (1933), Morale. *Enc. Soc. Sci.*, 10 : 640–642.

—— (1935a), *World Politics and Personal Insecurity*. New York: Whittelesey House.

—— (1935b), The Study and Practice of Propaganda. In: *Propaganda and Promotional Activities*. Minneapolis: University of Minnesota Press, pp. 1–27.

—— (1938), Foreword in *Allied Propaganda and the Collapse of the German Empire*, G. Bruntz. Palo Alto: Stanford University Press.

—— (1941), *Democracy Through Public Opinion*. Menasha, Wis.: George Banta.

LAZARSFELD, P. (1940), *Radio and the Printed Page.* New York: Duell, Sloan, Pearce.

LE BON, G. (1895), *The Crowd.* London: Unwin, 1920.

—— (1910), *La psychologie de la politique et la defense sociale.* Paris: Flammarion.

LEVY, D. M. (1928), Fingersucking and Accessory Movements in Early Infancy. *Amer. J. Psychiat.,* 7 : 881–918.

—— (1934), Experiments on the Sucking Reflex and Social Behavior of Dogs. *Amer. J. Orthopsychiat.,* 4 : 203–224.

—— (1943), *Maternal Overprotection.* New York: Columbia University Press.

—— (1947), On the Problem of Movement Restraint. *Amer. J. Orthopsychiat.,* 14 : 644–671.

LEWIN, B. D. (1939), Some Observations on Knowledge, Belief and the Impulse to Know. *Int. J. Psycho-Anal.,* 20:426–431.

—— (1950), *The Psychoanalysis of Elation.* New York: Norton.

—— (1952), Phobic Symptoms and Dream Interpretation. *Psychoanal. Quart.,* 21 : 295–322.

—— (1953a), The Forgetting of Dreams. In: *Drives, Affects, Behavior,* ed. R. M. Loewenstein. New York: International Universities Press, pp. 191–202.

—— (1953b), Reconsideration of the Dream Screen. *Psychoanal. Quart.,* 22 : 174–199.

LEWIN, K. (1938), The Conceptual Representation and the Measurement of Psychological Forces. *Contributions to Psychological Theory,* Ser. 4, Vol. I, No. 3. Durham, N.C.: Duke University Press.

—— (1946), Behavior and Development As a Function of the Total Situation. In: *Manual of Child Psychology,* ed. L. Carmichael. New York: Wiley, pp. 791–844.

LEWIS, A. (1942), Incidence of Neuroses in England under War Conditions. *Lancet,* 243 : 176–183.

LITTLE, M. (1951), Countertransference and the Patient's Response to It. *Int. J. Psycho-Anal.,* 32 : 32–40.

LOEWENSTEIN, R. M. (1935), Phallic Passivity in Men. *Int. J. Psycho-Anal.,* 16 : 334–340.

—— (1951a), The Problem of Interpretation. *Psychoanal. Quart.,* 20 : 1–14.

—— (1951b), Ego Development and Psychoanalytic Technique. *Amer. J. Psychiat.,* 107 : 617–622.

—— (1954), Some Remarks on Defences, Autonomous Ego, and Psycho-Analytic Technique. *Int. J. Psycho-Anal.,* 35 : 188–193.

LOOMIE, L. S., ROSEN, V. H., & STEIN, M. H. (1958), Ernst Kris and the Gifted Adolescent Project. *The Psychoanalytic Study of the Child,* 13 : 44–63.

LORAND, S. (1944), *Psychoanalysis Today.* New York: International Universities Press.

———— (1946), *Technique of Psychoanalytic Therapy.* New York: International Universities Press.

———— (1948), Comments on the Correlation of Theory and Technique. *Psychoanal. Quart.,* 17 : 32–50.

LOURIE, R. S. (1949), The Role of Rhythmic Patterns in Childhood. *Amer. J. Psychiat.,* 105 : 653–660.

McCULLOCH, W. S. (1949), [Discussion remarks in:] *Transactions of the 6th Conference on Cybernetics, Circular Causal and Feedback Mechanisms in Biological and Social Problems,* ed. H. v. Foerster. New York: Josiah Macy, Jr. Foundation.

McCOLLUM, A. T. (1956), A Clinical Caseworker in Interdisciplinary Research. *Social Work,* 1 : 88–102.

MacIVER, R. (1937), *Society.* New York: Farrar Rinehart.

MAHLER, M. S. (1952), On Child Psychosis and Schizophrenia: Autistic and Symbiotic Infantile Psychoses. *The Psychoanalytic Study of the Child,* 7 : 286–305.

———— & ELKISCH, P. (1953), Some Observations on Disturbances of the Ego in a Case of Infantile Psychosis. *The Psychoanalytic Study of the Child,* 8 : 252–261.

MALCOVE, L. (1945), Margaret E. Fries' Research in Problems of Infancy and Childhood. *The Psychoanalytic Study of the Child,* 1 : 405–414.

MALONEY, J. C. (1949), *The Magic Cloak.* Wakefield, Mass.: Montrose Press.

MANNHEIM, K. (1939), *Man and Society in an Age of Reconstruction.* London: Kegan Paul.

MEAD, G. H. (1925/26), The Nature of Aesthetic Experience. *Int. J. Ethics.,* 36 : 251–287.

MEAD, M. (1946), Research on Primitive Children. In: *Manual of Child Psychology,* ed. L. Carmichael. New York: Wiley, pp. 667–706.

MENNINGER, K. A. (1938), *Man Against Himself.* New York: Harcourt Brace.

———— (1942), *Love Against Hate.* New York: Harcourt Brace.

MIDDLEMORE, M. P. (1941), *The Nursing Couple.* London: Hamish Hamilton.

MOWRER, O. H. (1940), An Experimental Analogue of "Regression" with Incidental Observations on "Reaction-Formation." *J. Abnorm. Soc. Psychol.,* 35 : 56–87.

———— & KLUCKHOHN, C. (1944), Dynamic Theory of Personality. In: *Personality and Behavior Disorders,* ed. J. McV. Hunt. New York: Ronald Press, 1 : 69–135.

MURPHY, G. (1947), *Personality.* New York: Harpers.

———— & MURPHY, L. B. (1931), *Experimental Psychology.* New York: Harpers.

MURRAY, H. A. (1933), The Effect of Fear upon Estimates of the Maliciousness of Other Personalities. *J. Soc. Psychol.,* 4 : 310–329.

———— (1938), *Explorations in Personality.* New York: Oxford University Press.

NAUMBURG, M. (1950), *Schizophrenic Art: Its Meaning in Psychotherapy.* New York: Grune & Stratton.

Nowlis, V. (1952), The Search for Significant Concepts in the Study of Parent-Child Relationships. *Amer. J. Orthopsychiat.*, 22 : 286–299.

Nunberg, H. (1926), The Will to Recovery. In: Nunberg (1948), pp. 75–88.

—— (1931), The Synthetic Function of the Ego. In: Nunberg (1948), pp. 120–136.

—— (1932), *Principles of Psychoanalysis.* New York: International Universities Press, 1955.

—— (1937), Theory of the Therapeutic Results of Psychoanalysis. In: Nunberg (1948), pp. 165–173.

—— (1939), Ego Strength and Ego Weakness. In: Nunberg (1948), pp. 185–208.

—— (1947), Circumcision and the Problem of Bisexuality. *Int. J. Psycho-Anal.*, 28 : 145–179.

—— (1948), *Practice and Theory of Psychoanalysis.* New York: International Universities Press, 1955.

Odier, C. (1948), *Anxiety and Magic Thinking.* New York: International Universities Press, 1956.

Orlemans, A. C. (1949), *The Development of Freud's Conception of Anxiety.* Amsterdam: North Holland Publishing Company.

Payne, S. M. (1946), Notes on Developments in the Theory and Practice of Psycho-Analytical Technique. *Int. J. Psycho-Anal.*, 27 : 12–19.

Peiper, A. (1936), Die Saugtätigkeit. *Ergebnisse der inneren Medizin und Kinderheilkunde,* 50. Berlin: Springer.

Peller, L. E. (1946), Incentives to Development and Means of Early Education. *The Psychoanalytic Study of the Child,* 2 : 397–415.

Piaget, J. (1932), *The Moral Judgment of the Child.* Glencoe, Ill.: Free Press, 1948.

Postman, L., Jenkins, W. O., & Postman, D. L. (1948), An Experimental Comparison of Active Recall and Recognition. *Amer. J. Psychol.*, 61 : 511–519.

Prinzhorn, H. (1923), *Die Bildnerei der Geisteskranken.* Berlin: Springer.

Provence, S. A. & Lipton [Coleman], R. W. (1962), *Infants in Institutions.* New York: International Universities Press.

—— & Ritvo, S. (1961), Effects of Deprivation on Institutionalized Infants: Disturbances in Development of Relationship to Inanimate Objects. *The Psychoanalytic Study of the Child,* 16 : 189–205.

Putnam, M. C., Rank, B., & Kaplan, S. (1951), Notes on John I.: A Case of Primal Depression in an Infant. *The Psychoanalytic Study of the Child,* 6 : 38–58.

—— —— Pavenstedt, E., Andersen, I., & Rawson, I. (1948), Case Study of an Atypical Two-and-a-Half-Year-Old. *Amer. J. Orthopsychiat.*, 18 : 1–30.

Rabinovitch, R. D. (1950), Psychogenetic Factors. Contribution to the Round Table: The Psychopathic Delinquent Child. *Amer. J. Orthopsychiat.*, 20 : 232–236.

RADO, S. (1942), Pathodynamics and Treatment of Traumatic War Neurosis. *Psychosom. Med.*, 4 : 362–368.

RANK, B. (1949a), Adaptation of the Psychoanalytic Technique for the Treatment of Young Children with Atypical Development. *Amer. J. Orthopsychiat.*, 19 : 140–144.

———— (1949b), Aggression. *The Psychoanalytic Study of the Child*, 3/4 : 43–48.

———— & MacNAUGHTON, D. (1950), A Clinical Contribution to Early Ego Development. *The Psychoanalytic Study of the Child*, 5 : 53–65.

———— PUTNAM, M. C., & ROCHLIN, G. (1948), The Significance of the "Emotional Climate" in Early Feeding Difficulties. *Psychosom. Med.*, 10 : 279–283.

RANK, O. (1924), *The Trauma of Birth*. New York: Harcourt Brace, 1929.

RAPAPORT, D. (1942), Freudian Mechanisms and Frustration Experiments. *Psychoanal. Quart.*, 11 : 503–511.

———— (1950), On the Psycho-Analytic Theory of Thinking. *Int. J. Psycho-Anal.*, 31 : 161–170.

———— ed. (1951), *Organization and Pathology of Thought*. New York: Columbia University Press.

REICH, A. (1951), The Discussion of 1912 on Masturbation and Our Present-Day Views. *The Psychoanalytic Study of the Child*, 6 : 80–94.

REICH, W. (1928), On Character Analysis. In: *The Psychoanalytic Reader*, ed. R. Fliess. New York: International Universities Press, 1948, pp. 129–147.

———— (1931), Character Formation and the Phobias of Childhood. *Int. J. Psycho-Anal.*, 12 : 219–230.

———— (1933), *Character Analysis*. New York: Orgone Institute Press.

REIDER, N. (1953a), Reconstruction and Screen Function. *J. Amer. Psychoanal. Assn.*, 1 : 389–405.

———— (1953b), A Type of Transference to Institutions. *Bull. Menninger Clin.*, 17 : 58–63.

REIK, T. (1937), *Surprise and the Psychoanalyst*. New York: Dutton.

RHEINGOLD, H. L. (1956), *The Modification of Social Responsiveness in Institutional Babies*. Lafayette, Ind.: Society for Research in Child Development Monographs.

RIBBLE, M. A. (1941), Disorganizing Factors in Infant Personality. *Amer. J. Psychiat.*, 98 : 459–463.

———— (1943), *The Rights of Infants*. New York: Columbia University Press.

RICHFIELD, J. (1954), An Analysis of the Concept of Insight. *Psychoanal. Quart.*, 23 : 390–408.

RITVO, S. & SOLNIT, A. J. (1958), Influences of Early Mother-Child Interaction on Identification Processes. *The Psychoanalytic Study of the Child*, 13 : 64–91.

———— ———— (1960), The Relationship of Early Ego Identifications to Superego Formation. *Int. J. Psycho-Anal.*, 41 : 295–300.

RIVIERE, J. (1952), General Introduction. In: *Developments in Psycho-Analysis,* by M. Klein, P. Heimann, S. Isaacs, & J. Riviere. London: Hogarth Press, pp. 1–36.

RÓHEIM, G. (1939), Racial Differences in the Neuroses and Psychoses. *Psychiatry,* 2 : 375–390.

ROSEN, V. H. (1955), The Reconstruction of a Traumatic Childhood Event in a Case of Derealization. *J. Amer. Psychoanal. Assn.,* 3 : 211–221.

ROSS, S. (1951), Sucking Behavior in Neonate Dogs. *J. Abnorm. Soc. Psychol.,* 46 : 142–149.

RUCKMICK, C. A. (1924), Bibliography of Rhythm. *Amer. J. Psychol.,* 35 : 407–413.

RUDEL, R. (1949), *The Function of the Daydream.* Master's thesis (directed by M. Scheerer). Graduate Faculty of Political and Social Science. New York: New School for Social Research.

SANDERS, C. R. (1953), *The Strachey Family 1588–1932: Their Writings and Literary Associations.* Durham, N.C.: Duke University Press.

SAUSSURE, R. DE (1933), Über genetische Psychologie und Psychoanalyse. *Imago,* 20 : 282–314.

SCHACHTEL, E. (1949), On Memory and Childhood Amnesia. In: *A Study of Interpersonal Relations,* ed. P. Mullahy. New York: Hermitage Press, pp. 3–49.

SCHILDER, P. & KAUDER, O. (1926), *The Nature of Hypnosis.* New York: International Universities Press, 1956.

SCHMIDEBERG, M. (1934), Intellektuelle Hemmung und Ess-störung. *Z. psychoanal. Päd.,* 8 : 107–116.

SEARS, R. R. (1943), Survey of Objective Studies of Psychoanalytic Concepts. *Soc. Sci. Res. Coun. Bull.,* 51.

——— (1944), Experimental Analysis of Psychoanalytic Phenomena. In: *Personality and Behavior Disorders,* ed. J. McV. Hunt. New York: Ronald Press, 1 : 306–332.

SEEMAN, W. (1951), The Freudian Theory of Daydreams: An Operational Analysis. *Psychol. Bull.,* 48 : 369–382.

SELIGMAN, C. G. (1924), Anthropology and Psychology. *J. Roy. Anthrop. Inst.,* 54 : 13–46.

SHARPE, E. F. (1930), The Technique of Psycho-Analysis. In: *Collected Papers on Psycho-Analysis.* London: Hogarth Press, 1950, pp. 9–106.

SHULMAN, M. D. (1942), Planetary Gangbusting. *J. Educ. Sociol.* [*Sociol. Educ.*], 15 : 394–403.

SIEGMAN, A. (1956), The Psychological Economy of *Déjà Raconté. Psychoanal. Quart.,* 25 : 83–86.

SILVERBERG, W. V. (1955), Acting Out versus Insight: A Problem in Psychoanalytic Technique. *Psychoanal. Quart.,* 24 : 527–543.

SMITH, B. (1942), Democratic Control of Propaganda Through Registration and Disclosure. *Publ. Opinion Quart.,* 6 : 27–40.

SMITH, H. W. (1949), Organism and Environment: Dynamic Oppositions. In: *Adaptation*, ed. J. Romano. Ithaca, N.Y.: Cornell University Press, pp. 23–52.

SPENCE, K. W. (1942), Theoretical Interpretations of Learning. In: *Comparative Psychology*, ed. F. A. Moss. New York: Prentice-Hall, pp. 280–329.

SPERLING, M. (1949), The Role of the Mother in Psychosomatic Disorders. *Psychosom. Med.*, 11 : 377–385.

SPITZ, R. A. (1937), Familienneurose und neurotische Familie. *Int. Z. Psychoanal.*, 23 : 548–559.

—— (1945), Hospitalism. *The Psychoanalytic Study of the Child*, 1 : 53–74.

—— (1946), Hospitalism: A Follow-up Report. *The Psychoanalytic Study of the Child*, 2 : 113–117.

—— (1948), La perte de la mère par le nourisson. *Enfance*, 1 : 373–79.

—— (1950), Relevancy of Direct Infant Observation. *The Psychoanalytic Study of the Child*, 5 : 66–73.

—— (1951), The Psychogenic Diseases in Infancy. *The Psychoanalytic Study of the Child*, 6 : 255–275.

—— (1954), Genèse des premieres relations objectales. *Rev. Franç. Psychanal.*, 18 : 479–575.

—— (1955), The Primal Cavity. *The Psychoanalytic Study of the Child*, 10 : 215–240.

—— & WOLF, K. M. (1946), Anaclitic Depression. *The Psychoanalytic Study of the Child*, 2 : 313–342.

—— —— (1949), Autoerotism. *The Psychoanalytic Study of the Child*, 3/4 : 85–120.

STAUB, H. (1943), A Runaway from Home. *Psychoanal. Quart.*, 12 : 1–22.

STERBA, E. (1945), Interpretation and Education. *The Psychoanalytic Study of the Child*, 1 : 309–317.

STERBA, R. (1934), The Fate of the Ego in Analytic Therapy. *Int. J. Psycho-Anal.*, 15 : 117–126.

—— (1940), The Dynamics of the Dissolution of the Transference Resistance. *Psychoanal. Quart.*, 9 : 363–379.

STONE, L. (1954a), On the Principal Obscene Word in the English Language. *Int. J. Psycho-Anal.*, 35 : 30–56.

—— (1954b), The Widening Scope of Indications for Psychoanalysis. *J. Amer. Psychoanal. Assn.*, 2 : 567–594.

STRACHEY, J. (1934), The Nature of the Therapeutic Action in Psycho-Analysis. *Int. J. Psycho-Anal.*, 15 : 127–159.

SUTTIE, J. D. (1935), *The Origins of Love and Hate*. London: Kegan Paul.

VARENDONCK, J. (1921), *The Psychology of Dreams*. London: Allen & Unwin.

WAELDER, R. (1929), Review of S. Freud's *Inhibitions, Symptoms and Anxiety*. *Int. J. Psycho-Anal.*, 10 : 103–111.

—— (1930), The Principle of Multiple Function. *Psychoanal. Quart.*, 5 : 45–62, 1936.

WAELDER, R. (1936), The Problem of the Genesis of Psychical Conflict in Earliest Infancy. *Int. J. Psycho-Anal.*, 18 : 406–473, 1937.

—— (1939a), Criteria of Interpretation. In: *Collected Papers of Robert Waelder*. New York: International Universities Press, 1975 (in press).

—— (1939b), *Psychological Aspects of War and Peace*. Geneva Studies, X. New York: Columbia University Press.

—— (1944), Present Trends in Psychoanalytic Theory and Practice. *Bull. Menninger Clin.*, 8 : 9–13.

—— (1949), Report of Panel B: Dream Theory and Interpretation. *Bull. Amer. Psychoanal. Assn.*, 5 (2) : 36–40.

—— (1951), The Structure of Paranoid Ideas. *Int. J. Psycho-Anal.*, 32 : 167–177.

WAPLES, D. & BERELSON, B. (1941), *Public Communications and Public Opinion*. Graduate School Library, University of Chicago (mimeographed).

WATSON, G., ed. (1942), *Civilian Morale* [*The Second Yearbook of the Society for the Psychological Study of Social Issues*]. New York: Houghton Mifflin.

WEISS, P. (1949), The Biological Basis of Adaptation. In: *Adaptation*, ed. J. Romano. Ithaca, New York: Cornell University Press, pp. 1–22.

WERTHEIMER, M. (1945), *Productive Thinking*. New York: Harpers.

WILLIAMS, F. (1934), *Soviet Russia Fights Neurosis*. London: Routledge.

WINNICOTT, D. W. (1953), Transitional Objects and Transitional Phenomena. *Int. J. Psycho-Anal.*, 34 : 89–97.

WOLF, K. M. (1944), Evacuation of Children in Wartime: A Survey of the Literature with a Bibliography. *The Psychoanalytic Study of the Child*, 1 : 389–404.

—— (1948), Unpublished seminar notes.

—— (1953), Observation of Individual Tendencies in the First Year of Life. In: *Problems of Infancy and Childhood*, ed. M. J. E. Senn. New York: Josiah Macy, Jr. Foundation, pp. 97–137.

WOLFENSTEIN, M. (1953), Trends in Infant Care. *Amer. J. Orthopsychiat.*, 23 : 120–130.

ZACHRY, C. B. (1941), The Influence of Psychoanalysis in Education. *Psychoanal. Quart.*, 10 : 431–444.

ZEIGARNIK, B. (1927), Über das Behalten erledigter und unerledigter Handlungen. *Psychol. Forsch.*, 9 : 1–5.

ZETZEL, E. R. (1956), An Approach to the Relation between Concept and Content in Psychoanalytic Theory. *The Psychoanalytic Study of the Child*, 11 : 99–121.

ZILBOORG, G. (1938), Propaganda from Within. *Ann. Amer. Acad. Polit. Soc. Sci.*, 198 : 116–123.

—— (1941), *History of Medical Psychology*. New York: Norton.

—— (1952), The Emotional Problem and the Therapeutic Role of Insight in Psychoanalysis. *Psychoanal. Quart.*, 21 : 1–24.

Index